UK CHR...   ...NDBOOK

RELIGIOUS TRENDS
No.2

2000/01 Millennium Edition

EDITED BY DR PETER BRIERLEY

ASSISTANT EDITOR: GEORGINA SANGER

Section 12 English Church Attendance Survey sponsored by:

The Centre for Black & White Christian Partnership
Campaigners
Christian Aid
Christian Book Club
Christian Healing Mission
Covenanters
Church Pastoral-Aid Society
Ecclesiastical Insurance Company
English Heritage
Moorlands Bible College
Operation Mobilisation
Premier Radio
Scripture Union
Youth For Christ

CHRISTIAN RESEARCH
Vision Building, 4 Footscray Road, Eltham, London SE9 2TZ
Telephone: 020 8294 1989   Fax: 020 8294 0014

HARPERCOLLINS*RELIGIOUS*
77 Fulham Palace Road, Hammersmith, London W6 8JB
Telephone: 020 8741 7070   Fax: 020 8307 4064

Council of Reference for Religious Trends

Ven Douglas Bartles-Smith, Archdeacon of Southwark

Dr Grace Davie, University of Exeter

Mr Paul Hanley, Editor, Church Times

Rev Bob Hunt, Deputy Principal, All Nations Christian College

Rev Richard Tiplady, Associate Director, EMA

British Library Cataloguing in Publication Data

UK Christian Handbook Religious Trends No.2 – 2000/01

1. Great Britain Christian Church

I. Brierley, Peter, 1938

ISBN's 1 85321 134 6 (Christian Research)

0 551 03237 5 (HarperCollins*Religious*)

Christian Research aims to provide Christian leaders with factual information, surveys, and other resource material to help them in the long-term in their strategic planning for evangelism and growth, and in the short-term with leadership training for greater efficiency, effectiveness, and cost-effectiveness. Christian Research also publishes and distributes related books and papers. The Christian Research Association is a registered charity, number 2792246.

Material similar to that in Religious Trends is published every other month in the Christian Research Association's bulletin, Quadrant. This is available only to members. Details of membership may be obtained from Pamela Poynter, Christian Research, Vision Building, 4 Footscray Road, Eltham, London SE9 2TZ.

Typeset by WestKey Ltd, WestKey House, Tregoniggie Estate, Falmouth, Cornwall TR11 4SN.

Printed for Christian Research at the above address and HarperCollins*Religious*, 77–85 Fulham Palace Road, Hammersmith, London W6 8JB.

Printed by Woolnough Bookbinding Ltd, Church Street, Irthlingborough, Northamptonshire NN9 5SE

FOREWORD

by Rev. Douglas A. O. Nicol
General Secretary of the Board of National Mission of the Church of Scotland

Christians in Britain today live at a time of enormous challenge – but with that challenge come opportunities for mission and evangelism that are without parallel!

It is in this context that I warmly commend the latest edition of *Religious Trends* – a volume which is the definitive statistical history of the UK Church in the twentieth century. It is a volume that deserves study at local, regional and national level and one that has the potential of inspiring Christians to action to meet the challenges and accept the opportunities of our generation.

As General Secretary of the Board of the Church of Scotland General Assembly charged with 'planning and resourcing the mission of the Church in Scotland today' I have read with great interest the statistics and stories that make up this volume. They have stimulated thoughts that I now offer as a background to your own consideration of *Religious Trends*.

First thoughts centre on the issue of the models of church appropriate to our generation. The decline in existing models is highlighted in the text with Baptist numbers peaking in 1905, Methodists in 1910 and 1930, Anglican in 1930, Presbyterians in 1935 and Catholics in 1960. Since these dates decline has been

the order of the day. Indeed when the statistics on churchgoing are analysed we find a decline that is accelerating as the century closes with a drop of 13% across the ten years 1979 to 1989 but an alarming 22% in the nine years 1989 to 1998.

Faced with these statistics of decline I find myself advocating not only programmes to develop the life of the model of church we have inherited and by and large loved but also ones to develop new models of church relevant to the 'pick and mix' society in which today our lives are set. These models must be less about maintaining an institution and more about recruiting, training and encouraging Christian disciples to 'gossip the Gospel' in every area of life. For those willing to rise to this personal challenge the opportunities are great – belief in a personal God has declined from 43% in the 1950s to 31% in the 1990s and disbelief in God has risen from 2% to 27% in the same period. The Lord's challenge to Isaiah comes alive: 'Whom shall I send? And who will go for us?' We need today models of church that inspire the personal response: 'Here I am'. Send me!'

Second thoughts centre on the issue of age. I am sure that other readers will identify with my feelings that as the years of life march relentlessly on I don't think that I myself am ageing – rather there just seem to be more younger people about! The statistics tell facts, however, and not just feelings and these facts encouragingly report that the number of older people attending church has actually increased in numerical terms – from 900,000 in 1989 to 930,000 in 1998.

We ought never to complain that there are too many old people in church or indeed dismiss their role in our congregations. In the 15 years in which I was a parish minister in congregations in Dumfries and Kilmacolm the contribution of our senior members never ceased to amaze and thrill me. I think of a programme – devised by others, not me – which 'linked' senior members to younger families. In a society where all too often the generations of a family are separated by distance, this 'adopt a Gran' scheme brought new depths of relationships and care to young and old alike – and our Christian fellowship was strengthened without measure! Then there was the self-sacrificial giving and prayer of both those able to come to Church and the housebound. Let's thank God for committed senior folk and seek ways to let them truly be part of an all-age body of Christ.

This brings me to my third thought – the challenge of communicating the Good news of Jesus Christ to children and young people. The statistics recorded in this volume are stark. The English Church Attendance Survey reveals that the proportion of those aged under 15 attending church has dropped in the

ten short years from 1989 to 1999 from 25% to 19%. Today only 5% of those in their 20s are in church in England. Both parents and children have dropped out of church in the 1990s; but more children than parents.

Some say we need to reach the young 'because they are the church of the future'; my contention is that they are part of the church today and that all our fellowships are the poorer if there are no, or very few, children and young people. I equally believe that we cannot expect the children and young people of a new Millennium to feel part of a church which has stayed static at a time of enormous social change. It is only by establishing positive relationships with the children and young people around us that bridges for communicating faith will be established; and it is only be seeking new all-age models of church that new Christians will grow into disciples to ensure that our faith will be passed on from generation to generation.

So we have come round the full circle – a circle that has at its poles the words 'challenge' and 'opportunity'.

It was Helen Keller who said: 'Each dawn is a new beginning'. May *Religious Trends* offer us all a new dawn of understanding of the challenges of our time and may that dawn be the beginning of our accepting the God-given opportunities that are ours!

UKCH RELIGIOUS TRENDS No.2

Contents

EDITOR'S NOTE

We are grateful for the warm reception given to the first volume of *Religious Trends*, which gave an overview of the state of the church in Britain, and the world, in 1997, with 1995 the latest figures in most cases.

One aspect of it has not always been appreciated – the intention to use the Index in a cumulative sense. This means that the Index for Volume No 1 has been repeated in this Volume, whose entries are all indicated by a "1/" in front of them. It is intended to cumulate the Index for five issues at a time, DV, so that a comprehensive reference can be provided for researchers, librarians, and others searching for relevant information.

This Volume, Number 2, differs from the first in two major ways:

(1) Because it is the 2000/2001 edition it is naturally the Millennium edition. Whereas there are few figures which illustrate Christianity over the past 1,000, or even 2,000 years (but see Pages 1.2 and 2.2–4), much of this Volume is devoted instead to a history of Christianity over the last 100 years. In that sense this Volume could be sub-titled "A century of British Christianity 1900–2000".

(2) In 1998 the *English Church Attendance Survey* was carried out. Whilst the major report of its findings are published elsewhere, this Volume contains detailed information at a regional level, for the 10 regions in England in which the data was initially analysed. This information is given in an extra Section, Section 12. Page 12.3 gives the overall total figures. It is hoped it will be possible to analyse this information further down to county level and to include that information in *Religious Trends* No 3.

I wish to record many grateful thanks to the Council of Reference formed since the first Volume, and listed on Page 0.2, and for my colleagues who have helped in the preparation of this Volume, especially Keith Poynter, Georgina Sanger and Vicki Poynter. Also to a wide variety of people who helped with individual pages, gave me information over the phone and/or at the last minute, provided or amended maps, gave permission for their work to be mentioned, and in many other ways. This Volume may be my responsibility, especially for any errors, but behind it is a team, hardworking, small and dedicated.

Peter Brierley
October 1999

NOTES AND DEFINITIONS FOR STATISTICS IN SECTIONS 2, 8, 9 AND 10

Membership figures were given in answer to the following request:

"Total number of adult (aged 15 and over) members/adherents in the UK." Definitions of membership vary according to the church denomination or religious group in question. Adult church membership is defined as appropriate to each particular group, so that for example the Electoral Roll (not to be confused with the Local Authority Roll) has been used for the Church of England, whilst because there is no comparable equivalent to the Protestant definitions of membership, Roman Catholic adult mass attendance figures have mostly been used. Where adherents are defined as non-communicant members, as with some Scottish denominations, these have been added to the true members.

Ministers are full-time active clergy, or ordained officials, including those in administration, chaplaincies, etc. Many of the Afro–Caribbean clergy are part-time.

Churches are those religious buildings in regular use, normally wholly owned by the organisations. Numbers of buildings do not necessarily correspond to the number of congregations or groups within the particular denomination so the number of congregations has been used in some tables as indicated. Revised figures refer to changes from previous editions of the *UK Christian Handbook*.

Estimates indicated by footnotes are editorial estimates, rather than ones made by the individual denominations themselves, which are not identified in these tables.

Estimates for the year 2000 are based on the data for the previous years shown in the text and on other information where available, generally using a dampened linear regression, though other methods are used where necessary.

More extensive footnotes are supplied in many instances to help those requiring more information.

Contents

Sources:
World Churches Handbook, **Christian Research, London, 1997** and *Future Church*, **Monarch, 1998**

1

TABLE 1.2.1   The number of people who have ever lived and total Christians

Date	World population Millions	Assumed annual death rate Per 1,000	Total deaths between this date and the next Millions	Percentage who are Christian %	Total Christian deaths between this date and the next Millions
40,000 BC	½	50	500	-	-
35,000	4	50	6,750	-	-
8,000	6	50	3,450	-	-
5,000	40	50	9,350	-	-
1600 BC	70	40	1,360	-	-
1200	100	40	1,600	-	-
800	100	40	2,096	-	-
400	162	40	1,568	-	-
200	231	35	1,700	-	-
1 AD	255	35	893	-	-
100	255	35	3,227	0.6	19
500	206	35	3,821	22	856
1000	254	35	970	19	181
1100	301	35	1,225	19	229
1200	400	35	714	19	133
1250	416	35	742	19	139
1300	432	35	612	19	114
1340	443	40	979	19	183
1400	374	40	1,668	19	312
1500	460	35	1,816	19	345
1600	579	35	2,201	19	418
1700	679	35	1,267	19	241
1750	770	35	1,508	19	287
1800	954	35	1,920	23	444
1850	1,241	35	2,515	23	581
1900	1,633	25	2,618	34	900
1950	2,556	15	939	30	279
1970	3,707	12	490	29	142
1980	4,454	12	584	28	166
1990	5,277	11	624	29	178
2000 AD	6,073	10		28	
TOTAL			59,707		6,147

TABLE 1.2.2   Increase in World Population

Year	World population reached	Years to reach this level
1807	1 billion	Many!
1927	2 billion	120
1960	3 billion	33
1974	4 billion	14
1987	5 billion	13
1999	6 billion	12
2013	7 billion	14
2028	8 billion	15

Source: Future estimates in *Daily Telegraph* article of 12th October 1999

TABLE 1.2.3
The Six Biggest Countries

1950			1996			2020			2050		
555	China	1	1,232	China	1	1,449	China	1	1,517	China	2
358	India	2	945	India	2	1,407	India	2	1,787	India	1
158	USA	3	269	USA	3	322	USA	3	348	USA	4
102	Russia	4	148	Russia	6						
84	Japan	5									
80	Indonesia	6	200	Indonesia	4	264	Indonesia	4	318	Indonesia	6
			161	Brazil	5						
						248	Pakistan	5	357	Pakistan	3
						215	Nigeria	6	339	Nigeria	5

Numbers on left of each country are population figures given in millions.
Numbers on right of each country show the rank order of countries.

Source: *The Independent* 12th January 1998, amended with later estimates

Roger Thatcher, when Director and Registrar General of what was the Office of Population Censuses and Surveys, now part of the Office of National Statistics, was asked by the British Association for the Advancement of Science to answer the question "How many people have ever lived on earth?" This was partly to answer the assertion that more people were alive in the 1980s in the world than had ever lived before.

The details were published in the "Contributed Papers" of the 44th Session of the International Statistical Institute, Volume 2, 1983, Pages 841-843, and included a Table, of which the first three columns in **Table 1.2.1** are an extract. That Table went up to 1980, the later years have been taken from other sources, and the world population for 1950, 1970 and 1980 updated with the latest United Nations estimates. The fourth column in **Table 1.2.1** up to 1950 comes from the World Christian Encyclopedia, published by Oxford University Press in 1982, edited by Rev Dr David Barrett; thereafter the figures in the *World Churches Handbook*, Christian Research, 1997, have been used.

The two totals show:

- There have been almost 60 billion people who have ever lived on earth.

- This is almost exactly 10 times the current population on earth; that is, for every person alive today 9 others have already lived and died.

- Just over 10% of those who have ever lived would have called themselves Christian.

- Almost as many people lived *before* Christ (28.4 billion) as have lived *since* He did (31.3 billion).

- Of those who have lived in the Christian era the percentage who would say they were Christian is almost 20%.

The world population was said to pass the 6 billion mark on October 12th 1999 by the United Nations. **Table 1.2.2** shows the years between each successive billion and the speed of increase! The United Nations says we are sure to pass the 8 billion mark in the 21st century, but whether we reach the 9.4 billion projected for 2050 depends on many factors. The rate of increase in the world's population peaked in 1960 at 2.0%, and is currently 1.4% and still falling.

In Europe the population has already peaked and is likely to fall quite sharply in the next 2 or 3 decades. The same will happen in North America and later in East Asia. However the populations of Africa, Latin America, India and other parts of Asia will continue to grow rapidly.

If the projections of world population given for the six largest countries in **Table 1.2.3** prove accurate, India will have become the world's largest country well before 2050, with Pakistan the third and Nigeria the fifth.

FIGURE 1.3.1
World Population and Christian community from 0 AD to 1800

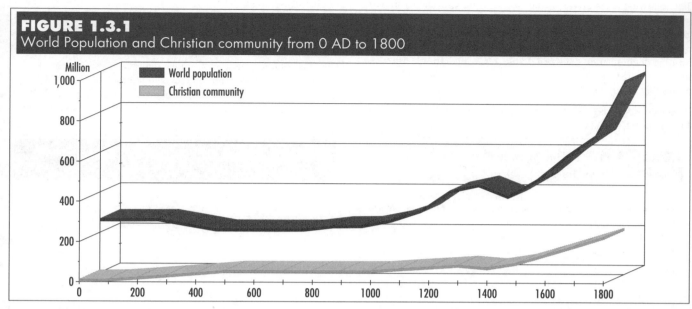

FIGURE 1.3.2
World Population and Christian community 1800 to 2000

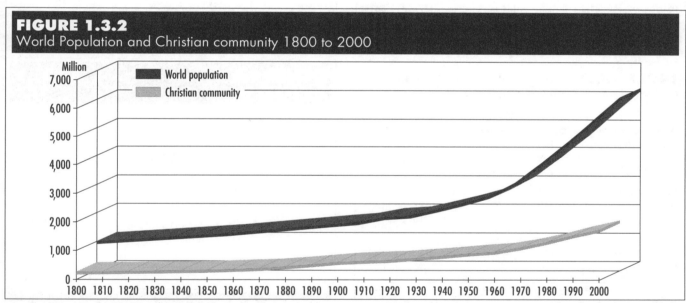

FIGURE 1.3.3
The world's religions 1900–2000

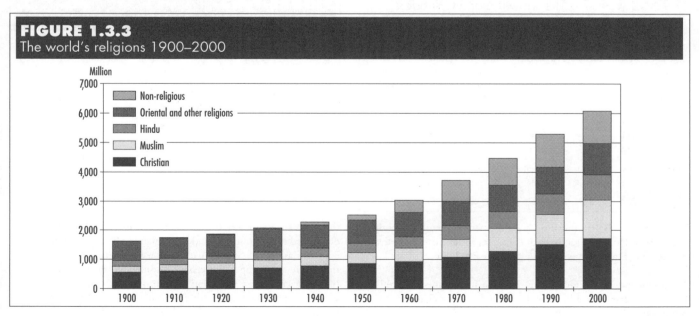

The following pages give a breakdown of world Christianity in two ways. Firstly they show the growth of each broad denominational group from 1960 to 2010. At the bottom of each Table are two numbers showing the total Christian Community in each continent for each denomination. Thus, in **Table 1.4.1**, underneath Africa in the line labelled "1960" is the number 27m. m = million. This means that in 1960 there were 27 million Catholics in Africa.

By the year 2010 if present trends continue that number will grow to 116 million. If we take the 1960 figure, 27 million, as an index

number of 100, then the 116 million is 420 ($116 \div 27 = 4.2$). The index figure for each decadal year is shown. To find the number of Catholics in Africa in 1980 say, multiply 27 million (the base figure for 1960) by 2.13, to get 57.5 million.

The final column gives total Catholic figures across the world. In 2010 if present trends continue they will number 1,055,000,000 people. The final line in each Table gives the percentage the 2010 figure is of this total for each continent. Thus Africa's 116 million is 11% of the world's total in 2010.

TABLE 1.4.1 The growth of the Catholic population by continent 1960–2010

Year	Africa	Europe	Oceania	North America	Asia	South America	World
1960	100	100	100	100	100	100	100
1970	154	104	144	123	129	126	118
1980	213	106	163	148	166	153	136
1990	292	107	200	169	222	175	154
2000	351	105	231	196	274	200	180
2010	420	104	267	220	320	220	188
1960	27m	241m	3m	110m	42m	137m	561m
2010	116m	251m	9m	244m	134m	302m	1,055m
% of total	11%	24%	1%	23%	13%	28%	100%

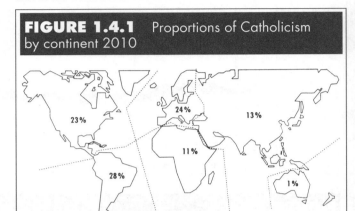

FIGURE 1.4.1 Proportions of Catholicism by continent 2010

TABLE 1.4.2 The growth of the Anglican Communion by continent 1960–2010

Year	Africa	Europe	Oceania	North America	Asia	South America	World
1960	100	100	100	100	100	100	100
1970	261	100	108	110	146	136	112
1980	395	97	106	117	195	161	123
1990	529	94	111	104	223	183	133
2000	679	90	112	92	254	197	137
2010	823	87	114	82	283	218	145
1960	3.0m	27.9m	4.6m	5.1m	0.2m	0.1m	40.9m
2010	24.7m	24.1m	5.3m	4.2m	0.6m	0.2m	59.1m
% of total	42%	41%	9%	7%	1%	0%	100%

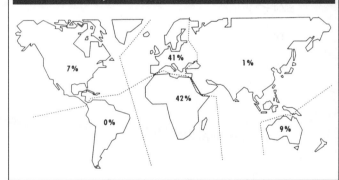

FIGURE 1.4.2 Proportions of the Anglican Communion by continent 2010

TABLE 1.4.3 The growth of the Orthodox Community by continent 1960–2010

Year	Africa	Asia + Europe	Oceania	North America	South America	World
1960	100	100	100	100	100	100
1970	125	110	131	120	119	113
1980	163	119	152	125	138	126
1990	191	128	210	126	156	138
2000	211	135	234	126	173	146
2010	234	135	263	126	191	150
1960	14m	75m	0.2m	6.3m	0.3m	96m
2010	33m	101m	0.6m	7.9m	0.5m	143m
% of total	23%	71%	0%	6%	0%	100%

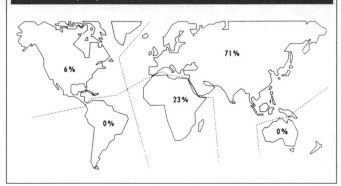

FIGURE 1.4.3 Proportions of Orthodox Community by continent 2010

The map for each denomination gives the percentage of the world total of that denomination in each continent in the year 2010; they are the same figures as given at the foot of each Table.

The continents of Asia and Europe have been combined in **Table 1.4.3** and **Figure 1.4.3** because the United Nations changed the definition of Europe in 1992, after the collapse of the USSR. It took

the 6 most western countries of the newly formed CIS and designated them "Europe" and the remaining 9 most eastern countries as "Asia". Since it had previously designated the whole of the USSR as "Europe" this caused considerable dislocation in numbers across these two continents for the Orthodox church, which is especially strong in these continents. For simplicity therefore the two continents have been combined.

For an explanation of what these Tables contain and how they work, and what the maps illustrate, please see top of **Page 1.4.**

TABLE 1.5.1 Changes to the Lutheran Community by continent 1960–2010

Year	Africa	Europe	Oceania	North America	Asia	South America	World
1960	100	100	100	100	100	100	100
1970	161	97	176	102	149	114	101
1980	240	93	233	103	203	123	100
1990	370	91	283	101	268	141	103
2000	480	85	326	99	315	155	102
2010	577	77	376	97	358	170	98
1960	1.4m	62.9m	0.3m	14.1m	1.8m	0.9m	81.5m
2010	8.3m	48.6m	1.2m	13.7m	6.6m	1.5m	79.9m
% of total	10%	61%	2%	17%	8%	2%	100%

FIGURE 1.5.1 Proportions of Lutheran Community by continent 2010

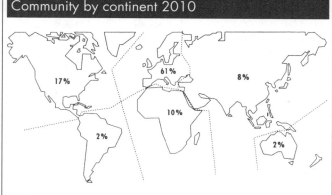

TABLE 1.5.2 The growth of the Presbyterian Community by continent 1960–2010

Year	Africa	Europe	Oceania	North America	Asia	South America	World
1960	100	100	100	100	100	100	100
1970	137	101	106	109	157	125	117
1980	183	101	55	135	235	181	138
1990	220	98	58	151	313	239	159
2000	237	94	58	154	356	274	167
2010	261	92	60	156	394	304	176
1960	4.9m	13.1m	1.5m	5.4m	4.3m	0.3m	29.5m
2010	12.7m	12.0m	0.9m	8.4m	17.0m	1.0m	52.0m
% of total	24%	23%	2%	16%	33%	2%	100%

FIGURE 1.5.2 Proportions of the Presbyterian Community by continent 2010

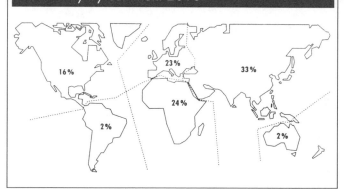

TABLE 1.5.3 The growth of the Pentacostal Community by continent 1960–2010

Year	Africa	Europe	Oceania	North America	Asia	South America	World
1960	100	100	100	100	100	100	100
1970	264	156	272	145	248	275	203
1980	516	217	501	257	461	587	385
1990	1001	307	919	478	741	1233	729
2000	1205	327	1295	646	1029	1739	1003
2010	1814	383	1665	773	1280	2259	1262
1960	1.7m	1.1m	0.1m	5.3m	1.4m	2.6m	12.2m
2010	31.4m	4.3m	1.1m	40.9m	17.6m	58.2m	153.6m
% of total	20%	3%	1%	27%	11%	38%	100%

FIGURE 1.5.3 Proportions of Pentecostal Community by continent 2010

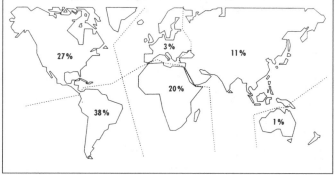

The Lutheran Church is the only major denomination with members in 2010 estimated as lower than in 1960. This is primarily because of the defection of large numbers in Germany, ostensibly becaused of the high extra tax, 9% of income, they have to pay. The Pentecostal churches are the fastest growing in the world, going from 12 million in 1960 to an estimated 154 million by 2010. These are the mainline denominations—Elim, Assemblies of God, Church of God (Anderson), Church of God (Cleveland), Apostolic Church, etc. Two-thirds (65%) of all Pentecostals will be in North or South America by 2010, mainly the United States and Brazil.

For an explanation of what these Tables contain and how they work, and what the maps illustrate, please see top of **Page 1.4.**

TABLE 1.6.1 The growth of the Baptist Community by continent 1960–2010

Year	Africa	Europe	Oceania	North America	Asia	South America	World
1960	100	100	100	100	100	100	100
1970	239	107	132	107	152	184	114
1980	533	119	160	127	214	309	145
1990	793	153	211	140	319	486	174
2000	986	163	246	153	427	621	198
2010	1186	182	287	167	508	766	223
1960	1.0m	1.8m	0.2m	30.6m	2.0m	0.5m	36.1m
2010	11.7m	3.3m	0.5m	51.1m	10.3m	3.7m	80.6m
% of total	14%	4%	1%	63%	13%	5%	100%

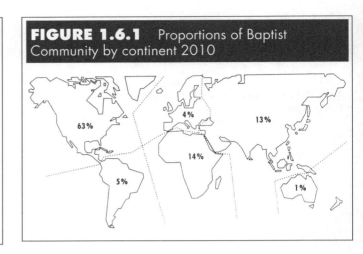

FIGURE 1.6.1 Proportions of Baptist Community by continent 2010

TABLE 1.6.2 Changes to the Methodist Community by continent 1960–2010

Year	Africa	Europe	Oceania	North America	Asia	South America	World
1960	100	100	100	100	100	100	100
1970	133	85	104	94	136	132	101
1980	165	83	31	89	173	175	100
1990	222	80	36	85	231	196	107
2000	275	77	36	83	247	236	114
2010	317	73	38	81	260	270	118
1960	2.9m	2.0m	1.3m	15.6m	1.2m	0.2m	23.2m
2010	9.1m	1.5m	0.5m	12.6m	3.2m	0.5m	27.4m
% of total	33%	5%	2%	46%	12%	2%	100%

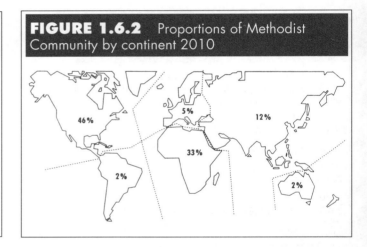

FIGURE 1.6.2 Proportions of Methodist Community by continent 2010

TABLE 1.6.3 The growth of Indigenous churches by continent 1960–2010

Year	Africa	Asia	Oceania	North America	South America	World
1960	100	100	100	100	100	100
1970	176	188	168	120	117	177
1980	284	332	189	159	131	289
1990	419	555	238	188	173	438
2000	524	766	276	220	196	561
2010	629	1015	317	251	223	692
1960	5.4m	1.4m	0.1m	0.2m	0.0m	7.1m
2010	34.2m	14.0m	0.2m	0.4m	0.1m	48.9m
% of total	70%	29%	0%	1%	0%	100%

FIGURE 1.6.3 Proportions of Indigenous Community by continent 2010

Almost two-thirds (63%) of the world's Baptists will be in North America by 2010 if present trends continue, but only half the world's Methodists (46%). The Baptists have however grown almost as twice as fast as the Methodists in the 50 years 1960–2010.

Indigenous Churches are mostly indistinguishable from Pentecostal churches. They are given separately however because these churches are by and large found only in one country, or one group of people within a country, whereas the mainline Pentecostal churches are found in numerous countries around the world. They are local churches belonging often to one linguistic, cultural or socio-economic group living in a particular area. Two-thirds (70%) of the world's indigenous churches are in Africa.

For an explanation of what **Table 1.7** contains and how it works, and what **Figure 1.7.1** illustrates, please see top of **Page 1.4**.

TABLE 1.7 Growth of Other Churches Community by continent 1960–2010

Year	Africa	Europe	Oceania	North America	Asia	South America	World
1960	100	100	100	100	100	100	100
1970	213	100	136	94	149	196	124
1980	354	93	224	98	490	286	210
1990	564	96	212	107	991	508	339
2000	726	95	215	116	1393	621	441
2010	894	97	226	127	1778	753	542
1960	4.8m	3.9m	0.9m	19.3m	6.6m	1.0m	36.5m
2010	43.0m	3.8m	2.1m	24.5m	116.8m	7.8m	198.0m
% of total	22%	2%	1%	12%	59%	4%	100%

FIGURE 1.7.1 Proportions of Other Churches Community by continent 2010

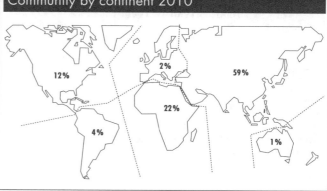

12%   2%   59%   22%   4%   1%

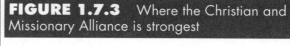

FIGURE 1.7.2 Where the Seventh-Day Adventists are strongest

FIGURE 1.7.3 Where the Christian and Missionary Alliance is strongest

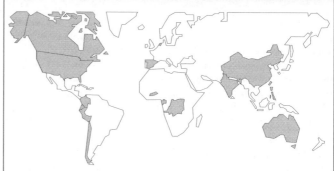

FIGURE 1.7.4 Where the Christian Brethren are strongest

FIGURE 1.7.5 Where the Churches of Christ are strongest

The many "Other Churches" are those smaller denominations but which are world-wide in their reach. For example, they include the following each of which will have a community worldwide of at least half a million people by the year 2010 and will be working in at least 20 countries: The Christian & Missionary Alliance, Christian brethren,

Church of the Nazarene, Churches of Christ, Moravians, the Mennonite groups (taken together for this purpose), Salvation Army and Seventh-day Adventists. The key countries for four of these denominations are illustrated in **Figures 1.7.3, 4, 5** and **6**. Other churches which don't quite meet these criteria include the Disciples of Christ, and the Wesleyan

Church and Wesleyan Holiness Church.

The fastest growing of these churches are the Seventh-Day Adventist and the Christian & Missionary Alliance. Both achieved this growth partly by moving into new countries. Perhaps this strategy is the denominational equivalent of church planting within a country!

TABLE 1.8.1
Christian Community by continent 1900, 1960 and 1990

Continent	1900 %	1960 %	1990 %
Europe	71	46	30
North America	11	23	21
Oceania[3]	1	1	1
Africa	2	7	15
Asia	4	7	14
South America	11	16	19
TOTAL (=100%)	554 mill.	924 mill.	1,512 mill.

TABLE 1.8.2
Percentage of Christians in institutional[1] denominations

Continent	1960 %	1990 %
Europe	98	97
North America	67	68
Oceania[3]	80	80
Africa	76	63
Asia	80	55
South America	97	86
OVERALL	88	78

TABLE 1.8.3
Numbers of churches or congregations 1960 and 1990

Number in thousands		Per 10,000 population		Members[2] per church	
1960	1990	1960	1990	1960	1990
302	325	4.6	4.1	811	786
346	493	12.8	11.6	393	402
21	38	13.3	14.1	215	219
126	476	4.5	7.4	272	228
104	529	0.6	1.7	322	200
35	220	2.4	7.5	2,656	806
934	2,081	3.1	3.9	585	410

[1] Anglican, Catholic, Lutheran, Orthodox or Presbyterian
[2] NOT the Community; in 1960 members were 59% of the Community; in 1990 56%
[3] Mainly Australia and New Zealand

Whilst UK church life is remarkably institutional, the same is true of all the Western world (**Table 1.8.1** top half). Over the 30 years 1960 to 1990, that institutionalism has not changed (**Table 1.8.2**), whereas it has reduced in the Third World (bottom half). This is because of the rapid growth worldwide of the smaller denominations, including Pentecostalism; this last has increased from 1% of Christendom in 1960 to 6% in 1990, and is forecast to grow to 8% by 2010.

The differences between the institutional Christianity of the Western World and the expansionist Christianity in the Third World in the latter part of the 20th century is readily portrayed in **Table 1.8.3**. The number of churches increased 28% 1960 to 1990 in the Western World, but 362% in the Third World. This is illustrated in **Figure 1.8** showing a fourfold rise in Africa, fivefold in Asia, but sixfold in South America. Pentecostalism has replaced some Roman Catholicism in Latin America, seen in **Table 1.8.3** by the huge number of churches they have started, and the subsequent large fall in numbers per church; a change which David Martin observes with great perceptiveness in his book *Tongues of Fire* (Blackwell, Oxford, 1990).

In 1990 the UK had 15% of Europe's churches, but twice as many per 10,000 population than across Europe as a whole.

They are however only a fifth (1960) or a sixth (1990) the size of a European church, reflecting the Protestant heritage of the UK, and the relatively small proportions of Catholics, Lutherans and Orthodox Christians.

Table 1.8.3 shows that South American churches are the largest in the world, due to their large proportion of Catholic churches. The same is true in the UK: in 1990 the Catholics had a Mass attendance in the UK averaging 507 people per church, the Presbyterians a membership of 221, Anglicans 105, and all others 74. However the number of priests available for those churches is decreasing, as seen in **Table 1.8.4**.

TABLE 1.8.4 Number of Catholic Priests for selected European Countries

	1976	1995	% change
Austria	6,099	4,891	−20
Belgium	13,432	9,158	−32
Czechoslovakia	4,054	3,858	−5
France	41,163	28,694	−30
Germany	24,001	20,896	−13
Great Britain	7,861	6,572	−16
Ireland	5,906	5,888	0
Italy	61,784	56,752	−8
The Netherlands	6,083	4,521	−26
Poland	18,529	25,838	+39
Portugal	5,035	4,407	−12
Spain	33,369	29,019	−13
Switzerland	4,308	3,457	−20
TOTAL	231,623	203,951	−12

Source: Article by Jan Kerkhofs, *The Tablet*, 27th July 1999

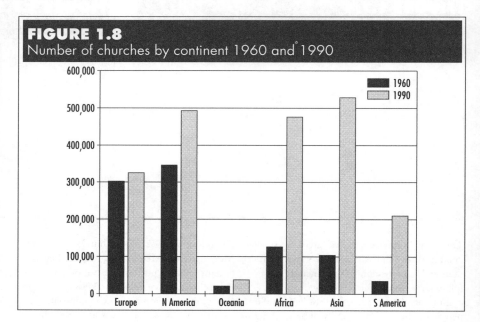

FIGURE 1.8
Number of churches by continent 1960 and 1990

FIGURE 1.9.1
Change in number of churches, Europe, 1960–1980

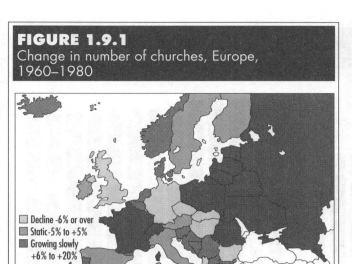

- □ Decline -6% or over
- Static -5% to +5%
- Growing slowly +6% to +20%
- ■ Growing fast +21% or over

FIGURE 1.9.2
Change in number of churches, Europe, 1980–2000

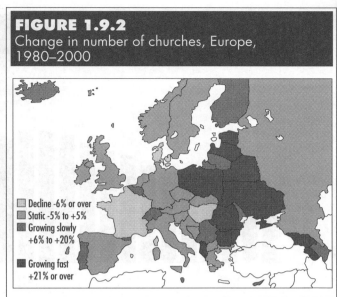

- □ Decline -6% or over
- Static -5% to +5%
- Growing slowly +6% to +20%
- ■ Growing fast +21% or over

FIGURE 1.9.3
Change in number of denominations, Europe, 1960–1980

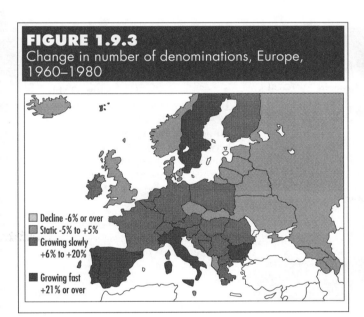

- □ Decline -6% or over
- Static -5% to +5%
- Growing slowly +6% to +20%
- ■ Growing fast +21% or over

FIGURE 1.9.4
Change in number of denominations, Europe, 1980–2000

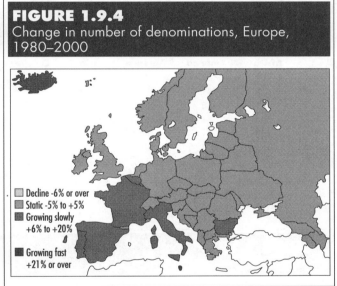

- □ Decline -6% or over
- Static -5% to +5%
- Growing slowly +6% to +20%
- ■ Growing fast +21% or over

These maps are in two pairs: one showing the change in the number of churches and the other the change in the number of denominations. They divide the time period 1960–2000 into two halves. Both pairs show a high time of growth 1960 to 1980 and a much slower or static position in the second 20 year period. These changes are similar to those which occurred on other continents. Part of the reason in Europe for lesser growth is the high proportion of the Christian population who belong to the institutional churches as shown on the previous page.

FIGURE 1.10.1
Percentage of United States population with religious affiliation 1865–2010

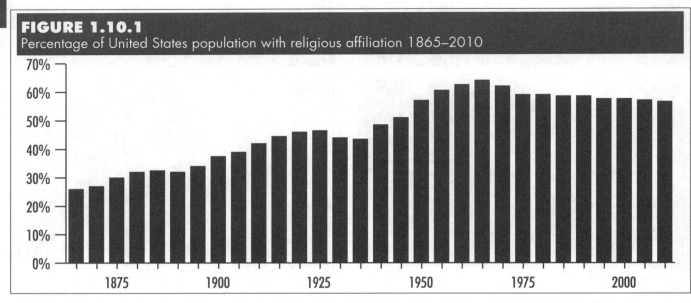

Sources: *Historical Atlas of Religion in America*, Harper & Row,1976, for 1865 to 1970, and adapted from *World Churches Handbook*, Christian Research, 1997, for 1975 to 2010.

TABLE 1.10.1
US Catholic Overseas Mission Personnel 1960–1996

	Africa	N America	S America	Asia	Europe	Oceania	TOTAL
1960	781	1,761	981	2,070	203	986	**6,782**
1965[2]	1,105	2,041	2,091	2,525	53	900	**8,715**
1970	1,141	2,038	2,080	2,176	38	900	**8,373**
1975	1,065	1,684	1,669	1,885	37	808	**7,148**
1980	909	1,541	1,556	1,641	35	711	**6,393**
1985	986	1,504	1,441	1,444	31	650	**6,056**
1990	945	1,509	1,413	1,317	27[1]	560	**5,771**
1995[3]	799	1,035[1]	980[1]	965	172	213	**4,164**

[1]Estimate [2]Average of years 1964 and 1966 [3]1996 figures
Source: *International Bulletin of Missionary Research*, Volume XX, 1999, using United Nations definitions of continents, so that North America includes Central America and the Caribbean.

FIGURE 1.10.2
Reactions of Catholic lay people to five issues, 1996

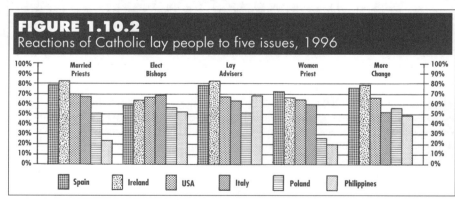

Married Priests | Elect Bishops | Lay Advisers | Women Priest | More Change

Spain | Ireland | USA | Italy | Poland | Philippines

Source: Article "The people cry reform" in *The Tablet*, 22nd March 1997, Page 388.

A series of surveys were carried out in 1996 by professional agencies (including Gallup in the United States) in six countries. They were analysed by Michael Hout and Father Andrew Greeley, Professor of Sociology of the Universities of Chicago and Arizona. Five of the issues polled are illustrated in **Figure 1.10.2**. All the suggested reforms received majority support in both Spain and Ireland; the most conservative of the countries was the Philippines. Only one proposal made majority support across all six: a return to the practice of priests and people electing bishops in their own Diocese. Catholics under 40, and those with an academic education, were more in favour of reform. In the United States, women gave more support to every reform except the ordination of women!

Figure 1.10.1 shows the increasing religious affiliation in the United States with the decrease during the years of depression in the 1920s, and the slower decrease in the last quarter of the 20th century. **Table 1.10.1** shows the number of personnel serving with the US Catholic Overseas Mission, the halving of total numbers between 1970 and 1996, and the changing disposition of them. The increase in Europe in 1996 presumably reflects the shortage of priests highlighted in **Table 1.8.4**.

Table 1.10.2 gives the composition of the World Council of Churches Central Committee elected in Harare, Zimbabwe, December 1998 to serve until 2005. The Central Committee chooses its own executive Committee. The outgoing moderator of the Central Committee, His Holiness Aram I, was re-elected.

TABLE 1.10.2
Composition of WCC Central Committee

Orthodox	37
Reformed	33
Anglican	15
Methodist	15
Lutheran	13
Free, Pentecostal, African Instituted	10
United and Uniting	10
Baptist	7
Others	10
Men	91
Women	59
Ordained	85
Lay	65
Under 30	22
30 or over	128
TOTAL	**150**

Source: *Report of 8th General Assembly of the WCC, Harare, December 1998*, by Col Earl Robinson to Lausanne Committee

CHURCHES IN THE UNITED KINGDOM

Contents

See Notes and Definitions on Page 0.6

Sources:
Individual denominations, UK Christian Handbook 1996/97, Church Censuses in England, Scotland and Wales and others as indicated

2

FIGURE 2.2.1
Dioceses of the Church 1035

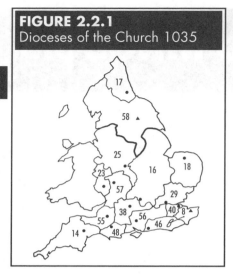

Source: Anglo-Saxon England, Sir Frank Stenton, OUP.

FIGURE 2.2.2
Dioceses of the Church 1135

Source: Anglo-Norman England 1066–1166, Marjorie Chibnall, Blackwell, Oxford, Page 41.

FIGURE 2.2.3
Dioceses of the Church 1450

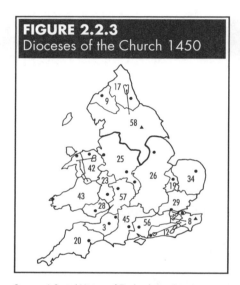

Source: A Social History of England, Asa Briggs.

FIGURE 2.2.4
Dioceses of the Church 1541

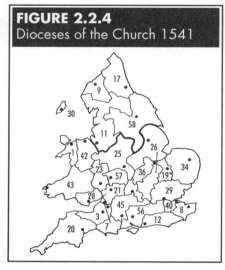

Source: The English Dioceses: A History of their Limits, G Will, Elliot Stock, 1900, Page 387.

FIGURE 2.2.5 Dioceses of the Church of England 1836

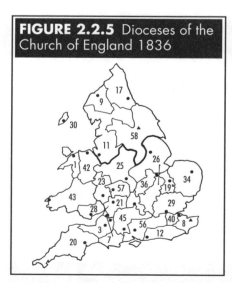

Source: Religion and Society in Industrial England, A D Gilbert, Longman, London, 1976, Page 103.

FIGURE 2.2.6 Dioceses of the Church of England 1998

Source: Religious Trends, No 1, 1998/1999, Paternoster Publishing and Christian Research, 1997, Page 11.2.

Dioceses 1035–1998

1 Bangor
2 Bath
3 Bath and Wells
4 Birmingham
5 Blackburn
6 Bradford
7 Bristol
8 Canterbury
9 Carlisle
10 Chelmsford
11 Chester
12 Chichester
13 Coventry
14 Crediton
15 Derby
16 Dorchester
17 Durham
18 Elmham
19 Ely
20 Exeter
21 Gloucester
22 Guildford
23 Hereford
24 Leicester
25 Lichfield
26 Lincoln
27 Liverpool
28 Llandaff
29 London
30 Man
31 Manchester
32 Monmouth
33 Newcastle
34 Norwich
35 Oxford
36 Peterborough
37 Portsmouth
38 Ramsbury
39 Ripon
40 Rochester
41 St Albans
42 St Asaph
43 St David's
44 St Edmundsbury & Ipswich
45 Salisbury
46 Selsey
47 Sheffield
48 Sherborne
49 Sodor & Man
50 Southwark
51 Southwell
52 Swansea and Brecon
53 Truro
54 Wakefield
55 Wells
56 Winchester
57 Worcester
58 York

● Bishopric
▲ Archbishopric

TABLE 2.3 Number of Churches Built or Congregations Started by Century 450–1998

Date	Anglican	Roman Catholic	Free Churches	Orthodox	TOTAL	Percentage
450–700	174	0	0	0	174	1
700–799	80	0	0	0	80	0
800–899	329	0	0	0	329	1
900–999	399	0	0	0	399	1
1000–1099	1,495	0	0	0	1,495	4
1100–1199	2,332	0	2	0	2,334	6
1200–1299	2,132	0	2	0	2,134	6
1300–1399	916	0	0	0	916	2
1400–1499	430	0	2	0	432	1
1500–1599	221	4	8	0	233	1
1600–1699	149	23	667	0	839	2
1700–1799	285	71	690	0	1,046	3
1800–1899	4,622	1,392	8,103	0	14,117	37
1900–1998	2,717	2,281	7,933	258	13,189	35
Total	16,281	3,771	17,407	258	37,717	100

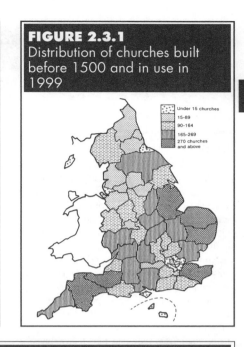

FIGURE 2.3.1 Distribution of churches built before 1500 and in use in 1999

Under 15 churches
15–89
90–164
165–269
270 churches and above

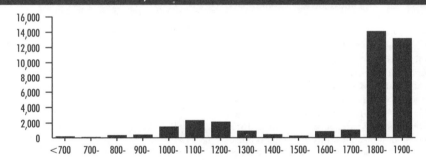

FIGURE 2.3.2 Number of churches built in England per century since the seventh century

Large building programme

The final column of **Table 2.3** and **Figure 2.3.2** shows the huge church building programme that operated in the 11th to 13th centuries, and which still accounts for 1 in 6 (16%) of our churches in use today. The rapid expansion of the church, especially into urban areas as the industrial revolution got under way, in the 19th century, is also seen. Three in every eight of churches today (37%) date from the 19th century.

One in three (35%) of today's churches were built this century, just over one in three (37%) were built in the 19th century, and almost one in three (28%) in all the earlier times since Christianity first came to England with the Roman conquerors. That so many have survived and are still in use today is a testimony to the craftmanship that went into their building, and underlines the importance of the heritage that our churches give to this country.

Although dwarfed by the 19th and 20th centuries, **Figure 2.3.2** shows the importance of the building programme undertaken in the 11th to 13th centuries. How did such a programme happen?

Why so much building?

King Harold II was slain by the victorious William the Conqueror at Hastings in 1066. William proceeded to unite England, defend England, open England up, and institutionalise England. He came from Normandy, and allowed fellow Normans to join him in Britain. The largest immigration in British history took place in the years after 1066, not parallelled until a million came from the West Indies in the aftermath of World War II in the 1950s. Trade links with the continent were encouraged. In addition the population of Europe was generally expanding in the 11th and 12th centuries and

that larger population caused new living areas to be opened.

Amongst those newer places to live were the rural areas of England, now safer because Viking attacks were decreasing and William had a superior army. He built many castles to keep such raiders out. So people felt safe to settle in small rural communities, often quite isolated from each other. Each of these many communities required its own church.

Prosperity and peace

The central and northern parts of Britain were also more generally amenable to habitation as the overall weather saw a gradual warming in the 12th and 13th centuries. At that stage, especially in Lincolnshire and Norfolk, Britain had a feudal system of government, with many "sokemen" and slaves under control of the Lords. The people were mainly sheep and arable farmers, so were less busy in the winter months each year; thus labour was available for building. The Lords were powerful and rich, partly through the sale of grain, other farm products and sheep. Thus they could afford to build churches.

It was a time of peace, both physically and

intellectually. The Hundred Years War had yet to start, sapping wealth and diverting manpower. The Renaissance had yet to begin in earnest, although some religious changes were being heralded through the Lollards and the ideas of John Hus. The motive for building the churches may have been in part to provide Masses for the dead of rich families, but once built others could attend.

The churches may have replaced existing buildings. The 1086 Domesday Book listed some 15,000 "priests", but excluded some further 25,000 assistant clergy. Not always would there be only one clergyman to a church. If there were on average 3 or 4 clergy per church, then that would mean some 10 to 12,000 churches in the areas the Domesday Book covered (it omitted London and Winchester for example). Some 6,000 churches which survive to today, were built in the 11th to 13th centuries, made mostly of costly stone. They were built to last, and initially would have been larger than for the immediate village population. As the population grew in successive decades there was no need to rebuild as the church remained large enough.

TABLE 2.4 Proportions of churches built in various periods, and average number per year

	1975–	450–1500	1500–1799	1800–1849	1850–1874	1875–1899	1900–1924	1925–1949	1950–1974	Total (=100%)
	%	%	%	%	%	%	%	%	%	
	22	6	12	12	13	8	8	9	10	37,717
Interval in years	1,050	300	50	25	25	25	25	25	24	1,548
Churches per year	8	7	91	184	199	126	114	135	155	24

Principles

Thus the Norman invaders effectively aided the Christianisation of the land by building churches, replacing old ones where necessary, wherever a suitable number of people lived. Small congregations, conveniently situated within walking distance. These were accepted by the community – who had helped to build the church in the first place, and helped to construct the community in the process. There was public visibility and professional leadership. It could be argued that these principles are similar to those used today by the New Churches, Pentecostals and other denominations as they start new fellowships.

Changes

In the 14th century, the Black Death decimated villages, causing some to be burnt completely, though not the central church. In parts of East Anglia, Derbyshire and elsewhere a new village would be built perhaps a mile away from the ashes of the old, but leaving the church in the middle of what today are cornfields! Strong religious forces were unleashed with Erasmus' translation of the Bible and Martin Luther nailing his 95 Theses to the door of Wurtenburg Cathedral in 1517. The rise of non-conformity as a result of the Reformation caused many chapels to be built, and the great Norman churches still continued but with smaller congregations perhaps than before. The consequence of all this was to drastically reduce the need for new village and town churches, and the building programme suffered accordingly. In the 16th century only 230 churches were built in the entire 100 years that are still in use, 10% of the number erected four hundred years earlier.

Thus the first heyday of church building was between 1100 and 1300 under the stabilising influence of the Normans. They also built many of the country's cathedrals in the same period, as were the French cathedrals.

Denominational variations

Table 2.3 breaks down the numbers built by broad denominational group. It should also be noted that many of the New Churches, a group within the Free Churches, do not, for the most part, actually build churches, but rather hire school halls or other public premises in which to meet. They may also occasionally buy a redundant church. Likewise the Orthodox churches in by far the majority of cases, start new congregations using existing Anglican (mostly) or Catholic churches. Thus the numbers are not strictly all of church buildings. The Free Churches include 300 residential schools and colleges where services are held, mostly in private chapels. About 600 of the Catholic churches are not ecclesiastical buildings as such but where Mass is publicly conducted in retreat houses, etc.

Table 2.3 shows that there are 8,000 Anglican churches currently in use which were built before the year 1400. That is virtually half (49%) of all the Anglican churches in the country. Many of the problems of the Church of England are summarised in this one figure! It is a huge burden to look after so many historic buildings, many of which are listed and therefore worthy of preservation. Bodies like English Heritage play a crucial role in this.

There are no current Roman Catholic churches from before 1500 since all the Catholic churches were requisitioned by Henry VIII when he formed the Church of England. All churches before this date are therefore now deemed to be Anglican.

Closed churches

When such churches are closed, some are taken over by the Churches Conservation Trust (formerly the Redundant Churches Fund), established by law in 1969. They are responsible for preserving churches of historical and archaeological interest or architectural quality which are no longer required for regular worship. By the end of March 1999 315 churches had been vested to the Trust. Redundant churches not so fortunate as to owned by the Trust are usually sold or used in a variety of ways. Some are turned into cultural centres, others into flats or businesses. A few have been demolished. Others are now used as mosques or temples or have been purchased by other Christian churches. One of the Anglican churches in Lewisham, for example, was bought by the New Testament Church of God.

Churches built per year

Table 2.4 shows the proportions of churches built in smaller time periods than a century, and the average number built per year. It may be readily seen that the 19th and 20th centuries have had very large numbers of new churches built, but the 19th century eclipsed the 20th in terms of numbers per year. In the last half of the 19th century, a new church was being opened every other day!

Anglican Churches

Figure 2.4 gives the number of Anglican churches built by century. The peak in the 12th and 13th was not surpassed until the latter half of the 19th century, and as these are of surviving churches still in use with the likelihood of 19th centuries being more likely to have survived to the present day, the achievement of our forefathers can be the more readily appreciated. Over half, 51%, of Anglican churches in use today were built *before 1500*.

The latter half of the nineteenth century saw a huge church building programme. This was partly in response to the finding in the 1851 Population Census, the first to include a religious question, that there were not enough seats in churches should everyone in the country wish to attend. This was especially true in the urban areas to which many of the population had moved.

Horace Mann's Report said that 1,645,000 "inhabitants of England would not be able ... to join in public worship" and suggested that some 2,000 churches be built to remedy this deficiency. His Report was published in 1854. In the next 45 years some 8,700 would be built, many times more than strictly necessary, and many therefore inevitably rarely if ever filled.

It was these facts that lay behind the analysis by Professor Robin Gill in his book *The Myth of the Empty Church* in which he meticulously shows that many churches in the nineteenth century were mostly empty. The Victorians did not fill the churches in their church attendance.

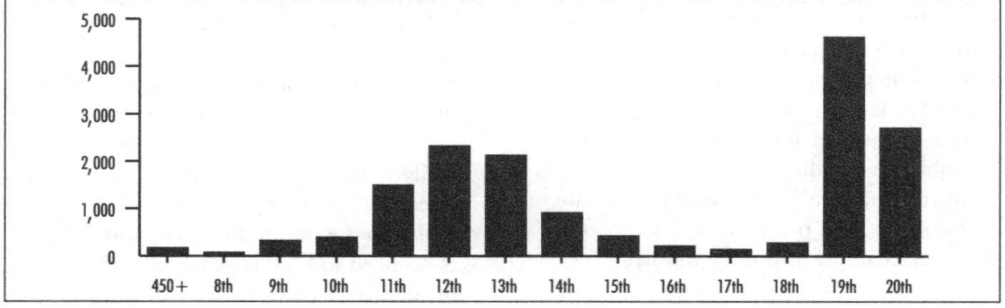

Sources: The Domesday Geography of England, "The End of Anglo-Saxon England" Volume, H C Darby, Cambridge University Press, 1952; Domesday, A Search for the Roots of England, Michael Wood; 'Christian' England, Peter Brierley, MARC Europe, 1991; English Church Attendance Survey, Christian Research, 1998; Religious Worship in England and Wales, Census of Great Britain, 1851, George Routledge & co., 1854, Page 102; The Myth of the Empty Church, Professor Robin Gill, SPCK, London, 1993.

FIGURE 2.4
Number of Anglican churches built per century

TABLE 2.5.1
Number of churches built and congregations started in 19th and 20th centuries by broad denominational group

Date	Anglican	Roman Catholic	Free Churches	Orthodox	TOTAL	Percent-age
1800–1824	195	46	1,064	0	1,305	3
1825–1849	1,411	213	1,615	0	3,239	9
1850–1874	1,801	508	2,295	0	4,604	12
1875–1899	1,215	625	3,129	0	4,969	13
1900–1924	848	553	1,760	0	3,161	8
1925–1949	634	577	1,604	25	2,840	8
1950–1974	793	750	1,721	105	3,369	9
1975–1998	442	401	2,848	128	3,819	10

TABLE 2.5.2
Number of churches built and congregations started every five years since 1975 by broad denominational group

Date	Anglican	Roman Catholic	Free Churches	Orthodox	TOTAL	Percent-age
1975–1979	92	178	495	30	795	2
1980–1984	80	113	586	25	804	2
1985–1989	79	78	845	18	1,020	3
1990–1994	110	12	654	40	816	2
1995–1998	81	20	268	15	384	1

TABLE 2.5.3
Period when churches now in use were built by current environment

	City Centre	Inner City	Council Estate	Suburban/ Urban Fringe	Separate Town	Commuter Rural Area	Other Rural Area	Overall
Before 1500	348	87	87	544	678	2,530	4,449	8,723
1500–1799	200	100	25	361	586	424	797	2,493
1800–1849	190	237	95	869	839	854	1,661	4,745
1850–1899	294	1,013	356	2,352	1,861	1,344	2,826	10,046
1900–1949	132	492	654	2,492	1,178	689	919	6,556
1950–1989	286	614	1,201	1,925	1,206	445	367	6,044
TOTAL (=100%)	1,550	2,543	2,418	8,543	6,348	6,286	11,019	38,607

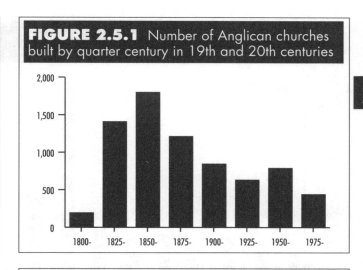

FIGURE 2.5.1 Number of Anglican churches built by quarter century in 19th and 20th centuries

FIGURE 2.5.2 Number of Free churches built or congregations started in 19th and 20th centuries

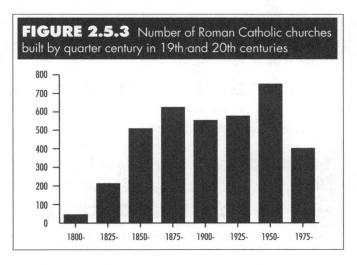

FIGURE 2.5.3 Number of Roman Catholic churches built by quarter century in 19th and 20th centuries

The percentages in the final column of **Tables 2.5.1** and **2.5.2** are of the total number of churches in England in 1998. **Table 2.5.1** is illustrated in **Figures 2.5.1–3** and **Table 2.5.2** in **Figure 2.6.1**. The Anglicans concentrated their building programme after 1854 when Horace Mann's Report on the Census of Population in 1851 showed the need for more churches. The Free Churches built more at the end of the 19th century, and, when the Pentecostal and

New Churches began or began expanding, in the last quarter also of the 20th century. The Roman Catholics built more immediately after the Second World War.

The data in **Table 2.5.3** is based on that obtained from the 1989 English Church Census, a question which was not asked in the 1998 Survey. The base numbers therefore are a little higher than those used in the previous Tables.

Whilst the oldest churches are predominantly in rural areas, the expansion in the latter half of the 19th century was not confined to the urban or suburban areas – over 4,000 new churches were also built in the rural areas, largely as the Free Churches built there, especially the Methodists, which like other major denominations now were then split into various segments. The 20th century increase has mostly been in towns, suburban areas and Council Estates.

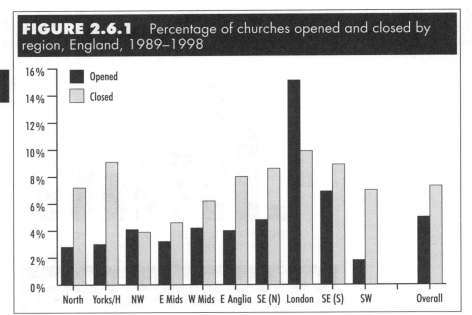

FIGURE 2.6.1 Percentage of churches opened and closed by region, England, 1989–1998

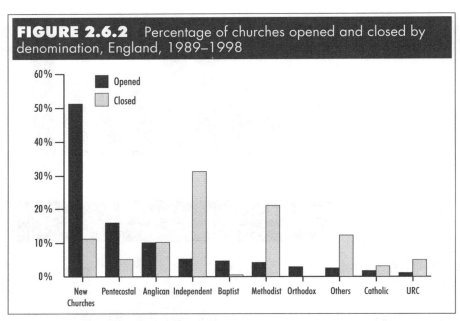

FIGURE 2.6.2 Percentage of churches opened and closed by denomination, England, 1989–1998

TABLE 2.6 Churches Opening and Closing by Period and Region 1989–1998

Date	North	Yorks/ Humb	North West	East Mids	West Mids	East Angl.	South E (N)	South E (L)	South E (S)	South West	TOTAL
Total churches 1989	2,550	3,827	4,039	3,911	3,868	2,769	3,943	3,549	4,297	5,854	38,607
Started 1989–1998	+70	+107	+164	+124	+158	+107	+182	+565	+291	+99	+1,867
Closures of these churches	–3	–5	–8	–6	–8	–6	–9	–27	–14	–4	–90
Closures of churches built prior to 1989	–174	–323	–151	–173	–228	–208	–316	–344	–362	–388	–2,667
Net change 1989–1998	–107	–221	+5	–55	–78	–107	–143	+194	–85	–293	–890
Total churches 1998	2,443	3,606	4,044	3,856	3,790	2,662	3,800	3,743	4,212	5,561	37,717

Figure 2.6.1 shows where church numbers have grown most in England in the 1990s – Greater London and the North West. The high closure programme in the South West shows the continuing policy of the Methodist Church in that region. The closing of some rural churches, often through combining with other parishes, by the Church of England partly accounts for the decline in the North, and East Anglia. Some of the Anglican closures are also in the inner city areas, as evidenced by the high numbers in the East and West Midlands, a closure policy shared with the United Reformed Church and the Methodists. Often Local Ecumenical Projects (LEPs) are created when two or three churches in an area are closed and a new one built, or three are merged into one, newly furnished, building. The main decline, however, is in the number of small independent churches, which frequently have no, or insufficient, wider group to help them.

Figure 2.6.2 shows where the main emphasis has been in the church planting initiatives – the work of the New Churches in its various streams, of which New Frontiers, Ichthus and Pioneer are the largest and perhaps most well known. There are however at least another 20 smaller streams as well. The Pentecostals also have started many churches in these 9 years (nearly 300 in total), and whilst the Anglicans have closed more than they have opened, they still have opened well over 100 new churches.

It is equally clear which are the major denominations closing churches: the small independent churches, the Methodist Church and those in other smaller denominations. The Methodists are essentially engaged in a rationalising policy of closing small, uneconomic and less used churches; the others tend to close because those attending, often elderly, die and the remainder are unable to start it afresh.

The line labelled "Closure of these churches" in **Table 2.6** is estimated. There are four columns where there is a positive net change over the decade: the three South East areas and the North West region. Elim (a Pentecostal denomination) have held a strong campaign in the North west to plant more churches in that region, and many of those started in this Region are Pentecostal. Kensington Temple in central London has also had a strong church planting programme over the past few years and of the 454 new churches started 129 are through their work. Many of the rest will be in the burgeoning numbers of African and West Indian churches and those of other ethnic minority groups in and around the capital.

Where there was such a positive net change the number of church closures was also smaller. Could this suggest that in areas where vigorous church planting was taking place such activity acts as an inhibitor to some extent in the closure of other churches? If so, this is an interesting corollary to a church planting programme.

TABLE 2.7
UK Christian and Religious Community in millions 1900–2000

Year	Anglican	Roman Catholic	Presby-terian	Methodist	Baptist	Others[2]	Total Christianity Number	Total Christianity % Pop[3]	Other Religions	Total all Religions Number	Total all Religions % Pop[3]
1900	23.1	2.5	3.2	1.7	0.7	1.6	**32.8**	86%	0.2	**33.0**	86%
1905	24.2	2.6	3.3	1.7	0.8	1.7	**34.3**	86%	0.3	**34.6**	86%
1910	25.4	2.7	3.4	1.8	0.8	1.8	**35.9**	85%	0.3	**36.2**	86%
1915	25.6	2.9	3.4	1.7	0.8	1.8	**36.2**	85%	0.4	**36.6**	86%
1920	26.3	2.9	3.5	1.7	0.8	1.8	**37.0**	84%	0.4	**37.4**	85%
1925	26.9	3.1	3.5	1.7	0.8	1.8	**37.8**	84%	0.5	**38.3**	85%
1930	27.1	3.2	3.5	1.8	0.8	1.8	**38.2**	83%	0.5	**38.7**	84%
1935	27.4	3.5	3.5	1.8	0.8	1.8	**38.8**	82%	0.6	**39.4**	84%
1940	27.6	3.5	3.5	1.7	0.8	1.8	**38.9**	82%	0.7	**39.6**	83%
1945	27.8	3.5	3.5	1.7	0.7	1.7	**38.9**	80%	0.7	**39.6**	81%
1950	28.5	4.0	3.5	1.7	0.7	1.7	**40.1**	80%	0.8	**40.9**	81%
1955	27.8	4.3	3.5	1.7	0.6	1.7	**39.6**	77%	0.9	**40.5**	79%
1960	27.6[1]	4.8	3.5	1.7	0.6	1.7	**39.9**	76%	1.1	**41.0**	78%
1965	27.4[1]	5.3	3.3	1.6	0.6	1.7	**39.9**	74%	1.5	**41.4**	77%
1970	27.8[1]	5.4	3.1	1.5	0.6	1.6	**40.0**	72%	1.9	**41.9**	75%
1975	28.2	5.6	2.9	1.5	0.6	1.4	**40.2**	72%	2.1	**42.3**	76%
1980	27.7	5.7	2.8	1.4	0.6	1.6	**39.8**	71%	2.6	**42.4**	75%
1985	27.1	5.6	2.7	1.4	0.6	1.7	**39.1**	69%	3.2	**42.3**	74%
1990	26.6	5.6	2.7	1.4	0.6	1.7	**38.6**	67%	3.6	**42.2**	73%
1995	26.1	5.7	2.6	1.3	0.6	1.8	**38.1**	65%	4.1	**42.2**	72%
2000[4]	25.6	5.8	2.6	1.3	0.5[1]	1.9	**37.7**	64%	4.5	**42.2**	71%

[1] Revised figure
[2] Independent, Orthodox, Pentecostal, New and Other Churches
[3] Including Northern Ireland population prior to 1921
[4] Estimate

FIGURE 2.7
Percentage of population Religious and Christian

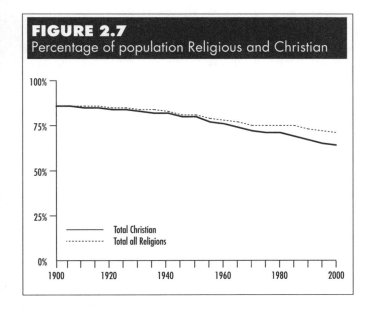

Total Christian
Total all Religions

Table 2.7 gives the size of the Christian community in the UK across the 20th Century. From being 86% of the population at the turn of the last century, seven people in every eight, it has decreased to 64%, five in every eight.

Anglican figures are estimates of the number of people baptised in the Church of England or other Episcopal church, a number which peaked in 1950, though was also high in 1975.

Likewise the *Roman Catholic* figures represent the Catholic population of this country, that is, those baptised as Catholics. This number has steadily increased across the century though fell slightly in the 1980s. This number is reported by Parish Priests in their annual return and the figure is simply a total of all those figures.

The *Presbyterian* figures are largely the numbers in Scotland who belong either to the Church of Scotland or other like Presbyterian churches. The decrease in numbers reflects the decrease in membership of the Church of Scotland.

The figures in the *Methodist* column show the Methodist Community Roll, a figure collected regularly by their headquarters.

The *Baptist* figures are an estimate and are taken as roughly double the number of Baptist members in the UK. Likewise the figures for *other denominations* are estimated; the low figure in 1975 reflects the decline in many of these prior to the increase that took place in the 1980s with the increasing numbers joining the New Churches.

Since all these numbers include children as well as adults the percentages of the population given twice in this Table are of the entire population.

The figures in the *Other Religions* column are estimated in a variety of ways. The later figures (1975–2000) were given in more detail in *Religious Trends* No 1 Table 2.3.

Figure 2.7 graphs the two percentage columns and shows that the increasing religious diversity in the UK by the widening gap between the two lines especially since about 1960.

For a similar analysis of church *membership* see Page 8.15.

	Membership	Churches	Ministers
TABLE 2.8.1			
Total Institutional Churches[1]			
1900	6,802,529	28,274	32,021
1910	7,641,564	29,261	31,787
1920	7,747,518	29,858	30,209
1930	8,194,473	30,093	29,141
1940	7,985,910	30,265	30,533
1950	7,752,713	29,929	28,272
1960	8,106,144	29,563	28,077
1970	7,453,550	29,008	27,209
1980	6,243,820	29,629	25,244
1990	5,324,616	28,856	23,732
2000	4,565,652	27,913	18,932
1991	5,244,856	28,786	23,556
1992	5,233,503	28,724	23,399
1993	5,180,459	28,727	23,173
1994	5,101,151	28,635	22,956
1995	4,983,092	28,463	22,010
1996	4,766,046	28,296	20,545
1997	4,739,149	28,345	20,092
1998	4,715,761	28,104	19,722

	Membership	Churches	Ministers
TABLE 2.8.2			
Total Anglican Churches[2]			
1900	3,241,450	20,079	22,486
1910	3,880,350	20,707	21,285
1920	3,824,750	20,976	19,913
1930	4,166,100	21,152	18,561
1940	3,911,320	21,393	18,685
1950	3,444,130	20,956	15,714
1960	3,340,750	20,677	14,749
1970	2,987,040	20,417	14,767
1980	2,179,808	19,399	12,472
1990	1,727,967	18,823	12,373
2000	1,657,150	18,307	10,011
1991	1,764,980	18,790	12,358
1992	1,786,932	18,736	12,330
1993	1,790,269	18,809	12,277
1994	1,793,820	18,752	12,162
1995	1,785,033	18,663	11,781
1996	1,604,641	18,550	10,640
1997	1,631,579	18,620	10,464
1998[1]	1,649,928	18,416	10,395

	Mass Attendance	Churches	Priests
TABLE 2.8.3			
Total Roman Catholic[3]			
1900	1,911,960	2,272	3,903
1910	1,995,310	2,566	4,908
1920	2,107,000	2,765	5,137
1930	2,189,735	3,075	5,617
1940	2,232,270	3,452	7,230
1950	2,431,540	3,850	8,350
1960	2,844,570	3,972	9,490
1970	2,746,203	4,058	9,570
1980	2,454,803	4,156	9,004
1990	2,198,364	4,334	8,081
2000	1,721,500	4,276	6,083
1991	2,100,706	4,317	7,965
1992	2,086,930	4,322	7,886
1993	2,058,493	4,338	7,658
1994	2,004,002	4,379	7,601
1995	1,914,066	4,275	7,309
1996	1,889,496	4,258	7,025
1997	1,859,349	4,297	6,753
1998	1,832,907	4,288	6,503

	Membership	Churches	Priests
TABLE 2.8.4			
Total Orthodox Churches[4]			
1900	–	–	–
1910	–	–	–
1920	–	–	–
1930	10,000	9	7
1940	20,000	21	13
1950	80,650	33	26
1960	107,240	92	77
1970	159,170	124	108
1980	171,735	154	135
1990	184,745	207	156
2000	207,930	256	197
1991	186,444	208	158
1992	188,525	212	158
1993	190,767	215	159
1994	192,996	221	163
1995	195,895	234	174
1996	198,487	238	184
1997	199,733	243	190
1998	202,236	248	192

	Membership	Churches	Ministers
TABLE 2.8.5			
Total Presbyterian Church[5]			
1900	1,649,119	5,923	5,632
1910	1,765,904	5,988	5,594
1920	1,815,768	6,117	5,159
1930	1,828,638	5,857	4,956
1940	1,822,320	5,399	4,605
1950	1,796,393	5,090	4,182
1960	1,813,584	4,822	3,761
1970	1,559,137	4,409	2,764
1980	1,437,474	5,920	3,633
1990	1,213,540	5,492	3,122
2000	979,072	5,074	2,641
1991	1,193,626	5,471	3,075
1992	1,171,116	5,454	3,025
1993	1,140,930	5,365	3,079
1994	1,119,333	5,283	3,030
1995	1,088,098	5,284	2,746
1996	1,073,422	5,250	2,696
1997	1,048,488	5,185	2,685
1998	1,030,690	5,152	2,632

	Membership	Churches	Ministers
TABLE 2.8.6			
Total Free Churches[6]			
1900	1,861,297	20,714	13,387
1910	2,062,397	21,983	13,486
1920	2,055,151	22,177	13,828
1930	2,162,680	23,966	14,559
1940	2,031,320	24,663	14,469
1950	1,861,271	24,742	13,382
1960	1,811,701	25,197	13,134
1970	1,625,853	24,207	12,072
1980	1,285,175	20,209	10,450
1990	1,299,435	20,739	13,164
2000	1,296,144	20,782	14,777
1991	1,292,813	20,681	13,517
1992	1,291,759	20,556	13,680
1993	1,295,162	20,563	13,680
1994	1,290,516	20,581	14,090
1995	1,299,981	20,631	14,203
1996	1,299,369	20,681	14,311
1997	1,292,223	20,675	14,354
1998	1,296,470	20,655	14,435

[1] Total of Tables 2.8.2–5
[2] Table 8.2.1
[3] Table 8.6.1
[4] Table 8.11.1
[5] Table 8.14.1
[6] Total of Tables 2.10.1–6

2

FIGURE 2.9.1
Total Church Membership, UK 1900–2000

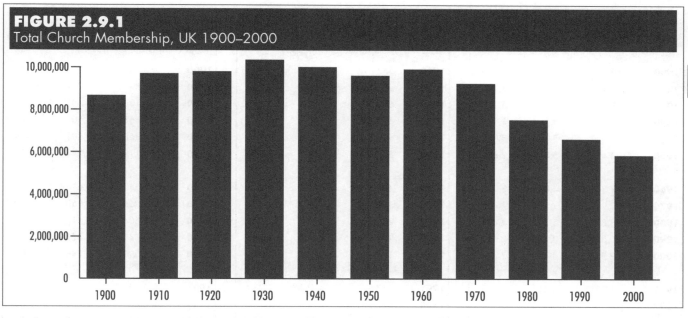

FIGURE 2.9.2
Anglican Church Members, UK 1900–2000

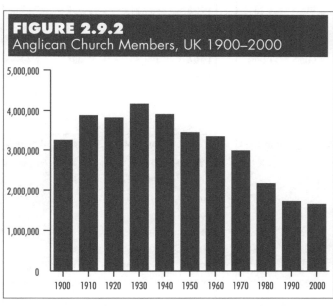

FIGURE 2.9.3
Roman Catholic Attendance, UK 1900–2000

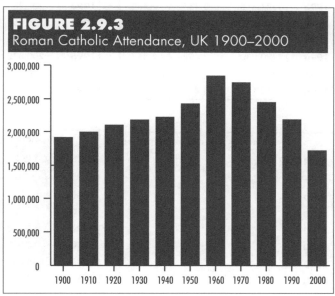

FIGURE 2.9.4
Orthodox Church Members, UK 1900–2000

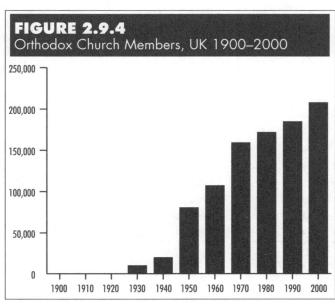

FIGURE 2.9.5
Presbyterian Church Members, UK 1900–2000

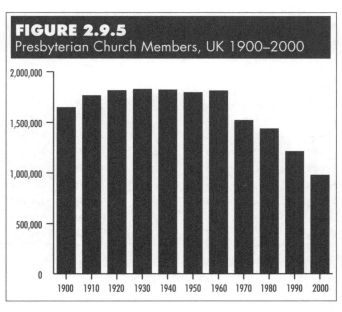

	Membership	Churches	Ministers
TABLE 2.10.1 Total Baptist Churches[2]			
1900	359,855	4,424	2,910
1910	412,165	5,048	3,195
1920	398,811	4,990	3,118
1930	400,005	5,107	3,102
1940	376,347	5,104	3,069
1950	334,476	5,045	2,872
1960	317,301	4,882	3,005
1970	292,976	3,588	2,459
1980	238,805	3,317	2,414
1990	230,377	3,438	2,615
2000	209,234	3,430	2,774
1991	231,386	3,412	2,755
1992	228,502	3,406	2,814
1993	227,878	3,437	2,883
1994	225,227	3,430	2,866
1995	223,151	3,446	2,860
1996	220,980	3,438	2,817
1997	216,920	3,430	2,815
1998	213,612	3,418	2,777

	Membership	Churches	Ministers
TABLE 2.10.2 Total All Independent Churches[3]			
1900	532,797	7,015	3,249
1910	601,507	7,231	3,290
1920	608,829	7,184	3,196
1930	619,660	7,588	3,127
1940	590,547	7,568	3,113
1950	528,079	7,287	3,046
1960	493,506	7,181	2,987
1970	422,544	7,280	3,044
1980	236,706	4,294	1,274
1990	222,918	4,101	1,242
2000	195,498	3,889	1,274
1991	217,237	4,051	1,239
1992	212,991	4,005	1,252
1993	207,286	3,955	1,251
1994	206,053	3,940	1,275
1995	203,594	3,907	1,251
1996	200,872	3,905	1,230
1997	198,462	3,906	1,239
1998	198,974	3,904	1,254

	Membership	Churches	Ministers
TABLE 2.10.3 Total Methodist Church[4]			
1900	849,446	7,404	3,952
1910	917,897	7,772	4,270
1920	877,106	8,121	4,057
1930	917,661	8,507	4,243
1940	862,358	8,891	4,005
1950	809,119	9,249	3,750
1960	788,562	9,613	3,646
1970	673,256	9,950	3,090
1980	539,804	8,517	2,430
1990	477,540	7,625	2,467
2000	386,590	6,746	2,408
1991	469,326	7,543	2,461
1992	460,849	7,439	2,461
1993	453,213	7,352	2,475
1994	444,396	7,259	2,465
1995	434,410	7,156	2,441
1996	424,531	7,086	2,437
1997	414,394	6,998	2,428
1998	405,039	6,918	2,411

	Membership	Churches	Ministers
TABLE 2.10.4 Total New Churches[5]			
1900	–	–	–
1910	–	–	–
1920	–	–	–
1930	–	–	–
1940	–	–	–
1950	–	–	–
1960	–	–	–
1970	225	1	20
1980	10,037	205	156
1990	76,485	1,113	1,145
2000[1]	137,225	1,818	1,805
1991	78,950	1,203	1,226
1992	85,468	1,226	1,255
1993	91,763	1,272	1,308
1994	97,859	1,348	1,377
1995	104,101	1,414	1,435
1996	108,594	1,495	1,530
1997	113,730	1,574	1,574
1998	122,887	1,659	1,604

	Membership	Churches	Ministers
TABLE 2.10.5 Total All Pentecostal Churches[6]			
1900	–	–	–
1910	50	2	1
1920	1,100	26	16
1930	18,040	402	321
1940	36,050	782	632
1950	37,050	809	652
1960	52,905	1,092	960
1970	86,090	1,357	1,362
1980	117,582	1,808	2,279
1990	153,962	2,178	3,279
2000	233,234	2,649	4,322
1991	158,005	2,210	3,425
1992	165,910	2,252	3,513
1993	177,499	2,292	3,593
1994	179,854	2,334	3,707
1995	197,602	2,429	3,897
1996	207,491	2,463	3,997
1997	212,929	2,481	4,038
1998	221,520	2,529	4,138

	Membership	Churches	Ministers
TABLE 2.10.6 Total All Other Denominations[7]			
1900	119,169	1,871	3,276
1910	130,778	1,930	2,730
1920	169,305	1,856	3,441
1930	207,314	2,362	3,766
1940	166,018	2,318	3,650
1950	152,547	2,352	3,062
1960	159,427	2,429	2,536
1970	150,762	2,031	2,097
1980	142,241	2,068	1,897
1990	138,153	2,284	2,416
2000	134,363	2,250	2,194
1991	137,909	2,262	2,411
1992	138,039	2,228	2,385
1993	137,523	2,255	2,398
1994	137,127	2,270	2,400
1995	137,123	2,279	2,319
1996	136,901	2,294	2,300
1997	135,276	2,286	2,277
1998	134,438	2,227	2,251

[1] The total of these six Tables is given in Table 2.8.6
[2] Table 9.2.1
[3] Table 9.8.1
[4] Table 9.10.1
[5] Table 9.12.1
[6] Table 9.15.1
[7] Table 9.32.1

NB Charts not drawn to same vertical scale

FIGURE 2.11.1
Baptist Church Members, UK 1900–2000

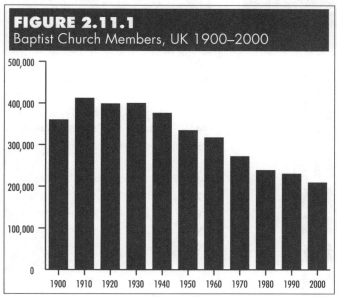

FIGURE 2.11.2
Independent Church Members, UK 1900–2000

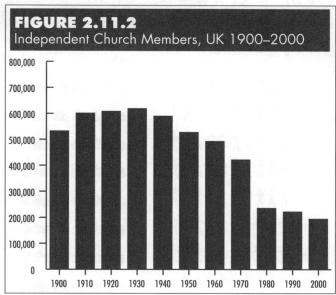

FIGURE 2.11.3
Methodist Church Members, UK 1900–2000

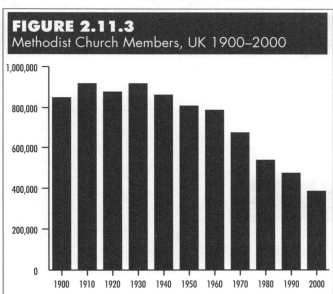

FIGURE 2.11.4
New Church Members, UK 1900–2000

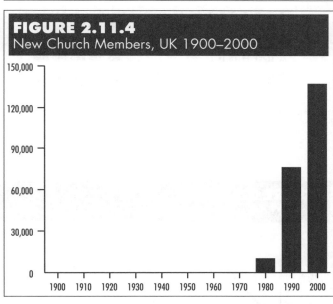

FIGURE 2.11.5
Other Churches Members, UK 1900–2000

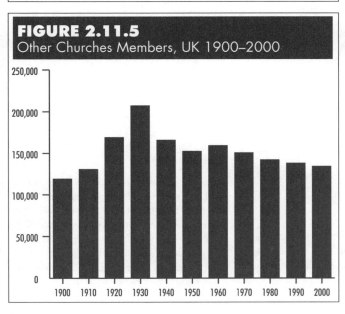

FIGURE 2.11.6
Pentecostal Church Members, UK 1900–2000

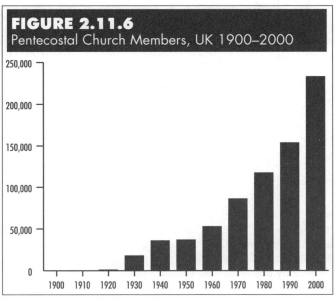

FIGURE 2.12.1
Total Church Members, Churches and Ministers, UK, 1900–2000

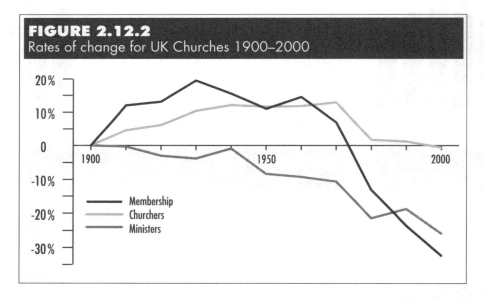

	Membership	Churches	Ministers
TABLE 2.12 Total UK Members, Churches and Ministers 1900–2000			
1900	8,663,826	48,988	45,408
1910	9,703,961	51,244	45,273
1920	9,802,669	52,035	44,037
1930	10,357,153	54,059	43,700
1940	10,017,230	54,928	45,002
1950	9,613,984	54,671	41,654
1960	9,917,845	54,760	41,211
1970	9,079,403	53,215	39,281
1980	7,528,995	49,838	35,694
1990	6,624,051	49,595	36,896
2000	5,861,796	48,695	33,709
1991	6,537,669	49,467	37,073
1992	6,525,262	49,280	37,079
1993	6,475,621	49,290	36,853
1994	6,400,667	49,216	37,046
1995	6,283,073	49,094	36,213
1996	6,065,415	48,977	34,856
1997	6,031,372	49,020	34,446
1998	6,012,231	48,759	34,157

FIGURE 2.12.2
Rates of change for UK Churches 1900–2000

Membership
Churchers
Ministers

The membership figures in **Table 2.12** are illustrated in **Figure 2.9.1. Table 2.12** and **Figures 2.12.1** and **2.12.2** show that the 20th century may be divided into three parts as far as the church is concerned:

- 1900-1930 when church membership and numbers of congregations were growing, although not as it happens the number of ministers

- 1930-1960 when the church was largely static, although in reality membership slightly declined and then recovered because of a massive influx of Irish labourers in the 1950s most of whom were Catholic

- 1960-2000 when church membership has dropped 40%, a net 6,000 churches have closed, and there are 7,500 fewer ministers.

At its peak in 1930, the 10 million plus church members were 31% of the adult population, whereas by 2000 it will have fallen to 12%.

The number of adults per church in the population in 1900 was 500, which rose to 620 by 1930, to 710 by 1960, and will be 970, virtually double the 1900 figure, by the year 2000.

When the number of ministers was highest, in 1900, they each had 190 members on average. By 1930 that had become 240, the same figure as in 1960, whereas by the 2000 it will be back to 170, showing that the number of leaders did not rise as fast as membership at the beginning of the century and is not shrinking as fast as membership at the end.

Tables **2.13.1** and **2.13.2** are based on the 1989 English Church Census. A question on church environment was not asked in the 1998 English Church Attendance Survey, so the figures in these Tables cannot be updated at present. The Independent churches in these Tables include the New (House) Churches.

The two Tables show the widespread nature of churches in England, with 45% in rural areas, though attended by only 22% of those going to church. On the other hand, a fifth (22%) of churches are in suburban areas, but are attended by a third (35%) of the churchgoers. (See bottom line of each Table).

Table 2.13.1 shows the exceptionally high proportion, over half, five times the average for the country, of Orthodox and Afro-Caribbean churchgoers who go to church in inner city areas, ten times the number of Methodist and URC. Likewise it is the Catholics and the two Pentecostal groups who are especially active on Council Estates. The Anglicans, Independents and Methodists are particularly strong in the rural areas.

Table 2.13.2 shows the denominational distribution by environment. Whilst broadly similar to **Table 2.13.1**, it is not identical. So there are fewer Orthodox churches in the inner city than their congregations would suggest, fewer suburban Anglicans likewise, and rather more Orthodox and URC churches in rural commuter areas than their congregations would suggest. Over a third of Anglican and Methodist churches are in the remoter rural areas, and explains why some of these are being merged or closed.

Table 2.13.3 is derived from the first two Tables and shows the average congregation as it was in October 1989. The numbers include children and adults, and are across all services.

TABLE 2.13.1
Percentage of church attendance by church environment 1989

	City Centre %	Inner City %	Council Estate %	Suburban/ Urban Fringe %	Separate Town %	Other built-up area %	Rural: Commuter dormitory %	Rural: Other areas %	Total (=100%)
Anglican	7	7	5	30	12	4	18	17	1,266,300
Baptist	3	6	4	39	23	5	12	8	270,900
Catholic	4	12	13	39	15	4	7	6	1,715,900
Independent	4	8	5	36	20	5	14	8	465,500
Methodist	3	5	5	35	18	5	11	18	512,300
Orthodox	9	46	1	24	13	2	3	2	12,300
Pentecostal: Afro-Caribbean	5	58	13	11	5	6	2	0	104,100
Pentecostal: Mainstream	11	13	10	29	21	8	4	4	132,600
URC	4	4	3	42	24	6	9	8	149,300
Other Churches	3	10	6	33	29	6	5	8	113,600
All Churches	**5**	**10**	**8**	**35**	**16**	**4**	**11**	**11**	**4,742,800**

TABLE 2.13.2
Percentage of churches by church environment 1989

	City Centre %	Inner City %	Council Estate %	Suburban/ Urban Fringe %	Separate Town %	Other built-up area %	Rural: Commuter dormitory %	Rural: Other areas %	Total (=100%)
Anglican	6	6	5	18	7	3	20	35	16,373
Baptist	3	8	6	29	16	5	14	19	2,339
Catholic	4	10	13	27	18	4	11	13	3,824
Independent	4	8	8	30	18	6	11	15	4,123
Methodist	2	5	5	21	11	5	13	38	6,740
Orthodox	9	20	3	29	18	6	12	3	114
Pentecostal: Afro-Caribbean	7	50	14	14	7	6	1	1	949
Pentecostal: Mainstream	3	13	13	25	25	7	6	8	1,002
URC	3	7	4	33	20	5	12	16	1,681
Other Churches	3	10	9	29	24	5	7	13	1,462
All Churches	**4**	**7**	**6**	**22**	**12**	**4**	**16**	**29**	**38,607**

TABLE 2.13.3
Average Sunday congregation size by church environment 1989

	City Centre	Inner City	Council Estate	Suburban/ Urban Fringe	Separate Town	Other built-up area	Rural: Commuter dormitory	Rural: Other areas	Total (=100%)
Anglican	90	90	80	130	130	100	70	40	**80**
Baptist	120	90	70	160	170	110	100	50	**120**
Catholic	440	530	460	650	370	450	270	220	**450**
Independent	110	110	70	140	130	90	140	60	**110**
Methodist	120	70	70	130	120	80	70	40	**80**
Orthodox	110	250	30	90	80	30	30	90	**110**
Pentecostal: Afro-Caribbean	80	130	100	90	80	100	190	40	**110**
Pentecostal: Mainstream	480	140	100	150	110	140	100	70	**130**
URC	110	60	70	110	110	100	70	40	**90**
Other Churches	80	80	50	90	90	90	60	50	**80**
All Churches	**150**	**180**	**160**	**200**	**160**	**120**	**80**	**50**	**120**
All Churches excluding Catholic	**120**	**120**	**90**	**130**	**130**	**90**	**70**	**40**	**90**

FIGURE 2.13
Average size of Protestant Sunday Congregation 1989

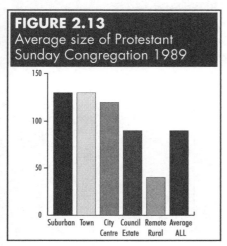

2

TABLE 2.14.1 Adult church attendance in England 1980–2005

England	1980	1985	1990	1995	2000	2005
Anglican	968,000	920,900	917,600	839,200	793,700	748,200
Baptist	201,300	196,200	197,700	212,600	223,700	229,800
Catholic	1,601,400	1,424,200	1,346,400	1,100,800	1,030,700	889,700
Independent	164,200	176,500	179,700	148,400	128,200	108,000
Methodist	437,900	420,800	395,200	347,000	313,100	279,200
New Churches	50,300	81,000	114,200	152,500	187,500	222,400
Orthodox	7,200	8,400	9,600	16,400	21,100	24,900
Pentecostal	147,200	152,400	164,700	166,300	163,100	162,800
United Reformed	139,000	121,400	104,100	102,500	100,000	89,600
Other Churches	97,700	81,400	83,000	77,600	75,500	70,300
TOTAL	3,814,200	3,583,200	3,512,200	3,163,300	3,036,600	2,824,900
Percentage of adult population	10.2%	9.3%	9.0%	8.0%	7.7%	7.0%

Source: Anglicans: UK Christian Handbook 1996/97 edition for Church of England, plus latest information from Church House, all increased by +0.001% to allow for other Anglican churches outside the Church of England. Baptists, Independents and Methodists: Estimated from the English Church Census results, published in Prospects for the Nineties, MARC Europe, 1991, the latest figures on church membership, and the results of the 1998 English Church Attendance Survey (ECAS). Catholics: Table 2.8.3 in this volume. New, Orthodox, Pentecostal, United Reformed and Other Churches: Estimated from the English Church Census results, published in Prospects for the Nineties and 'Christian' England, MARC Europe, 1991, and the 1998 ECAS.

TABLE 2.14.2 Adult church attendance in Scotland 1980–2005

Scotland	1980	1985	1990	1995	2000	2005
Baptist	22,300	21,000	19,900	18,300	16,900	15,600
Catholic	296,000	284,700	283,600	250,100	224,800	198,200
Church of Scotland	272,700	256,600	236,200	216,300	196,200	177,600
Episcopal	14,500	15,500	16,100	16,600	17,100	17,900
Independent	28,100	27,500	31,700	35,100	37,000	39,500
Other Presbyterian	27,000	23,700	21,100	17,900	15,000	12,000
Other Churches	17,300	19,100	20,500	22,600	24,300	26,000
TOTAL	677,900	648,100	629,100	576,900	531,300	486,800
Percentage of adult population	16.6%	15.7%	15.2%	13.9%	13.1%	12.0%

Source: Prospects for Scotland 2000, Report of the Scottish Church Census 1994, Christian Research and National Bible Society of Scotland, 1995, and the Roman Catholic Church in Scotland for their 1995–98 mass attendance figures. Figures for 2000 and 2005 estimated from these.

TABLE 2.14.3 Adult church attendance in Wales 1980–2005

Wales	1980	1985	1990	1995	2000	2005
Baptist	31,900	30,000	25,600	21,800[1]	18,600	15,100
Catholic	56,700	57,000	50,500	45,700	41,500	36,000
Church in Wales	78,100	76,000	67,300	60,200	54,800	48,600
Methodist	18,000	17,000	14,700	12,700	11,000	9,200
Presbyterian Church of Wales	38,200	35,000	28,000	22,000	16,900	11,300
Union of Welsh Independents	25,400	24,000	19,700	16,200[2]	13,400	10,200
Other Churches	30,400	34,000	31,500	30,500	31,000	30,800
TOTAL	278,700	273,000	237,300	209,100	187,200	161,200
Percentage of adult population	12.5%	12.0%	10.2%	8.9%	7.9%	6.6%

[1] Total of Baptist Union of Wales, Baptist Union of Great Britain and Scottish Baptists
[2] Total of Annibynwr, Congregational Federation and Evangelical Fellowship of Congregational Churches
Source: Prospects for Wales, Results of the 1982 Welsh Church Census, MARC Europe and Bible Society, 1983 for the 1980 and 1985 figures, and Challenge to Change, Results of the 1995 Welsh Churches Survey, Bible Society, 1996 for the 1995 figures. Figures for the years 1990, 2000 and 2005 are estimated from these.

TABLE 2.14.4 Total adult church attendance in Great Britain 1980–2005

Great Britain	1980	1985	1990	1995	2000	2005
TOTAL	4,770,800	4,513,300	4,378,600	3,949,300	3,755,100	3,472,900
Percentage of adult population	10.9%	10.1%	9.6%	8.6%	8.1%	7.4%

Table 2.14.1 gives the latest estimates of adult (taken as 15 or over) church attendance in England. The 1980 and 1990 figures are based on the English Churches Censuses of 1979 and 1989, and later figures on the 1998 English Church Attendance Survey. They show a drop of a million adult church attenders over the 25 years 1980 to 2005, an average loss of 760 a week, though the years 2000 to 2005 show a projected loss slightly higher than this of 810 a week.

Table 2.14.2 gives similar figures for Scotland, based on the 1984 and 1994 Church Censuses, with that of 1994 having a response rate of 81%, giving a fairly firm basis for the estimates.

Table 2.14.3 gives the figures for Wales, based on a Church Census in 1982 and another large scale study in 1995 with an 85% response. There are no equivalent figures on church attendance for Northern Ireland, where it may be expected to be considerably higher, around 30–35%. **Table 2.14.4** therefore simply gives the total for the three countries, showing a drop in adult attendance from one person in 9 in 1980 to one person in 13 by 2005. The drop of 1.3 million people is against a rise of 3.1 million in the adult population over the same 25 year period.

The percentage figures underneath the totals in **Tables 2.14.1–3** are graphed in **Figure 2.14** below.

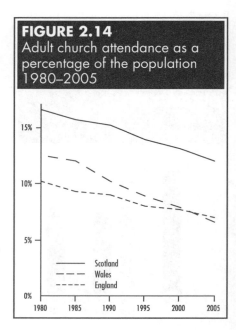

FIGURE 2.14
Adult church attendance as a percentage of the population 1980–2005

Scotland
Wales
England

TABLE 2.15
Sunday School Scholars by denomination in thousands

Year	Church of England	Other Anglican[6]	Pres C of E + Cong[2]	Pres Church in Wales	Church of Scotland[3]	Methodist[5]	Other Methodists[7]	Baptist	Other Baptists[8]	Brethren[9]	Pentecostal & New Churches[9]	All Others[10]	TOTAL Number	TOTAL % Pop[1]
1900	2,302	316	768	177	458	1,739	162	525	38	17	–	294	6,796	55%
1905	2,398	311	820	195	480	1,807	155	578	39	18	–	293	7,094	56%
1910	2,437	307	784	187	476	1,761	147	573	40	18	–	292	7,022	54%
1915	2,255	285	698	173	428	1,655	140	545	37	19	–	281	6,516	54%
1920	2,010	264	661	166	392	1,538	132	509	35	20	–	271	5,998	49%
1925	1,915	245	616	160	386	1,501	122	521	34	21	3	259	5,783	49%
1930	1,802	221	568	145	361	1,357	113	478	34	21	5	247	5,352	48%
1935	1,645	204	497	129	350	1,187	95	432	30	22	7	209	4,807	43%
1940	1,400[1]	187	393	101	251	930	76	372	27	23	9	171	3,940	36%
1945	1,440[1]	176	319	86	255	717	70	293[1]	29	22	9	167	3,583	33%
1950	1,342[1]	189	325	82	290	800	64	318	30	22	10	163	3,635	32%
1955	1,310	160	334	77	326	770	55	320	27	22	12	147	3,560	30%
1960	1,039	149	231	63	296[1]	587	45	260	24	21	14	131	2,860	24%
1965	834[1]	125	185	51	263[1]	482	35	190	22	20	18	111	2,336	19%
1970	671[1]	96	161	40[1]	227	287[1]	24	190	20	19	22	92	1,849	14%
1975	468[1]	72	123[1]	22	165[1]	228[1]	20	176	21	19	25	74	1,413	11%
1980	273[4]	46	89[1]	18	99	176	17	156	21	19	33	55	1,002	9%
1985	259	44	40[12]	14	94	136[1]	14	140	21	19	45	53	879	8%
1990	226	43	32[12]	12	91[1]	97	11	124	21	19	56	51	783	7%
1995	153	29	23[12]	10	76[1]	74	9	139	24	12	64	45	658	6%
2000[1]	88	16	12	8	66[1]	52	7	131	26	8	77	39	530	4%

[1] Estimate
[2] Presbyterian Church of England and Congregational Unions of England & Wales and Scotland 1900 to 1970; United Reformed Church 1975 to 2000
[3] Including United Free Church of Scotland prior to Union in 1929, and the continuing United Free after 1929
[4] Figures for 1980 to 2000 are Sunday attendance figures, as per Table 8.5, and not necessarily Sunday School
[5] Given in more detail in Table 9.11
[6] Membership total of Tables 8.2.3-5 as a percentage of the Church of England and taken pro rata to the previous column
[7] Membership total of Tables 9.10.3-6 as a percentage of the Methodist Church of Great Britain and taken pro rata to the previous column
[8] Membership total of Tables 9.2.5, 9.3.1–6 as a percentage of the Baptist Union of Great Britain and taken pro rata to the previous column
[9] Taken as 78% of the percentage of children in Table 4.9 for 1979, 1989 and 1998 for 1980, 1990 and 1995 respectively, with similar proportions for earlier years.
[10] Membership total of Tables 8.14.2,4 and 5, 8.15.1–5, 9.7.1 and 3, 9.8.2–5, 9.9.1–9, and 9.32.1 (all denominations not elsewhere included) as a percentage of the total for all UK members (Table 2.12) and taken pro rata to the total of all Sunday School scholars in the previous columns
[11] Child population (under 15), including Northern Ireland population prior to 1921
[12] Taken as 89% of children in worship in 1985 (English Church Census percentage), 81% in 1990, and 73% (estimate) in 1995

FIGURE 2.15
Percentage of child population in Sunday School, UK, 1900–2000

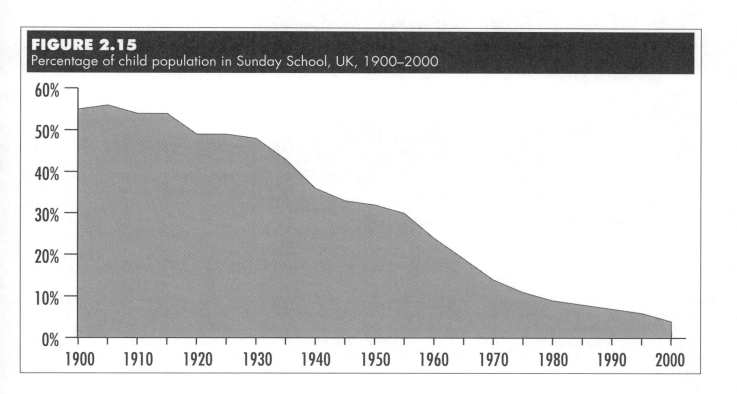

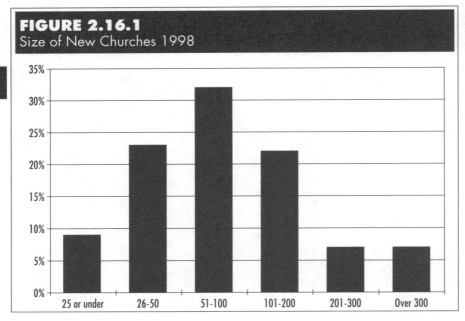

FIGURE 2.16.1
Size of New Churches 1998

The Body Book, a voluntary listing of charismatic churches is now in its 7th edition. Published in 1998 it lists 900 churches, more than double the 402 listed in the 1st edition of 1987. A quarter, 24%, of these are of denominational churches, a third, 35%, are of independent churches, and the remaining two-fifths, 41%, are of New Churches.

Figure 2.16.1 shows the size distribution of these churches, which has changed very little over the 1990s, but differs from churches in general because these churches are on average about double the size of a typical (non–Catholic) English church. In 1998 the average size of the churches listed was 126 adults and 47 children, a total of 173. In 1990 the figures were 121 adults and 41 children, showing that churches have not on average increased in size, suggesting the past decade has been a time of consolidation to some extent for individual churches.

As **Table 9.12.1** shows, the total *number* of New Churches, however, has grown vigorously from 1,110 in 1990 to 1,660 in 1998, an increase of 49% in 8 years or 4 new churches every 3 weeks. Those given in *The Body Book* represent almost a quarter, 23%, of these. The ones listed have a total Sunday attendance of 60,500, which when grossed up for all the churches comes to 263,000 people or more than double (2.14 times) the membership.

Source: The Body Book, edited by Mervyn Love, Pioneer Publishing, 1998.

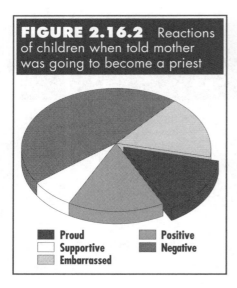

FIGURE 2.16.2 Reactions of children when told mother was going to become a priest

■ Proud   ■ Positive
□ Supportive   ■ Negative
▨ Embarrassed

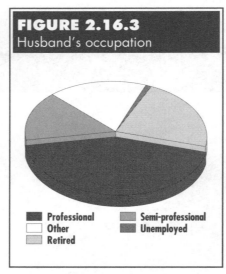

FIGURE 2.16.3
Husband's occupation

■ Professional   ▨ Semi-professional
□ Other   ■ Unemployed
▨ Retired

In 1996, Rev Patsy Kettle, an ordained married Anglican, carried out a survey of other married women priests. Because the first women priests were only ordained in 1994 many women who are now priests have been in parish ministry for some years. On average in this study it was 10 years, 56% under 10 years, 36% between 10 and 20, and 8% over 20 years.

The 167 stipendiary women priests of this study excluded those married to a priest (about 230 in total), and represent about a third of married ordained women in like position. Half, 49%, were in their 50s or 60s, 36% in their 40s, the remaining 15% were younger. Half, 51%, had two children, a

third, 31%, three or more, with 5% one, and 13% none. **Figure 2.16.2** shows what their children's reactions had been when they learned that their mother was going to be a priest. Two-thirds, 64%, were not in favour, but the remaining third was. What their husband's thought was not asked!

Figure 2.16.3 shows the husband's occupation. How did the women cope with having a home which had to be used for both private and public duties? A third, 30%, said they found this difficult, but another third, 35%, said it was not a problem. The remainder coped by declaring certain rooms private (21%), by use of an answerphone (6%), and having the privilege of having the woman's office outside her home (8%).

With regard to domestic duties, a quarter, 24%, said "it works out", a third, 32%, had cleaning help, another third, 30%, shared as necessary with her husband, with the remaining one in 7, 14%, coping "with difficulty".

Source: Ministry and Marriage, Survey of Women Priests in the Church of England, Rev Patsy Kettle, Leaders Briefing No 9, Christian Research, 1997.

SECTION 3

BRITISH MISSION OVERSEAS

3

Contents

Source:
UK Christian Handbook 2000/01 and dedicated sector surveys

3

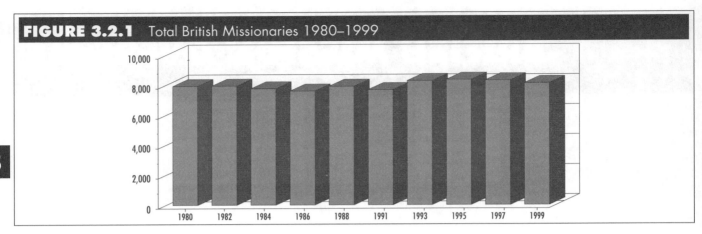

FIGURE 3.2.1 Total British Missionaries 1980–1999

TABLE 3.2 Total British Missionaries 1980–1999[2]

	1980	1982	1984	1986	1988	1991	1993	1995	1997	1999
Anglican Societies	1,428	1,319	1,068	1,044	1,088	998	940	912	906	919
Roman Catholic Societies[1]	1,799	1,783	1,717	1,588	1,723	1,625	1,540	1,496	1,396	1,287
Other Denominational Societies	1,080	1,114	1,203	1,276	1,267	1,215	1,191	1,261	1,243	1,261
Interdenominational Societies	3,058	3,212	3,315	3,218	3,351	3,346	4,116	4,160	4,220	4,125
Direct Sending Churches	560	512	452	469	478	491	480	508	529	513
Total	7,925	7,940	7,755	7,595	7,907	7,675	8,267	8,337	8,294	8,105

[1] Numbers include those serving in the UK   [2] This includes estimates for missing data

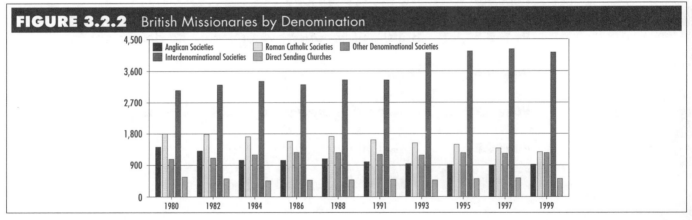

FIGURE 3.2.2 British Missionaries by Denomination

Legend: Anglican Societies · Roman Catholic Societies · Other Denominational Societies · Interdenominational Societies · Direct Sending Churches

The total number of British missionaries, shown in **Table 3.2**, and illustrated in **Figure 3.2.1**, declined slightly between 1997 and 1999, falling by 189 people or 2% of the total. Similar variations have occurred on the year by year figures over the last 20 years, and is nothing unusual on this occasion. The overall number of missionaries serving overseas in 1999 is virtually the same as the total in 1980, 2% higher, varying from a high in 1995 of 8,300 to a low in 1986 of 7,600. Figures for earlier years are not available.

British missionaries are those serving overseas, mostly in cross-cultural settings, but includes some working in the UK (often amongst immigrants), and those on home leave.

Figure 3.2.2 depicts the detail of **Table 3.2** and shows the growth in the number serving in Interdenominational Societies, that is, societies whose missionaries come from a variety of denominational backgrounds. They do not give up their denominational allegiance in serving with such societies, but are those preferring to serving with such a society to one whose missionaries are *only* of one denomination.

The number serving with Interdenominational Societies has increased by over a third, 35%, in the 19 years shown in the Table. Those in Anglican Societies have seen a decline of over a third, 36%, in the same period, partly because of the much smaller number of missionaries now serving in India. Roman Catholic missionaries have likewise declined 28%.

The line "Direct Sending Churches" gives the total number of missionaries sent out directly by individual churches, who do not work overseas under the auspices of a missionary society. They have dropped 8% in the same period.

Other Denominational Societies, that is, those working within a specific denomination (such as the Methodist Church World Church Office or the Pentecostal Assemblies of God World Ministries) have seen an increase of 18% between 1980 and 1999.

Part of the reason for this change is because many of the Interdenominational Societies are evangelical, and it is this sector which is growing, as **Table 3.6.6** shows. In 1995, the first year such an analysis was undertaken, 63% of serving missionaries were with societies in membership with the Evangelical Missionary Alliance, now called Global Connections. In 1999 the percentage was 75%.

The 10 countries with most British missionaries, by denomination. Total taken as number of UK serving members. Position in 1997 shown in brackets. The country where most British missionaries were working in 1999 was Kenya with 323 missionaries.

TABLE 3.3.1
Anglican Societies

		1999	1997	1995	1993	1991
1	Uganda (2)	72	73	62	63	67
2	Tanzania (1)	54	75	68	63	84
3	Kenya (5=)	46	31	31	36	38
4	Zimbabwe (7)	27	28	28	40	30
5	France (5=)	26	31	26	26	21
6=	Argentina (–)	23	17	21	25	22
6=	Israel (3)	23	34	34	33	38
8	Chile (–)	21	13	19	25	28
9=	Pakistan (8)	19	27	21	28	41
9=	Paraguay (–)	19	16	22	20	23
9=	South Africa (4)	19	32	34	28	35

TABLE 3.3.2
Roman Catholic Societies[1]

		1999	1997	1995	1993	1991
1	South Africa (1)	90	104	107	118	102
2	Kenya (4)	77	41	101	86	98
3	Zimbabwe (2)	54	72	43	61	148
4	Nigeria (3)	35	44	64	69	96
5	Tanzania (7)	34	34	21	33	32
6	Peru (6)	30	35	35	38	46
7	Zambia (5)	29	40	68	80	43
8	Uganda (9)	28	27	28	35	36
9	India (8)	25	28	35	34	26
10	Philippines (–)	24	18	20	22	14

[1]Excluding the Republic of Ireland

TABLE 3.3.3
Other Denominational Societies

		1999	1997	1995	1993	1991
1	Nepal (1)	66	69	63	44	45
2	Kenya (4)	61	49	36	45	44
3	USA (2)	60	64	61	57	45
4	Brazil (3)	51	60	65	64	69
5=	Malawi (–)	37	25	26	32	29
5=	South Africa (5)	37	46	51	47	48
7	Spain (6=)	36	38	39	33	24
8	France (6=)	33	38	32	37	22
9	India (–)	31	25	30	37	38
10	Zimbabwe (9)	29	32	40	59	51

TABLE 3.3.4
Interdenominational Societies

		1999	1997	1995	1993	1991
1	Kenya (3)	139	122	122	105	102
2	France (2)	122	124	131	102	88
3	Nepal (1)	108	150	142	115	98
4	Brazil (4=)	89	85	88	109	96
5	Philippines (4=)	73	85	67	71	76
6=	India (8)	69	55	54	54	50
6=	Spain (6)	69	77	65	61	55
8	Papua New Guinea (–)	61	28	26	39	47
9	Thailand (9)	53	50	48	59	54
10	Japan (10=)	52	46	53	60	48

FIGURE 3.3
Top Missionary Sending Countries 1990

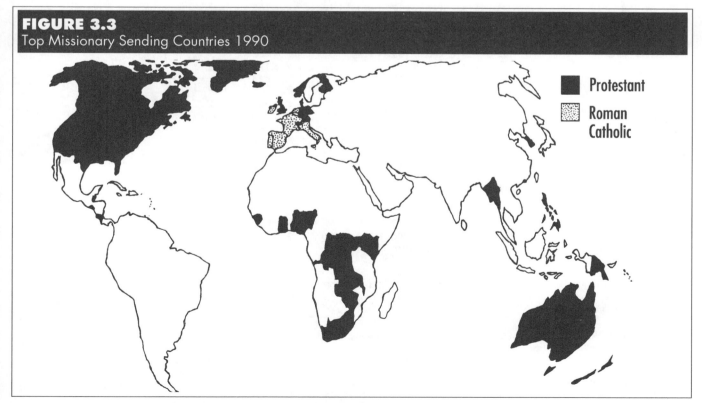

Protestant
Roman Catholic

Source: *Operation World*, Patrick Johnstone, fifth edition, WEC International and OM Publishing, 1993

3

TABLE 3.4.1
Missionary Personnel by size of Society

	Total members with Societies 1997				Total members with Societies 1999			
	Less than 50	50–100	More than 100	Total	Less than 50	50–100	More than 100	Total
Anglican								
Cross-Culture Overseas	123	73	380	**576**	167	48	418	**633**
Own-Culture Overseas	0	66	2	**68**	0	0	7	**7**
Cross-Culture UK	0	18	14	**32**	17	0	29	**46**
Own-Culture UK	7	0	12	**19**	8	0	0	**8**
On furlough/home leave	10	24	30	**64**	3	0	13	**16**
Secondments	1	0	26	**26**	0	0	78	**78**
UK Executive staff	11	19	91	**121**	20	8	103	**131**
Sub-total: Serving members	**151**	**200**	**555**	**906**	**215**	**56**	**648**	**919**
UK Office Staff	23	48	82	**153**	58	0	89	**147**
Associates	3	47	25	**75**	28	0	108	**136**
Retired personnel	42	57	503	**602**	19	2	566	**587**
Total Missionary personnel	219	352	1,165	**1,736**	320	58	1,411	**1,789**
Number of Societies	7	3	3	**13**	9	1	4	**14**
Average serving members per Society	22	67	185	**70**	24	56	162	**66**
Other Denominational								
Cross-Culture Overseas	142	210	614	**966**	85	272	560	**917**
Own-Culture Overseas	0	9	7	**16**	1	2	10	**13**
Cross-Culture UK	13	20	0	**33**	2	31	3	**36**
Own-Culture UK	2	0	55	**57**	0	0	0	**0**
On furlough/home leave	0	4	47	**51**	8	12	26	**46**
Secondments	2	4	45	**51**	2	0	40	**42**
UK Executive staff	22	14	33	**69**	31	18	23	**72**
Sub-total: Serving members	**181**	**261**	**801**	**1,243**	**129**	**335**	**662**	**1,126**
UK Office Staff	12	44	75	**131**	24	19	88	**131**
Associates	1	9	2	**12**	2	0	2	**4**
Retired personnel	53	176	438	**667**	59	186	449	**694**
Total Missionary personnel	247	490	1,316	**2,053**	214	540	1,201	**1,955**
Number of Societies	12	4	5	**21**	11	5	5	**21**
Average serving members per Society	15	65	160	**59**	12	67	132	**54**
Interdenominational								
Cross-Culture Overseas	557	580	1,390	**2,527**	518	402	1,492	**2,412**
Own-Culture Overseas	9	6	87	**102**	26	0	61	**87**
Cross-Culture UK	75	13	129	**217**	90	12	61	**163**
Own-Culture UK	67	109	649	**825**	85	173	644	**902**
On furlough/home leave	29	70	146	**245**	28	15	195	**238**
Secondments	12	4	26	**42**	18	20	67	**105**
UK Executive staff	124	50	88	**262**	126	54	88	**268**
Sub-total: Serving members	**873**	**832**	**2,515**	**4,220**	**891**	**676**	**2,608**	**4,175**
UK Office Staff	173	244	185	**602**	335	255	238	**828**
Associates	30	124	2	**156**	94	42	13	**149**
Retired personnel	184	78	195	**457**	134	89	185	**408**
Total Missionary personnel	1,260	1,278	2,897	**5,435**	1,455	1,072	3,044	**5,560**
Number of Societies	58	11	10	**79**	58	9	11	**78**
Average serving members per Society	15	76	252	**53**	15	75	237	**54**
Roman Catholic								
Cross-Culture Overseas	519	124	111	**754**	531	107	0	**638**
Own-Culture Overseas	0	0	0	**0**	1	0	0	**1**
Cross-Culture UK	0	0	0	**0**	0	0	0	**0**
On furlough/home leave	n/a	n/a	n/a	**n/a**	3	0	0	**3**
Secondments	n/a	n/a	n/a	**n/a**	0	0	0	**0**
UK Executive staff	204	168	270	**642**	600	93	0	**693**
Sub-total: Serving members	**723**	**292**	**381**	**1,396**	**1,135**	**200**	**0**	**1,335**
UK Office Staff	n/a	n/a	n/a	**n/a**	n/a	n/a	n/a	**n/a**
Associates	0	0	7	**7**	0	7	0	**7**
Retired personnel	49	66	54	**169**	370	20	0	**390**
Total Missionary personnel	772	358	442	**1,572**	1,450	227	0	**1,732**
Number of Societies	100	4	3	**107**	106	2	0	**108**
Average serving members per Society	7	73	127	**13**	5	54	0	**6**

Table 3.4.1 breaks down the information given in **Table 3.2** in two ways — it gives information by size of missionary society (in three classifications), and by the type of work and location of missionaries. Thus

- *Cross-culture overseas* are those working in a non-English culture outside the UK
- *Own-culture overseas* are those working in an English culture outside the UK, such as with British sailors when visiting trading ports
- *Cross-culture UK* are those working in the UK but in an overseas culture, such as those working with immigrants
- *Own-culture UK* are those working in the UK amongst English speaking people. These are only included if the particular society has personnel in the other categories given above

- *On furlough or home leave*. Many missionaries return home for 4 to 6 months every three years, or longer if away longer. The number included here will also include those on leave of absence, sick leave, undertaking training courses, etc.
- *Secondments* are the number of missionaries lent to other societies but still financially supported by their parent organisation. It does not include those seconded from other societies since these are included in their primary society.
- *UK Executive staff* include permanent home staff who may be regarded as full mission members
- *Serving members* is a sub-total of the above 7 categories. It is this total which is reflected in **Table 3.2** and other Tables of primary analysis
- *UK Office staff* are mainly clerical staff, some of whom are not strictly mission members. The distinction between these and executive staff is sometimes not possible, especially in Roman Catholic societies
- *Associates* includes those working abroad, not financially dependent on their society. Societies have different qualifications for them
- *Retired personnel* are only counted if partly financially dependent on the society
- *Total missionary personnel* is the total of all the above
- *Number of societies* is the total number listed in the *UK Christian Handbook* of that size within that denominational grouping
- *Average serving members* is the Serving Member Sub-total divided by the number of societies

Although not shown on this page, 57% of all missionary personnel serve with the 20 societies with more than 100 serving members (one-sixth, or 18%, of the total), and a further quarter, 26%, with the 78 smallest (69% of the total).

Totals of the final column within each denominational group, plus those for Direct Sending Churches (not given separately here) are given in **Table 3.4.2**.

TABLE 3.4.2 Missionary Personnel by type of work 1997 and 1999

	1997	1999	Percentage Change %
Cross-Culture overseas	5,298	5,023	−5
Own-Culture overseas	211	106	−50
Cross-Culture UK	292	257	−12
Own-Culture UK	901	984	+9
On furlough/home leave	412	316	−23
Secondments	216	235	+9
UK Executive staff/ Home staff	964	1,184	+23
Sub-total: Serving members	**8,294**	**8,105**	**−2**
UK Office staff	905	1,079	+19
Associates	257	303	+18
Retired personnel	1,895	2,079	+10
TOTAL Missionary Personnel	**11,351**	**10,983**	**−3**
Number of societies	228	228	0
Average serving members per Society	36	32	−11

TABLE 3.5.1 UK Missionaries by Continent

	Anglican Societies		Other Denominational Societies		Inter-denominational Societies		Roman Catholic Societies[2]		Direct Sending Churches		Total Societies	
	1997 %	1999 %	1997 %	1999 %	1997 %	1999 %	1997 %	1999 %	1997 %	1999 %	1997 %	1999 %
Africa	47	49	29	26	28	33	66	63	36	28	36	37
Americas	16	16	22	22	11	14	17	16	13	11	15	16
Asia (South, East, Australasia)	6	8	9	8	13	18	9	13	6	7	10	14
Europe[3]	15	11	25	27	23	19	0	0	32	38	20	19
Indian Subcontinent and Middle East	16	16	15	17	21	15	8	8	13	16	17	14
Boat Ministry	0	0	0	0	4	1	0	0	0	0	2	0
TOTAL[1] (=100%)	783	620	999	940	2,990	2,760	761	698	499	504	6,032	5,522

[1] Based on the number of missionaries abroad and on furlough, and associates from those societies giving the necessary detail
[2] Europe and North America are not recognised as 'overseas mission' destinations by the National Missionary Council of England & Wales.
[3] Excluding the United Kingdom

FIGURE 3.5.1 1999 All Societies

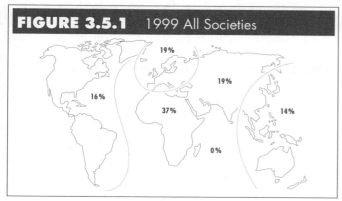

19%

19%

16%

37%

14%

0%

TABLE 3.5.2 Denomination of Protestant Missionaries

Denomination	1982 %	1998 %	Missionaries per 10,000 members 1998	
			1982	1998
Anglican	40	34	14	17
Baptist	26	16	86	61
Brethren	10	7	88	70
Presbyterian	9	7	5	6
Pentecostal	6	5	41	17
Methodist	5	6	7	13
Others	4	25	11	52
TOTAL (=100%)	7,940	8,068	16	21

The various Interdenominational Societies do not usually keep a total of their missionaries by denomination, and it has only been ascertained twice through a special survey to that end.

The first, undertaken in 1982 when Rev Stanley Davies was at Moorlands Bible College, is repeated in **Table 3.5.2**. The second, undertaken last year, courtesy of the Christian Medical Fellowship and the Evangelical Missionary Alliance, is summarised in the second column of this Table.

It is obvious that in the intervening years the number of missionaries coming from the newer denominations has risen quite dramatically, these numbers affecting the proportion of Baptist missionaries most. Further information on New Church missionaries is given on **Page 3.8**. Slightly more Methodist missionaries now serve with interdenominational than that of their denomination.

FIGURE 3.5.2
Denomination of Protestant Missionaries

1982 · 1998

- Anglican
- Baptist
- Brethren, Presbyterian, Pentecostal and Methodist
- Others

TABLE 3.5.3
Total Income of Missionary Societies[1]

	Anglican Societies[8] Millions	Other Denominational Societies Millions	Inter-denominational Societies Millions	Roman Catholic Societies Millions	Direct Sending Churches Millions	Total Societies[8] Millions
1991	£16.45	£n/a[2]	£51.42	£17.24	£2.45	£87.56
1993	£16.06	£20.18[9]	£36.94	£19.08	£2.55	£94.81
1995	£16.84	£21.59[9]	£45.10[4]	£22.84[5]	£3.07	£109.44
1997	£17.16	£21.91[9]	£57.08[6]	£23.75[3]	£3.39	£123.29
1999	**£21.15**	**£22.16**	**£68.28[7]**	**£27.58**	**£4.84**	**£144.01**
Increase 99 over 97	+23%	+2%	+20%	+16%	+43%	+13%

[1] Total income grossed up for all societies, estimated by grossing up on number of serving members
[2] Included with the 1991 Interdenominational Societies figure
[3] Estimate
[4] Five Societies (Latin Link, MAF, OMF, Wycliffe Translators and YWAM) accounted for 53% of this increase
[5] Hospitallers accounted for £3 million of this increase
[6] Four societies (Internatioanl Teams, MAF, Siloam Ministers and SIM) accounted for 78% of this increase
[7] Four societies (MAF, OM, Dohnavur Fellowship, OMF International) accounted for 76% of this increase
[8] Excluding Church Army
[9] Revised figure

The 10 Societies with most missionaries by denomination. Total taken as number of UK serving members. Position in 1997 shown in brackets. The largest British Society sending missionaries overseas is Youth With A Mission with 486 missionaries in 1999, the same number as it had in 1997.

TABLE 3.6.1 Anglican Societies

	1999	1997	1995	1993	1991
1 Church Mission Society (1)	257	287	269	267	295
2 South American Mission Society (5)	162	75	100	102	111
3 United Society for the Propagation of the Gospel (3)	124	163	163	159	184
4 Crosslinks (4)	105	105	109	110	87
5 Intercontinental Church Society (6)	56	71	71	71	61
6= Church's Ministry Among Jewish People (9)	44	40	45	47	39
6= Right Hand Trust (–)	44	47	20	10	6
8 Mid-Africa Ministry (CMS) (8)	36	45	43	36	32
9 The Missions to Seamen (7)	33	54	39	61	69
10 Church Missionary Society Ireland (CMS Ireland) (10)	28	31	27	26	42

TABLE 3.6.2 Roman Catholic Societies

	1999	1997	1995	1993	1991
1 St Joseph's Missionary Society, Mill Hill (1)	56	149	83	83	56
2 Society of Jesus (6)	51	62	57	57	67
3 Missionaries of Africa (White Fathers) (5)	32	85	46	52	61
4 Fidei Donum Priests (8)	31	40	39	51	50
5 Franciscan Missionaries of Divine Motherhood (3)	28	102	204	204	28
6 Franciscan Missionaries of Mary (2)	24	130	44	44	44
7 Orders of Friars Minor (–)	20	24	n/a	n/a	n/a
8 Sisters of Notre Dame de Namur (–)	19	24	29	29	29
9 Medical Missionaries of Mary (10)	15	32	n/a	n/a	n/a
10 Institute of Our Lady of Mercy (–)	14	10	15	15	n/a

TABLE 3.6.3 Other Denominational Societies

	1999	1997	1995	1993	1991
1 Baptist Missionary Society (1)	186	304	255	170	202
2 New Tribes Mission (–)	126	n/a	n/a	n/a	n/a
3 Church of Scotland Board of World Mission (4)	125	106	136	110	106
4 Assemblies of God World Ministries (3)	121	120	134	142	87
5 World-Wide Advent Missions (5)	105	105	105	115	149
6 Presbyterian Church in Ireland Overseas Board (8)	88	56	51	61	59
7 Methodist Church World Church Office (6)	85	93	115	115	150
8 Free Presbyterian Church of Ulster Mission Board (7)	59	59	59	59	39
9 Elim International Missions (9)	55	53	35	51	40
10 Grace Baptist Mission (10)	50	49	46	43	40

TABLE 3.6.4 Interdenominational Societies

	1999	1997	1995	1993	1991
1 Youth with A Mission (1)	486	486	486	451	173
2 Operation Mobilisation (3)	366	379	370	295	355
3 WEC International (2)	312	388	388	398	333
4 OMF International (5=)	266	218	218	273	250
5 Wycliffe Bible Translators (4)	255	320	287	308	288
6 SIM UK (9)	228	123	111	111	118
7 Africa Inland Mission International (8)	175	129	130	121	128
8 World Horizons (5=)	170	218	220	224	n/a
9 Interserve (7)	138	146	159	148	156
10 Latin Link UK (–)	107	78	60	61	56

TABLE 3.6.5 EMA[1] Member Societies v Non-EMA Member Societies[2] 1999

	EMA Member Societies				Non-EMA Member Societies				Percentage of overall total with EMA Societies %
	Less than 50	50–100	More than 100	Total	Less than 50	50–100	More than 100	Total	
Cross Culture overseas	446	572	1,888	2,906	309	150	422	881	77
Own-Culture overseas	2	0	75	77	29	2	3	34	69
Cross-Culture UK	51	16	92	159	57	27	1	85	35
Own-Culture UK	55	173	648	876	38	0	0	38	96
On furlough/home leave	21	36	231	278	58	1	2	61	82
Secondments	7	20	155	182	13	0	30	43	81
UK Executive staff	87	66	175	328	90	14	39	143	70
Sub-total: Serving members	**671**	**873**	**3,438**	**4,982**	**1,072**	**194**	**354**	**1,620**	**75**
UK Office staff	192	274	335	801	219	10	70	299	73
Associates	85	52	121	258	33	0	1	41	86
Retired personnel	91	117	796	1,004	112	160	404	676	60
Total Missionary personnel 1999	**983**	**1,316**	**4,204**	**6,503**	**928**	**364**	**956**	**2,248**	**74**
Number of Societies	35	12	16	63	43	3	4	50	56
Average serving members per society	19	73	215	79	25	65	89	32	71

[1] Evangelical Missionary Alliance, now Global Connections [2] Excludes Roman Catholic Societies and Direct Sending Churches

TABLE 3.6.6 Serving Members

Serving members 1995	362	761	3,211	4,334	756	287	1,526	2,569	63
Serving members 1997	631	868	3,330	4,829	574	425	1,211	2,210	69
Serving members 1999	**671**	**873**	**3,438**	**4,982**	**1,072**	**194**	**354**	**1,620**	**75**

TABLE 3.7.1
Short-term[1] v Career[2] Missionaries by gender and denomination

	Anglican Missionies 1999			Other Denominational Missionaries 1999			Interdenominational Missionaries 1999			Roman Catholic Missionaries 1999			Direct Sending Churches Missionaries 1999		
	Men	Women	Total	Men	Women	Total	Men	Women	Total	Men	Women	Total	Men	Women	Total
Short-term[1]	14%	14%	28%	5%	9%	14%	9%	10%	19%	1%	1%	2%	2%	2%	4%
Career[2]	45%	27%	72%	38%	48%	86%	36%	45%	81%	53%	45%	98%	42%	54%	96%
TOTAL	59%	41%	100%	43%	57%	100%	45%	55%	100%	54%	46%	100%	44%	56%	100%

[1] Short-term missionaries are those who are not expected to complete more than one term of service (normally a maximum of 4 years).
[2] All others supported by a church or Society.

Table 3.7.2 shows that in 1999 the proportion of career missionaries, those serving with an agency for more than one term of service, was 84% of all workers, marginally lower than the 87% in 1997, 85% of 1995 or the 87% of 1993. The proportion of career missionaries working in a cross–cultural context in the UK was 85%, rather higher than the 77% in 1997, and that despite the fact that Church Army officers have

TABLE 3.7.2
Short-term v Career Missionaries by Culture

	Cross Culture Work 1999			Own Culture Work 1999			All Types of Work 1999		
	Overseas	UK	Total	Overseas	UK	Total	Overseas	UK	Total
Short-term	16%	1%	17%	0%	5%	5%	15%	1%	16%
Career	79%	4%	83%	10%	85%	95%	70%	14%	84%
TOTAL	95%	5%	100%	10%	90%	100%	85%	15%	100%

TABLE 3.7.3
Short-term v Career Missionaries 1972–1999

						All Missionaries							
	1972[1]	1976[1]	1980[1]	1982	1984	1986	1988	1991	1993	1995	1997	1999
Short-term	0%	5%	12%	30%	25%	25%	10%[2]	15%	13%	15%	13%	16%
Career	100%	95%	88%	70%	75%	75%	90%	85%	87%	85%	87%	84%

[1] Excludes Roman Catholic societies
[2] Sharp drop in proportion of short-term missionaries caused in part by a number of societies changing their classification of some missionaries

been excluded from the 1999 figures but were included in the 1997 figures.

A comparison of the 1999 figures with those of 1993, the first year such information was analysed, is given in **Figure 3.7.2.**

The percentage of career missionaries is highest, 98%, in Roman Catholic societies (**Table 3.7.1**) but lowest, 72%, in Anglican ones.

The sharp decline in the number of missionaries working worldwide from societies based in the UK, **Table 3.7.4**, is because of drastic drop in the number of Roman Catholic mission workers.

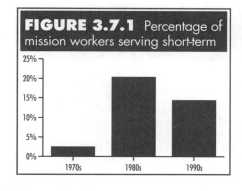

FIGURE 3.7.1 Percentage of mission workers serving short-term

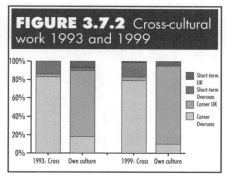

FIGURE 3.7.2 Cross-cultural work 1993 and 1999

TABLE 3.7.4
Missionaries of all Nationalities[1,2]

	Anglican Societies		Other Denominational Societies		Interdenominational Societies		Roman Catholic Societies		Total Societies	
	Number of Missionaries	Number of Societies[3]	Number of Missionaries	Number of Societies[3]	Number of Missionaries	Number of Societies[3]	Number of Missionaries	Number of Societies[3]	Number of Missionaries	Number of Societies[3]
1991	1,684	12	n/a[4]	n/a[4]	45,313[5]	84	80,511[8]	55	127,508	151
1993	1,195	12	n/a[4]	n/a[4]	45,105[5]	85	84,544[9]	54	130,844	151
1995	886	13	2,800	19	45,586[6]	67	92,999[10]	63	144,372	162
1997	897	12	2,777	21	49,121[7]	74	89,000[10]	59	141,795	166
1999	**746**	**14**	**5,517**	**21**	**39,823**	**78**	**69,743**	**108**	**115,829**	**221**

[1] Working with societies with at least one UK person
[2] Total missionaries and other workers worldwide
[3] Number of societies giving details
[4] 1991 and 1993 figures for Other Denominational Societies are included in 1991 and 1993 figures for interdenominational societies
[5] Includes 15,000 with Agapé (Campus Crusade for Christ) and 7,000 with Youth With A Mission
[6] Includes 15,000 with Agapé (Campus Crusade for Christ), 6,543 with Wycliffe Bible Translation and 10,000 with Youth With A Mission

[7] Includes 14,200 with Agapé (Campus Crusade for Christ), 5,900 with Wycliffe Bible Translation and 10,000 with Youth With A Mission
[8] Includes 8,000 with Franciscan Missionaries of Mary, 7,600 Salesian Fathers and Brothers, and 7,275 Dominicans
[9] Includes 8,713 with Franciscan Missionaries of Mary, 17,000 Salesian Fathers, and 6,000 Redemptionists
[10] Includes 7,000 Dominicans, 9,000 Franciscan Missionaries of Mary, 6,000 Redemptionists, and 17,000 Salesian Fathers

FIGURE 3.8.1
Factors Starting Mission Initiatives

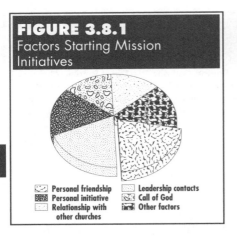

- 😊 Personal friendship
- Personal initiative
- Relationship with other churches
- Leadership contacts
- Call of God
- Other factors

FIGURE 3.8.2
Preferred Forms of Mission Involvement

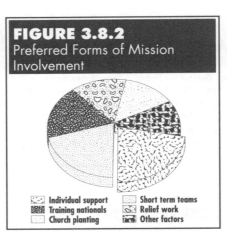

- 😊 Individual support
- Training nationals
- Church planting
- Short term teams
- Relief work
- Other factors

FIGURE 3.8.3
Focus of Involvement

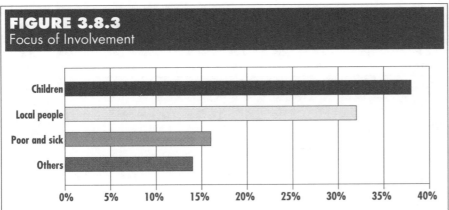

FIGURE 3.8.4
Impact of International Involvement

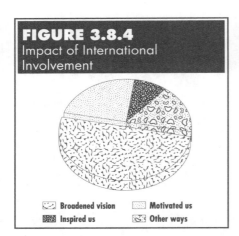

- 😊 Broadened vision
- Inspired us
- Motivated us
- Other ways

FIGURE 3.8.5
Under 25s' Interest in Mission

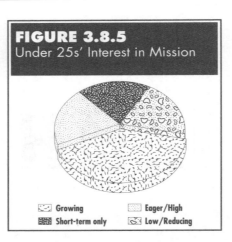

- 😊 Growing
- Short-term only
- Eager/High
- Low/Reducing

FIGURE 3.8.6
Percentage of Budget New Churches Spend on International Mission

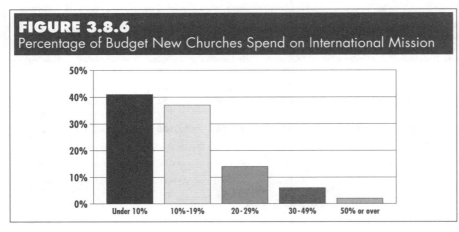

In 1997 a detailed survey was undertaken of the involvement by New Churches in world mission, bibliographical details of which are given below. It was a wide ranging and thorough study, and a few of the findings are given on this page. 240 New Churches answered the questionnaire, about 1 in 6 of all New Churches. These churches had 228 people active overseas, with an additional 493 members working abroad, averaging 3 people per church. Sunday attendance at these churches averaged 169, about double the national average for Free Churches.

Figure 3.8.1 shows the factors which initiated mission involvement overseas in New Churches. Personal friendship (21%), leadership contacts (19%) and personal initiatives (17%) were the top reasons.

Figure 3.8.2 indicates the ways in which New Churches prefer to work overseas. They are keen on supporting individuals (22%), and sending short-term teams (20%). They like to train national workers (18%), and engage in relief work (15%) or church planting (14%). No one form of working was predominant, but involvement in the local situation was desired by all churches.

Figure 3.8.3 shows that young people are at the front of attention for New Churches. Orphans, children and young people, and street children were the highest concern, collectively 38%, followed by work with local people at 32%. Helping the poor, deaf, sick, AIDS victims and those with drug problems were the concern of 16% of churches, with 14% involved in other areas, such as local pastors, students or the business community.

Figure 3.8.4 identifies the impact international involvement has made on the life of the church. 50% said it "has broadened our vision", 24% that it "has motivated us and increased our prayer life", 9% that it "has inspired us and challenged us spiritually", and 17% made other comments.

Figure 3.8.5 reflects the interest young people under 25 in New Churches have in overseas mission. Two-fifths, 40%, reported that it was growing, and a further 20% said there was high, eager interest. Another fifth, 20%, said it was only for short-term work, with the remaining fifth stating there was little interest.

Figure 3.8.6 gives the proportion New Churches' give of their budget to international mission. Two-fifths (41%) give under 10%, but almost as many, 37%, give between 10 and 19%. One in seven, 14%, gives between 20 and 29%, with the remaining 8% giving at least 30%. Four churches in the sample said they gave over 50% of their budget, and one church said 60%.

Source: Britain's New Churches and World Mission, Andrew McClintock, Forward Together, Clarendon House, Cavendish Road, Sheffield S11 9BH. Phone: 0114 258 3707.

POPULATION

Contents

Sources:
Population Trends and other government statistics, and specialist studies

TABLE 4.2
European Union Population in Thousands

Country	1980	1985	1990	1995	2000	% increase 1980–2000	% aged under 15 1996	% aged 65+ 1996
Austria	7,549	7,574	7,690	8,040	8,076	+7	18	15
Belgium	9,852	9,858	9,948	10,131	10,171	+3	18	16
Denmark	5,123	5,111	5,135	5,216	5,271	+3	18	15
Finland	4,780	4,894	4,974	5,099	5,135	+7	19	14
France	53,880	55,157	56,577	58,027	58,815	+8	19	15
Germany	73,304	77,709	79,113	81,539	82,323	+5	17	14
Greece	9,643	9,920	10,121	10,443	10,539	+9	17	16
Irish Republic	3,401	3,544	3,507	3,580	3,591	+5	25	12
Italy	56,434	56,588	56,694	57,269	56,911	−1	15	17
Luxembourg	364	366	379	407	428	+14	18	14
Netherlands	14,144	14,454	14,893	15,424	15,684	+10	18	13
Portugal	9,766	10,014	9,920	9,912	9,911	+1	18	15
Spain	37,542	38,345	38,805	39,178	39,239	+4	16	16
Sweden	8,310	8,343	8,527	8,816	8,852	+6	19	17
United Kingdom	56,355	56,850	57,808	58,606	59,404	+5	19	15
Total EU	**355,447**	**358,727**	**364,091**	**371,687**	**374,350**	**+5**	**18**	**15**

Table 4.2 shows that in the European Union all countries, with the exception of Italy, are increasing in population size, the Netherlands and Luxembourg at an especially high rate. Germany continues to be the largest country in terms of population, followed by the UK and France. Although Italy declined slightly between 1995 and 2000 it is still the fourth largest country in Europe.

Figure 4.2.2 shows that the Irish Republic remains the most religious country in Europe with 97% of the population professing the Christian faith although this is a decrease since 1995 when 98% did so. Iceland is very close behind with 96% claiming to be Christian, and Greece, Portugal and Poland follow with over 94% of their populations who are Christian. Much of this Christianity is nominal.

In the European Union the 2 countries with the lowest percentage of the population who are Christian are the United Kingdom and the Netherlands with 63% and 59% respectively. Outside the Union the lowest number of Christians in a European country is in Turkey where only 0.2% of the population profess allegiance. Azerbaijan only has 2%.

FIGURE 4.2.1
Population change in Europe, 1980–2000

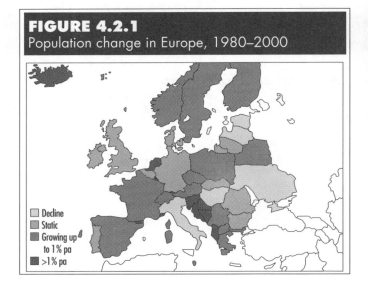

Decline
Static
Growing up to 1% pa
>1% pa

FIGURE 4.2.2
Percentage of population who are Christian, 2000

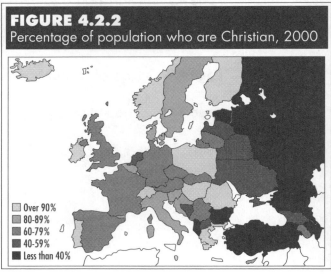

Over 90%
80-89%
60-79%
40-59%
Less than 40%

TABLE 4.3
UK Population in Thousands
The percentages represent the proportion of men in that age group

UK	1991	%	1996	%	2001	%	2006	%	2011	%	2016	%	2021	%	2026	%	2031	%
0–14	11,065	51.4	11,360	51.2	11,288	51.5	10,861	51.5	10,508	51.4	10,357	51.3	10,368	51.3	10,390	51.3	10,274	51.3
15–19	3,744	51.5	3,522	51.4	3,727	51.4	3,950	51.6	3,820	51.4	3,655	51.3	3,524	51.3	3,467	51.3	3,505	51.3
20–29	9,304	51.0	8,380	51.0	7,469	51.1	7,476	51.2	7,899	51.1	7,990	50.8	7,698	50.8	7,408	50.8	7,217	50.8
30–44	12,211	50.3	12,936	50.3	13,747	50.4	13,334	50.4	12,171	50.4	11,456	50.7	11,687	50.6	11,975	50.6	11,908	50.6
45–64	12,388	49.4	13,354	49.6	14,086	49.5	15,200	49.7	16,477	49.5	16,959	50.4	17,015	50.7	16,431	50.7	15,541	50.6
65 or over	9,096	40.0	9,249	40.6	9,301	41.5	9,466	41.8	10,052	41.1	11,188	44.5	11,952	44.9	13,016	45.1	14,377	45.5
TOTAL	57,808	48.9	58,801	49.0	59,618	49.2	60,287	49.2	60,927	49.2	61,605	49.6	62,244	49.7	62,687	49.6	62,822	49.6

England

	1991	%	1996	%	2001	%	2006	%	2011	%	2016	%	2021	%	2026	%	2031	%
0–14	9,154	51.4	9,444	51.3	9,435	51.5	9,106	51.6	8,827	51.5	8,716	51.3	8,749	51.3	8,803	51.3	8,743	51.3
15–19	3,083	51.5	2,905	51.3	3,082	51.3	3,294	51.4	3,197	51.3	3,070	51.3	2,966	51.3	2,919	51.3	2,960	51.3
20–29	7,790	51.0	6,990	50.9	6,228	50.9	6,243	51.0	6,628	51.0	6,743	50.7	6,521	50.7	6,292	50.7	6,141	50.7
30–44	10,231	50.3	10,842	50.3	11,558	50.4	11,233	50.4	10,249	50.4	9,652	50.8	9,880	50.6	10,167	50.6	10,156	50.6
45–64	10,319	49.6	11,155	49.7	11,784	49.6	12,726	49.8	13,831	49.7	14,245	50.6	14,317	50.9	13,848	50.8	13,097	50.7
65 or over	7,631	40.1	7,753	40.7	7,784	41.7	7,924	42.1	8,429	41.4	9,406	44.7	10,051	45.0	10,952	45.2	12,127	45.7
TOTAL	48,208	48.9	49,089	49.1	49,871	49.2	50,526	49.3	51,161	49.2	51,832	49.7	52,484	49.8	52,981	49.7	53,224	49.7

Wales

	1991	%	1996	%	2001	%	2006	%	2011	%	2016	%	2021	%	2026	%	2031	%
0–14	558	51.4	564	51.7	551	51.6	522	51.7	509	51.5	508	51.4	513	51.5	512	51.3	498	51.4
15–19	188	51.5	178	52.0	192	51.7	200	51.7	187	51.7	179	51.4	172	51.2	174	51.1	178	51.1
20–29	422	50.8	383	51.6	353	52.2	369	52.1	392	51.8	386	50.8	365	51.0	350	50.9	346	50.9
30–44	587	50.0	601	49.7	624	49.8	600	49.8	559	49.9	543	50.6	568	50.4	576	50.2	563	50.3
45–64	641	49.4	689	49.2	719	49.0	763	49.4	803	49.3	808	50.1	797	50.4	776	50.5	753	50.5
65 or over	496	40.1	506	40.1	508	41.2	512	41.3	539	41.0	594	44.3	628	44.7	669	44.8	718	45.0
TOTAL	2,892	48.7	2,921	48.7	2,947	48.9	2,966	48.9	2,989	49.2	3,018	49.4	3,043	49.5	3,057	49.4	3,056	49.4

Scotland

	1991	%	1996	%	2001	%	2006	%	2011	%	2016	%	2021	%	2026	%	2031	%
0–14	959	51.3	962	51.1	924	51.3	877	51.3	837	51.3	816	51.3	800	51.3	780	51.4	752	51.3
15–19	344	51.3	314	51.3	324	51.1	327	51.3	313	51.1	289	51.2	279	51.3	273	51.3	269	51.3
20–29	831	51.2	752	51.2	651	51.4	634	51.4	646	51.1	635	50.7	598	50.8	564	50.9	547	50.8
30–44	1,087	50.3	1,147	50.4	1,195	50.7	1,128	51.0	1,008	50.5	921	50.2	906	50.1	904	50.1	871	50.2
45–64	1,117	48.3	1,175	48.6	1,224	48.9	1,317	49.2	1,420	48.8	1,457	49.4	1,435	49.6	1,348	49.7	1,246	49.7
65 or over	769	38.9	778	39.5	788	40.0	801	40.2	833	39.8	913	43.3	975	43.7	1,065	44.0	1,164	44.3
TOTAL	5,107	48.5	5,128	48.7	5,106	48.8	5,084	49.0	5,057	48.8	5,031	49.0	4,993	49.0	4,934	49.0	4,849	49.0

Northern Ireland

	1991	%	1996	%	2001	%	2006	%	2011	%	2016	%	2021	%	2026	%	2031	%
0–14	394	51.2	390	51.0	378	51.7	356	51.5	335	51.5	317	50.9	306	51.1	295	51.5	281	51.2
15–19	129	51.9	125	51.2	129	51.9	129	52.1	123	51.9	117	51.3	107	51.4	101	51.5	98	51.0
20–29	261	52.4	255	52.5	237	52.1	230	52.7	233	51.8	226	52.7	214	52.3	202	52.5	183	52.5
30–44	306	49.2	346	49.9	370	50.3	373	49.8	355	49.9	340	50.9	333	51.1	328	51.2	318	50.9
45–64	311	48.2	335	48.9	359	48.8	394	49.0	423	48.8	449	48.6	466	48.7	459	49.5	445	49.9
65 or over	200	40.9	212	40.1	221	40.3	229	39.9	251	40.0	275	43.2	298	44.3	330	44.4	368	44.2
TOTAL	1,601	49.2	1,663	49.2	1,694	49.4	1,711	49.3	1,720	49.0	1,724	49.3	1,724	49.4	1,715	49.7	1,693	49.4

Source: Government Actuary's Department

FIGURE 4.3
Population of UK by age-group 1971–2031

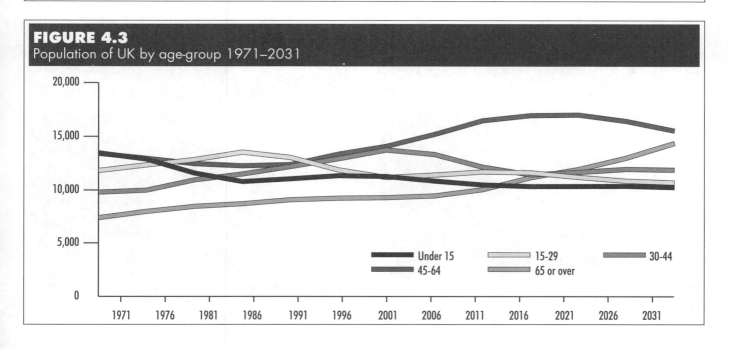

TABLE 4.4
Births and Abortions 1970–1998

	Number of births[2]	Births per 1,000 population	% births outside marriage	Number of Abortions[3]	Cumulative abortions since 1967 Act[3]
1970	903,900	16.2	8.2	75,962	148,113
1975	603,400	10.7	9.0	106,224	677,485
1980	753,700	13.4	12.5	128,927	1,243,463
1985	750,700	13.2	21.0	141,101	1,905,431
1990	798,600	13.9	29.8	173,900	2,721,902
1995	732,000	12.5	33.6	154,300	3,518,441
1996	733,400	12.5	35.5	167,900	3,686,341
1997	725,800[1]	12.3	36.7	170,100	3,856,441
1998	715,300[1]	12.1	37.8	177,332	4,033,773

[1] Estimate
[2] United Kingdom
[3] Rersident in England and Wales only
Source: Population and Health, Abortion Monitors and Health Statistics 01, Office for National Statistics

Table 4.4.1 shows that although the number of births has fallen slightly between 1996 and 1997, the number of abortions is rising. Since the 1967 Abortion Act the figures gradually rose to a peak in 1990, but then fell in 1995 only to start rising again to an all time high in 1998. The increases and decreases can be seen clearly in **Figure 4.4.1**; the number of conceptions being terminated is very high, contributing to the decrease in the birth rate.

The *Daily Telegraph* suggested that one reason for the increase in terminated pregnancies could be the government warning that the Pill carries an increased risk of thrombosis for women using it. Many women therefore stopped using the Pill as a contraceptive, have not found another suitable, become pregnant and in effect are using abortion as a means of contraception.

The two maps **Figures 4.4.2** and **4.4.3** show the trend of growing numbers of abortions in the UK from 1970 to 1995, even though 1995 was one of the lowest years recently for terminations. However, compared to some Eastern European countries, UK figures are relatively low. Between 1970 and 1995 abortion numbers have *decreased* in some countries, especially in Poland.

Source: Daily Telegraph, February 1999

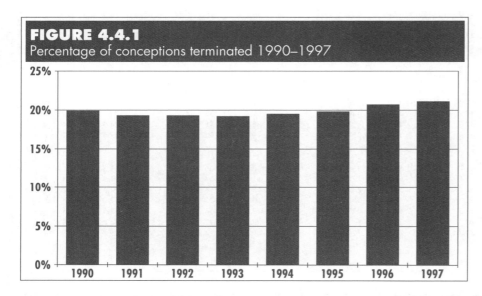
FIGURE 4.4.1
Percentage of conceptions terminated 1990–1997

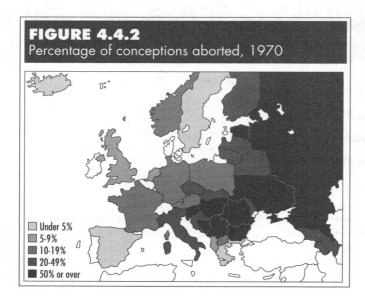
FIGURE 4.4.2
Percentage of conceptions aborted, 1970

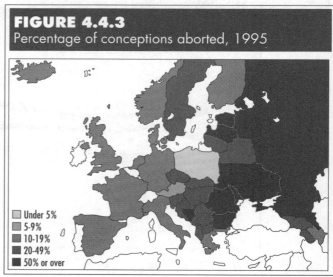
FIGURE 4.4.3
Percentage of conceptions aborted, 1995

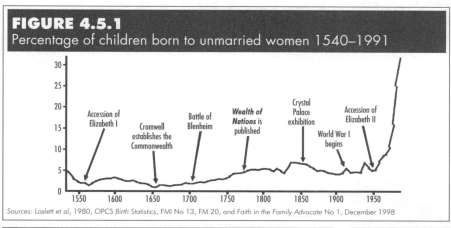

FIGURE 4.5.1
Percentage of children born to unmarried women 1540–1991

Sources: Laslett et al, 1980, OPCS *Birth Statistics*, FMI No 13, FM 20, and *Faith in the Family Advocate* No 1, December 1998

TABLE 4.5
Babies conceived by those under 20, 1996

Age	Under 16	16 to 19	Total under 20
Conception rate[1]	0.94%	6.85%	6.30%
Number conceived	8,800	85,600	94,400
Terminated by abortion	52%	35%	37%

[1] Rates for under 16 and under 20 are based on the number of women aged 13–15 and 15–19 respectively
Source: *Health Statistics*, No 1, Spring 1999.

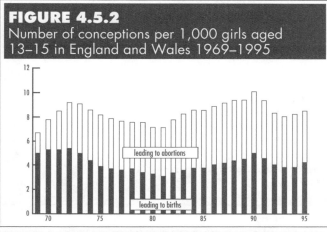

FIGURE 4.5.2
Number of conceptions per 1,000 girls aged 13–15 in England and Wales 1969–1995

leading to abortions

leading to births

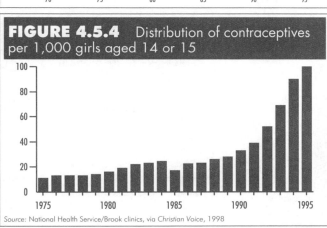

FIGURE 4.5.4 Distribution of contraceptives per 1,000 girls aged 14 or 15

Source: National Health Service/Brook clinics, via *Christian Voice*, 1998

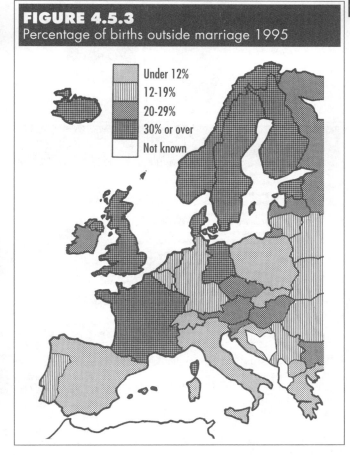

FIGURE 4.5.3
Percentage of births outside marriage 1995

Under 12%
12-19%
20-29%
30% or over
Not known

The number of children born to unmarried women has been well under 5% for the 400 years 1550 to 1950, except for a few years around 1850. In the 30 years 1950 to 1980 it climbed to 12½%, in the next 10 years it more than doubled again to 30%, and in 1998 was 38%. Actual figures for the most recent years are in **Table 4.4.1.**

Figure 4.5.3 shows that Great Britain has one of the higher rates of birth for unmarried women in Europe, though not as high as in Scandinavia, where in Sweden for example the percentage was 54% in 1997. In general the Catholic countries of southern Europe, and Poland, have much lower rates.

Of the 39 countries shown on the map, the rate is under 20% in 21 of them.

Figure 4.5.2 gives the number of conceptions for every 1,000 girls aged 13 to 15 in England and Wales from 1969, and whether they lead to an abortion or a birth. The proportion having an abortion grew in the 1970s, and has remained at about 50 to 55% of the total since.

Figure 4.5.4 shows the number of contraceptives distributed for every 1,000 girls aged 14 or 15 in England since 1975. In the 20 years since then the number has increased ten-fold. The sudden drop in 1985 reflects the

Gillick ruling which outlawed pill secrecy for most of that year. The "Safe Sex" campaign began in 1986, but the most substantial increase took place in the early 1990s when the number distributed went from 35 for every 1,000 girls in 1990 to 100 in 1995. Whilst this may show young teenagers to be increasingly sexually active, it may also reflect the greater availability and awareness of safe sex.

The outcome of conceptions is shown in **Table 4.5.** In 1996 in England and Wales, 7% of these under 20 conceived a baby, 1 in every 16, although only 1 in every 106 for those under 16. Of the 94,000 babies thus conceived, 35,000 were aborted.

FIGURE 4.6.1
Percentage cohabiting by age, 1989–1996

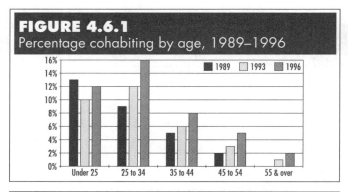

FIGURE 4.6.2 Why the 25% of cohabiting women who stop each year do so

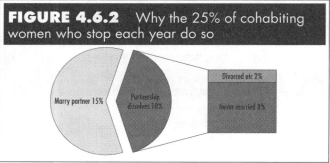

Marry partner 15% — Partnership dissolves 10% — Divorced etc 2% — Never married 8%

FIGURE 4.6.3 Women aged 20–39 who never attend church by first partnership

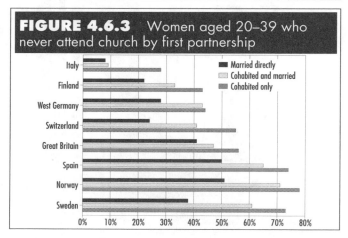

Italy, Finland, West Germany, Switzerland, Great Britain, Spain, Norway, Sweden

- Married directly
- Cohabited and married
- Cohabited only

TABLE 4.6.1 Percentage of the population of England and Wales cohabiting, 1989 to 1996

| | 1989 | | 1993 | | 1996 | |
Age:	Men %	Women %	Men %	Women %	Men %	Women %
16–19	1	3	1	2	1	3
20–24	8	13	7	10	7	13
25–34	11	8	14	11	19	14
35–44	5	4	6	5	8	7
45–64	2	2	3	3	5	4
55 or over	1	0	1	1	1	2
All ages	**4**	**4**	**7**	**7**	**7**	**7**

Source: Cohabitation, Families Policy Studies Centre, Population Trends, No 72, Summer 1993; Lifestyle Pocket Book, 1999, quoting General Household Survey, Office for National Statistics

TABLE 4.6.2 First reason for marrying by those who cohabited before marriage, Great Britain, 1995

Reason:	Men %	Women %	Total %
Wanted to strengthen relationship/make it more secure	34	34	**34**
Wanted to have/ was having/ had just had children	20	23	**21**
Decided that "trial marriage" worked	11	6	**8**
Influence of parents, friends	4	7	**5**
Financial reasons	4	4	**4**
Freedom to marry, eg divorce came through	1	3	**2**
Other reasons	26	23	**25**

Source: Populations Trendsd No 96, Summer 1999, Office for National Statistics

TABLE 4.6.3 Percentage of Marriages in England and Wales where the couple cohabited first, 1994

Denomination/Religion	Cohabit-ing %	Number of marriages
Unitarian	75	900
Religious Society of Friends	70	70
United Reformed Church	65	5,400
Methodist	62	14,300
Presbyterian	58	300
Independent Congregationalist	51	800
Roman Catholic	48	16,400
Baptist	41	3,200
Others, including Mormons	41	3,000
Salvation Army	40	300
Muslim	39	100
Calvanistic Methodist	37	400
Church of England	36	86,100
Jews	34	800
Denomination not given	27	300
Church of Wales	23	4,500
Christian Brethren	20	200
Jehovah's Witnesses	7	900
Sikh	7	800
TOTAL RELIGIOUS	**41**	**138,770**
TOTAL CIVIL	76	152,000
ALL MARRIAGES	60	290,770

Source: Article by John Haskey "Spouses with identical residential addresses before marriage: an indicator of pre-marital cohabitation", Population Trends No 89, Autumn 1997, Office for National Statistics.

- 22% of men aged 25 to 29 in 1996 had never had a partner; 16% of women
- 13% of men aged 30 to 34 in 1996 had never had a partner; 6% of women
- In Great Britain 50% of cohabiting women aged 20 to 39 did so for up to 17 months, 50% longer, when cohabitation ended in marriage
- In Great Britain 50% of cohabiting women aged 20 to 39 did so for up to 19 months, 50% longer, when cohabitation dissolved
- 37% of women aged 25 to 29 married directly for their first partnership, and 72% aged 35 to 39
- 27% of all women in Great Britain started cohabiting in 1997; 17% of these were single, 5% divorced, 4% separated, and 1% widowed
- Peter Vardy's book, *The Puzzle of Sex*, 1997, reports on a survey of 3,000 A-level students at a sixth form RE Conference. 85% Roman Catholics and 80% Anglicans do not think it "morally wrong" to have sex with a long-term partner when the couple are not married
- Those marrying in the early 1980s after cohabiting were by 1992 60% more likely to be divorced than other couples, after 8 years

Table 4.6.3 assumes that if a couple about to be married give the same address that they are co-habiting. However it could be that the same address is given for convenience or to prove they both live in the required area; on the other hand, some who may be cohabiting give their parents addresses. The figures in the Table are thus only a guide, and not necessarily definitive.

Even as a guide they show that two in five marrying in church are likely to be cohabiting first. The General Household Survey (GHS) however asks couples directly if they are cohabiting, and on the basis of this survey many more do so than are ascertained by the identical addresses, especially amongst those in their 20s. This data pushes the religious cohabiting percentage closer to 60%, and the civil figure closer to 90%, with the overall figure at about 75%.

Sources: Article in the *Daily Telegraph* 18th June 1997; *High Divorce Rates*, Lord Chancellor's Department, report in *Church Times* 26th February 1999; *Population Trends* No 96, Summer 1999, Office for National Statistics

TABLE 4.7.1 Marriages 1970–2000

	England & Wales	& religious	Scotland	N Ireland	TOTAL UK
1971	404,700	60	42,500	12,200	459,400
1976	358,600	52	37,500	9,900	406,000
1981	352,000	50	36,200	9,600	397,800
1986	347,900	51	35,800	10,200	393,900
1991	306,800	53	33,800	9,200	349,800
1992	311,600	51	35,100	9,400	356,100
1993	299,200	49	33,400	9,000	341,600
1994	291,100	48	31,500	8,700	331,300
1995	283,000	46[1]	30,700	8,600	322,300
1996	279,000	41	30,200	8,300	317,500
1997	272,500	38[1]	29,600	8,100	310,200
2000[1]	250,000	31	27,000	7,000	284,000

[1] Estimate
Source: Population Trends No 96, Summer 1999, Office for National Statistics © Crown copyright

TABLE 4.7.2 Divorces 1970–2000

	England	Wales	Scotland	N Ireland	TOTAL UK
1971	74,400		4,800	300	79,500
1976	126,700		8,100	600	135,400
1981	145,700		9,900	1,400	157,000
1986	146,000	7,900	12,800	1,500	168,200
1991	150,100	8,600	12,400	2,300	173,400
1992	151,500	8,900	12,500	2,300	175,200
1993	156,100	8,900	12,800	2,200	180,000
1994	149,600	8,600	13,100	2,300	173,600
1995	147,500	8,000	12,200	2,300	170,000
1996	148,700	8,400	12,300	2,300	171,700
1997	138,700	8,000	12,200	2,200	161,100
2000[1]	133,000	8,000	12,000	2,000	155,000

[1] Estimate
Source: Population Trends No 96, Summer 1999, Office for National Statistics © Crown copyright

TABLE 4.7.3
Religious marriages by denomination, England and Wales, 1837–2000

Year	All religious marriages	Anglican %	Roman Catholic %	All others %
1837	58,048	97.9		2.1
1840	122,391	95.6		4.4
1850	146,537	89.4	3.8	6.8
1860	158,899	86.6	4.9	8.5
1870	163,807	84.4	4.5	11.1
1880	167,785	82.3	4.9	12.8
1890	192,652	81.6	5.0	13.4
1900	218,009	80.0	4.7	15.3
1910	213,043	78.1	5.4	16.5
1920[1]	224,900	78.1	6.8	15.1
1930[1]	237,500	76.3	8.1	15.6
1940[1]	250,100	75.4	9.2	15.4
1950[1]	230,900	75.1	14.3	10.6
1960[1]	241,400	67.8	17.6	14.6
1970	251,368	68.2	17.4	14.4
1980	186,627	66.5	15.4	18.1
1990	174,275	66.5	13.0	20.5
1995	127,522	66.0	12.0	22.0
2000[1]	77,500	66.0	10.8	23.2

[1] Estimate

TABLE 4.7.4
Children under 16 of divorced couples, England and Wales, 1971–1996

Year	Number	0 to 4 %	5 to 10 %	11 to 15 %
1971	82,304	25	49	26
1981	159,403	25	42	33
1991	160,684	33	42	25
1992	168,428	32	42	26
1993	175,961	32	43	25
1994	164,834	30	43	27
1995	160,563	29	43	28
1996	159,671	28	44	28

FIGURE 4.7.1
Marriages and divorces 1961–1996

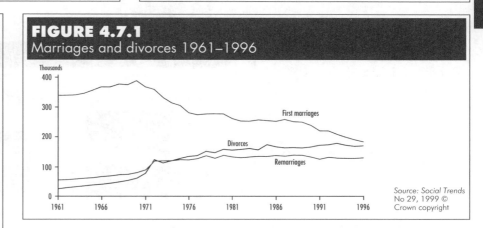

Source: Social Trends No 29, 1999 © Crown copyright

FIGURE 4.7.2
Estimated percentage of marriages which survived up to 50th anniversary, England and Wales, 1947

FIGURE 4.7.3
Percentage of marriages which would survive up to 50th anniversary, if divorce and death rates remain constant, England and Wales, 1994

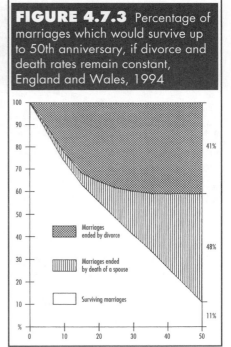

Marriages ended by divorce

Marriages ended by death of a spouse

Surviving marriages

Tables 4.7.1, 4.7.2, and Figure 4.7.1 reflect the decreasing number of marriages and increasing numbers of divorces and remarriages. It is estimated that two in five current marriages will end in divorce. Figures 4.7.2 and 4.7.3 show the proportion of marriages likely to celebrate their Golden Anniversary – down from 28% in 1947 to 11% in 1994, with the decrease the increasing number of divorces, not any major change in the proportion of deaths. Table 4.7.3 gives the number of religious marriages, and their sharp decline in the last 30, and especially the last 10, years. As Table 4.7.1 indicates an increasing number are now married somewhere other than a church building.

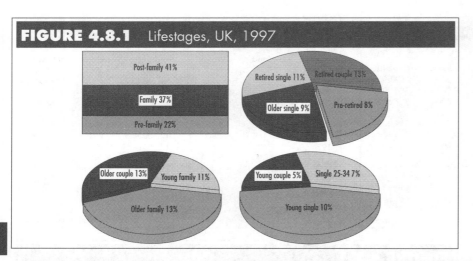

FIGURE 4.8.1 Lifestages, UK, 1997

Post-family 41%

Family 37%

Pre-family 22%

Retired single 11%   Retired couple 13%

Older single 9%   Pre-retired 8%

Older couple 13%   Young family 11%

Older family 13%

Young couple 5%   Single 25-34 7%

Young single 10%

Figure 4.8.1 shows several things. In the first instance the bar chart breaks down the population as to whether they are in the pre-family, family or post-family stage. Each of these three is then broken down as a pie chart showing the composition of these three groups, with the post-family on the right of the bar chart, the pre-family underneath it, and the family itself underneath the bar chart. It might be of interest for churches to analyse their congregations in a similar manner and compare the resulting percentages. The pre-retired couples are sometimes also called the "empty nesters" because their children have left home.

TABLE 4.8.1
Deaths ands cremations, UK, 1900–2000

Year	Number of deaths	Deaths per 1,000 population	Percentage cremated %	Catholic proportion of cremations %
1900	670,126	17.5	0.1	–
1905	594,567	14.8	0.1	–
1910	555,515	13.2	0.2	–
1915	643,884	15.1	0.2	–
1920	534,309	12.1	0.3	–
1925	538,348	11.9	0.5	–
1930	519,712	11.3	0.9	–
1935	542,732	11.5	1.8	–
1940	654,312	13.7	3.9	–
1945	550,763	11.3	7.8	–
1950	574,297	11.4	16	–
1955	580,209	11.3	24	–
1960	588,032	11.2	35	–
1965	612,247	11.3	44	0.4
1970	638,834	11.4	55	2.0
1975	645,966	11.5	61	3.1
1980	644,684	11.4	65	3.8
1985	654,701	11.5	68	3.3
1990	641,800	11.2	68	4.2[1]
1995	641,712	10.9	71	4.7[1]
2000[1]	621,300	10.5	72	5.1

[1] Estimate
Source: Cremation Society Deaths Monitor, Population Trends, Number 96, Summer 1999, Office for National Statistics © Crown copyright

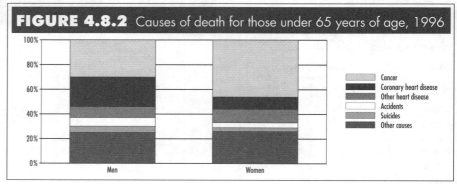

FIGURE 4.8.2 Causes of death for those under 65 years of age, 1996

Men   Women

Legend:
- Cancer
- Coronary heart disease
- Other heart disease
- Accidents
- Suicides
- Other causes

Whilst the number of funerals conducted with a Christian service is not definitively known, it is usually estimated at about 90 to 95% of the total. The Church of England proportion of these is probably similar to their proportion of marriages, about 65 to 70%. However there are two trends which are likely to cause both figures to diminish.

One of these is the increasing number of secular funerals, as small firms are bought up by international companies selling pre-paid funeral packages. For example, the Co-operative Society owns a 25% share of the market, and the American-based Service Corporation International 14%. A Church of England Report, *Good Funerals*, published in October 1998, suggested the recycling of burial grounds to reduce the distance between the funeral service and place of burial.

The second is the trend towards more do-it-yourself funerals, as reported in *Time* magazine 31st May 1999, using dedicated woodland sites, going from 17 in 1996 in the UK to 90 in 1999. One of these, Hinton Park Woodland Burial Ground, for example, allows a person "to be buried in a low-cost, eco-friendly manner, with a tree and name plaque instead of a headstone". Such cost about £1,000. When they opened in 1995 they expected 12 such burials a year, but in 1999 were getting about 300.

Figure 4.8.2 shows the cause of death for the 55,030 men and 33,582 women under 65 who died in 1996. One cause is accidents, about three-quarters of which are traffic accidents. Road users killed in Britain in 1996, 3,598, was almost identical to the number killed in 1997, 3,599.

Table 4.8.1 suggests a total of 60.13 million deaths this century. Catholic Roadwatch, an organisation devoted to trying to reduce the number of traffic accidents, and named after the first person killed by a car – Bridget Driscoll, a Catholic, in 1896 – estimates half a million of these, one in every 120, was a traffic accident. **Table 4.8.2** shows that half the traffic accidents in 1997 were in a car – either driving or travelling as a passenger.

TABLE 4.8.2
Types of fatal road accidents, Great Britain, 1997

Car users	50%
Pedestrians	27%
Motor/pedal cyclists	19%
Goods vehicles	3%
Others	1%

Sources: Jesus Life, Number 43, 1st quarter, 1998, Page 18; Road Casualties Great Britain, Main Results 1997, The Department of Environment, Transport and the Regions; personal correspondence with Antony Porter, OSB, Catholic Roadwatch, P O Box 1580, London W7 3ZP.

500 women are widowed every day in the UK. These are one eighth of the 1½ million people who suffer a major bereavement in the UK each year. The CRUSE bereavement helpline gets over 100,000 calls a year. 18,000 children lost a parent in 1997, part of the 200,000 children under 16 who have a lost a parent through death. CRUSE has opened a special helpline for children.

TABLE 4.9.1
Age distribution of English churchgoers by denomination 1979–1998

Category	Year	Under 15 %	15–19 %	20–29 %	30–44 %	45–64 %	65 or over %	Total (=100%)	Average[1]	Men %	Women %
English	1979	26	9	11	16	20	18	5,441,000	37	45	55
Churchgoers:	1989	25	7	10	17	22	19	4,742,800	38	42	58
TOTAL	1998	19	6	9	17	24	25	3,714,700	43	–	–
Anglicans	1979	27	9	10	17	18	19	1,671,000	36	45	55
	1989	24	5	8	17	24	22	1,491,900	41	39	61
	1998	18	4	7	16	26	29	980,600	46	–	–
Baptists	1979	30	8	9	16	19	18	290,000	36	43	57
	1989	26	7	10	18	20	19	270,900	37	40	60
	1998	22	6	9	18	22	23	277,600	41	–	–
Catholics	1979	24	12	12	19	20	13	1,991,000	35	46	54
	1989	24	8	11	18	23	16	1,715,900	37	45	55
	1998	18	6	10	19	25	22	1,230,100	42	–	–
Independent and	1979	31	9	13	17	14	16	299,000	33	47	53
New Churches	1989	31	16	13	18	13	9	425,500	29	49	51
	1998	23	7	12	21	20	17	392,100	37	–	–
of which:											
Independent	1998	19	5	8	16	23	28	161,600	44	–	–
New Churches	1998	26	9	15	25	18	7	230,500	32	–	–
Methodist	1979	28	5	5	12	25	25	621,000	41	40	60
	1989	23	5	7	12	23	30	512,300	44	37	63
	1998	19	4	4	11	24	38	379,700	49	–	–
Orthodox	1979	27	12	6	13	23	19	10,000	37	45	55
	1989	24	7	12	14	25	18	12,300	38	44	56
	1998	17	12	11	17	20	23	25,200	41	–	–
Pentecostal:	1979	33	11	12	18	16	10	228,000	30	44	56
Mainline and Afro-	1989	31	9	15	18	17	10	236,700	31	43	57
Caribbean	1998	27	8	14	22	19	10	214,600	33	–	–
of which:											
Mainline	1979	29	11	13	17	16	14	121,000	33	46	54
	1989	28	9	13	20	17	13	132,000	33	44	56
Afro-Caribbean	1979	38	12	10	18	17	5	107,000	27	41	59
	1989	34	9	17	16	18	6	104,100	28	41	59
United Reformed	1979	27	5	7	14	21	26	190,000	41	43	57
	1989	24	4	6	13	23	30	149,300	44	37	63
	1998	18	3	5	12	24	38	121,700	49	–	–
Other denominations	1979	25	9	11	16	20	19	141,000	37	44	56
	1989	27	6	8	14	21	24	113,600	40	41	59
	1998	18	5	9	16	23	29	93,100	45	–	–
English Population	1979	21	8	14	19	23	15	46.4 mn	37	49	51
	1989	19	8	16	20	22	15	47.7 mn	38	49	51
	1998	20	6	13	22	23	16	49.7 mn	38	49	51

[1] Taking "65 and over" as having an average age of 75.
Sources: Prospects for the Nineties, Results of the English Church Census, MARC Europe, 1991; Results of the *English Church Attendance Survey,* Christian Research, 1998.

TABLE 4.9.2
Age distribution of Welsh and Scottish churchgoers by denomination 1982–1995

Category	Year	Under 15 %	15–19 %	20–29 %	30–44 %	45–64 %	65 or over %	Total (=100%)	Average[1]	Men %	Women %
Welsh Churchgoers	1982	26	7	8	14	22	23	280,000	40	38	62
	1995	17	4	7	14	26	32	253,100	47	33	67
of which:											
3% "younger"[2]	1995	17	4	7	14	26	32	10,800	33	39	61
8% "normative"	1995	24	10	16	23	18	9	32,800	42	35	65
89% "older"	1995	17	7	12	19	24	21	209,500	49	32	68
Welsh Population	1982	21	8	14	19	23	15	2.7 mn	37	49	51
	1995	20	6	14	20	23	17	2.9 mn	39	49	51
Scottish Churchgoers	1984	25	5	9	15	24	22	863,000	40	37	63
	1994	23	5	8	16	25	23	746,000	42	39	61
Scottish Population	1984	21	9	15	19	22	14	5.1 mn	37	48	52
	1994	19	6	16	21	23	15	5.1 mn	38	48	52

[1] Taking "65 and over" as having an average age of 75.
[2] This classification is taken from the 1995 report. "Younger" are Covenant Ministries, the Non-aligned churches and Pioneer. "Normative" are those denominations whose average age is about the same as the national population: Apostolic, Associating Evangelical Churches of Wales, Baptist Union of GB, Chinese, Christian Brethren, EFCC, Elim, FIEC, Nazarenes, Orthodox and Salvation Army. "Older" are Annibynwr, Assemblies of God, Baptist Union of Wales, Church in Wales, Roman Catholic Church, Congregational Federation, Lutheran Church, Methodist, Presbyterians, Religious Society of Friends, Scottish Baptist, Seventh Day Adventist and the United Reformed Church.

Sources: Prospects for Wales, Results of the Welsh Church Census, Bible Society and MARC Europe, 1983; *Challenge to Change,* Results of the Welsh Churches Survey, Bible Society, 1995; *Prospects for Scotland 2000,* Results of the Scottish Church Census, National Bible Society of Scotland and Christian Research, 1995.

TABLE 4.10.1 Population in thousands by age-group and old county boundaries, including unitary authorities, England, 1998[2]

English county	Under 15	15 to 19	20 to 29	30 to 44	45 to 64	65 or over	TOTAL
Avon	182.2	61.3	136.4	226.6	226.8	161.4	**994.7**
Bedfordshire	115.9	35.7	75.1	132.4	125.8	72.0	**556.9**
Berkshire	160.3	51.0	115.6	199.9	180.0	99.7	**806.5**
Buckinghamshire	138.7	42.7	89.3	164.2	163.3	86.6	**684.8**
Cambridgeshire	136.6	47.3	107.0	163.6	163.2	102.0	**719.7**
Cheshire	189.0	59.8	122.4	218.6	245.6	151.6	**987.0**
Cleveland	115.0	37.8	70.8	123.1	126.7	81.8	**555.2**
Cornwall	86.1	28.4	53.8	95.8	126.9	97.6	**488.6**
Cumbria	88.6	28.0	58.6	105.2	124.6	87.8	**492.8**
Derbyshire	180.6	56.1	123.9	217.0	233.1	156.6	**967.3**
Devon	187.4	66.3	123.5	218.4	261.4	213.7	**1,070.7**
Dorset	115.7	38.9	82.7	139.1	164.9	151.9	**693.2**
Durham	113.1	40.2	74.3	134.7	147.8	97.6	**607.7**
East Sussex	87.0	27.3	49.2	94.8	120.1	112.4	**490.8**
Essex	301.4	92.9	209.2	347.8	387.0	262.6	**1,600.9**
Gloucestershire	104.2	33.5	67.6	123.3	135.8	96.4	**560.8**
Greater London	1,398.1	412.9	1,121.4	1,848.6	1,450.8	914.1	**7,145.9**
Greater Manchester	522.4	166.6	351.4	578.4	576.1	375.0	**2,569.9**
Hampshire	310.7	103.3	224.2	374.0	382.2	255.8	**1,650.2**
Herefordshire[3]	31.1	9.3	18.5	34.6	42.2	32.0	**167.7**
Hertfordshire	201.4	59.6	131.4	242.2	238.4	153.4	**1,026.4**
Humberside	172.2	57.4	113.0	191.1	210.5	145.9	**890.1**
Isle of Wight	21.4	6.9	12.5	23.1	32.9	29.4	**126.2**
Kent	302.1	94.5	196.2	337.3	377.7	258.6	**1,566.4**
Lancashire	277.8	90.3	183.0	304.0	338.5	235.7	**1,429.3**
Leicestershire	182.7	64.5	129.9	210.4	213.6	137.9	**939.0**
Lincolnshire	112.0	35.6	74.3	128.7	157.6	118.2	**626.4**
Merseyside	277.1	92.1	183.1	308.7	318.1	227.3	**1,406.4**
Norfolk	136.9	45.4	96.4	157.7	196.3	153.9	**786.6**
North Yorkshire	132.8	45.4	87.5	159.8	186.2	132.3	**744.0**
Northamptonshire	122.9	39.2	79.0	138.8	145.1	87.4	**612.4**
Northumberland	55.7	18.6	35.4	65.5	80.0	52.8	**308.0**
Nottinghamshire	195.7	67.3	137.6	232.0	241.1	162.6	**1,036.3**
Oxford	118.3	42.1	87.6	142.2	138.0	85.4	**613.6**
Shropshire	81.5	26.0	52.4	91.1	107.1	68.7	**426.8**
Somerset	89.8	29.0	55.9	98.2	120.5	94.7	**488.1**
South Yorkshire	248.3	80.5	173.4	297.4	297.6	206.5	**1,303.7**
Staffordshire	197.7	65.6	135.4	234.1	262.7	161.5	**1,057.0**
Suffolk	127.8	38.8	85.2	138.7	159.3	118.3	**668.1**
Surrey	194.9	62.0	122.4	245.0	261.4	170.9	**1,056.6**
Tyne & Wear	210.5	74.3	148.7	254.1	252.2	182.3	**1,122.1**
Warwickshire	93.1	29.1	62.5	110.6	128.8	80.3	**504.4**
West Midlands	544.9	175.4	360.0	580.5	572.8	402.3	**2,635.9**
West Sussex	174.5	55.0	127.3	219.2	229.4	195.7	**1,001.1**
West Yorkshire	423.0	139.6	289.5	481.0	469.5	311.8	**2,114.4**
Wiltshire	116.9	35.1	79.3	138.5	139.9	92.9	**602.6**
Worcestershire[3]	99.7	31.7	63.6	116.2	139.2	87.3	**537.7**
Channel Islands: Jersey[1]	14.7	4.5	13.1	22.4	21.0	12.4	**88.1**
Channel Islands: Guernsey	10.5	3.4	8.4	13.3	14.4	9.2	**59.2**
Isle of Man	12.8	4.3	9.2	15.2	18.1	13.0	**72.6**
TOTAL	**9,513.7**	**3,052.5**	**6,608.1**	**11,237.1**	**11,452.2**	**7,797.2**	**49,660.8**

TABLE 4.10.2 Population in thousands 1800-2000

Year[2]	England and Wales	Scot- land	N Ireland[5]	TOTAL UK	15 & over %[4]
1800	8,893				
1810	10,164				
1820	12,000				
1830	13,897				
1840	15,914	2,624[1]	689[1]	19,227	64.2[1]
1850	17,928	2,942[1]	775[1]	21,645	64.6
1860	20,066	3,139[1]	862[1]	24,067	64.3
1870	22,712	3,415[1]	971[1]	27,098	63.9
1880	25,974	3,624[1]	1,100[1]	30,698	63.9[1]
1890	29,003	4,025	1,227[1]	34,255	64.8[1]
1900	32,528	4,472	1,237	38,237	67.6
1905[1]	34,213	4,603	1,242	40,058	68.5
1910	36,070	4,761	1,251	42,082	69.1
1915[1]	36,541	4,808	1,253	42,602	71.6
1920	37,887	4,882	1,258	44,027	72.2
1925[1]	39,001	4,880	1,257	45,138	74.1
1930	39,952	4,843	1,269	46,064	75.9
1935[1]	40,811	4,961	1,274	47,046	76.2
1940	41,460[3]	5,007	1,302	47,769	77.0
1945[1]	42,245	5,042	1,337	48,624	77.6
1950	43,758	5,096	1,371	50,225	77.7
1955[1]	44,769	5,133	1,408	51,310	77.1
1960	46,105	5,179	1,425	52,709	77.0
1965[1]	47,422	5,206	1,474	54,102	77.5
1970	48,750	5,236	1,520	55,506	76.2
1975	49,459	5,233	1,514	56,206	77.1
1980	49,635	5,180	1,538	56,353	79.4
1985	50,162	5,121	1,567	56,850	81.0
1990	51,100	5,107	1,601	57,808	80.9
1995	51,852	5,134	1,620	58,606	80.6
2000[1]	52,476	5,024	1,622	59,122	80.0

[1] Estimate [2] Figures relate to a date in April of the year following that shown (except for 1801, 1851 and 1901 when it was March, 1811, 1821 and 1831 when it was May, and 1841 and 1921 when it was June). [3] Mid-year estimate for 1939; there was no census in 1941. [4] Based on figures for Great Britain 1900-1965. [5] Until 1922 the whole of Ireland was part of the United Kingdom. Population figures for 1900 to 1920 come from official estimates, 1890 is trend estimated backwards from these, and the years 1840 to 1880 are estimated pro rata to the total for Great Britain.

Sources: *Preliminary Report*, 1981 Census, CEN 81 PR(1), Office of Population Censuses and Surveys, June 1981; articles in *Population Trends* No 48, Summer 1987; personal communication with Office for National Statistics, Census marketing; *Churches and Churchgoers*, Robert Currie, OUP, 1977. All figures in column 2 and most in column 3 are © Crown copyright.

Footnotes for Table 4.10.1:
[1] Increased by 2% to allow for the population of Alderney and Sark [2] Based on 1996 projections [3] Formerly combined
Source: Subnational population projections 1996.
© Crown copyright 1996. Reproduced by permission of the Office for National Statistics

FIGURE 4.10 Social class of church members

Church Membership (estimated)	Upper class	
	Middle class	Population
	Upper working class	
	Working class etc	

Source: *The Irrelevant Church*, Robin Gamble, Monarch, 1991

TABLE 4.10.3 Social class of Roman Catholic and Church of Scotland and their fathers 1992 and 1997

	Respondents 1992			Respondents 1997			Fathers of respondents 1992			Fathers of respondents 1997		
	RC %	CS %	All %	RC%	CS%	All %	RC%	CS%	All %	RC%	CS%	All %
I	3	2	**2**	2	4	**4**	1	2	**3**	3	4	**6**
II	21	20	**22**	18	23	**23**	19	19	**19**	16	17	**21**
IIN	16	25	**25**	22	29	**25**	4	9	**8**	8	6	**8**
IIM	24	24	**22**	22	18	**21**	47	44	**46**	48	48	**43**
IV	25	18	**20**	22	14	**17**	20	21	**18**	15	17	**16**
V	10	11	**10**	12	12	**10**	9	6	**6**	10	6	**6**

Source: *Scottish Election Surveys*, 1992, 1997, quoted in *Conservative Protestant Politics*, Professor Steve Bruce, OUP, 1998, Page 11.

The Office for National Statistics now publishes population information separately for "counties" and for "unitary authorities". **Table 4.10.1** combines these into the counties established in 1974, except for Hereford and Worcestershire which are separated.

Table 4.10.2 gives UK population figures since 1800 based on the census. At the beginning of the century, children (under 15) were one-third of the population; at the end one-fifth, reflecting both the increasing longevity and the decreasing number of births.

Figure 4.10 is an estimate of the variation between church members and the population by social class. **Table 4.10.3** shows that the class differences, at least in Scotland, between Roman Catholics and the Church of Scotland are much less than they were.

Table 4.12.4 in *Religious Trends* No 1 showed much greater variations in a 1973 survey. There is however a large generational difference in **Table 4.10.3**, especially between the manual class IIIM and the non-manual IIIN. 1998 UK population percentages for the various classes are, respectively, 5%, 29%, 23%, 20%, 17% and 6%, suggesting Scotland has rather fewer in Class II and more in Class III than England.

Contents

Sources:
Government statistics, and specialist studies; UK Christian Handbook 2000/2001

TABLE 5.2.1
A-level Religious Studies examination results 1995–1999

A-level Grade	Religious Studies 1995 %	1996 %	1997 %	1998 %	1999 %	All Subjects 1995 %	1996 %	1997 %	1998 %	1999 %
A	13	14	14	15	17	16	16	16	16	17
B	18	20	19	19	20	17	18	19	19	19
C	23	24	24	24	24	19	20	20	21	21
D	20	20	20	20	18	18	18	19	19	18
E	14	12	13	12	11	14	14	13	13	13
N	7	6	6	6	6	9	8	8	8	7
U	5	4	4	4	4	7	6	5	4	5
Total (=100%)	8,924	9,053	9,281	9,138	8,997	725,992	776,115 739,163		783,692 777,710	
Increase on previous year	–	+1.4%	+4.0%	–1.5%	–1.5%		+1.7%	+6.9%	+0.2%	+0.8%

Sources: A-level results *The Times* 15th August 1996, 14th August 1997, The *Daily Telegraph* 20th August 1998, 19th August 1999

TABLE 5.2.2
GCSE Religious Studies examination results 1995–1999

GCSE Grade	Religious Studies 1995 %	1996 %	1997 %	1998 %	1999 %	All Subjects 1995 %	1996 %	1997 %	1998 %	1999 %
A+	3	4	5	6	7	3	3	4	4	4
A	12	12	12	13	13	10	10	11	11	11
B	20	19	19	18	18	18	18	18	17	17
C	21	21	21	20	20	22	22	22	22	24
D	15	15	15	14	14	19	19	19	19	19
E	12	12	12	12	11	14	14	13	13	13
F	9	9	9	8	8	9	9	8	8	7
G	5	4	4	5	5	4	4	4	4	3
U	3	3	3	4	4	1	1	1	2	2
Total (=100%)	108,055	118,545 116,549	115,679 113,381			4,971,667	5,415,176 5,475,872	5,374,751 5,353,095		
Increase on previous year	–	+7.9%	+1.7%	–4.4%	+2.0%		+2.1%	–1.1%	–1.1%	+0.4%

Sources: A-level results *The Times* 15th August 1996, 14th August 1997, The *Daily Telegraph* 27th August 1998, *The Times* 13th September 1999

TABLE 5.2.3
Top 10 names in 1998

The names in bold are from the Bible

	Boys		Girls
1)	Jack	1)	**Chloe**
2)	**Thomas**	2)	Emily
3)	**James**	3)	Megan
4)	**Daniel**	4)	Jessica
5)	**Joshua**	5)	Sophie
6)	**Matthew**	6)	Charlotte
7)	**Samuel**	7)	**Hannah**
8)	Callum	8)	Lauren
9)	**Joseph**	9)	**Rebecca**
10)	**Jordan**	10)	Lucy

Source: The *Daily Telegraph* 5th January 1999

FIGURE 5.2
Defining spiritual development

- Development of personal values
- Development of the ability to form relationships with others
- Reflecting on community upheld value and attitudes
- Development of a sense of awe, mystery and wonder
- Reflecting that our understanding of the world is limited
- Reflecting on the meaning and purpose of life
- Responsding to challenging experiences, eg death
- Development of individual creativity
- Reflecting on questions of a philosophical or religious nature
- Developement of Christian beliefs
- Development of a relationship with God

0%   20%   40%   60%   80%   100%

■ Agree   ▫ Not certain   ▨ Disagree

Source: Article "What is Spiritual Development?" by G Davies in *International Journal of Children's Spirituality*, Volume 3 Number 2, December 1998, Page 129.

Figure 5.2 reflects the results of a questionnaire returned by 204 headteachers in nursery (2), primary (171), infant (20) or junior (11) schools in three counties in south Wales in the summer term of 1996, 33 of which were church schools. The large majority, 97%, said that for them spiritual development meant developing personal values, followed by, for 96%, an ability to form relationships with others. Linking spiritual development with religion was agreed by a much smaller percentage, 56% (but still a majority over half), of a relationship with God, or the development, by 62%, of Christian beliefs.

TABLE 5.2.4
Places and Fees at Theological Colleges and Bible Schools

	Number of Colleges Residential	Totally non-residential	Total	Giving Details %	Residential Student Places Men	Women	Mixed	Total	Men: Women: mixed ratio	Tuition and Accommodation fees Annual Average	Increase p/a %	Average length of full course Years
1972	33	1	34	91	981	659	425	2,065	48:32:20	£325	–	2.6
1976	36	4	40	100	1,007	736	1,492	3,235	31:23:46	£675	+20	2.4
1980	68	18	86	94	1,652	967	2,419	5,038	33:19:48	£1,380	+20	2.6
1982	70	18	88	97	1,620	1,033	2,704	5,357	30:19:51	£1,680	+10	2.6
1984	79	22	101	94	1,639	1,112	3,090	5,841	28:19:53	£2,050	+10	2.6
1986	97	22	119	90	1,770	1,242	3,553	6,565	27:19:54	£2,350	+7	2.7
1988	96	21	117	96	1,768	1,335	3,497	6,600	27:20:53	£2,560	+4	2.8
1991	98	33	131	98	2,016	1,066	4,113	7,195	28:15:57	£3,180	+7	2.9
1993	96	53	149	97	1,914	1,310	4,113	7,357	26:18:56	£3,562	+6	2.8
1995	93	66	159	94	2,053	1,352	4,004	7,409	28:18:54	£3,751	+3	2.6
1997	91	56	147	92	2,300	1,903	4,242	8,425	27:23:50	£3,994	+6	2.4
1999	96	58	154	94	2,671	1,968	3,209	7,848	34:25:41	£4,146	+4	2.5

The number of actual students in 1997 is estimated at 3,750 men and 2,500 women, a total of 6,250 or 74% of places; in 1999 the numbers are estimated at 4,450 men and 2,700 women, a total of 7,150 or 91% of places.

The Christian Medical Fellowship helped sponsor a survey in 1998 seeking the activities of UK missionaries. The results are given in **Table 5.3.1**, and show that about 570 missionaries are involved in health activities, 7% of the total. The kind of work they do is shown in **Figure 5.3.1**:

- Two-fifths, 41%, work in preventative health care (abbreviated to "Prev" in the piechart), two-thirds of whom are men;
- A third, 36%, in institutional medical work ("Inst"), three-fifths of whom are women;
- 17% in primary health care ("Prim"), four-fifths of whom are women;
- The remaining 6%, all women, in midwifery ("Mid").

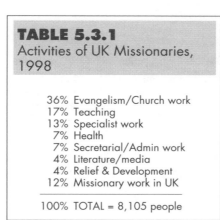

TABLE 5.3.1
Activities of UK Missionaries, 1998

36%	Evangelism/Church work
17%	Teaching
13%	Specialist work
7%	Health
7%	Secretarial/Admin work
4%	Literature/media
4%	Relief & Development
12%	Missionary work in UK

100% TOTAL = 8,105 people

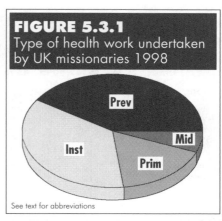

FIGURE 5.3.1
Type of health work undertaken by UK missionaries 1998

See text for abbreviations

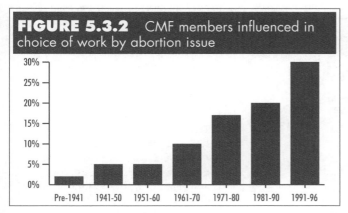

FIGURE 5.3.2 CMF members influenced in choice of work by abortion issue

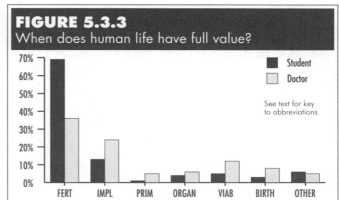

FIGURE 5.3.3
When does human life have full value?

■ Student
□ Doctor

See text for key to abbreviations

A study by Dr Harold Koenig of the Duke University Medical Centre of 4,000 people in North Carolina found those attending church weekly were 28% less likely to die over a 6 year period than those who went less often or not at all. This is equivalent to not smoking cigarettes. "Religious people have lower blood pressure, less depression and anxiety, stronger immune systems and cost the health care system less".

An analysis of the medical obituaries in the UK in 1991 suggested that about 12% had been Christians. If the percentage is true in 1999, then some 14,000 of the nation's 112,000 doctors are Christian, and nearly a third, 32%, of these are members of the Christian Medical Fellowship (CMF).

In 1996 the CMF undertook a survey of its members about their attitude to abortion. **Figure 5.3.2** illustrates how much the abortion issue affected their choice of work or speciality by their year of graduation ; it seems clear that the 1967 Abortion Act had a real influence. Many Christian doctors are likely to hold pro-life views.

The survey also asked members when they felt human life had "full value", a deliberately vague phrase not defined on the form. Their answers are given in **Figure 5.3.3** and show that students do not always have the same view as registered doctors! In the barchart:

FERT = when the embryo is fertilised
IMPL = when it is implanted in the womb
PRIM = after about 14 days when the

TABLE 5.3.2 Sequels to sexual exploitation of Catholic Nuns

Level of sexual behaviour →	Non-physical %	Physical, non-genital %	Genital %
Past effects			
Difficulty praying	18	38	62
Difficulty working/concentrating	18	47	60
Depression	9	39	55
Difficulty sleeping	18	32	53
Relationship with God disrupted	27	28	51
Considered leaving religious life	9	22	40
Suicidal thoughts	0	4	20
Current effects			
Shame or embarrassment	18	36	60
Anxiety	9	14	31
Depression	9	7	29
Self blame	9	1	20
TOTAL number on which replies are based	11	72	55

development of a primitive streak shows the beginnings of a central nervous system
ORGAN = when organs have developed after about 10 weeks
VIAB = when the foetus is viable, after about 24 weeks
BIRTH = at birth, or
OTHER = at other times

One doctor, seeing his own unborn children on an ultra-scan, put "value" much earlier.

A 1997 random survey of 2,500 Roman Catholic Sisters across most American Orders had a 48% response. The respondents had a mean age of 62 years and had been in the religious life for 42 years. 19% had experienced sexual abuse as a child, and 13% sexual exploitation since entering the religious life.

This latter was defined as "any sexual advance, request for sexual favours, or other verbal, nonverbal, or physical conduct of a sexual nature that occurs in the context of a relationship wherein a woman trusts her property, body, mind, or spirit to another person acting in a professional role."

Their reactions are given in **Table 5.3.2**. It shows that the greater the level of sexual behaviour the greater the impact, and that the results affected them spiritually as well as physically. 88% subsequently received therapy.

Sources: Christian Medical Fellowship, 157 Waterloo Road, London SE1 8XN, phone 020 7928 4694; article in the *Daily Telegraph* 23rd July 1999, quoting the *Journal of Gerontology* and the *International Journal of Psychiatry in Medicine*; *Members' Attitudes to Abortion*, Christian Medical Fellowship, July 1996; article "A national survey of the sexual trauma experiences of Catholic Nuns" in *Review of Religious Research*, Vol 40, No 2, December 1998, Pages 142–167.

5

TABLE 5.4.1
Age structure of male Church of England clergy 1963–2007

Year	Under 29 %	30 to 34 %	35 to 39 %	40 to 44 %	45 to 49 %	50 to 54 %	55 to 59 %	60 to 64 %	65 to 69 %	70 or over %	TOTAL (=100%)
1963	9	10	9	9	12	15	14	10	6	6	13,343
1968	8	11	11	9	10	12	16	13	7	3	13,552
1971	8	9	11	11	9	11	15	16	7	3	12,905
1978	4	10	10	14	14	12	11	14	8	3	10,753
1983	5	9	13	12	16	15	13	11	4	2	10,107
1988	6	10	12	15	13	17	15	9	2	1	10,431
1993	2	8	12	13	17	15	18	13	2	0	9,816
1998	1	6	10	14	15	19	16	16	3	0	8,653
2007	3	7	10	13	15	18	17	15	2	0	7,679

TABLE 5.4.2
Age structure of female Church of England clergy 1988–2007

Year	25 to 29 %	30 to 34 %	35 to 39 %	40 to 44 %	45 to 49 %	50 to 54 %	55 to 59 %	60 to 64 %	65 to 69 %	70 or over %	TOTAL (=100%)
1988	7	13	12	18	17	16	14	2	1	0	516
1993	5	10	12	18	21	17	12	4	1	0	756
1998	3	7	11	15	22	23	13	6	0	0	983
2007	3	7	12	16	19	21	15	6	1	0	1,514

Table 5.4.1 shows how the age structure of Church of England clergy has changed in the 44 years covered by the Table. Whilst the first column says "Under 29" in reality the majority here are aged "25 to 29"; likewise in the penultimate column "70 or over" is in the large majority of cases "70 to 74".

The average age, 49 years, has changed very little over this period, partly because, prior to the 1976 Synod Act requiring all to retire at 65 in any new incumbency, many stayed on into their late 60s or 70s, and a few into their 80s. The decreasing numbers of older people (never quite zero as a few clergy hang on, and bishops need not retire till 70) – which tend to extend the average age – are then compensated by fewer coming in at a younger age.

The consequence is seen in **Figure 5.4.1** where over half, 51%, of clergy are aged 45 to 64 between 1963 and 1978, 55% 1983, 54% in 1988, but climbing to two-thirds, 66%, in 1988. As older people are ordained the number of years service they can give becomes fewer, unless the retirement age is altered again.

The picture for female clergy is quite different. Allowed to become deacons in 1987 and ordained as priests in 1994, **Table 5.4.2** shows that in 1998 half, 50%, were under 45 years of age. That shrank to 36% by 1998. Likewise those aged 55 to 64 were 16% of the total in 1988 and 1993, but grew to 19% by 1998 and are likely to become 21% by 2007. These numbers are illustrated in **Figure 5.4.2.**

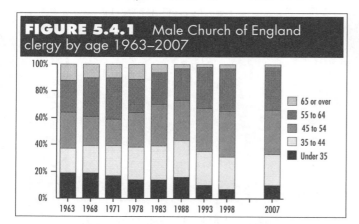

FIGURE 5.4.1 Male Church of England clergy by age 1963–2007

Legend: 65 or over; 55 to 64; 45 to 54; 35 to 44; Under 35

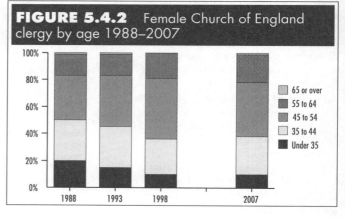

FIGURE 5.4.2 Female Church of England clergy by age 1988–2007

Legend: 65 or over; 55 to 64; 45 to 54; 35 to 44; Under 35

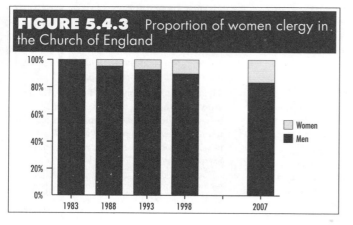

FIGURE 5.4.3 Proportion of women clergy in the Church of England

Legend: Women; Men

Figure 5.4.3 illustrates the growing percentage of women priests in the Church of England, with the years 1988 and 1993 counting those as deacons. The 5% in 1988 doubled to 10% by 1998, and is set to increase to one-sixth, 17%, by 2007. If the proportion continues to grow at the same rate, women form a majority of the clergy in 2058!

Sources: Successive issues of the *Church of England Yearbook*, Church House Publishing, and material kindly supplied by the Statistics Unit, Archbishops' Council, Church House.

According to Ecclesiastical Direct Insurance (EDI) there were 4,000 claims of burglary or vandalism against Anglican churches in 1998. The January 1999 National Churchwatch Conference report, *Church Crime ... Who Cares?*, gave figures for crimes against churches which in a single year outnumber the churches themselves! In England and Wales an estimated 20,600 crimes are committed against churches each year, but as only 22% of crimes are reported according to the Home Office, the real figure could be as high as 94,000.

Table 5.5.1 shows the number of fires dealt with by the Fire Brigade in places of worship which has remained at about the same level for the years 1994–1998. The percentage of deliberate arson attacks has decreased between1994 and 1998, although it rose between 1996 and 1997. EDI state that each incident causes an average of £45,000 worth of damage and the cost of replacing a burnt out church is £2 million.

EDI paid out £1.5 million to Anglican churches for criminal damage in 1997. This sum covers only stolen or damaged goods, and does not include antique valuables, damage to churches of other denominations, or cover paid out by other insurance companies or the cost of re-building churches.

Young people's attitudes to crime are shown in **Table 5.5.2**. More than twice as many who believed in God thought that taking religion seriously would reduce crime.

Statistics from the Rutherford Institute state that only 51% of prison inmates worldwide finish high school and that 60% are illiterate, but not all the young people surveyed for **Table 5.5.2** thought that better school discipline would prevent crime. **Figure 5.5.1** illustrates that almost two–fifths of offenders cautioned or convicted for offences in 1996 were under the age of 21.

Figure 5.5.2 shows that a growing number of prisoners in the UK are either of no religion at all or of a non–Christian religion such as Jews, Sikhs or Muslims. There was a steep increase in the number of Protestant prisoners between 1972 and 1975, in those of other religions and in those of no religion between 1990 and 1992. These changes in the religious affiliation of prisoners reflect the overall religious situation in the UK but much more starkly, that is, the percentage changes are much greater than in the UK as a whole.

Figure 5.5.3 shows the application numbers to the European Court of Human Rights, established in 1955. There has been a considerable increase in applications to the Court in the last 18 years, from 335 new applications in 1978 (of which 16 or 5% were declared admissible) to 4,758 in 1996 (of which 624 or 13% were admissible).

Sources: Eccesiastical Direct Insurance, Beaufort House, Brunswick Road, Gloucester GL1 1JZ, Email gbeigmkg@ibmmail; and The Rutherford Institute, PO Box 7482. Charlottesville, Virginia 22906-7482, United States of America, Email tristaff@rutherford.org

TABLE 5.5.1
Fire in buildings of worship 1994–1998

	Total[1]	Deliberate or possibly deliberate %	Accidental or unknown causes %
1994	289	82	18
1995	238	72	28
1996	295	69	31
1997	280	73	27
1998	209	73	27

[1] Figures are based on sample data weighted to brigade totals
Source: Home Office Fire Statistics and Research Section

TABLE 5.5.2 Young people's opinions on how effective crime prevention measures would be

	Those who do not believe in God %	Believe in God now, did not before %	Have always believed in God %
Less poverty	79	76	78
School discipline	77	78	80
Family discipline	76	79	81
More prison	56	62	58
Less crime on TV	43	56	54
Less prison	22	20	18
Religion	16	39	43

Source: Young People's Social Attitudes, edited by Roger Jowell & others, Social & Community Planning Research and Barnado's, 1996

FIGURE 5.5.1 Offenders as a percentage of the population, by gender and age, 1996

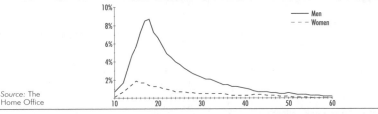

Source: The Home Office

FIGURE 5.5.2
The changes in religious affiliation of UK prison inmates, 1972–1997

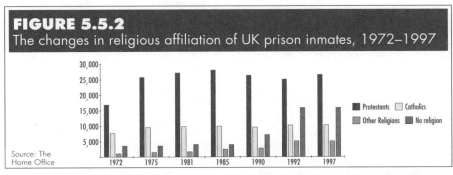

Source: The Home Office

FIGURE 5.5.3 Development of the number of applications of the European Court of Human Rights

TABLE 5.6.1
Primary purpose of Christmas 1964–1995

	Opportunity to meet family and friends	Religious Festival	Holiday	Occasion for eating and drinking	Don't know/ None of these
	%	%	%	%	%
1960s	23	37	26	8	6
1970s	30	33	24	11	2
1980s	38	27	17	15	3
1990s	36	28	19	12	5
Average	**32**	**31**	**22**	**11**	**4**

FIGURE 5.6.1
Spending per person at Christmas, 1997

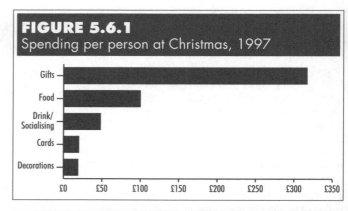

FIGURE 5.6.2 Percentage of population saying they attend church at Christmas

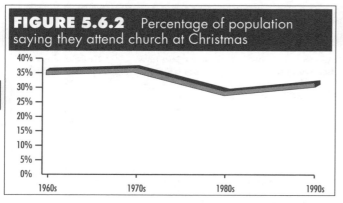

FIGURE 5.6.3 Percentage of population saying they attend church at Easter

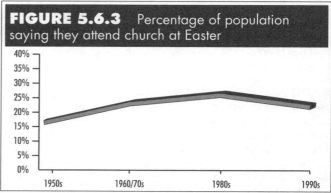

TABLE 5.6.2 Knowledge of the Nativity Story, 1996

Correct answer %	Fact
88	Myrrh was one of the Kings' gifts
87	Frankincense was one of the Kings' gifts
84	Jesus was born in Bethlehem
83	Jesus was laid in a manger
80	Gold was one of the Kings' gifts
61	Gabriel was the Angel sent to Mary
52	Herod was King of Judaea

TABLE 5.6.3
Belief in a physical or spiritual resurrection of Christ, 1984 and 1996

Person	Physical		Spiritual		Neither		No View/ Unsure	
	1984 %	1996 %	1984 %	1996 %	1984 %	1996 %	1984 %	1996 %
Laity	52	49	31	41	1	2	16	8
Churchgoing Anglicans	30	29	35	40	4	12	31	19
All Anglicans	59	55	26	22	3	9	12	14
Roman Catholics	34	53	38	34	5	13	23	0
Free Churches								
ALL adults	**34**	**34**	**33**	**38**	**5**	**9**	**28**	**19**
Anglican Clergy	77	79	10	13	8	6	5	2
Full-time	81	82	12	11	2	4	5	3
Retired								

Table 5.6.1 gives the percentage indicating the primary purpose of Christmas as given by various sample polls, taking the average of answers per decade. The full information is given in Dr Clive Field's paper "When a Child is Born". It shows that marginally more think of Christmas as an opportunity to meet family and friends than as a religious festival overall, but this has changed since the 1960s.

The information in **Figure 5.6.1** and **Table 5.6.2** come from Gallup surveys for the *Daily Telegraph*, and show that about five-sixths of the population know some of the key facts of the nativity story. **Figure 5.6.1** shows that of the average £504 spent per adult at Christmas 1997 on the items indicated, three-fifths, 63%,

was on presents, and another fifth, 20%, on food.

Figure 5.6.2 suggests an average of about a third of the population, 32%, go to church at Christmas. This is the percentage who *say* they go rather than as measured by the churches. Again the figures are averages of appropriate sample polls for each decade from Clive Field's paper, in which he suggests that the *real* figure for attendance is probably only half what people say.

A comparison with Christmas attendance by Easter is given in **Figure 5.6.3**, again based on another paper by Clive Field. The data behind this graph are much less robust however and are averages of local samples as well as national polls. Taking this and **Figure 5.6.2** together, it suggests that attendance at Easter is decreasing whilst that

at Christmas is increasing, and also that attendance at Easter is lower than that at Christmas. In a society where church attendance is generally less, fewer focus on the event which makes Christianity unique amongst the world's religions – that Jesus died and rose from the dead. In some ways this is confirmed by **Table 5.6.3** which shows fewer people believing in a physical resurrection. Both surveys whose results are given in this Table were undertaken by Gallup.

Sources: Article "When a Child is Born", Dr Clive Field, in *Modern Believing*, Journal of the Modern Churchpeople's Union, Volume 40, Number 3, 1999, Pages 29–40; *Facts and Figures on Christmas*, Evangelical Alliance, 1997 quoting Gallup survey for the *Daily Telegraph*; article "All Chicks and Going Out", Dr Clive Field, in *Theology*, March/April 1998, Pages 82–90.

In 1998 the Teal Trust surveyed Christians on their prayer habits; 5,644 survey forms were completed from 344 churches making it one of the biggest researches into prayer. Although it was mainly conducted in the UK, 545 global surveys were received. The denominational breakdown of surveys received was Anglican (64%), Baptist (14%), Methodist (10%) and others (12%).

Figure 5.7.1 shows that 35% of people questioned spent an hour or more in personal prayer each week, ministers praying for the longest time period in a week with 23% praying for up to 5 hours. It is interesting that 14% of ministers spend less than 15 minutes a week in solitary prayer!

In prayer people devote most of their time to issues personal to them as can be seen in **Figure 5.7.2**. Family and friends was the top subject prayed about (89%) whereas world and regional issues was one of the lowest topics with only 29% of respondents praying regularly for them. Other prayers for people such as healing, wisdom for church leaders and for non-Christians to come to faith were also relatively high on the list showing that relationships in the Church are very important to members. Personal financial needs were least frequently prayed for (16%).

Some find it difficult to pray as **Figure 5.7.3** illustrates, wandering thoughts and the inability to focus on God is the most widely experienced problem, but 54% actually have problems finding the time to pray. Knowing what to pray for was the least taxing problem.

Table 5.7 confirms that those who pray more are most likely to have experienced answers to their prayers and to have experienced God talking back to them as they pray. The survey also showed that although 39% of people pray with others outside of church services on a weekly basis, another 19% do so once a month. 32% wrote that they regularly attend a church prayer group, but only one quarter of Christian couples pray together most days and a third never pray together at all.

Source: The Teal Trust, 11 Lincoln Road, Northburn Green, Cramlington NE23 9XT
Phone 01670 717 452

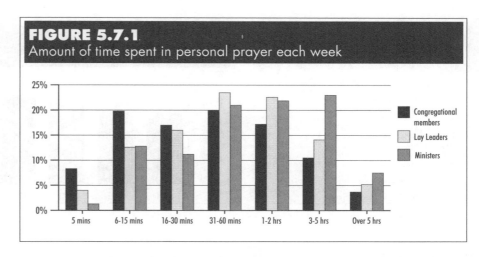

FIGURE 5.7.1
Amount of time spent in personal prayer each week

(Legend: Congregational members, Lay Leaders, Ministers)

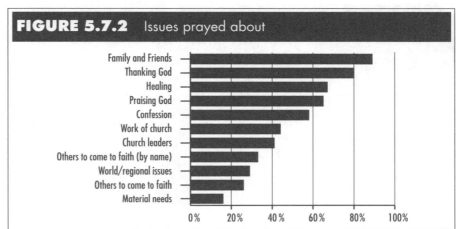

FIGURE 5.7.2 Issues prayed about

- Family and Friends
- Thanking God
- Healing
- Praising God
- Confession
- Work of church
- Church leaders
- Others to come to faith (by name)
- World/regional issues
- Others to come to faith
- Material needs

TABLE 5.7
Experiences in prayer by amount of time spent in prayer per week

% of respondents who...	Under 1 hour	More than 1 hour	Total
Believe God hears their prayers	90	98	93
Believe they have experienced answered prayer	81	96	86
Spend time listening to God	54	80	63
Have experienced God communicating with them	49	77	59
Read the Bible every day or most days	44	82	58
Pray with others at least once a week	31	52	39

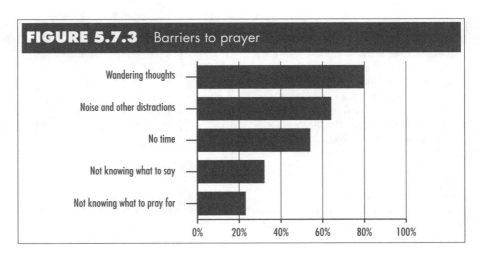

FIGURE 5.7.3 Barriers to prayer

- Wandering thoughts
- Noise and other distractions
- No time
- Not knowing what to say
- Not knowing what to pray for

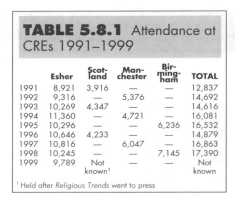

TABLE 5.8.1 Attendance at CREs 1991–1999

	Esher	Scot-land	Man-chester	Bir-ming-ham	TOTAL
1991	8,921	3,916	—	—	12,837
1992	9,316	—	5,376	—	14,692
1993	10,269	4,347	—	—	14,616
1994	11,360	—	4,721	—	16,081
1995	10,296	—	—	6,236	16,532
1996	10,646	4,233	—	—	14,879
1997	10,816	—	6,047	—	16,863
1998	10,245	—	—	7,145	17,390
1999	9,789	Not known[1]	—	—	Not known

[1] Held after *Religious Trends* went to press

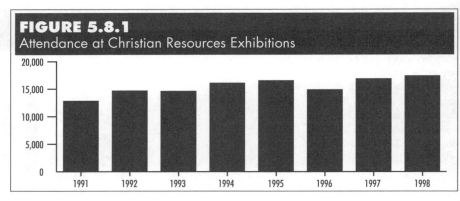

FIGURE 5.8.1
Attendance at Christian Resources Exhibitions

TABLE 5.8.2 Accommodation by Size and Type

	Conference Centres, Guest Houses and Hotels[1]							Retreat Houses[2]					
	1978	1982	1986	1991	1995	1997	1999	1982	1986	1991	1995	1997	1999
Average no. who can be accommodated by each	50	63	61	75	82	59	54	29	27	28	30	29	27
Proportion in Single Rooms	21%	18%	15%	16%	16%	16%	18%	54%	54%	49%	51%	45%	48%
Double Rooms	35%	30%	34%	36%	42%	43%	42%	36%	36%	36%	37%	40%	37%
Larger Rooms	44%	52%	51%	48%	42%	41%	42%	10%	10%	15%	12%	15%	15%
Average number in Day Room	n/a	n/a	n/a	96	104	108	110	n/a	n/a	20	53	54	56
Total number listed	143	161	219	250	245	261	268	81	130	114	110	128	123

	Hotels							Residential Homes for the Elderly[3]					
	1978	1982	1986	1991	1995	1997	1999	1986	1988	1991	1995	1997	1999
Average no. who can be accommodated by each	50	63	61	75	82	48	44	28	31	29	30	33	23
Proportion in Single Rooms	49%	54%	57%	61%	71%	69%	71%	76%	69%	68%	77%	44%	48%
Double Rooms	29%	24%	25%	30%	47%	15%	16%	17%	27%	30%	23%	11%	9%
Larger Rooms	22%	22%	18%	9%	12%	16%	13%	7%	4%	2%	0%	45%[4]	43%[4]
Average number in Day Room	n/a	n/a	n/a	40	94	80	87	–	–	–	–	–	–
Total number listed	34	68	76	123	122	168	153	39	53	99	103	163	174

[1] Including some Retreat Houses in 1978 [2] Figures for 1978 not separately available
[3] Figures prior to 1986 not available [4] Figure shows percentage of 'other' accommodation as opposed to larger rooms

The first annual Christian Resources Exhibition was held in the London Horticultural Halls in 1985, but after a couple of years its success was such that it moved to Sandown Park, Esher. Other like Exhibitions have since been held in Scotland, Manchester, Birmingham every three years. **Figure 5.8.1** graphs the total attendance at these Exhibitions in the 1990s, and **Table 5.8.1** gives the detailed figures. The 1999 attendance at Sandown Park was hit by a lorry protest on the M25 for one of its days.

Table 5.8.2 shows four types of Christian accommodation listed in the *UK Christian Handbook*. While the average number of people per establishment is decreasing, so is the total, as **Figure 5.8.2** indicates. In 1991 the number of beds in a Christian environment available in the UK was some 34,000 beds. By 1995 it had dropped to 31,000; rose to 32,600 in 1997, but dropped back to 28,500 beds in 1999, partly because of closures, and partly because the YWCA has retracted the majority of their hostels (about 600 beds) from the *Handbook* because they state that they are no longer Christian.

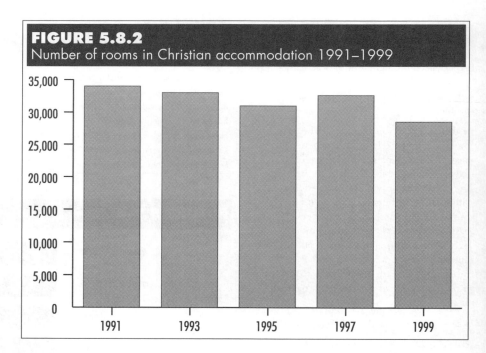

FIGURE 5.8.2
Number of rooms in Christian accommodation 1991–1999

About 38% of the 1999 accommodation is in single rooms, 31% in double rooms, and 31% in larger rooms. In 1995 the percentages were 43%, 32% and 25% respectively, and in 1997 40%, 29% and 31% suggesting that the newer centres are offering twin beds more than single bedrooms.

TABLE 5.9.1 Traditional belief, 1940s–1990s

Traditional Belief	1940/50s %	1960s %	1970s %	1980s %	1990s %
God	–	79	74	72	67
God as personal	43	39	32	32	31
God as spirit or life force	38	39	38	39	40
Jesus as Son of God	68	62	–	49	–
Heaven	––	––	52	55	52
Life after death	49	49	37	43	44
The devil	24	28	20	24	26
Hell	–	–	21	26	25

Source: Churchgoing and Christian Ethics, Professor Robin Gill, CUP, 1999

TABLE 5.9.2 Traditional disbelief, 1940s–1990s

Traditional Disbelief	1940/50s %	1960s %	1970s %	1980s %	1990s %
God	2[1]	10	15	18	27
Jesus as just a man/a story	18	22	–	38	–
Heaven	–	–	33	35	39
Life after death	21	23	42	40	42
The devil	54	52	70	64	67
Hell	–	–	68	65	66

[1] Estimate

Source: Churchgoing and Christian Ethics, Professor Robin Gill, CUP, 1999

TABLE 5.9.3 Non-traditional belief and disbelief, 1970s–1990s

	Belief			Disbelief		
	1970s %	1980s %	1990s %	1970s %	1980s %	1990s %
Foretelling future	48	54	47	41	40	46
Ghosts	19	28	32	73	65	58
Horoscopes	23	26	26	72	69	67
Reincarnation	24	26	25	53	57	59
Lucky charms	17	19	18	79	78	78
Exchange messages with the dead	11	14	14	79	77	80
Black magic	11	13	10	82	82	86

Source: Churchgoing and Christian Ethics, Professor Robin Gill, CUP, 1999

FIGURE 5.9.1 Belief and disbelief in God, 1940s–1990s

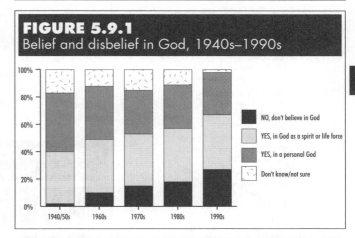

- NO, don't believe in God
- YES, in God as a spirit or life force
- YES, in a personal God
- Don't know/not sure

TABLE 5.9.4 A cross analysis of beliefs

Also believe in:		God	Heaven	Life after death	Reincarnation	Hell	The devil
God	%	—	98	95	93	96	98
Heaven	%	67	—	78	74	95	93
Life after death	%	47	57	—	70	75	76
Reincarnation	%	28	32	42	—	36	33
Hell	%	25	37	40	32	—	79
The devil	%	24	33	37	27	72	—

Column header "Believe in" spans God, Heaven, Life after death, Reincarnation, Hell, The devil.

Source: A 1973 Gallup survey quoted in The Becoming Church, John Adair, SPCK, 1977, Page 43.

FIGURE 5.9.2 Agreement of young people with statements on Christianity 1974–94

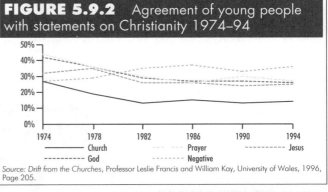

—— Church ---- Prayer ---- Jesus
----- God ······ Negative

Source: Drift from the Churches, Professor Leslie Francis and William Kay, University of Wales, 1996, Page 205.

Professor Robin Gill, together with Professor Penny Marler and C Kirk Hadaway, took a large number of Gallup and other sample surveys which asked questions about religious belief and averaged the answers for each decade. Full details are in Robin Gill's new book *Churchgoing and Christian Ethics*, CUP, August 1999. The results are given in **Tables 5.9.1, 2** and **3**. They show a decreasing belief in a personal God, but a rapidly increasing disbelief in God, shown in **Figure 5.9.1,** but suggesting that the population is dividing into two groups – the believers who are not very strong on what they believe, and the disbelievers.

The 1973 Gallup survey quoted in John Adair's book *The Becoming Church*, SPCK, 1973, indicates the inconsistencies of belief, at least in the 1970s. 98% of people who believe in heaven believe also in God, but only 67% of people who believe in God also believe in heaven! Personal belief systems are not necessarily rationally ordered.

A number of studies have looked at young people's beliefs. Leslie Francis has surveyed 500 secondary school pupils every 4 years by asking them 24 questions about Christianity, some positive and some negative. These are graphed in **Figure 5.9.2.** They show fewer agreements with positive statements on the church (27% in 1974, 14% in 1994), prayer (44% and 27%) and God (42% and 26%), but continue to agree about Jesus (32% to 25%).

In August 1998, MORI conducted a poll which included the following question: "At present, one of the functions of the monarchy is to be head of the Church of England, although many British citizens follow other religions or no religion at all. It has been suggested that being associated with one religion makes it difficult for the monarch to

FIGURE 5.9.3 Monarch should be head of Church of England

represent all British people. Do you think the monarch should or should not remain head of the Church of England?" Overall, half, 49%, of respondents felt the monarch should remain head, 38% felt the monarch should not. And the remainder gave neutral or "don't know" answers. The answers varied both by age and by the party the respondent last voted for, as shown in **Figure 5.9.3.**

TABLE 5.10.1 Key features of British life 1900–1979

1900–04	Flight of the first aeroplane Welsh Revival Book: The Tale of Peter Rabbit
1905–09	Boy Scout movement introduced London hosts the Olympic Games Book: Wind in the Willows
1910–14	War declared, first air raid on Britain Book: Sons and Lovers Film: Tarzan of the Apes Song: It's a Long Way to Tipperary
1915–19	Women over 30 given the right to vote Rutherford splits the atom Book: The Thirty Nine Steps Song: Good Bye-ee!
1920–24	The first ever newspaper crossword is printed Book: Ulysees Film: Robin Hood Song: Yes, We have no Bananas
1925–29	England wins the Ashes Book: Winnie the Pooh Film: Ben Hur Song: Charleston
1930–34	First Christmas Day Broadcast Book: Brave New World Film: The Invisible Man Song: Winter Wonderland
1935–39	The 999 number in operation Book: The Hobbit Film: Gone With the Wind Song: Pennies from Heaven
1940–44	King George VI calls for a National Day of Prayer Book: For Whom the Bell Tolls Film: Citizen Kane Song: The White Cliffs of Dover
1945–49	Formation of the NHS Book: Animal Farm Film: Great Expectations Song: Anything You Can Do
1950–54	First broadcast of the Archers Billy Graham's Haringay Crusade Book: The Lion, the Witch and the Wardrobe Film: The Cruel Sea
1955–59	8 miles of the M1 motorway are open Book: Doctor Zhivago Book: J B Phillips Letters to Young Churches Book: History of the English Speaking Peoples Film: Bridge on the River Kwai Film: The Ten Commandments
1960–64	BBC2 show Playschool Coventry Cathedral opened Book: A Clockwork Orange *Songs of Praise* begins
1965–69	Abortions legalised / The first heart transplant England wins the World Cup Book: Stig of the Dump
1970–74	Introduction of Decimal Currency Book: The Eye of the Storm Film: The Godfather Song: I'd Like to Teach the World
1975–79	Margaret Thatcher becomes Prime Minister Spring Harvest begins Book: Good News Bible Film: Star Wars Song: Amazing Grace top of the pops

TABLE 5.10.2 Alpha courses worldwide

Year	Number of registered courses	Number attending	Average number per course	Cumulative total of attenders
1992	5	100[1]	20[1]	100
1993	200	4,600	23	4,700
1994	750	22,100	29	26,800
1995	2,500	76,400	31	103,200
1996	5,000	156,750	31	259,950
1997	6,500	283,440	44	543,390
1998	10,500	435,980	42	979,370
1999	20,860[2]	834,420[1]	40[1]	1,813,790
2000[1]	25,000	950,000	38	2,763,790

[1] Estimate
[2] Taking HTB's own estimate for the first six months, and increasing it by 50% for the full year
Source: *Alpha News*, No 18, March–June 1999, with South Africa increased by 800 courses and United States by 1,000, per personal conversation with Rev Nicky Gumbel

The very rapid growth of Alpha courses is shown in **Table 5.10.1**. They began in 1992 at Holy Trinity, Brompton (HTB), an evangelical Anglican church in London, through the ministry of Rev Nicky Gumbel,

FIGURE 5.10.1 Alpha courses by continent, 1999

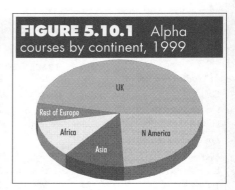

and have since grown worldwide. In 1999 just under half, 47%, were held in the UK, and almost a quarter, 24%, in Canada and the United States. Total courses worldwide are difficult to count precisely because not every one is registered. Perhaps two-thirds of the whole will be from the UK, equivalent to 2.6% of the adult population attending a course, one person in every 39 by the end of 1999.

FIGURE 5.10.2 Church attendance by gender, 1990–98

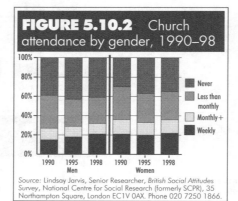

Source: Lindsay Jarvis, Senior Researcher, *British Social Attitudes Survey*, National Centre for Social Research (formerly SCPR), 35 Northampton Square, London EC1V 0AX. Phone 020 7250 1866.

FIGURE 5.10.3 Income of UK Christian organisations, 1999

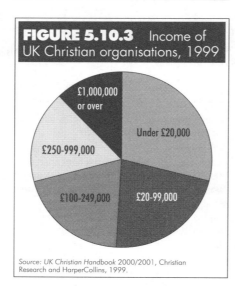

Source: *UK Christian Handbook 2000/2001*, Christian Research and HarperCollins, 1999.

The data reflected in **Figure 5.10.2** suggests that more men are saying they go to church weekly as the 1990s have passed. Perhaps they are more open about their need or search for spirituality.

TABLE 5.10.3 Why those under 20 leave the church

79%	Started making own decisions
72%	Aware of alternate ways of life/thought
68%	Do not need to go to church to be a Christian
66%	I changed, it wasn't the church's fault
62%	Church failed to connect with the rest of life
58%	Did not feel part of the church
51%	Participation became a chore
47%	Disagreed with the church on moral issues
45%	Church was stuck in its views
44%	Worship was too mechanical
38%	Made to go by my parents and it put me off
32%	Church was too hierarchical and status-conscious
31%	Left home
22%	Church was not supportive or caring

Source: *Gone but not Forgotten*, Philip Richter and Leslie Francis, Darton, Longman and Todd, 1998

One survey regularly asks people their four main topics with their family and friends. Top, at 38% in 1997, is the cost of living, followed by the problems of bringing up children at 31%, and sport at 30%. Consistently from 1986 "religion" has always been 7% plus or minus 1%. Perhaps part of that conversation is going to church! Or why they leave, as per the reasons given in **Table 5.10.3**.

There are nor many large Christian organisations, as **Figure 5.10.3** indicates. One in 8, 12%, have income or turnover in excess of £1,000,000, and a further sixth, 17%, between £250,000 and a million. Just over half, 51%, have less than £100,000, and a fifth, 22%, less than £20,000. However the top 12% account for two-thirds, 65%, of all the money given to Christian agencies, and the top 29% seven-eighths, 87%!

Source: ITV – TOM Attitudes to Advertising Survey, *Lifestyle Pocket Book*, 1993 and 1999, NTC Publications, Ltd, 1999. Phone 01491 411 000.

CHRISTIAN BOOKS AND BOOKSHOPS

Contents

6

Sources:
UK Christian Handbook 2000/2001, Bible Society, BBC and British Library

TABLE 6.2.1 Turnover and Titles by size of Christian Bookshops 1999

Total titles	Small shops (under 1,000 sq ft)							Large shops (1,000 sq ft or over)						
	Turnover							Turnover						
	Less than £10,000	£10,000–£30,000	£30,001–£75,000	£75,001–£150,000	More than £150,000	Not stated	TOTAL	Less than £30,000	£30,000–£75,000	£75,001–£150,000	£150,000–£300,000	More than £300,000	Not stated	TOTAL
Less than 1,000	5	4	6	1	1	39	56	–	–	–	–	1	2	3
1,000–3,000	3	18	31	24	10	98	184	1	3	4	–	1	9	18
3,000–5,000	–	–	9	22	12	44	87	–	3	5	10	3	11	32
5,001–7,500	–	–	1	3	2	18	24	–	2	–	4	1	4	11
More than 7,500	–	–	–	2	3	25	30	–	1	–	5	7	30	43
Not stated	–	1	1	1	–	11	14	–	–	1	1	–	2	4
TOTAL	8	23	48	53	28	235	395	1	9	10	20	13	58	111
Average titles	1,100	1,700	2,300	3,300	3,800	3,200	3,000	2,000	4,300	3,100	5,700	6,200	6,100	5,600

TABLE 6.2.2 Number of titles held by Christian Bookshops 1978–1999

Total titles	Small bookshops						Large bookshops						All bookshops					
	1978 %	1982 %	1986 %	1991 %	1995 %	1999 %	1978 %	1982 %	1986 %	1991 %	1995 %	1999 %	1978 %	1982 %	1986 %	1991 %	1995 %	1999 %
Less than 1,000	18	17	15	16	17	14	10	7	4	2	4	3	15	15	12	13	15	12
1,000–3,000	32	38	56	49	48	47	21	22	30	18	20	16	29	32	49	42	42	40
3,000–5,000	18	19	14	16	20	22	24	13	17	23	24	29	19	18	15	18	20	24
5,001–7,500	13	3	6	5	5	6	12	13	17	9	8	10	13	6	9	5	5	7
More than 7,500	4	7	3	7	6	8	24	20	24	40	398	39	10	12	9	14	13	14
Not stated	15	16	6	7	4	3	9	25	8	8	5	3	13	17	6	8	5	3
TOTAL	114	179	333	449	429	395	42	84	121	128	114	111	156	263	454	577	543	506
Average titles	3,100	2,800	2,500	2,900	2,900	3,000	4,600	4,700	4,800	6,300	6,000	5,600	4,200	4,100	4,200	3,500	3,600	3,600

TABLE 6.2.3 Average turnover of Christian Bookshops 1978–1999

	1978	1982	1984	1986	1988	1991	1993	1995	1997	1999
Small bookshops[1]	£31,700	£34,100	£43,700	£47,000	£53,000	£59,900	£46,500	£74,900	£92,400	£95,500
Large bookshops[2]	£77,800	£90,700	£91,900	£108,800	£135,500	£171,500	£152,100	£168,100	£238,200	£221,000
Index (1978=100)										
Small bookshops	100	108	138	148	167	189	147	236	291	301
L:arge bookshops	100	117	118	140	174	220	196	216	306	284
Rate of inflation	100	162	178	196	214	267	282	298	315	330

[1] Area under 1,000 sq ft   [2] Area 1,000 sq ft or over

FIGURE 6.2
Turnover of small and large bookshops 1978–1999

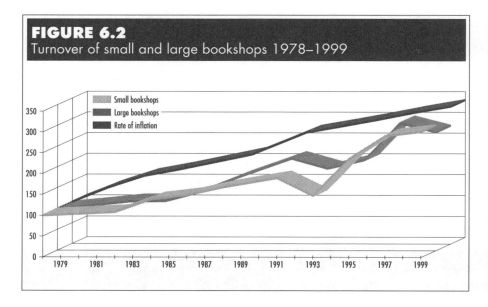

Small bookshops
Large bookshops
Rate of inflation

TABLE 6.2.4 Turnover of top Christian Chains 1998

Wesley Owen	£10.5m
SPCK	£7.1m
CLC	£3.1m

Source: *The Bookseller*, 18th June 1999, Page 21

Figure 6.2 shows how the turnover of the average small or large bookshop, defined as being smaller or larger than 1,000 sq ft, has fared compared with the rate of inflation. The actual figures are given in **Table 6.2.3**. Smaller shops slightly outstripped the larger ones in the mid-1980s, but suffered more from the recession in the early 1990s. They appear to be doing better in the last 2 years. Larger shops have almost twice as many titles as the smaller ones (**Table 6.2.1**), a feature since 1986 but not before (**Table 6.2.2**).

TABLE 6.3.1 Books published

	Total Books	Religious	Occult
1900	–	–	–
1910	–	–	–
1928[1]	13,981	951	28
1930	15,494	857	60
1940	11,053	519	42
1950	17,072	971	58
1960	23,783	1,247	75
1970	33,489	1,245	165
1980	48,158	1,725	258
1990	63,980	2,360	408
2000[2]	107,800	4,400	730
1991	67,704	2,466	425
1992	78,835	2,630	445
1993	83,322	2,635	413
1994	88,718	3,330	511
1995	95,064	4,442	502
1996	101,504	4,331	557
1997	100,029	4,109	569
1998	104,634	4,379	637

[1] First records started in 1928 [2] Estimate

TABLE 6.3.2 Total Books[1] Published by Selected Subjects

	1970	1975	1980	1985	1990	1992	1994	1996	1998
Biography	940	1,211	1,360	1,796	2,164	2,574	2,939	3,292	3,180
Children's Books	2,406	2,688	3,485	4,410	5,855	7,006	7,080	8,045	8,497
Education	973	1,036	1,258	1,292	1,311	1,621	1,948	2,170	2,011
Fiction	4,449	4,198	5,145	5,846	7,426	8,076	8,448	9,209	9,236
History	1,556	1,324	1,587	1,916	2,359	3,620	3,858	4,348	4,546
Law and Public Administration	960	1,062	1,548	1,800	1,403	2,053	2,320	2,562	2,947
Literature	1,320	907	1,185	1,671	1,706	2,337	2,646	3,107	2,930
Medical Science	1,285	1,804	3,323	3,655	2,686	3,235	3,625	3,964	3,842
Occult	165	240	258	239	408	445	511	557	637
Political Science & Economics	840	2,629	4,269	3,917	4,415	5,127	5,625	6,813	7,061
Religion and Theology	**1,245**	**1,098**	**1,725**	**1,992**	**2,360**	**2,630**	**3,330**	**4,331**	**4,379**
School Textbooks	1,875	2,099	2,317	1,824	1,968	2,340	2,730	3,629	4,141
Social Sciences	699	957	1,195	1,151	1,492	2,312	3,319	4,068	4,400
All other subjects	14,776	14,315	19,503	21,485	28,427	35,459	40,339	45,409	46,827
TOTAL all new books	33,849	35.608	48,158	52,994	63,980	78,835	88,718	101,504	104,634
% religious titles of all titles	3.7	3.1	3.6	3.8	3.7	3.3	3.7	4.3	4.2
% occult titles of all religious and occult titles	12	18	13	11	15	14	13	11	13

[1] Including revised and new editions, translations, and limited editions Source: J Whitaker, Bookseller

Figure 6.3 and Table 6.3.3 are based on the number of books recorded by the British Library acting in its copyright capacity of receiving a copy of every published book. The classification used is that of Dewey which breaks "religion" down into 10 sections, listed in full in Table 6.3.3. The numbers in Figure 6.3 are the *average* number published each year as the time periods are uneven. Four areas have grown over the last 50 years: books about the Bible, devotional books, books on comparative and other religions, and books on Christian theology. These have grown, respectively, 144%, 235%, 651%, and 127%. In the last 5 years more than 500 books a year have been published on comparative and other religions, more than a fifth, 21%, of all religious books published.

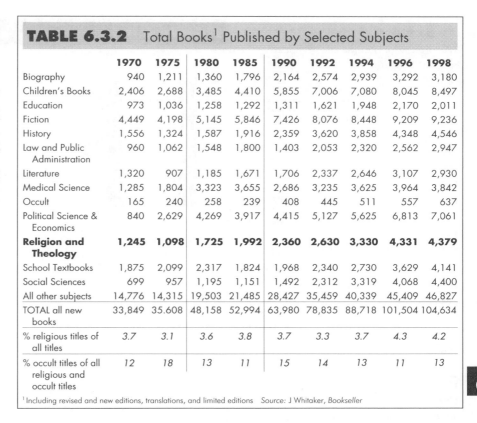

FIGURE 6.3
Types of religious books published 1950–1997

Legend: Others, Geography, Denominations, Theology, Other religions, Devotional, Bible, History

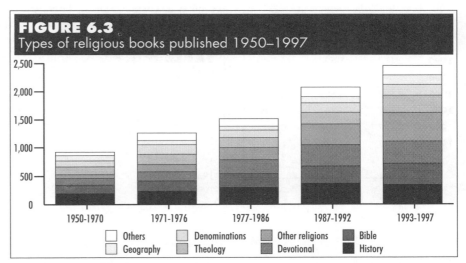

TABLE 6.3.3 Religious Books by Subject[2] 1950–1997

Religious Topic[1]	Number published in period						Average number published per annum						Proportion in each category					
	1950–1970	1971–1976	1977–1986	1987–1992	1993–1997	1950–1997	1950–1970	1971–1976	1977–1986	1987–1992	1993–1997	1950–1997	1950–1970	1971–1976	1977–1986	1987–1992	1993–1997	1950–1997
Social and ecclesiastical history (260)	4,058	1,421	3,032	2,222	1,728	12,461	193	237	303	370	346	260	21	19	20	18	14	19
Bible (220)	3,227	1,098	2,390	1,821	1,871	10,407	153	183	239	304	374	217	17	15	16	14	15	15
Christian moral and devotional theology (240)	2,458	948	2,426	2,233	1,962	10,027	117	158	243	372	392	209	13	13	16	18	16	15
Other and comparative religions (290)	1,421	759	2,123	2,250	2,554	9,107	68	126	212	375	511	190	7	10	14	18	21	13
Christian theology (230)	2,829	1,062	1,820	1,219	1,528	8,458	135	177	182	203	306	176	15	14	12	10	13	13
Christian denominations and sects (280)	2,154	1,024	1,365	1,026	1,005	6,574	103	171	137	171	201	137	11	13	9	8	8	10
History and geography of the church (270)	1,932	455	685	663	845	4,580	92	76	68	111	169	95	10	6	5	5	7	7
Religion not included elsewhere (200)	386	478	834	578	279	2,555	18	80	83	96	56	53	2	6	5	5	2	4
Local church and religious orders (250)	686	266	379	351	384	2,066	33	44	38	58	77	43	3	3	2	3	3	3
Natural religion (210)	169	76	109	118	153	625	8	13	11	20	31	13	1	1	1	1	1	1
TOTAL	19,320	7,587	15,163	12,481	12,309	66,860	920	1,265	1,516	2,080	2,463	1,393	100	100	100	100	100	100

[1] As given by the Dewey Decimal Classification (shown with number in brackets after the description) [2] Total number of books held in the British Library published between 1950 and 1997 Source: British Library

TABLE 6.4.1
Number of languages into which at least one book of the Bible has been translated

Year	Languages translated	World population in millions	Languages per million people
1400	12	374	0.032
1500	38	460	0.083
1600	51	579	0.088
1700	66	679	0.097
1800	73	954	0.077
1900	621	1,633	0.380
1910	725	1,805	0.402
1920	825	1,862	0.443
1930	975	2,070	0.471
1940	1,053	2,295	0.459
1950	1,197	2,556	0.468
1960	1,426	3,039	0.469
1970	1,657	3,707	0.447
1980	1,710	4,454	0.384
1990	1,946	5,277	0.369
2000[1]	2,300	6,073	0.379
1991	1,978	5,359	0.369
1992	2,009	5,442	0.369
1993	2,062	5,523	0.373
1994	2,092	5,603	0.373
1995	2,123	5,682	0.374
1996	2,167	5,761	0.376
1997	2,197	5,840	0.376
1998	2,212	5,919	0.374

[1] Estimate
Source: Bible Society

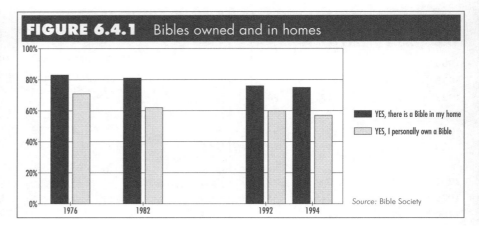

FIGURE 6.4.1   Bibles owned and in homes

■ YES, there is a Bible in my home
□ YES, I personally own a Bible

Source: Bible Society

Figure 6.4.1 shows that Bible ownership is high, with 57% of those interviewed in 1994 owning a Bible, and there being a Bible in a person's home in 75% of cases. But both figures had declined – from 71% and 83% respectively in 1976 which could imply that in 2000 only 53% would personally own a Bible but 72% of homes would have one.

Bible ownership may be high, but Bible knowledge is not. Only one person in 4 in Britain can recall having heard or read anything from the Bible, and half of secondary school pupils find it "boring". **Table 6.4.2** shows the frequency with

which the Bible is read from a succession of surveys commissioned by the Bible Society. All were personal interviews with adults aged 16 or over who attend church at least once a month. Whilst the overall trend is slightly downwards, the data suggests that it declined more in the 1980s than in the 1990s – indeed it is static or even increasing in the 1990s.

Figure 6.4.2 shows the frequency of Bible reading by age in one large evangelical Anglican church in the London Borough of Bromley in September 1998. The older a person the more likely they are to read the Bible more frequently.

TABLE 6.4.2
Frequency of Bible reading, regular churchgoers, 1982–1997

	Every day/ Several times a week %	Once a week/ Several times a month %	Occasionally (Once a month/ Several times a year) %	Seldom/ Never/Don't know (Once a year or less) %	Average number of times read per year[1]
1982	29	13	26	32	82
1989	22	7	36	34	62
1991	26	8	25	41	72
1995	24	9	27	40	68
1997	26	11	25	38	73

[1] Taking the number of times as 5 times a week, 3 times a month, 6 and 1 times a year respectively

Some churches are encouraging greater Bible knowledge and understanding by:

- Acting out the Scriptures

- Holding special services especially for non regular churchgoers to help make the Bible more easily understood

- Special teaching to help adults new, (or not so new!) to the faith to find their way around it

- Encouraging all their congregation to read the same passage every day

- Organising Alpha courses

Sources: Bible Society; Diocese of Rochester Evangelical Fellowship

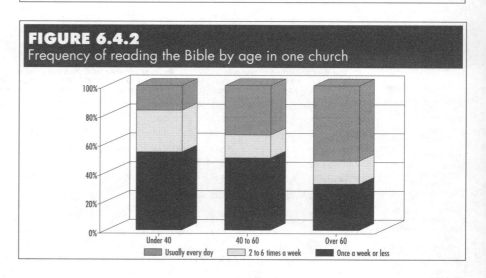

FIGURE 6.4.2
Frequency of reading the Bible by age in one church

▨ Usually every day   ▦ 2 to 6 times a week   ■ Once a week or less

Under 40   40 to 60   Over 60

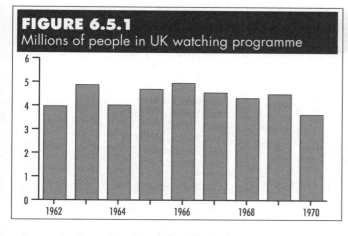

FIGURE 6.5.1
Millions of people in UK watching programme

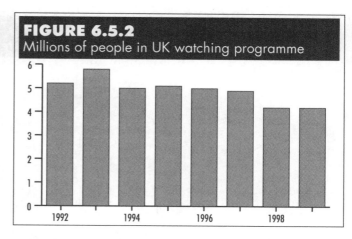

FIGURE 6.5.2
Millions of people in UK watching programme

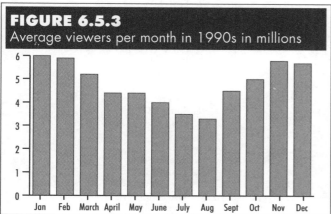

FIGURE 6.5.3
Average viewers per month in 1990s in millions

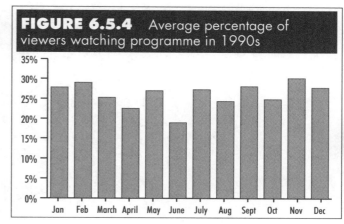

FIGURE 6.5.4   Average percentage of viewers watching programme in 1990s

6

Songs of Praise has been a very popular programme since it began in 1962. **Figure 6.5.1** shows the viewing audience of the Sunday programme in the 1960s, averaging 4.5 million over the decade, and **Figure 6.5.2** the audience in the 1990s, averaging 4.9 million viewers, 10% more than 30 years previous, although the population has increased 40% in the same period.

This excludes however the 0.4 million who watched the following Monday repeat in 1992 to 1994, almost another 10% assuming they were different people. It was switched to Wednesdays later in 1994, but the numbers halved and did not recover even when restored to Monday, and so the repeat was dropped altogether in July 1996.

The audience for the programme varies considerably during the year as shown in **Figure 6.5.3**, peaking in the winter months, and falling off during the summer. However the share of the television viewing audience is considerable, averaging 26% over the 1990s, with a high of 32% in June 1992. Whilst this share also varies during the year, as shown in **Figure 6.5.4**, the variation is not as great, showing the summer fall is due in part to a smaller number of people watching television.

On average during the 1990s 40% of the audience were male. Half, 51%, of the audience on average was 65 years or over. **Figure 6.5.5** shows the age-range of the audience, and this is compared with the age of church-goers in 1998 (estimated for the whole of the UK) aged over 5. It shows that there are a million more young people attending church than the number who watch the programme (who may not all be churchgoers). It also shows that there are at least a million people aged 65 or over watching the programme who do not go to church (likely to be more as not all churchgoers will watch *Songs of Praise*).

Finally, **Figure 6.5.6** compares the social class of those watching *Songs of Praise* with that of the population (the social class of churchgoers not being generally available). It shows that rather more in social classes D and E (C2, D and E used to be called the "working class") watch *Songs of Praise* than in the population generally. The church has always had problems reaching this segment of the population – *Songs of Praise* is doing it instead!

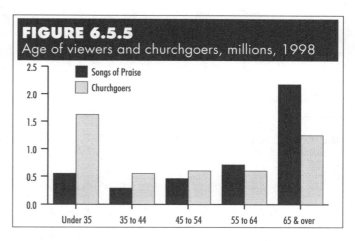

FIGURE 6.5.5
Age of viewers and churchgoers, millions, 1998

- ■ Songs of Praise
- □ Churchgoers

Under 35 | 35 to 44 | 45 to 54 | 55 to 64 | 65 & over

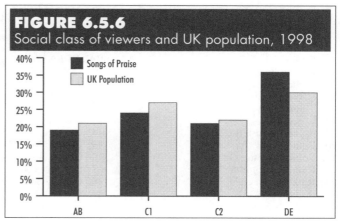

FIGURE 6.5.6
Social class of viewers and UK population, 1998

- ■ Songs of Praise
- □ UK Population

AB | C1 | C2 | DE

Sources: Data supplied by BBC Information & Analysis Department; Tables 4.9.2 and 12.3.5; *Churches and Churchgoers,* R M Currie et al, OUP, 1977; *Lifestyle Pocket Book,* 1999, Page 11.

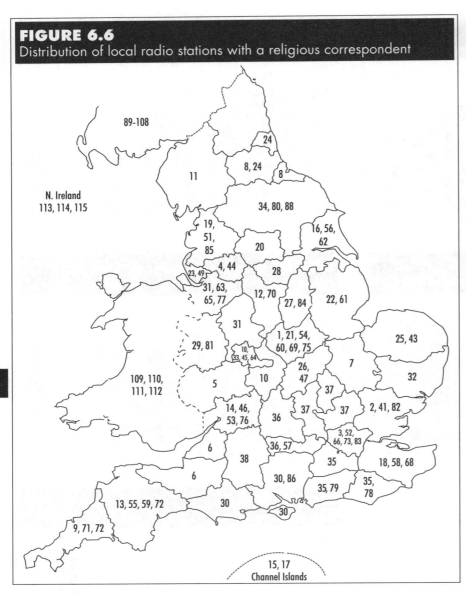

FIGURE 6.6
Distribution of local radio stations with a religious correspondent

52. FLR
53. The Falcon
54. Fosseway
55. Gemini FM
56. Huddersfield FM
57. Kestrel FM
58. KFM
59. Lantern FM
60. Leicester Sound
61. Lincs FM
62. Magic 1161 AM
63. Marcher Gold
64. Mercia FM
65. MFM
66. Millennium Radio
67. Mix 96
68. Neptune Radio
69. Oak FM
70. Peak FM
71. Pirate FM 102
72. Plymouth Sound
73. Premier Radio
74. Quay West Radio
75. Rutland Radio
76. Severn Sound FM
77. Silk FM
78. Sovereign Radio
79. Spirit FM
80. Stray FM
81. Sunshine 855
82. Ten 17
83. Thames FM
84. Trax FM
85. The Wave 96.5
86. Wave 105 FM
87. The Wolf
88. Yorkshire Dales Radio

Scotland
89. Aberdeen: NorthSound One & Two
90. Arbroath: RNA FM
91. Ayr: West Sound Radio
92. Douglas: Manx Radio
93. Dundee: Tay FM
94. Dundee: Radio Tay AM
95. Edinburgh: Forth AM
96. Edinburgh: Forth FM
97. Falkirk: Central FM
98. Fife: Kingdom FM
99. Fort William: Nevis Radio
100. Galashiels: Radio Borders
101. Glasgow: Clyde 1
102. Glasgow: Clyde 2
103. Inverness: Moray Firth Radio
104. Isles: Isles FM
105. Paisley: 96.3 QFM
106. Peterhead (Scot): Waves Radio
107. Pitlochry: Heartland FM
108. West Ross: Lochbroom

Wales
109. Aberystwyth: Radio Ceredigion
110. Colwyn Bay: Coast FM
111. Ebbw Vale: Valleys Radio
112. Swansea: Swansea Sound

Northern Ireland
113. Belfast: City Beat 96.7 FM
114. Downtown Radio
115. Newtown: Radio Maldwyn

Contact details for all these stations are given in the 2000/2001 edition of the *UK Christian Handbook*

BBC LOCAL RADIO STATIONS
1. Asian Network
2. Essex
3. GLR
4. GMR
5. Hereford & Worcester
6. Radio Bristol/Somerset Sound
7. Radio Cambridgeshire
8. Radio Cleveland
9. Radio Cornwall
10. Radio Coventry & Warwickshire
11. Radio Cumbria
12. Radio Derby
13. Radio Devon
14. Radio Gloucestershire
15. Radio Guernsey
16. Radio Humberside
17. Radio Jersey
18. Radio Kent
19. Radio Lancashire
20. Radio Leeds
21. Radio Leicester
22. Radio Lincolnshire
23. Radio Merseyside
24. Radio Newcastle
25. Radio Norfolk
26. Radio Northampton

27. Radio Nottingham
28. Radio Sheffield
29. Radio Shropshire
30. Radio Solent
31. Radio Stoke
32. Radio Suffolk
33. Radio WM (Birmingham)
34. Radio York
35. Southern Counties Radio
36. Thames Valley
37. Three Counties Radio
38. Wiltshire Sound

INDEPENDENT
39. 96.4 The Eagle
40. 97.4 Vale FM
41. 107.7 Chelmer FM
42. Arrow FM
43. Broadland 102
44. Century
45. Classic Gold 1359
46. Classic Gold 774
47. Connect FM
48. County Sound Radio
49. Crash FM
50. Delta FM 102
51. Dune FM

RECENT RESEARCH REPORTS

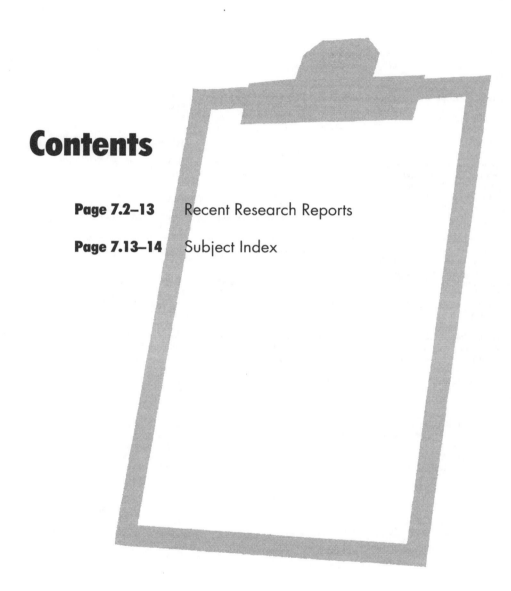

Contents

This section of the *UK Christian Handbook* records recent, past (and in a few cases known forthcoming) research on Christian topics. The entries are listed alphabetically by author, and the address from which the book or report may be obtained is given underneath each entry. Where there is more than one entry from a particular author, the address is given under the first entry only.

The number after each name in the Subject Index on Page 7.13 is the sequential number of the papers for a particular author listed. Thus *Back 2* is the second paper listed by P Back.

Source:
Individual authors

See Note on Page 7.1

Arhin Rev J | **The rise expansion and impact of Independent/Indigenous churches in Ghana**
Historical background of the Independent/Indigenous churches, missionaries contribution and impact on the Ghanaian society. | Submitted 1999; 45,000 words, Postgraduate Dissertation, Greenwich School of Theology

Astley J, L J Francis, L Burton & C Wilcox (1) | **Distinguishing between aims and methods in RE:** a study among secondary RE teachers
Trinity College, Carmarthen, Carmarthenshire SA31 3EP | Published 1997; *British Journal of Religious Education*, Vol 19, pp 171-185

Astley J & W K Kay (2) | **Will the real world please stand up?** Perceptions through a two-way mirror – teenagers and the media | Published 1998; *Muslim Education Quarterly*, Vol 15, No 1, pp 1-9

Atkinson Dr W P | **The Development of church based training schemes and its implications for established Bible Colleges**
A paper presented at the annual EPTA Conference in 1998 surveying the recent rise in the number of Pentecostal church based training schemes | Submitted 1999; 9 pages, British Journal of Theological Education

Attwood J | An examination of commitment making in the local church in people undergoing (a version of) the Good News Down The Street material in relation to preparation for the baptism or thanksgiving of their children
Cliff College, Calver, Hope Valley, Nr Sheffield S32 3XG | Published 1997; c20,000 words; MA Dissertation; Price £30

Back P (1) | **Transferring Biblical Concepts as meaningful equivalents for Arabic speakers within an Islamic worldview**
CLC Bookshop, 26-30 The Viaduct, Holborn, London EC7 6XP | Published 1999; 43 pages; Based on PhD research; Monograph 4 in Mission Theology; Publisher: Church and Mission: Building the Kingdom

Back P (2) | **Ethnotheology in the Light of the authority of Scripture and Linguistic Relevance Theory**
A critique of the theology underlining Kraft's Contextualization approach, which has a defective view of the Authority of Scripture | Published 1999; 37 page; Based on PhD research; Monograph 5 in Mission Theology

Back P (3) | **Is God Allah?**
An academic assessment of Allah as the "god" whom Muslims worship. A well argued case! | Published 1999; 42 pages; Monograph 8 in Mission Theology; Publisher: Church and Mission: Building the Kingdom

Back P (4) | **Principles of Reformed Mission Ministry**
An organisational and exegetical study. | Published 1999; 97 pages; Monograph 9 in Mission Theology; Publisher: Church and Mission: Building the Kingdom

Bagwell D | **Mind the Gap**
A study of the cultural gap that now exists between the church and society, with particular reference to use of language in worship; and how this gap needs to be bridged if the good news of Jesus is to be effectively communicated
Cliff College, Calver, Hope Valley, Nr Sheffield S32 3XG | Published 1998; c20,000 words; MA Dissertation; Price £30

Balchin Dr John | **Congregational Survey**
Above Bar Church, Southampton
24 Abbotts Way, Southampton SO17 1NS | Published 1998; *In Touch Newsletter*, pp 6-7

Banks Dr Robert | **The Quest for Community in Church and World Today**
Looks at the weakening of community and the quest for it is epitomised in different age groups. Challenges churches to be "community builders".
Zadok Institute, 59 Scotchmer Street, North Fitzroy, 3068, Australia | Published 1996; Zadok paper S81

Barker G | **An Ordinary Parish**
Cliff College, Calver, Hope Valley, Nr Sheffield S32 3XG | Published 1998; c20,000 words; MA Dissertation; Price £30

Barna George (1) | **What Effective Churches have Discovered**
Insights on ministry in the late nineties
Barna Research Group Ltd., 2487 Ivory Way, Oxnard, CA 93030-6290 USA | Published 1998; Seminar notes

Barna George (2) | **How to Increase Giving in your Church**
A book of research into the reason of giving | Published 1997; Publisher: Regal Books, California USA

Barna George (3) | **The Second Coming of the Church**
A challenging, and in some ways devastating, review of Christianity in America today | Published 1998; Publisher: Word Publishing, Thomas Nelson Inc, Tennessee USA

Barrett Sue & Stuart Baylis | **Action in Aspley, Nottingham**
Report on churches serving Aspley
St Margarets Parish Office, Aspley Lane, Aspley, Nottingham NG8 5GA | Published 1999

Batchelor Alan | **Don't Muzzle the Ox, Full time ministry in Local Churches**
Aimed primarily at churches with Brethren' origins providing guidance for churches planning to appoint a full-time worker
Paternoster Periodicals, Carlisle | Published 1997; 100 pages; Price: £4.75; Publisher: Paternoster Periodicals, Carlisle

Bazalgette John & Justin Tomkins | **Students Exploring Marriage Initiative; Report on Phase 1**
Report on commissioned research enabling 16-17 year olds to study the significance of Christian marriage in society
Grubb Institute of Behavioural Studies Ltd, Cloudesley Street, London N1 0HU | Published 1998; 33 pages; Price £4

Beardshaw Tom | **Church Leaders Questionnaire Report**
A study by Care of churches they have links with and their involvement in family ministry
Care for the Family, Garth House, Leon Avenue, Cardiff CF4 7RG | Published 1998; 37 pages

Beasley-Murray Rev Dr Paul | **Power for God's Sake**
A book looking at power and abuse in the local church
Any Christian Bookshop | Published 1998; Publisher: Paternoster, Carlisle

Bentley Peter & P J Hughes | **Australian Life and the Christian Faith: Facts and Figures**
A book looking at aspects of Australian people and life – a kind of Australian *Religious Trends*
CRA, Locked Bag 23, Kew, Victoria 2101, Australia | Published 1998; Publisher: Christian Research Association, Australia

Bird M | A critical analysis of the Evangelical Alliance's 'Groundswell' project and its relationship with missionary church thinking at the end of the 20th century
Cliff College, Calver, Hope Valley, Nr Sheffield S32 3XG | Published 1998; c20,000 words; MA Dissertation; Price £30

Bissett W | **Holistic Faith as the Foundation of Mission** | Published 1998; c20,000 words; MA Dissertation; Price £30
Why Christianity needs whole-life discipleship and what prevents it
Cliff College, Calver, Hope Valley, Nr Sheffield S32 3XG

Bouma Gary D (ed) | **Many Religions, All Australian** | Published 1998; Price Australian $39
Religious Settlement, Identity and Cultural Diversity
CRA, Locked Bag 23, Kew, Victoria 2101, Australia

Briant C P (1) | **Dunnington Village Survey** | Published 1999; 18 pages; Price £5; Publisher: St Nicholas & Dunnington Methodist Church
Local Survey of 1 in 10 households, demographic data, work, leisure, young people, transport, shopping, life in Dunnington, environment, health, traffic, religious affiliation
The Rectory, Church Street, Dunnington, York YO19 5PW

Briant C P (2) | **Congregational Survey** | Published 1997; 15 pages; Price £5; Publisher: St Nicholas & Dunnington Methodist Church
Local church survey of Anglican and Methodist congregations: demographic, work, leisure, life in village and church and reasons for attendance, newcomers and traditional lifetime congregation of churchgoers with few 25-45 year olds.

Brierley Dr P W (1) | **Nominalism Reconceived: the continuing phenomenon** | Published 1997; 36 pages; Price £5; *Christian Research Leaders' Briefing No 8*
What is nominalism?
Christian Research, Vision Building, 4 Footscray Road, Eltham SE9 2TZ

Brierley Dr P W (2) | **Religion in Britain 1900-2000** | Published 1998; 18 pages; Price £4; *Christian Research Leaders' Briefing No 12*
Trends in church community, membership and buildings, plus other Christian statistics across the century

Brierley Dr P W (3) | **Youth and Today's Church** | Published 1998; 7 pages; Price £4; *Christian Research Leaders' Briefing No 13*
A summary of recent research covering Church and Young People and Society and Young People

Brierley Dr P W (4) | **Everyday Faith Issues in the Coming Century** | Published 1998; 9 pages; Book contribution; Publisher: Winterbourne PCC
Small is Cosmic: Millennial issues in parochial perspective

Brierley Dr P W (5) | **Change in Society:** | Published 1997; 4 pages; free to members
Results of a survey amongst members of Christian Research

Brierley Dr P W (6) | **Bible Reading Materials for Children of different ages.** | Published 1997-1999
Research reports for Scripture Union on a variety of samples, types of material and methods.

Brierley Dr P W (7) | **Congregational Attitudes and Beliefs survey** | Published 1998; 18 pages
A survey amongst a variety of churches on a one-to-one basis

Brierley Dr P W (8) | **Background to the Anglican Scene** | Published 1998; 17 pages
Research report for Church Mission Society

Brierley Dr P W (9) | **Contacts Survey** | Published 1997; *FactFile* No 5; free to members
Research report for Youth for Christ

Brierley Dr P W (10) | **Christian Book Club** | Published 1998; 28 pages
Research report

Brierley Dr P W (11) | **Members of Christian Research** | Published 1998; 26 pages
Research report for Board of Christian Research

Brierley Dr P W (12) | **Baptismal Policy** | Published 1998
Research report for Church of Scotland

Brierley Dr P W & Heather Wraight (13) | **Social Concerns.** | Published 1996; 12,000 words
A Church and Society Survey for the United Reformed Church, through Rev Peter Brain

Brown P | A critical examination of the use of specific forms of apologetics in evangelism today(including C S Lewis, the Alpha Course & Evangelical Alliance 'Truth' Tours) | Published 1997; c20,000 words; MA Dissertation; Price £30
Cliff College, Calver, Hope Valley, Nr Sheffield S32 3XG

Burlet Stacey & Helen Reids | **Faith in our Future: People of Faith, Social Action and the City of Leeds** | Published 1998; Dept of Theology and Religious Studies, University of Leeds and Leeds Church Institute
Dept of Theology & Religious Studies, University of Leeds, West Yorkshire LS2 9JT

Campbell Dr William S (Ed) | Papers on a new Maslow typology of religion; death, myth and reality in C S Lewis | Published 1997; *Journal of Beliefs and Values; Studies in Religion and Education*, Vol 18, No 2
Carfax Publishing Ltd, PO Box 25, Abingdon, Oxfordshire OX14 3UE

Chamberlain J | **A Dynamic Model of Leadership Development** | Published 1998; 20,000 words MA Dissertation; Publisher: ANCC
Developing and evaluating models with particular references to WEC
All Nations Christian College, Easneye, Ware, Hertfordshire SG12 8LX

Charles Tessa | **Seeds of Redemption** | Published 1997; Publisher: Honest to Goodness Publishing Company, Gloucester
Story of a woman who finds healing and ability to forgive after suffering emotionally and physically at the hands of her husband and his family
Any Christian Bookshop

Chesworth P | **Preaching and personality type** | Published 1997; c20,000 words; MA Dissertation; Price £30
A study of typology and its application to preachers and preacher training
Cliff College, Calver, Hope Valley, Nr Sheffield S32 3XG

Christian Medical Fellowship | **Members' attitude to abortion** | Published 1996; Price £4
Survey of reported views and practice among members of the Christian Medial Fellowship
Dr Andrew Fergusson, General Secretary, Christian Medical Fellowship, 157 Waterloo Road, London SE1 8XN

Christian Voice | **Britain in Sin** | Published 1998; Price £4.50
A compilation of statistics and comment relating to social and economic trends in British today to the Ten Commandments
Christian Voice, PO Box 526, Sutton, Surrey

Church of Scotland, Mission & Evangelism Resources Committee | **Understanding the Times** | Published 1998
Report on a survey of barriers to belief in Scotland
Saint Andrew Press, 121 George Street, Edinburgh EH2 4YN

Cipkin Christopher | **The Information needs of Anglican Clergy in the Diocese of Newcastle** | Published 1997; MA Dissertation
An evaluation of CRA Literature
15 Fairwater Drive, Woodley, Reading RG5 3LG

Clarke Rev C D | **An Historical, Theological and Biblical Evaluation of John Wesley's Doctrine of Christian Perfection** | Published 1998; PhD Potchefstroom University of Christian Higher Education, South Africa
Available for study at St Deiniol's Library, Hawarden, Flintshire CH5 3DF

7

Clifford Bruce | **Christians in the Workplace** An evaluation in the Diocese of Gloucester *10 Carne Place, Gloucester GL4 3BE* | Published 1998

Coffey Rev David | **President's Report to EBF** (European Baptist Federation) Perspectives on such issues as identifying younger leaders, pressure on local pastors, missionary strategy and religious liberty *The Baptist Union of Great Britain, Baptist House, PO Box 44, 129 Broadway, Didcot OS11 8RT* | Published 1998

Coleman S | **Changing the Wineskins** Is structural change necessary to facilitate renewal in rural Methodism *Cliff College, Calver, Hope Valley, Nr Sheffield S32 3XG* | Published 1998; c15,000 words; Postgraduate Diploma Dissertation; Price £30

Cooke Professor Christopher C H, D Goddard & R Westall | **Knowledge and experience of drug use amongst church affiliated young people** Self report questionnaires assessing knowledge and experience of drug use completed by 7,666 young people aged 12-30 years attending Spring Harvest 1995 *Kent Institute of Medicine & Health Sciences, University of Kent at Canterbury, Canterbury, Kent CT2 7PD* | Published 1997; 9 pages; Publisher: Elsevier

Cooke Dr Dennis | **Persecuting Zeal: A Portrait of Ian Paisley** *From any bookshop* | Published 1996; 224 pages; Price £9.99; Publisher: Brandon

Corbitt Rev Otis & Sue Seeley | **Use of the Alpha Programme** Survey of Evangelism in the Eastern Area of the Baptist Union of Great Britain *Park Baptist Church, 14a Crown Road, Great Yarmouth, Norfolk NR30 2JN* | Published 1998

Coyne J | Communicating the gospel as Truth in a postmodern world *Cliff College, Calver, Hope Valley, Nr Sheffield S32 3XG* | Published 1997; c20,000 words; MA Dissertation; Price £30

Cranston Michael | **Reader Ministry in the Church of England** Understanding the function, the history, the training of the Reader ministry and providing a clear indication of whether Reader ministry is relevant to the needs of the contemporary church *24 Wilderness Heights, West End, Southampton SO18 3PS* | Published 1999; 101 pages; MA Religious Studies Dissertation, University of Southampton

Crisp Anne & Greg Smith | **Valuable Resources** Summary report regarding young people and the youth provision for them in Newham *greg3@uel.ac.uk* | Published 1977; undertaken for the Newham Safer Cities Project

Crooks C | **Mourning as a touchstone of authentic Renewal** *Cliff College, Calver, Hope Valley, Nr Sheffield S32 3XG* | Published 1997; c15,000 words; Postgraduate Diploma Dissertation; Price £30

Crumpton C | **An examination of the effectiveness of baptismal preparation in a parish church** *Cliff College, Calver, Hope Valley, Nr Sheffield S32 3XG* | Published 1997; c15,000 words; Postgraduate Diploma Dissertation; Price £30

Culham College Institute | **Collective Worship Reviewed** Report of the 1997 Consultation *Culham College Institute, The Malthouse, 60 East St Helen Street, Abingdon, Oxon OX1 5EB* | Published 1997

Curtis Dr A | **Re-reading the Gospel of Luke today** The study of Luke from the perspective of the disadvantaged and/or marginalised within an affluent first world context *Oxford Centre for Mission Studies, PO Box 70, Oxford OX2 6HB* | Published 1999; 100,000 words Doctoral Thesis Open University; Oxford Centre

Dandelion Dr P | **A Sociological Analysis of the Theology of Quakers** A complete survey and study of patterns of believing amongst Quakers in Britain *Woodbrooke College, 1046 Bristol Road, Birmingham B29 6LJ* | Published 1996; 425 pages; Price £59.95; Publisher: Edwin Mellen Press

Dew M | **Bridging the Gap** A research project into the churches' relationship with the local community and how it can be improved *Cliff College, Calver, Hope Valley, Nr Sheffield S32 3XG* | Published 1998; c20,000 words; MA Dissertation; Price £30

Dewar Ian | **Renewal and Culture in the English Tradition** 14th century English mystic Richard Rolle and 20th century Renewalist Michael Harper compared and contrasted *Cliff College, Calver, Hope Valley, Nr Sheffield S32 3XG* | Published 1997; c15,000 words; Postgraduate Diploma Dissertation; Price £30

Dowson J | **Mission in a local (Methodist) church setting** *Cliff College, Calver, Hope Valley, Nr Sheffield S32 3XG* | Published 1997; c20,000 words; MA Dissertation; Price £30

Drane Rev Dr John | **Cultural Change and the Future Shape of Christian Ministry** Looks at the major challenges to the church posted by the shift from modernity to postmodernity. Text of an address given to the Baptist Union of Scotland *Christian Research, Vision Building, 4 Footscray Road, Eltham SE9 2TZ* | Published 1996; 17 pages; Price £4; *Christian Research Leaders' Briefing No 6*

Eagles Christine & Robert Mountford | **The end of church as we know it** Survey of churches in Stoke-on-Trent *City Vision Ministries, 12a Moorland Road, Burslem, Stoke-on-Trent ST6 1DW* | Published 1997

Edwards Rev V | **Concepts of Inculturation in Roland Allen's Missiology: A Critique** An investigation into Roland Allen's theology compared with modern trends *Nazarene Theological College, Dene Road, Didsbury, Manchester M20 2GU* | Published 1998; 15,000 words; Postgraduate Dissertation; Liverpool University

Escott Major Dr Phillip | **Benchmarks** Details of Salvation Army corporate life in the UK in the second half of the 20th Century *Christian Research, Vision Building, 4 Footscray Road, Eltham SE9 2TZ* | Published 1998; 21 pages; Price £8; *Christian Research Leaders' Briefing No 11*

Evangelical Alliance | **The Inaugural Annual Report of the EA/EMA Commission on Strategic Evangelism in the UK** A report detailing the state of evangelism in the UK *Evangelical Alliance, Whitefield House, 186 Kennington Park Road, London SE11 4BT* | Published 1998; Price £5

Evangelical Missionary Alliance (1) | **The Body International** Survey of new Church ministry overseas – how new churches are looking at world mission today *EMA, Whitefield House, 186 Kennington Park Road, London SE11 4BT* | Published 1998; Price £8

Evangelical Missionary Alliance (2) | **EMA Personal Members Survey** Summary and analysis | Published 1998

Eyles Rev Brian | **Church members Survey** Survey of four United Reformed Churches in Wimbledon District *18 Sumburgh Road, London SW12 8LA* | Published 1998; part of M.Phil on Remnant Theology in the Small Urban Church

Ferri Elsa & K Smith | **Step-parenting in the 1990s** A study of the diversities in family life and relationships involved in living in a stepfamily *Family Policy Studies Centre, 9 Tavistock Place, London WC1H 9SN* | Published 1998; Price £9.95

Fewkes G, N Davies & A Jones	**Challenge to Change** Results of the 1995 Welsh Survey *PO Box 227, Cardiff CF3 7YR*	Published 1997; 70 pages; Price £6
Flynn John	**"Count me in"** Church Census report 1996 Hull and District Evangelical Alliance *43 Beechdale, Cottingham, E Yorkshire HU16 4RH*	Published 1996; 26 pages; Price £3
Foster Rev Fr Stephen	**A Theological and Sociological Perspective on Hospital Chaplaincy** *Available for study at St Deiniol's Library, Hawarden, Flintshire CH5 3DF*	Published 1998; PhD Potchefstroom University of Christian Higher Education, South Africa
Francis J & L J Francis (eds)	**Tentmaking: perspectives on self-supporting ministry** *Trinity College, Carmarthen, Carmarthenshire SA31 3EP*	Published 1998; Book; 454 pages; Publisher: Gracewing, Leominster
Francis L J (1)	**The Psychology of Gender Differences in Religion: a review of empirical research** *Trinity College, Carmarthen, Carmarthenshire SA31 3EP*	Published 1997; *Religion* Vol 27, pp 81-96
Francis L J (2)	**Personality Type and Scripture: exploring Mark's Gospel**	Published 1997; Book; 160 pages; Publisher: Mowbray, London
Francis L J (3)	**John Edmund Greer 1932-1996: an appreciation**	Published 1997; *British Journal of Religious Education*, Vol 19, pp 71-72
Francis L J (4)	**Coopersmith's model of self esteem: bias toward the stable extravert?**	Published 1997; *Journal of Social Psychology*, Vol 137, pp 139-142
Francis L J (5)	**Christianity, personality and concern about environment pollution among 13-15 year old's**	Published 1997; *Journal of Beliefs and Values*, Vol 18, pp 7-16
Francis L J (6)	**The impact of personality and religion on attitude towards substance use among 13-15 year old's**	Published 1997; *Drug and Alcohol Dependence*, Vol 44, pp 95-103
Francis L J (7)	**Personal and social correlates of the 'closed mind' among 16 year old adolescents in England**	Published 1997; *Educational Studies*, Vol 23, pp 429-437
Francis L J (8)	**Personality, prayer and church attendance among undergraduate students**	Published 1997; *International Journal for the Psychology of Religion*, Vol 7, pp 127-132
Francis L J (9)	**The socio-psychological profile of the teenage television addict**	Published 1997; *Muslim Education Quarterly*, Vol 15, pp 4-19
Francis L J (10)	**A Church for the Twenty-first Century: agenda for the Church of England** Education and schooling	Published 1998; 39 pages; Book contribution; Publisher: Gracewing, Leominster
Francis L J (11)	**Winterbourne: the church congregation survey** Small is Cosmic: millennial issues in parochial perspective	Published 1998; 12 pages; Book contribution; Publisher: Winterbourne PCC
Francis L J (12)	**The relationship between intelligence and religiosity among 15-16 year old's**	Published 1998; *Mental Health, Religion and Culture, Vol 1*, pp 185-196
Francis L J (13)	**Is there gender bias in the short form Coopersmith Self Esteem Inventory?**	Published 1998; *Educational Research*, Vol 40, pp 83-89
Francis L J (14)	**Dogmatism and Eysenck's two-dimensional model of personality revisited**	Published 1998; *Personality and Individual Differences*, Vol 24, pp 571-573
Francis L J (15)	**Self-esteem as a function of personality and gender among 8-11 year olds: is Coopersmith's index fair?**	Published 1998; *Personality and Individual Differences, Vol 25*, pp 159-165
Francis L J (16)	**The social scientific study of religion**	Published 1998; *Journal of Beliefs and Values*, Vol 19, pp 247-250
Francis L J & J Astley (17)	**The quest for the psychological Jesus: influences of personality on images of Jesus**	Published 1997; *Journal of Psychology and Christianity*, Vol 16, pp 247-259
Francis L J, J Astley, W Kay & M Carter (18)	**Is adult Christian education mainly for stable extraverts?**	Published 1997; *Studies in the Education of Adults*, Vol 29, pp 191-199
Francis L J & J Bolger (19)	**Personality, prayer and church attendance in later life**	Published 1997; *Social Behaviour and Personality, Vol 25*, pp 335-338
Francis L J & J Bolger (20)	**Religion and psychological well-being in later life**	Published 1997; *Psychological Reports*, Vol 80, No 1050 and *Irish Journal of Psychology*, Vol 18, pp 444-447
Francis L J & P W Brierley (21)	**Leaving Religion and Religious Life** The changing face of the British churches: 1975-1995	Published 1997; 26 pages; Book contribution; Publisher: JAI Press, Greenwich Connecticut; Editors: M Bar-Lev and W Shaffir
Francis L J, L B Brown, D Lester & R Philipchalk (22)	**Happiness as stable extraversion:** a cross-cultural examination of the reliability and validity of the Oxford Happiness Inventory among students in the UK, USA, Australia and Canada	Published 1998; *Personality and Individual Differences*, Vol 24, pp 571-573
Francis L J & E D Daniel (23)	**Personality and prayer among churchgoing Methodists in England**	Published 1997; *Journal of Beliefs and Values*, Vol 18, pp 235-237
Francis L J & T E Evans (24)	**The relationship between marital disruption and adolescent values: a study among 13-15 year old's**	Published 1997; *Journal of Divorce and Remarriage*, Vol 26, Nos 3/4, pp 195-213, and also as a contribution in *Divorce and Remarriage: International Studies*; Publisher: Haworth Press, New York
Francis L J & Z Grindle (25)	**Whatever happened to progressive education?** A comparison of primary school teachers' attitudes in 1982 and 1996	Published 1998; *Educational Studies*, Vol 24, pp 269-279
Francis L J & S H Jones (26)	**Personality and charismatic experience among adult Christians**	Published 1997; *Pastoral Psychology*, Vol 45, pp 421-428
Francis L J & S H Jones (27)	**Personality and Christian belief among adult churchgoers**	Published 1998; *Journal of Psychological Type*, Vol 47, pp 5-11
Francis L J, S H Jones & C Wilcox (28)	**Religiosity and dimensions of psychological well-being among 16-19 year olds**	Published 1997; *Journal of Christian Education*, Vol 40, No 1, pp 15-20

Francis L J & D W Lankshear (29) | **The rural church is different: the case of the Anglican confirmation** | Published 1997; *Journal of Empirical Theology*, Vol 10, No 1, pp 5–20

Francis L J, D W Lankshear & S H Jones (30) | **Evangelical identity among young people: A comparative Study in Empirical Theology** | Published 1998; *Anvil* Vol 15 No 4

Francis L J & D Lester (31) | **Religion, personality and happiness** | Published 1997; *Journal of Contemporary Religion*, Vol 12, No 1, pp 81–86

Francis L J & K Mullen (32) | **Denominational and sectarian influence on adolescent attitude towards drug use in England and Wales** | Published 1997; *Journal of Alcohol and Drug Education*, Vol 42, No 3, pp 81–96

Francis L J & Mandy Robbins (33) | **A Woman's Voice in a Man's World** Listening to Women Clergy in the Church in Wales before the vote | Published 1996; *Contemporary Wales* Vol 9, Cardiff University of Wales Press

Francis L J & C F J Ross (34) | **The perceiving function and Christian spirituality: distinguishing between sensing and intuition** | Published 1997; *Pastoral Sciences*, Vol 16, pp 93–103

Francis L J & T Hugh Thomas (35) | **Mystical Orientation and Personality among Anglican Clergy** | Published 1996; *Pastoral Psychology* Vol 45, No 2

Francis L J & T Hugh Thomas (36) | **Are Charismatic Leaders Less Stable?** A study among male Anglican clergy | Published 1997; *Review of Religious Research*, Vol 39, pp 61–69

Francis L J & C Wilcox (37) | **The relationship between Eysenck's personality dimensions and Bem's masculinity and femininity scales revisited** | Published 1998; *Personality and Individual Differences*, Vol 25, pp 683–687

Francis L J & C Wilcox (38) | **Religiosity and femininity: do women really hold a more positive attitude toward Christianity?** | Published 1998; *Journal for the Scientific Study of Religion*, Vol 37, pp 462–469

Frost Robert W | **Response of the Methodist Church Home Mission Division** to the British New Town Movement from 1960 to 1980 with special reference to its attempts to plant new churches in Skelmersdale and Milton Keynes *Department of Theology, King's College, London* | Published 1998; Doctor of Philosophy Degree

Gardiner G | **The Rise and Fall of a Suburban Methodist Church** *Cliff College, Calver, Hope Valley, Nr Sheffield S32 3XG* | Published 1998; c15,000 words; Postgraduate Diploma Dissertation; Price £30

Garnham N | **Making disciples of all nations** An evaluation of multi-cultural mission in an inner-city Salvation Army Corps *Cliff College, Calver, Hope Valley, Nr Sheffield S32 3XG* | Published 1998; c20,000 words; MA Dissertation; Price £30

Gates P | **Demotivating Factors and Relational Evangelism** An inquiry into why ordinary church members find it difficult to share their faith *Cliff College, Calver, Hope Valley, Nr Sheffield S32 3XG* | Published 1998; c20,000 words; MA Dissertation; Price £30

Gill Prof R, C Kirk Hadaway & Prof P Marler | **Is Religious Belief declining in Britain?** *Michael Ramsey, Chair of Modern Theology, School of European Culture and Languages, University of Kent at Canterbury, Cornwallis Building, Canterbury, Kent CT2 7NF* | Published 1998; *Journal for the Scientific Study of Religion*, Vol 37 No 3

Githiga Dr G | **The Church as the Bulward against Extremism** Development of church and state relations in Kenya 1963–1992 *Oxford Centre for Mission Studies, PO Box 70, Oxford OX2 6HB* | Published 1997; 100,000 words Doctoral Thesis, Open University; Oxford Centre

Goodhead A | **Where should the Christian 'voice' be heard? Is the secular radio the place for Christian broadcasting, or should it be confined to Christian radio stations?** *Cliff College, Calver, Hope Valley, Nr Sheffield S32 3XG* | Published 1998; c20,000 words; MA Dissertation; Price £30

Grange P | **An examination and evaluation of the role of a Baptist General Superintendent as motivator and encourager of mission in the Baptist church in Great Britain** *Cliff College, Calver, Hope Valley, Nr Sheffield S32 3XG* | Published 1997; c20,000 words; MA Dissertation; Price £30

Greeley Andrew & Michael Hout | **The people cry reform Six country Catholic study** *The Tablet, 1 King Street Cloisters, Clifton Walk, London W6 0QZ* | Published: 22 March 1997 *The Tablet*, pp 388–390

Greene Mark | **Is anybody listening?** Sermons preached in evangelical churches *Institute for Contemporary Christianity, St Peter's Church, Vere Street, London W1M 9HP* | Published 1997; *Anvil* Vol 14 No 4

Hadaway C Kirk & Prof P Marler | **The Measurement and Meaning of Religious Involvement in Great Britain** Comparison of statistical measures of church attendance and membership *UCBHM, 700 Prospect Avenue, Cleveland, Ohio USA* | Unpublished paper, 1998

Hanna P | **The Stresses of Leaders in the Management of Change in the Church** *Cliff College, Calver, Hope Valley, Nr Sheffield S32 3XG* | Published 1997; c15,000 words; Postgraduate Diploma Dissertation; Price £30

Hanson–Taylor Mrs J | **Is there a conversion which is always necessary?** Missiological approach to the place and nature of conversion in a religiously plural world *All Nations Christian College, Easneye, Ware, Hertfordshire SG12 8LX* | Published 1997; 20,000 words; MA Dissertation; Publisher: ANCC

Hart Colin, Simon Calvert & Iain Bainbridge | **Homosexuality and Young People** Challenges "the claims of gay rights" campaigners on their own territory *The Christian Institute, Eslington House, Eslington Terrace, Jesmond, Newcastle upon Tyne NE2 4RF* | Published 1998; Price £6.95

Hayes M | **The Effect of Renewal in Ministers on Infant Baptism Policies and Practices** *Cliff College, Calver, Hope Valley, Nr Sheffield S32 3XG* | Published 1997; c15,000 words; Postgraduate Diploma Dissertation; Price £30

Heino H, K Salonene & Jakko Rusama | **Response to Recession** Report about changes in attitude among the people of Finland, particularly during their recession years of 1992–1995 *The Research Institute of the Evangelical Lutheran Church of Finland, Box 239, FIN-33101, Tampere, Finland* | Published 1997; Publication No 47

Hibberts J | **Paradigm and other changes** in a city centre mission and their affects on both numerical and spiritual growth *Cliff College, Calver, Hope Valley, Nr Sheffield S32 3XG* | Published 1998; c20,000 words; MA Dissertation; Price £30

Hilborn Rev Dr David (on behalf of ACUTE) — **Faith, Hope and Homosexuality**
Report of the Evangelical Alliance Commission on Unity and Truth among Evangelicals (ACUTE)
Evangelical Alliance, 186 Kennington Park Road, London SE11 4BT
Published 1998; 20,000 words; Price £4.99; Publisher: ACUTE/Paternoster

Hill Christopher — **Flowers in the Cities**
A discussion of the mass outpouring of grief in the wake of the death of Princess Diana
Any Christian Bookshop
Published 1998; Price £5.99; Publisher: Marshal Pickering, HarperCollins-Religious, London

Hill Dr Clifford — **Family Matters**
An examination of trends in family life over the last 20 years which was presented to the Home Secretary in July 1998
The Centre for Contemporary Ministry, The Park, Moggerhanger, Bedford MK44 3RW
Published 1998; 48 pages; Price £10; Publisher: Centre for Contemporary Ministry

Hills Rev Paul — **Ministerial Appraisal**
Produces a practical plan for church appraisal amongst churches of the North District of Southern Baptist Association
Baptist Union of Great Britain; Eastern Area, 7 The Furrells, Linton, Cambridgeshire CB1 6JT
Published 1997; Sabbatical report

Hock Ricky Ho Kim — **Evangelising the youth in the Malaysian context**
A needed shift in strategy towards the Wesleyan tradition on the use of small groups
Cliff College, Calver, Hope Valley, Nr Sheffield S32 3XG
Published 1998; c20,000 words; MA Dissertation; Price £30

Hodgson Dr Janet — **Signs of Life in the Diocese of Durham**
Summary of the Report on the Archdeacons' Articles
Adviser for Local Mission, Diocese of Durham, 50 The Oval, Hartlepool TS26 9QH
Published 1996

Hofstede Professor Geert — **Religion, Masculinity and Sex: the taboo dimension of national cultures**
Institute for Research on Intercultural Cooperation, University of Limburg, PO Box 616, NL-6200 MD Maastricht, The Netherlands
Published 1998; 18 pages; Book contribution: Masculinity and Femininity, Geert Hofstede, *SAGE Publications (ISBN 0-7619-1029-8)*

Holmes Mrs D A — **Are Pastors under pressure?**
A quantitative study into occupational stress amongst Baptist clergy
8 Loch Road, Parkstone, Poole BH14 9EX
Published 1997; 10,000 words; Undergraduate Dissertation, Bournemouth University; Price £7.50

Honour Jon — **Is there a future for Evangelicalism in a postmodern society?**
Looking at the roots and future of evanglicalism
JHonour501@aol.com
Published 1998; Dissertation

Hudson Dr D N — **A Schism and its aftermath**
An historical analysis of denominational discerption in the Elim Pentecostal church, 1939-1940
Kings College, Strand, London WC2R 2LS
Published 1999; 100,000 words; Doctoral Dissertation; Publisher: UMI Dissertation Services – Kings College

Hughes J — **A Reflection on 30 years of Ministry in Renewal**
An evaluation of changes in church and ministry
Cliff College, Calver, Hope Valley, Nr Sheffield S32 3XG
Published 1997; 15,000 words; Postgraduate Diploma Dissertation; Price £30

Hughes Philip — **Religion in Australia, Facts and Figures**
Describes 17 major religious groups in Australia
CRA, Locked Bag 23, Kew, Victoria 2101, Australia
Published 1998; Price Australian $17.95

Hunt Rev David R G (1) — **Journeys to Faith**
A survey of people baptised in Scottish Baptist churches June 1996–May 1997
18 Edward Street, Hamilton ML3 6PW
Published 1997; 61 pages; Sabbatical Study

Hunt Rev David R G (2) — **What's going on in the churches?**
A survey of baptisms and church attendance in Scottish Baptist churches
Published 1997; 26 pages; Sabbatical Study

Hunt Rev David R G (3) — **Seeing ourselves as we are**
An in-depth look at the Baptist Union of Scotland statistics for 1996
Published 1997; 45 pages; Sabbatical Study

Hunt Rev David R G (4) — **Reflecting on our past**
A statistical look at Baptists in Scotland 1892-1997
Published 1997; 35 pages; Sabbatical Study

Hunter Dr M — **Appropriate development for Nomadic Pastoralists**
A study of the Waso Borana of Northern Kenya illustrating the value and meaning of a holistic understanding of development amongst nomadic peoples
Oxford Centre for Mission Studies, PO Box 70, Oxford OX2 6HB
Published 1997; 100,000 words; Doctoral Thesis, Open University

Hunter Professor Rodney J — **Implicit Religion from the perspective of Psychosocial Commitment Theory**
Network for the Study of Implicit Religion, Winterbourne Rectory, 58 High Street, Winterbourne, Bristol BS17 1JQ
Published 1998; Denton Conference on Implicit Religion

Ingleby Dr J — **Education as a Missionary Tool**
A study in Christian Missionary education by English Protestant missionaries in India with special reference to cultural change
Oxford Centre for Mission Studies, PO Box 70, Oxford OX2 6HB
Published 1998; 100,000 words; Doctoral Thesis, Open University

Inglis David J & Margaret Reid Martin — **Small Church – Big Mission**
Looks at small parishes in New Zealand which have changed from full-time to part-time ordained ministry
Christian Research Association, Private Bage 11903, Ellerslie, Auckland, New Zealand
Published 1996

Jacklin Mrs G — **Maybridge Community Survey**
Local needs social audit to inform for future holistic mission
30 Cavendish Close, Goring-by-Sea, Worthing West Sussex BN12 6DP
Published 1997; 4 page summary; 50 page full report, Price £2.50

Jackson R — **Exploring the role of a Methodist Superintendent Minister: Reflections from the journey**
Cliff College, Calver, Hope Valley, Nr Sheffield S32 3XG
Published 1998; c20,000 words; MA Dissertation; Price £30

Jackson S — **Taking the Temperature**
A pastoral approach to the problem of evangelism
Cliff College, Calver, Hope Valley, Nr Sheffield S32 3XG
Published 1998; c20,000 words; MA Dissertation; Price £30

Jayakumar Dr S — **Impact of Christian Mission on Dalit Consciousness**
A study of Dalit theology and Dalit Christian history
Oxford Centre for Mission Studies, PO Box 70, Oxford OX2 6HB
Published 1998; 100,000 words; Doctoral Thesis, Open University

7

Jeffrey Grant R — **The Signature of God** — A book summarising the reasons why we can trust the Bible as the inspired word if God — *Any Christian Bookshop* — Publication 1998; Price £8.99; Publisher: Marshall Pickering, HarperCollins-Religious, London

Johnson Dr B — **World view and International Development** — The effect of "world view" on community development initiatives in the two-thirds world — *Oxford Centre for Mission Studies, PO Box 70, Oxford OX2 6HB* — Published 1998; 100,000 words; Doctoral Thesis, Open University

Johnson P — **To Children's Children and for evermore** — OT perspectives on faith propagation to the next generation and the problem of nominalism — *All Nations Christian College, Easneye, Ware, Hertfordshire SG12 8LX* — Published 1998; 20,000 words MA Dissertation; Publisher: ANCC

Jones S H & L J Francis — **The fate of the Welsh clergy: an attitude survey** — *Trinity College, Carmarthen, Carmarthenshire SA31 3EP* — Published 1997; *Contemporary Wales,* Vol 10, pp 182-199

Jones Sydney — **Retention through the Teenage Years** — A careful analysis of the issues facing teenagers in the Boys' Brigade — *The Boys' Brigade, Felden Lodge, Felden, Hemel Hempstead HP3 0BL* — Published 1997; Working Party Report

Kaiga J — A theological examination of mission and evangelism in Kenya 1991-1995 — *Cliff College, Calver, Hope Valley, Nr Sheffield S32 3XG* — Published 1997; c20,000 words; MA Dissertation; Price £30

Kay W K (1) — **British comments on the Swedish PPI,** — Religious Education in Britain and British comments on the Russian PPI — Published 1997; 3, 29 and 3 pages respectively; Book contribution in *Religious Education in Great Britain, Sweden and Russia;* Publisher: Linköping, University of Linköping; Editors: E Almén and H C Øser

Kay W K (2) — **Historical development of church schools;** — the legal basis of religious education; and Action Research — Published 1997; 36, 28 and 22 pages respectively; Book contribution in *Religion in Education (1)*; Publisher: Gracewing, Leominster

Kay W K (3) — **Children's understanding of texts; and models of the curriculum** — Published 1998; 30 and 29 pages respectively; Book contribution in *Religion in Education (2)*; Publisher: Gracewing, Leominster

Kay W K (4) — **Response to Hargreaves** — *Trinity College, Carmarthen, Carmarthenshire SA31 3EP* — Published 1997; *Research Intelligence,* Vol 59, p 20

Kay W K (5) — **Jung and World Religions** — Published 1997; *Journal of Belief and Values,* Vol 18, No 1, pp 109-112

Kay W K (6) — **Phenomenology, Religious Education and Piaget** — Published 1997; *Religion,* Vol 27, pp 275-283

Kay W K (7) — **Bertrand Russell and World Religions** — Published 1997; *Journal of Beliefs and Values,* Vol 18, No 2, pp 239-242

Kay W K (8) — **Belief in God in Great Britain 1945-1996:** — Moving the scenery behind classroom RE — Published 1997; *British Journal of Religious Education,* Vol 20, No 1, pp 28-41

Kay W K (9) — **British Atheism Past and Present: a literary and empirical perspective** — Published 1997; *Panorama,* Vol 9, No 1, pp 65-72

Kay W K (10) — **Assemblies of God: distinctive continuity and distinctive change** — Published 1998; 23 pages; Book contribution in *Pentecostal Perspectives;* Publisher: Paternoster, Carlisle; Editor: K Warrington

Kay W K (11) — **Phenomenology, Religious Education and Piaget** — Published 1998; 11 pages; Book contribution in *Religionspädagogik und Phänomenologie;* Publisher: Deutscher Studien Verlag, Weinheim; Editor: Hans-Günter Heimbrock

Kay W K (12) — **Ludweig Wittgenstein: beliefs, values and world religions** — Published 1998; *Journal of Beliefs and Values,* Vol 19, No 1, pp 123-126

Kay W K (13) — **A demonised worldview: dangers, benefits and explanations** — Published 1998; *Journal of Empirical Theology,* Vol 11, No 1, pp 17-29

Kay W K (14) — **What, then, is understanding the Bible?** — Published 1998; *Engaging the Curriculum,* Vol 7 (Spring), pp 23-26

Kay W K & L J Francis (15) — **Drift from the Churches** — A thorough examination and compilation of many pieces of research brought critically together to focus on the key reasons why people leave the church — *Trinity College, Carmarthen, Carmarthenshire SA31 3EP* — Published 1996; Price £10.99 University of Wales Press, Cardiff

Kay W K & L J Francis (eds) (16) — **Religion in Education: volume 1** — Published 1997; Book; 384 pages; Publisher: Gracewing, Leominster

Kay W K & L J Francis (eds) (17) — **Religion in Education: volume 2** — Published 1998; Book; 437 pages; Publisher: Gracewing, Leominster

Kay W K & P Weaver (18) — **Pastoral Care and Counselling: a manual** — Published 1997; Book; 214 pages; Publisher: Paternoster, Carlisle

Kay W K & R Wilkins (19) — **Reading for readiness** — Published 1998; *Educations and Christian Belief,* Vol 2, No 1, pp 65-69

Keep Rev Dr David — **The Methodist Church: Plymouth and Exeter District Education Committee.** — Results of a Survey carried out to discover what chaplaincy and RS provision was available in the six colleges in Devon, Plymouth and Torbay — *Heatherdene, Woodbury, Exeter EX5 1NR* — Published 1998

Kettle Rev Patsy	**Ministry and Marriage** The results of a survey of married women priests and the issues they face in the Anglican ministry *Christian Research, Vision Building, 4 Footscray Road, Eltham SE9 2TZ*	Published 1998; 65 pages; Price £6; *Christian Research Leaders' Briefing No 9*
Kirk D	**What does a Church Plant do now?** *Cliff College, Calver, Hope Valley, Nr Sheffield S32 3XG*	Published 1997; c15,000 words; Postgraduate Diploma Dissertation; Price £30
Knight Rev Canon Roger	**Render unto Caesar?** A search for Anglican Clergy who have served as local councillors in England and Wales since 1945 *The Rectory, 79 Finedon Road, Irthlingboough, Northamptonshire NN9 5TY*	Published 1998
Kolaneci Redina	**Getting to know Evangelical Donors** Who gives to what and why? *38 Bishops Way, Sutton Coldfield, West Midlands B74 4XU*	Published 1997; Madedonian Evangelical Trust
Kounis G	**A Biblical, Theological and Philisophical Approach to 'The Fall' in Genesis Chapter Three** *Available for study at St Deiniol's Library, Hawarden, Flintshire CH5 3DF*	Published 1998; MA Potchefstroom University of Christian Higher Education, South Africa
Kuhrt Ven Gordon W (1)	**Clergy Security** Discussion paper as a result of a spate of attacks on clergy and their families *Advisory Board of Ministry, Church House, Great Smith Street, London SW1P 3NZ*	Published 1997
Kuhrt Ven Gordon W (2)	**Issues in Theological Education and Training** Identifies strategies for training, significant developments and listing 13 problem areas in theological training for ongoing debate *Church House Bookshop, 31 Great Smith Street, London SW1P 3BN*	Published 1997; ABM Paper No 15 (GS Misc 507); Price £3
Kušnierik Juraj & Milan Cicel	**Shadows of the Past, The Impact of Communism on the Way People Think in Postcommunist Society** Aims to help understanding of the current political, spiritual, economic and social situation in Central and Eastern Europe *CEMF, 3 Springfield Road, Hinkley, Leics LE10 1AN*	Published 1997; Price £11.50
Lamb Christopher	**The Implicit Religion of Love** Paper on love as the highest value in some religions *Network for the Study of Implicit Religion, Winterbourne Rectory, 58 High Street, Winterbourne, Bristol BS17 1JQ*	Published 1998; Denton Conference on Implicit Religion
Lane P	An examination into the role of 'Community' in Christian mission *Cliff College, Calver, Hope Valley, Nr Sheffield S32 3XG*	Published 1997; c20,000 words; MA Dissertation, Price £30
Lappin Rev John	**Perspectives of Mariology** *Available for study at St Deiniol's Library, Hawarden, Flintshire CH5 3DF*	Published 1998; Ph.D Potchefstroom University of Christian Higher Education, South Africa
Larsen Andrew	**Commuting Christians and Rural Free Churches** *4 Woodlands Close, Bransgore, Herts BH23 8NF*	Published 1998; Dissertation, Moorland Bible College
Letson Pastor Henry	**Pentecostal Ministry** Its history and influence *377 Hollinwood Avenue, New Moston, Manchester M40 0J9*	Published 1997; MTh Thesis Spurgeon's College
Linder Eileen	**Yearbook of American and Canadian Churches 1998** The 66th edition of collection of statistics and information about churches in North America *Any Christian Bookshop*	Published 1998; Publisher Abingdon Press, Nashville USA
Lopez Dr D	**The Evangelical Church and Human Rights in Peru** An analysis of the religious and political events of 1980-1982 and the rise of theological transformation *Oxford Centre for Mission Studies, PO Box 70, Oxford OX2 6HB*	Published 1997; 100,000 words; Doctoral Thesis, Open University
Marfleet David	**The New Church Mission Movement** Examining the mission theologies, models, strategies and activities of the New Church Movement *All Nations Christian College, Easneye, Ware, Hertfordshire SG12 8LX*	Published 1999; 20,000 words; MA Dissertation; Publisher: ANCC
Marler Prof Penny & C Kirk Hadaway (1)	**Methodists on the Margins: "Self authoring" Religious Identity** Paper highlighting the differences between unchurched Methodists and Protestants *C Kirk Hadaway, UCBHM, 700 Prospect Avenue, Cleveland, Ohio USA*	Published 1997; *Connectionalism: Ecclesiology, Missions and Identity*
Marler Prof Penny & C Kirk Hadaway (2)	**Towards a Typology of Protestant "Marginal Members"** A paper for those interested in nominal Christianity	Published 1993; *Review of Religious Research Vol 35, No 1*
Marshall B	**A History of The Catholic Community of Hyde: 1848-1997** *Available for study at St Deiniol's Library, Hawarden, Flintshire CH5 3DF*	Published 1998; MA Potchefstroom University of Christian Higher Education, South Africa
Marshall D	**Driven or Led?** Leadership styles investigated *Cliff College, Calver, Hope Valley, Nr Sheffield S32 3XG*	Published 1997; c15,000 words; Postgraduate Diploma Dissertation; Price £30
McClintock Andrew & Eric Graham	**Discovering and documenting the overseas mission activities of New Churches** To identify and increase resources going to international mission *Forward Together, Clarendon House, Cavendish Road, Sheffield S11 9BH*	Published 1997
Moffett B	**How should Christian youth ministry respond to Globalisation?** Causes and effects of Globalisation on youth culture with special reference to "Youth for Christ" *All Nations Christian College, Easneye, Ware, Hertfordshire SG12 8LX*	Published 1999; 20,000 words; MA Dissertation; Publisher: ANCC
Morgan G	**Anglican Mission and Liturgy in Kenya** The theory and practice of contextualised African Anglican liturgies *Oxford Centre for Mission Studies, PO Box 70, Oxford OX2 6HB*	Published 1997; 100,000 words; MPhil Thesis, Open University
Morgan Dr Gareth	**A practical guide to the Millennium Bug – for charities, churches and voluntary organisations** *The Kubernesis Partnership, 36 Acomb Wood Drive, York YO24 2XN*	Price £3.95
MORI (1)	**Belief, Divination and the Supernatural** Survey of a sample of 721 adults conducted for *The Sun* regarding what people believe in/do not believe in *Mary Russell, MORI, 95 Southwark Street, London SE1 0HX*	Published 1998; *British Public Opinion*

7

MORI (2) | **Modernising the Monarchy** Survey of a sample of 928 adults conducted for the *Independent on Sunday* regarding whether the Queen should/should not remain Head of the Church of England | Published 1998; *British Public Opinion*

MORI (3) | **The Facts of Life** The changing face of childhood. Considers how society has changed in the past 20 years and the effect on children. *Barnardo's, Tanners Lane, Barkingside, Ilford IG6 1QG* | Published 1998; MORI poll

Murphy Eila | **St John's Parish Survey** Church's role in the community *Frank Gray, 2 Ashdene Close, Wimborne BH21 1QT* | Published 1998

Murray Rev Derek | **The Implicit Religion of Letters of Consolation** the importance of the letter of condolence in religious expression *Network for the Study of Implicit Religion, Winterbourne Rectory, 58 High Street, Winterbourne, Bristol BS17 1JQ* | Published 1998; Denton Conference on Implicit Religion

Musson David J | **The personality profile of male Anglican clergy in England:** The findings of a 16PF questionnaire completed by 441 male Anglican clergy *77 Grantham Road, Sleaford, Lincolnshire NG34 7NP* | Published 1998; *Personality and Individual Differences*, Vol 25, pp 689-698

Myers Boyd | **Christian Radio Station for Central Scotland** Research report for Revival Radio *Christian Research, Vision Building, 4 Footscray Road, Eltham, London SE9 2TZ* | Published 1998

Mylliemngap Dr L | **A study of the relation between Christianity and Khasi-Jaintia culture** A study of the theology and practice of the Khasi-Jaintia Presbyterian church *Oxford Centre for Mission Studies, PO Box 70, Oxford OX2 6HB* | Published 1998; 100,000 words; Doctoral Thesis, University of Wales

Nicoll P | **Executive Coaching as an appropriate model** Evaluation of the model for developing field leaders in OM *All Nations Christian College, Easneye, Ware, Hertfordshire SG12 8LX* | Published 1998; 20,000 words MA Dissertation; Publisher: ANCC

Orchard A & L J Francis | **Neuroticism and strength of religious attitudes among churchgoers in England** *Trinity College, Carmarthen, Carmarthenshire SA31 3EP* | Published 1998; *Journal of Beliefs and Values*, Vol 19, pp 231-236

Overman Richard & Steve Deckard | **Origins beliefs among NSTA members** *Institute for Christian Research, PO Box 2667, El Cajon, CA 92021* | Published 1997; *Impact*

Pagolu Dr A | **The Religion of the Patriarchs** A comparison with ancient near eastern and later Israelite religions *Sheffield Academic Press, Mansion House, 19 Kingfield Road, Sheffield S11 9AS* | Published 1998; 296 pages; Price £50; Publisher: Sheffield Academic Press

Panagos Pastor Maureen (1) | **Out of Bondage** A glimpse into the spiritual and cultural state of modern day Greece and its potential for restoration *Christians Without Borders, Em. Xanthopoulou 4, Katerini 60100, North Greece* | Published 1997; Survey

Panagos Pastor Maureen (2) | **Survey of Australian Women Married to Greek Men** Exploring the advantages and pressures of marriage where the role of women differs substantially in the background culture of the man and woman | Published 1997; Survey

Panagos Pastor Maureen (3) | **Street Survey on Beliefs and Attitudes Carried out in a working area** of Brisbane, Australia, to discover the needs and problems which a Church-based Community programme could address | Published 1997; Survey

Patchett M | **A critical analysis of the use of drama in evangelism in contemporary Western society** *Cliff College, Calver, Hope Valley, Nr Sheffield S32 3XG* | Published 1998; c20,000 words; MA Dissertation; Price £30

Petersen Douglas | **Pentecostals: Who are they?** *Paternoster Press, PO Box 300, Carlisle, Cumbria CA3 0QS or Oxford Centre for Mission Studies, Oxford OX2 6HB* | Published 1998; 12 pages; *Transformation: Evangelical Dialogue on Mission and Ethos* Vol 15 No 2 April/June 1998

Philpott R | **Coming to Faith and choosing a Church** An exploration of the factors involved in a local setting *Cliff College, Calver, Hope Valley, Nr Sheffield S32 3XG* | Published 1997; c15,000 words; Postgraduate Diploma Dissertation; Price £30

Pocock N D (1) | **Measurement of Spiritual Maturity among Ordinands** The empirical measurement of spiritual functioning, against personality, ecclesiology and authoritarianism *Flat 14, 31 Westwood Hill, Sydenham, London SE26 6NU* | Published 1998; 400 pages; M.Phil University of Wales, Lampeter

Pocock N D (2) | **Breaking the Chains** History and social psychology of English slavery, with anticipations of future trends and strategies for ethnic reconciliation | Published 1999; 330 pages; Price £15; Research project for Christian charity

Porter M | **A critical examination of ecumenical thinking** with reference to the Salvation Army and its relationships with partner churches in the city of Liverpool *Cliff College, Calver, Hope Valley, Nr Sheffield S32 3XG* | Published 1997; c20,000 words; MA Dissertation; Price £30

Portmann Adrian | **Consuming Friendship: Cooking and Eating as Religious Practices** *Network for the Study of Implicit Religion, Winterbourne Rectory, 58 High Street, Winterbourne, Bristol BS17 1JQ* | Published 1998; Denton Conference on Implicit Religion

Presbyterian Church USA, Research Services (1) | **A survey of adult new members in Presbyterian Congregations** *Research Services, Presbyterian Church (USA), 100 Witherspoon Street, Louisville, KY 40202, USA* | Published 1998; Survey

Presbyterian Church USA, Research Services (2) | **Comparative Statistics** Statistical details of the 11,000 congregations and 2.6 million members of the PCUSA | Published 1997

Preston Dr John | **On our knees? Survey on prayer, mostly in the UK, lay people and ministers** *The Teal Trust, 11 Lincoln Road, Northburn Green, Cramlington NE23 9XT* | Published 1998

Priggis Nick | **From Dictatorship to Democracy** Malawi in transition *World Vision UK, 599 Avebury Boulevard, Milton Keynes MK9 3PG* | Published 1998; Price £3

Probert John C C (1) | **Charlestown Methodist Chapel 1828-1998 A Social History** Lists village occupations in 1851 and includes a table of village age structure in percentage terms for 1851 and 1991 which shows a complete reversal pattern. *1 Penventon Terrace, Redruth, Cornwall TR15 3AD* | Published 1998; 12 pages; Price £2.90

Probert John C C (2) — **1851 Religious Census, West Cornwall and the Isles of Scilly**
Shows strength of churchgoing in each parish with percentages for each denomination
Published 1998; 24 pages; Price £2.90

Richter P & L J Francis — **Gone but not Forgotten**
Church leaving and returning. Addressing the problem of church leavers, with theories developed from a variety of statistics
From any Christian Bookshop
Published 1998; Book; 208 pages; Publisher: Darton, Longman and Todd, London; Price £10.95

Robbins M (1) — **A different voice: a different view**
Trinity College, Carmarthen, Carmenthenshire SA31 3EP
Published 1998; *Review of Religious Research*, Vol 40, No 1, pp 75-80

Robbins M, L J Francis & C Rutledge (2) — **The personality characteristics of Anglican stipendiary parochial clergy in England: gender differences revisited**
Published 1997; *Personality and Individual Differences*, Vol 23, pp 199-204

Roberts Helen & Darshan Sachdev (eds) — **Young People's Social Attitudes**
Views of 12-19 year olds. A young people's equivalent of *British Social Attitudes*
Barnardo's Child Care Publications, Barnardo's Trading Estate, Paycocke Road, Basildon, Essex SS14 3DR
Published 1997

Robinson Alan — **A Pastor's Job Portfolio**
A critical theological evaluation of the expectations placed upon the pastor in Scottish Nazarene Churches
Church of Nazarene, Eglington Street, Irvine, Ayrshire KA12 8AS
Published 1997; MTh Thesis, School of Theology, Westminster College, Oxford

Rodríguez Esther — **Manual de Oración**
A key book to get an overview of evangelical Christianity in Spain
Pocket Testament League, Calle Elcano, 34 Bis, 08004 Barcelona, Spain
Published 1997; Publisher: Liga del Testamento de Bolsillo

Rowe J — **Holy to the Lord**
Universality in the Deuteronomic history and its relationship to the author's theology of idolatory
All Nations Christian College, Easneye, Ware, Hertfordshire SG12 8LX
Published 1997; 20,000 words; MA Dissertation; Publisher: ANCC

Rowley Rev A J — **The Challenge of the Face which commands, 'Thou shalt not kill'**
The use of Levinasian metaphysics in the search for truly radical and truly liberating Christian Discipleship: with special reference to the changing Christian attitude to war and peace as egotism
Available for study at St Deiniol's Library, Hawarden, Flintshire CH5 3DF
Published 1998; PhD Potchefstroom University of Christian Higher Education, South Africa

Rozario Sister R — **The role of Caste in Prostitution**
Culture and violence in the life histories of prostitutes in India
Oxford Centre for Mission Studies, PO Box 70, Oxford OX2 6HB
Published 1998; 100,000 words; M.Phil Thesis, Open University

Rush Margaret — **Studying Student Movements**
Reflections on the Role of Women in the Australian Student Christian Movement
Centre for the Study of Australian Christianity, PO Box 1505 Macquarie Centre, NSW Australia 2113
Published 1997

Salter K — **The role of Prison Chaplain as Evangelist**
Cliff College, Calver, Hope Valley, Nr Sheffield S32 3XG
Published 1997; c20,000 words; MA Dissertation; Price £30

Sanger Georgina — **UK Missionaries and their work**
Research report for Christian Medical Fellowship & Evangelical Missionary Alliance
Christian Research, Vision Building, 4 Footscray Road, Eltham, London SE9 2TZ
Published 1998; 22 pages

Schmied Gerhard (1) — **Images of the Deceased as a Problem of Implicit Religion**
A paper as part of a wider project on cemeteries and feelings and behaviour experienced there
Network for the Study of Implicit Religion, Winterbourne Rectory, 58 High Street, Winterbourne, Bristol BS17 1JQ
Published 1998; Denton Conference on Implicit Religion

Schmied Gerhard (2) — **The Network Dependancy of Personal Religious Belief Systems**
Published 1998; Denton Conference on Implicit Religion

Sealey Mrs Sue & Rev Otis Corbitt — **Survey of the use of the Alpha Programme**
of evangelism in the Eastern Area of the Baptist Union of Great Britain
Park Baptist Church, 14a Crown Road, Great Yarmouth, Norfolk NR30 2JN
Published 1998

Sheppard Lowell — **Mission to the New Young of Japan**
An exploration of changes taking place within Japanese youth culture and their missiological implications with special attention given to postmodernism in Japan
Cliff College, Calver, Hope Valley, Nr Sheffield S32 3XG
Published 1998; c20,000 words; MA Dissertation; Price £30

Simmonds David — **Training for a Change in the Church: An investigation of the Alpha Course**
58 Barrow Road, London SW16 5PG
Published 1998

Smith Dr Greg — **The churches contribution to community work in East London in the 1990s**
Draft paper which aims to quantify the contribution of East End churches in "building social capital"
gregs@xena.uel.ac.uk
Published 1998

Smith Joan, Sheila Gilford & Ann O'Sullivan — **The family background of homeless young people**
Looks in depth at issues such as family conflict, abusive behaviour, disrupted families
Family Policy Studies Centre, 231 Baker Street, London NW1 6XE
Price £9.95; Published jointly by: Family Policy Studies Centre and the Joseph Rowntree Foundation

Snell P — **Becoming Disciples to make Disciples**
Cliff College, Calver, Hope Valley, Nr Sheffield S32 3XG
Published 1998; c20,000 words; MA Dissertation; Price £30

Souter I — **Motivations for Evangelism**
Using Acts as a model, and applied to society in England today
Cliff College, Calver, Hope Valley, Nr Sheffield S32 3XG
Published 1997; c20,000 words; MA Dissertation; Price £30

Sparey D — **Spiritual Warfare and the practice of evangelism:**
Is the theory of territorial spirits one which should be taken seriously in the practice of evangelism for the 21" Century?
Cliff College, Calver, Hope Valley, Nr Sheffield S32 3XG
Published 1998; c20,000 words; MA Dissertation; Price £30

Speak Suzanne, Stuart Cameron & Rose Gilroy — **Young single fathers: participation in fatherhood – barriers and bridges**
One in a series on family and parenthood
Family Policy Studies Centre, 231 Baker Street, London NW1 6XE
Price £9.95; produced jointly by: Family Policy Studies Centre and the Joseph Rowntree Foundation

Spurgeon's College Students — **Ashby Fields Community Survey**
Investigating the need for a church plant in a large new housing development
Spurgeon's College, 189 South Norwood Hill, London SE25 6DJ
Published 1996; Community Survey

Stone G — **Area Ministry Unites in a Parish Setting**
Cliff College, Calver, Hope Valley, Nr Sheffield S32 3XG
Published 1997; c15,000 words; Postgraduate Diploma Dissertation; Price £30

7

Sultan Dr P | **The involvement of the Church of Pakistan in development of Multan and Hyderabad**
A critical examination in the development of the poor in the Diocese of Multan and Hyderabad
Oxford Centre for Mission Studies, PO Box 70, Oxford OX2 6HB
Published 1997; 100,000 words; Doctoral Thesis, Open University

Taylor J P | **Report of "Jesus in the City 1998" – The biennial UK Urban Mission Congress**
Overview of main addresses and workshop seminars
Stanley McDowell, 209 Bangor Road, Holywood, Belfast BT18 0JG
Published 1999; 15 pages; Price £2.50

Theology and Religious Studies Dept, University of Malawi | *Religion in Malawi*: **Social change and widowhood**
The Editor, Religion in Malawi, Dept of Theology and Religious Studies, Chancellor College, PO Box 280, Zomba, Malawi
Published 1997; *Religion in Malawi*, Issue No 7

Trapnell John | **A Sermon Audit from a Methodist Circuit**
An analysis of the content of sermons in the Wimborne Circuit over 12 months
Snails Lane, Ringwood, Hampshire BH24 3PG
Published 1998; 7 pages

Verweij Dr J | **The importance of femininity in explaining cross-national differences in secularization**
From any Bookshop
Published 1998; 12 pages; Book contribution: Masculinity and Femininity, Geert Hofstede, *SAGE Publications* (ISBN 0-7619-1029-8)

Viney Rev Peter | **Church Attendance statistics at St Johns, High Wycombe 1992-98**
5 Avery Avenue, Downley, High Wycombe HP13 5UE
Published 1998

Wakefield Rev Dr G T | **Finding a Church**
The reasons people give for joining and moving churches. Summarises and critiques existing research and gives results of surveys in Essex.
St John's College, 3 South Bailey, Durham DH1 3RJ
Published 1998; PhD Thesis; Price £10

Walker Canon Geoffrey | **Mission Perspectives Canada: A Study in Local Mission**
Bath & Wells Diocesan Missioner, 6 The Liberty, Wells BA5 2SU
Published 1997; Sabbatical research project

Walter Tony | **The ideology and organisation of spiritual care:**
three approaches – Religious Community, Calling in the Chaplain and The Search for Meaning
15 Southcot Place, Lyncombe Hill, Bath BA2 4PE
Published 1997; *Palliative Medicine*, Vol 11

Ward Rev J W (1) | **Polanyi's Ontological Hierarchy**
Discussion of Polanyi's epistemology and his understanding of biological entities
Appraisal, 20 Ulverscroft Road, Loughborough, Leics LE11 3PU
Published 1997; 22 pages; Price £2.50; *Appraisal*, supplementary issue Vol 1 Part 2, pp 49-70, 1970

Ward Rev J W (2) | **A critical evaluation of the Epistemology of Michael Polanyi and comparison with that of Kant**
An exposition of the epistemology and ontology of Polanyi and comparison of its realism with the transcendental idealism of Kant
John Rylands University Library, University of Manchester, Oxford Road, Manchester M13 9PL
Published 1997; 208 pages MPhil Thesis, University of Manchester

Ward Rev J W (3) | **Michael Polanyi and Christian Witness to the Secular Society**
Exposition of Polanyi's epistemology and ways of using it to counter humanism and postmodernism
Whitefield Institute, Frewin Court, Oxford OX1 3HZ
Published 1998; 4 pages; Price £5; *Whitefield Briefing Paper*, Vol 3 No 6

Ward Rev J W (4) | **Realism or Idealism?**
A comparison of Polanyi's epistemology with that of Kant
Published 1999; 13 pages; Price £5; *Appraisal* Vol 2 No 3

Warren Yvonne | **The Psychotherapeutic needs of the Anglican Clergy in an uncertain world**
Exploring the effect on the clergy's psychological health of living in a multi-facted society
The Archdeaconry, Rochester, Kent ME1 1SX
Published 1997

Warrington Dr K (1) | **The teaching & praxis concerning supernatural healing of British Pentecostals, John Wimber & Kenneth Hagin**
in the light of an analysis of the healing ministry of Jesus as recorded in the Gospels
Regents Theological College, London Road, Nantwich, Cheshire CW5 6LW
Published 1998; 400 pages; PhD Dissertation

Warrington Dr K (2) | **Pentecostal Perspectives**
Analysis of Pentecostal/Charismatic UK history of some doctrinal/praxis evaluation
Paternoster Publishing, PO Box 300, Carlisle, Cumbria CA3 0QS
Published 1998; 222 pages; Price £12.99

Watkins D | **From Maintenance to Mission:**
Steps towards a rural Methodist church becoming a missionary church
Cliff College, Calver, Hope Valley, Nr Sheffield S32 3XG
Published 1998; c20,000 words; MA Dissertation; Price £30

Watts Julian | **God's Business: Preparing the Church for dramatic growth**
A book urging leaders to seek God in preparation for the influx of new members following the coming flood of His Spirit'
From any Christian Bookshop
Published 1998; Publisher: Cornwallis Emmanuel Ltd; Price £14.95

White I | **Young People on Pilgrimage**
Cliff College, Calver, Hope Valley, Nr Sheffield S32 3XG
Published 1997; c20,000 words; MA Dissertation; Price £30

Wilcox C & L J Francis (1) | **Personality and religion among A level religious studies students**
Trinity College, Carmarthen, Carmarthenshire SA31 3EP
Published 1997; *International Journal of Children's Spirituality*, Vol 1, No 2, pp 48-56

Wilcox C & L J Francis (2) | **Beyond gender stereotyping:**
examining the validity of the Bem Sex Role Inventory among 16-19 year old females in England
Published 1997; *Personality and Individual Differences*, Vol 23, pp 9-13

Wilcox C & L J Francis (3) | **The relationship between neuroticism and the perceived social desirability of feminine characteristics among 16-18 year old females**
Published 1997; *Social Behaviour and Personality*, Vol 25, pp 291-294

Williams Dr D | **Then they will know that I am the Lord**
The missiological significance of Ezekiel's concern for the nations
All Nations Christian College, Easneye, Ware, Hertfordshire SG12 8LX
Published 1998; 20,000 words; MA Dissertation; Publisher: ANCC

Williams Dr Ted & Rev D Flanagan | **Cohabitation or Marriage**
Analysis of the impact of cohabitation in society with particular reference to health issues
Belmont House Publishing, 36 The Crescent, Belmont, Sutton, Surrey SM2 6BJ
Published 1997; 28 pages; Price £2.99

SUBJECT INDEX   *See Note on Page 7.1*

7

INSTITUTIONAL CHURCH STATISTICS

Contents

See Notes and Definitions on page 0.6

8

Sources:
Individual denominations, previous editions UK Christian Handbook and *Churches and Churchgoers* by Robert Currie, OUP 1997

TABLE 8.2.1 — Total

	Membership	Churches	Ministers
1900	3,241,450	20,079	22,486
1910	3,880,350	20,707	21,285
1920	3,824,750	20,976	19,913
1930	4,166,100	21,152	18,561
1940	3,911,320	21,393	18,685
1950	3,444,130	20,956	15,714
1960	3,340,750	20,677	14,749
1970	2,987,046	20,417	14,767
1980	2,179,808	19,399	12,472
1990	1,727,967	18,823	12,373
2000[1]	1,657,150	18,307	10,011
1991	1,764,980	18,790	12,358
1992	1,786,932	18,736	12,330
1993	1,790,269	18,809	12,277
1994	1,793,820	18,752	12,162
1995	1,785,033	18,663	11,781
1996	1,604,641	18,550	10,640
1997	1,631,579	18,620	10,464
1998	1,649,928	18,416	10,395

TABLE 8.2.2 — Church of England

	Electoral Roll	Churches	Ministers[8]
1900	2,796,000[1]	17,468	20,953
1910	3,391,600[1]	18,026	19,701[1]
1920	3,323,000[1]	18,270	18,312[1]
1930	3,656,000[1]	18,417	16,942
1940	3,389,000[1]	18,666	17,070[1]
1950	2,959,000[1]	18,220	14,095[1]
1960	2,862,000	17,973	13,151
1970	2,559,000	17,760	13,080[1]
1980	1,815,000	16,884	11,053
1990	1,396,000	16,380	11,072[12]
2000[18]	1,360,000	15,906	8,720
1991	1,437,000	16,350[9]	11,076
1992	1,459,000	16,285[10]	11,049
1993	1,467,000	16,364	10,954
1994	1,475,000	16,303	10,817[13]
1995	1,468,000	16,255[7]	10,459[11]
1996	1,290,000	16,128	9,314
1997	1,324,700	16,202[2]	9,132[3]
1998	1,345,000	16,000	9,068[1]

TABLE 8.2.3 — Church in Wales

	Easter Communicants	Churches	Ministers[14]
1900	141,000	1,745[1]	905[1]
1910	153,000	1,750[1]	908[1]
1920	160,000	1,755[1]	911[1]
1930	185,000	1,774[1]	920[1]
1940[1]	194,000	1,766	916
1950[1]	168,000	1,774	920
1960	182,000	1,783	925[1]
1970	154,567	1,780	1,004
1980	131,518	1,697	800
1990	108,200	1,593	696[21]
2000[18]	80,200	1,515	674
1991	103,600	1,578	688
1992	104,900	1,577[15]	678[22]
1993	100,400	1,565	703
1994	97,100	1,555[16]	707[23]
1995	95,400	1,537	702[4]
1996	93,700	1,525	684
1997	87,000	1,521	688
1998	86,400	1,521	682

TABLE 8.2.4 — Total Scottish Episcopal Church

	Membership	Churches[17]	Ministers
1900	116,000	354	268[1]
1910	142,000	404	306[1]
1920	144,000	416	315[1]
1930	124,000	415	314[1]
1940	124,000	404	306[1]
1950	109,000	397	300[1]
1960	94,000	369	279[1]
1970	77,279[1]	341	260
1980	67,590	311	235
1990	58,299	310	233
2000[18]	49,900	316	157
1991	57,196	311[1]	230[1]
1992	56,742	312	225
1993	55,929	316	230[1]
1994	54,495	315	235
1995	54,352	316	230[5]
1996	53,553	316	210[1]
1997	52,661	316	190[1]
1998	51,353	316	175

TABLE 8.2.5 — Total Church of Ireland (Northern Ireland)

	Community[6]	Membership[20]	Churches	Ministers[19]
1900	316,825	183,800	467[1]	314[1]
1910	327,076	189,700	482[1]	324[1]
1920[1]	333,800	193,600	492	331
1930[1]	340,300	197,400	502	338
1940[1]	346,800	201,100	512	344
1950	353,245	204,900	521[1]	350[1]
1960	344,800	200,000	509[1]	342[1]
1970	334,318	194,000	493	365[1]
1980	281,472	163,300	462	330
1990	279,500	162,100	475	300
2000[1]	277,300	160,800	437[18]	277
1991	279,280	162,000	483	290
1992	279,100	161,900	480	286
1993	278,850	161,700	477	288
1994	278,600[1]	161,600	480	285
1995	278,400	161,500	450	245
1996[1]	278,200	161,400	447	260
1997[1]	278,000	161,200	445	275
1998	277,800[1]	161,100	442	291

[1] Estimate
[2] 12,976 parishes in 1997
[3] Of whom 859 were female
[4] Of whom 20 were female
[5] Of whom 20 were female
[6] Taken from the Census of Population. Figures 1900–1970 exclude estimated numbers of the Church in the Republic of Ireland
[7] 13,025 parishes in 1995
[8] Full-time stipendiary clergy within the Diocesan framework
[9] 13,099 parishes in 1991
[10] 13,060 parishes in 1992
[11] Of whom 783 were female
[12] This was 542 in excess of the so-called "Sheffield" ideal numbers
[13] This was 737 in excess of the "Sheffield" ideal numbers. In 1994, 39 ministers were out of work; the number would have been larger had 232 not left by then because of the ordination of women
[14] Includes non-stipendiary clergy 1900–1980, 1900–1960 based on the same proposition as in 1970 and 1980
[15] 1,142 parishes and 594 benefices
[16] 1,131 parishes and 590 benefices
[17] Excluding preaching points
[18] Revised figure
[19] Northern Ireland proportion of total is based on 1990 split with Republic of Ireland
[20] Taken as 58% of the community
[21] Of whom 24 were female
[22] Of whom 34 were female
[23] Of whom 38 were female

	Membership	Churches	Ministers[8]
TABLE 8.3.1 Anglican Orthodox Freechurch[7]			
1960[1]	–	–	–
1970[1]	–	–	–
1980[1]	200	6	5
1990	438	15	10
2000[1]	1,000	20	10
1991[1]	1,000	16	10
1992[1]	1,000	17	10
1993[1]	1,000	18	10
1994[1]	1,000	19	10
1995	1,000	20[9]	10
1996[1]	1,000	20	10
1997[1]	1,000	20	10
1998	1,000	20	10

	Membership	Churches	Ministers[10]
TABLE 8.3.4 Anglican Catholic Church[3]			
1960	–	–	–
1970	–	–	–
1980	–	–	–
1990	–	–	–
2000[1]	660	27[12]	25
1991	–	–	–
1992	500	10	13
1993	550	15	17
1994	600	26	21
1995	650	27	25
1996	650	27	25
1997	655	27	25
1998	655	27	25

	Membership	Churches	Ministers
TABLE 8.3.5 Other Anglican Churches[14]			
1960	–	–	–
1970	–	–	–
1980	–	–	–
1990	–	–	–
2000[1]	400	23	33
1991	–	–	–
1992	–	–	–
1993	–	–	–
1994	160	5	6
1995	185	7	10
1996	338	22	30
1997	338	23	33
1998	375	23	33

	Membership	Churches	Ministers
TABLE 8.3.2 Free Church of England			
1900[1]	4,500	40	40
1910[1]	4,500	40	40
1920[1]	4,000	38	38
1930[1]	3,500	37	37
1940[1]	3,000	37	37
1950[1]	3,000	35	35
1960[1]	2,500	33	37
1970	1,700	30	40
1980	1,875	29	29
1990	1,850	29	26
2000[1]	1,410	30[12]	45[12]
1991[1]	1,824	28	27
1992	1,810	28[1]	28[1]
1993	1,610	27	29
1994	1,585[13]	26	31
1995	1,510	30	40
1996[1]	1,490	30	43
1997[1]	1,470	30	45
1998[1]	1,450	30	45

	Membership	Churches	Ministers[4]
TABLE 8.3.6 Anglian Apostolic Episcopal Free Church			
1900	150	5	6
1910	150	5	6
1920	150	5	6
1930	150	5	6
1940	150	5	6
1950	150	5	6
1960	150	5	6
1970[12]	150	5	6
1980	200	5	10
1990	1,000	18	28
2000[11]	2,700	33[1]	62
1991	1,600	21	32
1992	2,000	24	35
1993	2,000	24	40
1994	2,200	26[6]	44
1995	2,336	28	53[5]
1996[1]	2,410	29	55
1997[1]	2,450	30	57
1998[1]	2,500	31	59

	Membership	Churches	Ministers
TABLE 8.3.3 Protestant Evangelical Church of England[2]			
1900	–	–	–
1910	–	–	–
1920	–	–	–
1930[1]	50	2	4
1940[1]	70	3	6
1950[1]	80	4	8
1960[1]	100	5	9
1970[1]	150	5	10
1980	125	5	10
1990	80	3	8
2000[1]	80	3	5
1991	80[1]	3	7
1992	80	3	6
1993	80	3	6
1994	80	3	6
1995	100	3	7
1996	100	3	7
1997	100	3	7
1998	90	3	5

8

[1] Estimate
[2] Began 1922
[3] Began 1992
[4] All unpaid
[5] Of whom 19 were female
[6] Congregations include 10 in France and Spain
[7] Includes the breakaway Church of England Homechurches Union
[8] All male and non-stipendiary
[9] Services largely held in homes, each with an average 12 attenders
[10] All male
[11] Church's own estimate
[12] Revised estimate
[13] Excluding 809 young people in Sunday School and youth organisations
[14] See list in Table 2.18 *Religious Trends* No 1

TABLE 8.4.1 Other Church of England Statistics

	Baptisms			Confirmations			Easter Day Communicants[5]		Christmas Communicants		Baptised population[6]
	Infants under 1 year	Percentages of births	Older people	Male	Female	Total	Number	Percentage of adult population	Number	Percentage of adult population	
1900	564,000	65.0%	11,000	73,000	108,000	181,000	1,902,000	8.9%	Not available		23,133,000
1905	576,000	65.7%[1]	13,000[1]	96,000	135,000	231,000	2,053,455	9.0%	Not available		24,235,000
1910	573,000	68.9%	16,000	95,000	132,000	227,000	2,212,000	9.2%	Not available		25,417,000
1915	528,000	67.5%[1]	13,000[1]	94,000	132,000	226,000	2,203,000	8.8%	Not available		25,646,000
1920	604,000	67.8%	11,000	83,000	116,000	199,000	2,171,619	8.2%	Not available		26,328,000
1925	470,000	69.5%[1]	10,000[1]	92,000	127,000	219,000	2,388,419	8.6%	Not available		26,857,000
1930	424,000	69.9%	10,000	84,000	112,000	197,000	2,261,857	8.0%	Not available		27,132,000
1935	385,000	62.5%[1]	10,000[1]	87,000	110,000	197,000	2,299,573	7.7%	Not available		27,428,000
1940	365,000	64.1%	10,000	65,000	79,000	144,000	1,997,820	6.4%	Not available		27,563,000
1945	525,000[2]	82.3%[1]	7,000[2]	45,000[2]	69,000[2]	114,000	1,728,940[2]	5.5%	Not available		27,759,000
1950	441,000	67.2%	9,000	60,000	82,000	142,000	1,847,998	5.8%	Not available		28,535,000
1955	427,000[1]	59.7%[1]	10,000[1]	68,000	95,000	163,000	2,092,002[1]	6.3%	Not available		27,758,000
1960	412,000	55.4%	11,000	78,000	113,000	191,000	2,159,356	6.5%	2,074,000	6.2%	27,629,000[7]
1965	413,000[3]	51.1%[3]	10,000[3]	59,000	87,000	146,000	1,899,469[3]	5.9%[3]	2,024,000[2]	5.9%[2]	27,500,000
1970	347,000	46.6%	8,000	45,000	68,000	113,000	1,631,506	4.6%	1,689,000	4.8%	27,736,000
1975	237,000[4]	42.8%[4]	8,000[4]	38,000	58,000	96,000	1,681,000[4]	4.7%[4]	1,695,000[3]	4.7%[3]	27,242,000[8]
1980	226,000	36.5%	40,000	37,000	61,000	98,000	1,551,000	4.2%	1,807,000	4.9%	26,769,000
1985	201,000	32.3%	38,000	29,000	48,000	77,000	1,624,000	4.2%	1,747,000	4.6%	26,287,000
1990	186,000	28.5%	45,000	21,000	34,000	55,000	1,376,000	3.5%	1,556,000	4.0%	25,805,000
1995	148,000	24.0%	46,000	17,000	27,000	44,000	1,265,000	3.2%	1,393,000[2]	3.5%[2]	25,323,000
2000[1]	122,000	21.1%	54,000	13,000	19,000	32,000	1,059,000	2.7%	1,228,000	3.1%	24,841,000
1991	180,000	27.2%	45,000	21,000	34,000	55,000	1,310,000	3.4%	1,590,000	4.1%	25,709,000
1992	170,000	26.0%	46,000	22,000	35,000	57,000	1,350,000	3.4%	1,483,000	3.8%	25,612,000
1993	160,000	25.1%	46,000	20,000	32,000	52,000	1,317,000	3.3%	1,481,000	3.8%	25,516,000
1994	157,000	24.9%	46,000	18,000	30,000	48,000	1,300,000	3.3%	1,488,000	3.8%	25,419,000
1995	148,000	24.0%	46,000	17,000	27,000	44,000	1,365,000	3.2%	1,393,000	3.5%	25,323,000
1996	141,000	22.9%	47,000	17,000	26,000	43,000	1,236,000	3.1%	1,344,000	3.4%	25,227,000
1997	139,000	22.8%	49,000	16,000	25,000	41,000	1,172,000	2.9%	1,344,000	3.4%	25,130,000

[1] Estimate
[2] 1947 Figure
[3] 1966 Figure
[4] 1976 Figure
[5] Communicants in the rest of Easter week no longer collected
[6] All figures estimated, based in part on birth and death figures each decade, and the percentage baptised each quinquennium
[7] 1962 figure was 27,384,000
[8] 1979 figure was 26,967,000

TABLE 8.4.2 Church of England Schools

	Primary Schools			Secondary Schools		
	Schools	Pupils	Average pupils per school	Schools	Pupils	Average pupils per school
1975	5,727	837,679	145	227	133,581	588
1980		Not available			Not available	
1985		Not available			Not available	
1990	4,718	668,888	142	220	138,257	628
1995	4,614	731,067	158	204	143,870	705
2000[1]	4,517	766,100	170	188	149,600	796
1991	4,685	675,721	144	218	138,431	635
1992	4,665	680,952	146	210	134,370	640
1993	4,653	697,969	150	211	142,526	675
1994	4,636	714,423	154	204	141,032	691
1995	4,614	731,067	158	204	143,870	705
1996	4,597	746,087	162	200	144,004	720
1997	4,575	758,191	166	199	145,857	733

Source: Culham College Institute, Abingdon
[1] Estimate

In 1995, the number of Church of England Primary Schools was 23% of the total in England and Wales, and the number of pupils 16%, with average size 219. For Secondary Schools the percentages were 5.3% and 4.5% respectively, with average size 831. In both cases therefore, Church of England schools are smaller.

TABLE 8.4.3 Church of England Electoral Roll

	Unadjusted As published by the Church of England	Adjusted To smooth out 6 yearly revisions
1983	1,761,000	1,638,600
1984	1,507,000	1,619,500
1985	1,551,000	1,600,300
1986	1,567,000	1,581,100
1987	1,584,000	1,562,000
1988	1,585,000	1,542,800
1989	1,601,212	1,523,700
1990	1,396,000	1,504,500
1991	1,437,000	1,485,400
1992	1,458,500	1,466,200
1993	1,474,400	1,447,100
1994	1,485,513	1,427,900
1995	1,500,000	1,408,800
1996	1,290,000	1,389,600
1997	1,325,000	1,370,500
1998	Not available	1,351,300
1999	Not available	1,332,200
2000	Not available	1,313,000

TABLE 8.5
Church of England Statistics Cont'd

	Number	Marriages[2] Percentage of All marriages	Religious marriages	Usual Sunday attendance Children[3]	Adults
1900	172,679	67%	79%	2,302,000	N/a
1905	165,747	64%	78%	2,398,000[4]	N/a
1910	164,945	62%	77%	2,437,000	N/a
1915	172,660[1]	58%	77%	2,255,000	N/a
1920	171,890[1]	60%	78%	2,010,000	N/a
1925	172,250[1]	58%	76%	1,915,000	N/a
1930	178,070[1]	56%	76%	1,802,000	N/a
1935	183,890[1]	53%	75%	1,645,000	N/a
1940	182,470[1]	52%[1]	74%[1]	Not available	
1945	177,050[1]	51%[1]	73%[1]	Not available	
1950	174,030[1]	50%	71%	Not available	
1955	171,020[1]	50%	69%	Not available	
1960	168,000[1]	47%	67%	1,039,000	N/a
1965	171,848	46%	68%	Not available	
1970	170,146	41%	68%	Not available	
1975	133,074	35%	67%	Not available	
1980	123,400	33%	66%	273,000	967,000
1985	110,121	34%	66%	259,000	920,000
1990	109,369	35%	67%	226,300	916,000
1995	79,616	30%	66%	153,300	892,000
2000[1]	44,800	18%	58%	88,000	847,000
1991	97,446	34%	67%	223,000	914,000
1992	96,828	33%	67%	220,000	903,000
1993	96,060	32%	66%	189,400	901,000
1994	86,143	31%	66%	185,000	896,000
1995	79,616	30%	66%	153,300	892,000
1996	71,400	27%	63%	133,000[1]	883,000[1]
1997[1]	64,000	23%	62%	Not published	

[1] Estimate
[2] Includes those in the Church in Wales
[3] Figures for 1900 to 1935 and 1960 give total Sunday School Scholars; figures for 1980 onwards are for those aged 16 or under who may be in church and not attending Sunday School
[4] These Sunday School Scholars were taught by 206,873 teachers

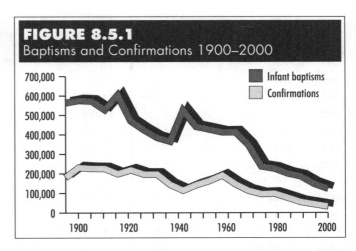

FIGURE 8.5.1
Baptisms and Confirmations 1900–2000

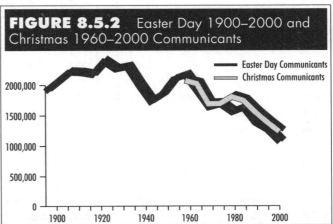

FIGURE 8.5.2 Easter Day 1900–2000 and Christmas 1960–2000 Communicants

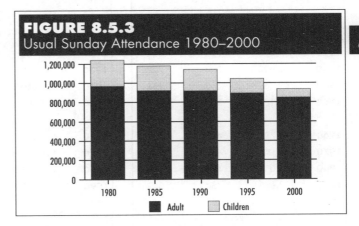

FIGURE 8.5.3
Usual Sunday Attendance 1980–2000

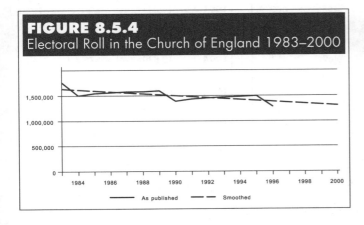

FIGURE 8.5.4
Electoral Roll in the Church of England 1983–2000

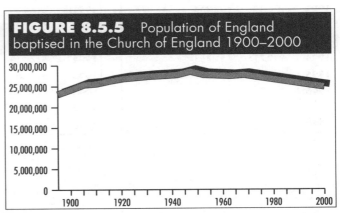

FIGURE 8.5.5 Population of England baptised in the Church of England 1900–2000

8

TABLE 8.6.1
Total Roman Catholic

	Mass Attendance	Churches	Priests
1900	1,911,960	2,272	3,903
1910	1,995,310	2,566	4,908
1920	2,107,000	2,765	5,137
1930	2,189,735	3,075	5,617
1940	2,232,270	3,452	7,230
1950	2,431,540	3,850	8,350
1960	2,844,570	3,972	9,490
1970	2,746,203	4,058	9,570
1980	2,454,803	4,156	9,004
1990	2,198,364	4,334	8,081
2000	1,721,500	4,276	6,083
1991	2,100,706	4,317	7,965
1992	2,086,930	4,322	7,886
1993	2,058,493	4,338	7,658
1994	2,004,002	4,379	7,601
1995	1,914,066	4,275	7,309
1996	1,889,496	4,258	7,025
1997	1,859,349	4,297	6,753
1998	1,832,907	4,288	6,503

TABLE 8.6.2
Roman Catholic Church in England

	Mass Attendance[8]	Churches[2]	Priests[3]
1900	1,109,020	1,517	2,710
1910	1,160,730	1,737	3,536
1920	1,236,120	1,901	3,724
1930	1,337,150	2,154	4,117
1940	1,392,750	2,418	5,443
1950	1,495,390	2,701	6,300
1960	1,869,665	2,794[1]	6,873
1970	1,863,263	2,877[1]	7,165
1980	1,587,524	2,980	6,750
1990	1,332,826	3,129[1]	6,043[1]
2000[10]	922,000	3,105	4,385
1991	1,244,235[1]	3,137[1]	5,950[1]
1992	1,237,770	3,145	5,907
1993	1,225,922	3,163	5,725
1994	1,175,889	3,203	5,673
1995	1,087,890	3,105	5,453
1996	1,065,262	3,086[1]	5,195
1997	1,044,088	3,126[1]	4,960[1]
1998[1]	1,021,900	3,118[1]	4,725[1]

TABLE 8.6.3
Roman Catholic Church in Wales[4]

	Mass Attendance[8]	Churches[2]	Priests[3]
1900	42,610	90	113
1910	44,500	120	147
1920	47,490	124	155
1930	51,375	134	172
1940	53,510	190	227
1950	57,460	212	263
1960[1]	71,835	211	286
1970[1]	71,590	210[10]	350
1980	56,700	209[1]	340[1]
1990	54,609	211[1]	311[1]
2000[10]	39,720	200	248
1991[1]	54,540	209	307
1992	54,300	207	303
1993	51,695	207	291
1994	50,308	207	293
1995	47,154	203	279
1996	45,472	203	275[1]
1997	45,034	202	268[1]
1998	44,300	202	262[1]

TABLE 8.6.4
Roman Catholic Church in Scotland

	Mass Attendance[9]	Churches[5]	Priests[3]
1900	341,660	279	475
1910	371,530	322	619
1920	407,690	352	652
1930	386,620	397	722
1940	369,360	453	954
1950	420,100	506	1,104
1960	417,720	495	1,437
1970	311,000[1]	485[10]	1,264
1980	296,030	475	1,174
1990	283,633	484	1,049
2000	226,500[10]	463[1]	861[10]
1991	276,100[1]	464	1,037
1992	268,508	464	1,014
1993	253,528	462	992
1994	249,716	463	990
1995	250,142	461	946
1996	248,935	463	935
1997	239,232	463	913
1998	235,613	463	907

TABLE 8.6.5 Roman Catholic Church in Northern Ireland[6]

	Mass Attendance[11]	Churches	Priests
1900	408,870	370[1]	589[1]
1910	408,650	370[1]	588[1]
1920	405,650	370[1]	587[1]
1930	404,290	370[1]	586[1]
1940	406,250	371[1]	585[1]
1950	447,890	409[1]	660[1]
1960	472,670	432[1]	859[1]
1970	487,460	445[1]	756
1980	502,400	459	707
1990	515,700	467	643
2000	521,500[1]	470[10]	554[10]
1991	514,800	468	640[1]
1992	515,600[1]	468	631[1]
1993	516,500	469	620[1]
1994	517,250	469	614[1]
1995[1]	518,000	470	600
1996[1]	519,000	470	587
1997[1]	520,000	470	580
1998[1]	520,000	470	578

TABLE 8.6.6
Total Other Catholic Churches[7]

	Mass Attendance	Churches	Priests
1900[1]	9,800	16	16
1910[1]	9,900	17	18
1920[1]	10,050	18	19
1930[1]	10,300	20	20
1940[1]	10,400	20	21
1950[1]	10,700	22	23
1960	12,680	40	35
1970	12,890	41	35
1980	12,149	33	33
1990	11,596	43	35
2000	11,780	38	35
1991	11,031	39	31
1992	10,822	38	31
1993	10,848	37	30
1994	10,839	37	31
1995	10,880	36	31
1996	10,827	36	33
1997	10,995	36	32
1998	11,094	35	31

[1] Estimate
[2] Taken as the full number of church buildings (1995, England 2,687, Wales 169) and half of the other buildings open for mass from 1980 onwards. Earlier figures based on the total for Great Britain
[3] Secular or Diocesan Priests and Regular Priests from the religious orders; all are male. Estimates for 1900–1960 made pro rata to totals for Great Britain
[4] Includes old English County of Herefordshire
[5] Parishes, 1980 onwards
[6] The Northern Ireland proportion is based on the following percentages of the four Dioceses that straddle the border: 95% of Derry, 75% of Armagh, 60% of Clogher and 5% of Kilmore, plus 100% of the two Dioceses within Northern Ireland: Down and Conner and Dromore
[7] Totals of Tables 8.6.1–9, plus estimate of other Catholic churches of 1,000 mass attendances ,15 churches, 10 priests 1960 and 1970 reduced to 500, 4 and 4 1980 onwards
[8] Figures for 1960 and 1970 are only available as a total for England and Wales. They have been split in the same proportions as for 1980 and 1990, 3.7% Wales, 96.3% England. Figures for 1940 to 1950 are taken as the same percentage of Catholic population as they were 1958 to 1962, namely 52.7%, and with an increasing percentage up to 75% in 1900
[9] The same proportions of mass attendance to population for 1900 to 1960 are used as for England and Wales
[10] Revised estimate
[11] Mass attendance taken as 89% of Catholic population, as given by Census of Population in 1980, the percentage coming from sample surveys. It was 85% in 1990. It has been taken as 95% in 1960 and all previous years

TABLE 8.7.1 Old Roman Catholic Church of Great Britian

	Mass Attendance	Churches	Priests[2]
1960[1]	350	6	8
1970[1]	350	6	7
1980	456	6	6
1990	70	4[1]	5[1]
2000[8]	40	4	6
1991[1]	66	4	6
1992[1]	62	4	6
1993[1]	58	4	6
1994[1]	54	4	6
1995[1]	50	4	6
1996[1]	47	4	6
1997[1]	45	4	6
1998[1]	44	4	6

TABLE 8.7.2 Croation Catholic Churches

	Mass Attendance	Churches	Priests[2]
1960	2,000[1]	1	1
1970	1,700[1]	1	1
1980	1,570	1	1
1990	1,206	1	1
2000[1]	2,000	1	3
1991	1,300[1]	1	1
1992	1,350[1]	1	1
1993	1,400[1]	1	1
1994	1,450[1]	1	1
1995	1,550[1]	1	1
1996	1,590	1	3
1997	1,750	1	3
1998	1,900	1	3

TABLE 8.7.3 German Catholic Church[3]

	Mass Attendance	Churches	Priests[2]
1960[1]	1,300	1	0
1970	1,300	1	0
1980	1,400	1	1
1990	1,400	1	1
2000[1]	1,400	1	1
1991	1,400	1	1
1992	1,400	1	1
1993	1,400	1	1
1994	1,400	1	1
1995	1,400	1	1
1996	1,400	1	1
1997	1,400	1	1
1998	1,400	1	1

TABLE 8.7.4 Hungarian Catholic Churches

	Mass Attendance	Churches	Priests[2]
1960[1]	4,500	2	1
1970	4,800[1]	2	1
1980	4,153	2	1
1990	4,350	2	2
2000[1]	4,100	2	2
1991	4,200	2	2
1992	4,000	2	2
1993	4,000	2	2
1994	4,000	2	2
1995	4,000[1]	2	2
1996	4,000[1]	2	2
1997	4,000[1]	2	2
1998	4,000[1]	2	2

TABLE 8.7.5 Latvian Catholic Church[5,6]

	Mass Attendance	Churches	Priests[2]
1960	500[1]	1	1
1970	500	1	1
1980	500	1	1
1990	500	1	1
2000[1]	500	1	1
1991	500	1	1
1992	500	1	1
1993	500	1	1
1994	500	1	1
1995	500	1	1
1996	500[1]	1	1
1997	500[1]	1	1
1998	500[1]	1	1

TABLE 8.7.6 Lithuanian St Casimir Catholic Church

	Mass Attendance	Churches	Priests[2]
1960[1]	200	1	1
1970	200[1]	1	1
1980	300	1	1
1990	320	1	1
2000[1]	420	1	2
1991	320	1	1
1992	320	1	1
1993	350	1	1
1994	350	1	1
1995	350	1	1
1996	350	1	1
1997	400	1	1
1998	400	1	1

TABLE 8.7.7 Slovene Catholic Churches

	Mass Attendance[4]	Churches	Priests[2]
1960[1]	230	1	1
1970	240[1]	1	1
1980	270	1	1
1990	400	9	1
2000[1]	760	9	1
1991	500[1]	9	1
1992	550[1]	9	1
1993	600[1]	9	1
1994	650[1]	9[1]	1
1995	700	9	1
1996[1]	720	9	1
1997[1]	730	9	1
1998[1]	740	9	1

TABLE 8.7.8 Tridentine Institute of our Lady of Walsingham[9]

	Mass Attendance	Churches	Priests[2]
1960	–	–	–
1970	–	–	–
1980	–	–	–
1990[1]	350	6	7
2000[1]	300[7]	4	4
1991[1]	345	6	6
1992[1]	340	5	6
1993[1]	340	5	5
1994[1]	335	5	5
1995	330[8]	5[8]	5
1996[1]	320	5	5
1997[1]	320	5	5
1998[1]	310	5	5

TABLE 8.7.9 Ukranian Catholic Churches

	Mass Attendance	Churches	Priests[2]
1960[1]	2,600	12	12[7]
1970	2,800[7]	13	13[7]
1980	3,000[1]	16	17
1990	2,500	14	12
2000[1]	1,750	11	11
1991[1]	2,400	14	12
1992[1]	2,300	14	12
1993[1]	2,200	13	12
1994[1]	2,100	13	13
1995	2,000	12	13
1996[1]	1,900	12	13
1997[1]	1,850	12	12
1998[1]	1,800	11	11

[1] Estimate
[2] All male
[3] St. Boniface
[4] Weekly mass attendance taken as about a third of the community
[5] Including Polish
[6] Latvian Communities in Bedford, Bradford, Corby, Coventry, Leicester, London and Nottingham have mass once every 2 months in Latvian; at other times they go to local Roman Catholic church
[7] Revised estimate
[8] Based on numbers in *Daily Telegraph* article 22/7/97
[9] Began 1982

TABLE 8.8
Other Roman Catholic Statistics

	Infant Baptisms			Confirmations[2]	Adult Conversions[4]	First Communions	Marriages, England and Wales				Marriages, elsewhere	
	England & Wales	Scotland	Percentage of births				Number		Percentage of		Scotland	N Ireland
							Both parties Catholic	Other marriages	All marriages	Religious marriages		
1900	Not available			Not available	N/a	N/a	10,267		4.0%	5.7%	3,322	2,131[8]
1905	Not available			Not available	N/a	N/a	10,812		4.1%	5.1%	3,376	2,324[8]
1910	59,700[1]		6.0%	Not available	2,930[1]	N/a	11,312		4.2%	5.3%	3,171	2,237[8]
1915	83,361		9.0%	Not available	9,367	N/a	14,400[1]		4.8%	6.3%	3,907	2,497[8]
1920	100,814		10.5%	Not available	12,621	N/a	15,500[1]		5.1%	6.9%	5,318	2,635
1925	84,851		10.4%	Not available	11,948	N/a	16,700[1]		5.6%	7.4%	3,865	2,231
1930	83,494		11.8%	Not available	11,980	N/a	19,700[1]		6.1%	8.3%	4,162	2,095
1935	82,871		12.2%	Not available	11,648	N/a	22,700[1]		6.6%	9.2%	5,069	2,413
1940	86,700[1]		13.4%	Not available	10,240[1]	N/a	25,750[1]		7.0%	10.1%	7,230	2,554
1945	90,033		12.8%	Not available	9,767	N/a	24,750[1]		6.7%	9.8%	6,025	3,027
1950	91,815	14,952	14.1%	Not available	11,010	N/a	29,500[1]		8.5%	12.1%	5,660	2,638
1955	97,753	16,784	13.7%	100,424[3]	13,291	N/a	22,527[3]	21,440[3]	12.6%	17.9%	6,734	3,032
1960	123,430	23,679	16.3%	80,602	14,803	N/a	23,217	23,263	13.4%	18.9%	6,789	3,312
1965	134,055	24,311	18.2%	69,672	10,308	90,776[6]	20,808	25,304	12.4%	18.2%	6,687	3,574
1970	108,187	16,995[1]	14.4%	71,956	7,341[5]	95,382	17,251	28,854	11.1%	18.3%	7,099	4,678
1975	75,815	14,467	13.9%	74,013	6,000[1]	84,877	12,321	22,876	9.2%	17.7%	6,003	4,759
1980	76,352	14,334	12.9%	54,803	5,850[1]	68,365	10,581	20,943	8.5%	16.9%	5,665	4,419
1985	74,857	13,238	12.1%	46,427	5,213	53,334	9,560	17,862	7.8%	15.6%	4,813	4,028
1990	69,364	12,632	10.7%	39,650	5,075	56,909	8,068	16,204	7.4%	13.9%	4,134	3,759
1995	74,848	11,214	12.2%	40,180	6,133	54,800[1]	5,691	11,084	5.9%	12.9%	2,948	3,278
2000[1]	62,500	9,360	10.7%	37,800	4,960	61,500	4,250	7,150	4.5%	13.0%	1,858	2,770
1991	77,352	12,309	11.7%	39,761	5,020	55,571	7,395	14,205	7.0%	13.3%	3,911	3,590
1992	78,386	12,099	12.0%	39,687	5,179	55,976	6,884	13,676	6.6%	13.2%	3,726	3,545
1993	75,529	11,570	11.8%	38,778	5,198	58,719	6,582	12,988	6.5%	13.3%	3,355	3,582
1994	75,236	11,284	11.9%	39,690[1]	6,205	58,200[1]	6,097[1]	11,928[1]	6.2%	12.9%	3,029	3,312
1995	74,848	11,214	12.2%	40,180	6,133	54,800[1]	5,691	11,084	5.9%	12.9%	2,948	3,278
1996	67,412[7]	10,718	11.0%	39,921	5,180	59,069	5,290	10,492	5.7%	13.5%	2,500	3,074
1997	67,384	10,344	11.1%	38,558	5,089	59,931	5,193	9,601	5.4%	13.6%	2,488	3,058

Source: Catholic Media Office; Archdioceses of Glasgow; Office for National Statistics: General Register Office for Scotland

[1] Estimate
[2] England and Wales only
[3] 1958 figure
[4] Great Britain
[5] 1968 figure
[6] 1969 figure
[7] There was a particularly large drop between 1995 and 1996.
[8] 1900–1915 pro rata to N Ireland proportion of all Catholic marriages in the whole of England 1920

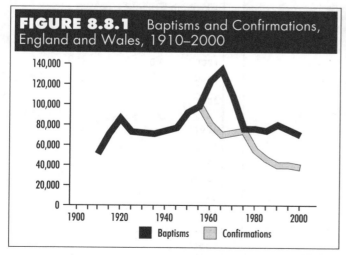

FIGURE 8.8.1 Baptisms and Confirmations, England and Wales, 1910–2000

■ Baptisms ▢ Confirmations

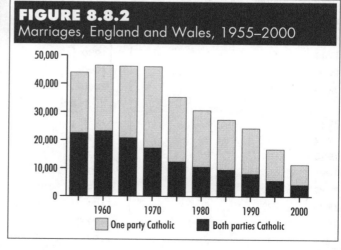

FIGURE 8.8.2 Marriages, England and Wales, 1955–2000

▢ One party Catholic ■ Both parties Catholic

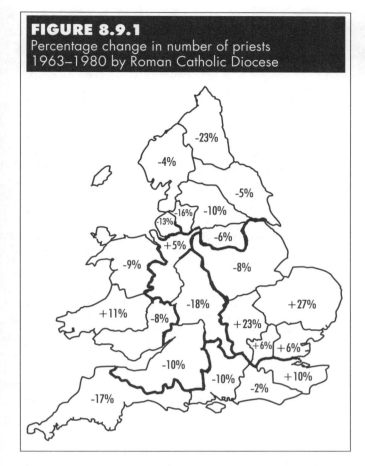

FIGURE 8.9.1
Percentage change in number of priests 1963–1980 by Roman Catholic Diocese

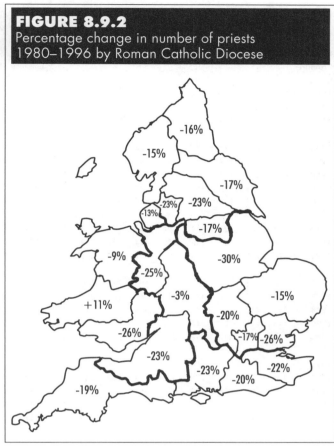

FIGURE 8.9.2
Percentage change in number of priests 1980–1996 by Roman Catholic Diocese

The number of priests has declined in the Roman Catholic church in England and Wales as it has in many other Western countries. In the 17 years between 1963 and 1980 the number dropped from 7,400 to 6,900, a fall of 7%. In the 16 years 1980 to 1996, the number dropped at almost three times that rate, 18%, down to 5,600 in 1996, with a further projected fall of 140, or 2%, by the year 2000. This change is graphed in **Figure 8.9.3**, and is shown Diocese by Diocese in **Figures 8.9.1** and

8.9.2, based on the data in **Table 8.10**.

Mass attendance has also declined but more drastically. Between 1963 and 1980 it dropped from 2.10 million to 1.64 million, a fall of 22%. Between 1980 and 1996 it has fallen a further 32% to 1.11 million (**Tables 8.8.2** and **8.8.3**).

In contrast the number of churches has increased from 3,005 in 1960 (the 1963 figure is not available) to 3,289 in 1996, an increase of 9%, as the church builds new

plant often in middle-class areas. These churches are often smaller churches, which can be staffed by one priest, akin to the Protestant model.

The Catholic population has in the same period increased quite substantially from 4.00 million in 1963 to 4.42 million in 1996, an increase of 11%. This means that whereas in 1963 there was 1 priest for every 540 Catholics, now there is 1 priest for every 790.

8

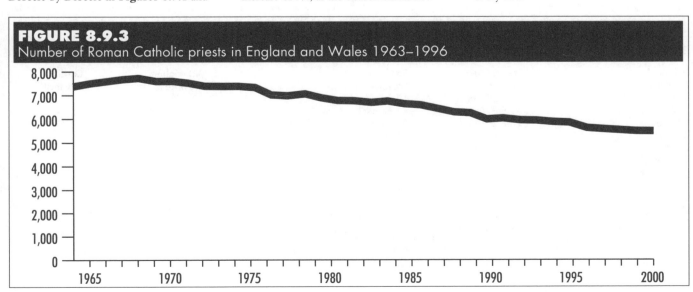

FIGURE 8.9.3
Number of Roman Catholic priests in England and Wales 1963–1996

TABLE 8.10
Roman Catholic Priests in England and Wales by Diocese

Province	Liverpool							Westminster					Southwark				Birmingham			Cardiff			TOTAL
Diocese	1	2	3	4	5	6	7	8	9	10	11	12	13	14	15	16	17	18	19	20	21	22	E & W
1963	432	229	124[4]	332[4]	609	703	278	293[4]	103[3]	200	887	146[3]	516[2]	350[2]	357	218	297	633	252	212	80[5]	124[5]	7,375
1964	443	230	125[4]	336[4]	609	713	286	292[4]	105[3]	208	892	150[3]	525[2]	356[2]	356	226	299	677	255	208	81[5]	124[5]	7,496
1965	447	239	126[4]	337[4]	605	713	282	293[4]	107[3]	217	919	151[3]	548[2]	371[2]	361	225	303	668	244	213	84[5]	130[5]	7,583
1966	429	248	122[4]	335[4]	598	723	287	278[4]	111[3]	216	935	157[3]	556	396	359	223	307	713	259	210	82[5]	127[5]	7,671
1967	432	252	124[4]	344[4]	595	743	286	278[4]	114[3]	209	948	161[3]	554	388	352	232	305	721	263	203	86[5]	134[5]	7,724
1968	436	253	121[4]	339[4]	598	718	299	268[4]	109[3]	198	953	156[3]	549	380	332	228	295	667	282	201	82[5]	128[5]	7,592
1969	430	249	126[4]	353[4]	570	723	301	277[4]	112[3]	214	935	158[3]	601	386	323	232	269	670	269	197	79[5]	122[5]	7,596
1970	428	245	121[4]	342[4]	577	696	295	264[4]	116[3]	211	920	165[3]	580	374	342	228	277	658	274	199	80[5]	123[5]	7,515
1973[6]	384	243	121[4]	333[4]	604	665	293	273[4]	115[3]	232	972	163[3]	577	347	334	193	287	599	279	190	71[5]	111[5]	7,386
1974	380	244	122[4]	342[4]	602	684	287	268[4]	112[3]	234	975	159[3]	565	351	333	198	282	581	279	194	73[5]	114[5]	7,379
1975	373	247	120[4]	338[4]	591	661	289	265[4]	115[3]	239	971	163[3]	578	357	347	200	278	592	287	188	71[5]	109[5]	7,379
1976	367	248	122[4]	344[4]	565	660	293	269[4]	113[3]	229	970	160[3]	593	355	343	196	268	584	283	193	69[5]	106[5]	7,330
1977	359	247	117[4]	333[4]	535	644	279	255[4]	110	232	883	157	556	347	326	197	263	545	271	192	65[5]	101[5]	7,014
1978	353	242	116[4]	388[4]	523	634	272	245[4]	118	218	888	168	573	348	317	183	274	545	266	196	63[5]	98[5]	6,978
1979	348	225	120[4]	344[4]	529	633	266	256[4]	130	225	933	170	573	354	324	183	274	548	266	196	63[5]	97[5]	7,057
1980	334	217	117	298	511	611	266	271	131	212	942	180	567	343	320	180	267	519	264	196	57[5]	87[5]	6,890
1981	332	203	118	304	503	611	260	255	118	210	888	180	549	344	351	184	268	510	258	187	56[5]	87[5]	6,776
1982	340	208	106	299	490	583	265	250	125	214	937	182	573	332	320	188	246	522	258	186	55[5]	86[5]	6,765
1983	340	208	103	299	478	563	258	250	125	212	926	182	573	331	320	178	246	526	239	186	55[5]	86[5]	6,694
1984	340	209	107	299	492	599	258	243	125	214	926	181	565	332	355	179	246	527	241	186	53[5]	83[5]	6,750
1985	357	216	106	293	475	578	253	243	119	214	907	172	564	328	302	177	250	530	230	186	53[5]	83[5]	6,636
1986	354	218	109	300	467	566	248	234	124	210	898	166	578	312	303	172	249	517	232	191	56[5]	86[5]	6,590
1987	335	211	104	293	469	531	240	244	120	210	872	173	566	311	298	169	249	484	232	186	54[5]	83[5]	6,434
1988	335	171	100	282	445	527	230	243	120	210	892	159	554	306	289	163	249	478	226	147	63	97	6,286
1989	309	171	104	282	472	512	238	243	120	192	889	159	541	306	284	163	249	478	226	158	61	92	6,249
1990	309	210	100	225	455	515	228	224	112	188	839	154	518	295	282	164	242	426	226	163	59	94	6,028
1991	312	210	103	265	454	509	232	246	114	188	849	147	510	286	273	162	237	410	221	153	50	95	6,026
1992	316	195	92	262	440	509	232	224	113	187	841	123	505	308	266	151	235	424	218	155	64	89	5,949
1993	300	195	98	262	453	503	229	224	113	188	828	149	498	311	266	143	228	419	221	154	63	89	5,934
1994	290	197	103	243	407	497	226	225	109	176	828	138	498	318	259	152	224	477	216	144	62	85	5,874
1995	370	198	98	263	403	493	246	218	111	170	814	136	465	289	260	193	219	475	194	147	61	85	5,848
1996	280	181	97	228	391	531	225	189	111	156	786	144	442	276	246	145	205	501	199	146	63	79	5,621
of which																							
Active	243	155	90	189	343	472	200	171	102	140	717	131	394	250	223	128	182	447	184	139	61	76	5,037
Retired	37	26	7	39	48	59	25	18	9	16	69	13	48	26	23	17	23	54	15	7	2	3	584
% retired	13	14	7	17	12	11	11	10	8	10	9	9	11	9	9	12	11	11	8	5	3	4	10
2000[1]	273	171	97	246	347	509	234	181	109	143	766	132	410	287	229	160	188	549	179	133	68	71	5,482

Liverpool Province
1 Hexham and Newcastle
2 Middlesbrough
3 Hallam
4 Leeds
5 Salford
6 Liverpool (incl Isle of Man)
7 Lancaster

Westminster Province
8 Nottingham
9 East Anglia
10 Brentwood
11 Westminster
12 Northampton

Southwark Province
13 Southwark
14 Arundel & Brighton
15 Portsmouth (incl Channel Islands)
16 Plymouth (incl Scilly Islands)

Birmingham Province
17 Clifton
18 Birmingham
19 Shrewsbury

Cardiff Province
20 Cardiff
21 Menevia
22 Wrexham

[1] Estimate assuming the trends from 1990 to 1996 continue.
[2] The Diocese of Arundel and Brighton was formed in 1965 by a division of the Diocese of Southwark. The allocation of priests prior to that date are pro rata to the actual proportions afterwards.
[3] The Diocese of East Anglia was formed in 1976 by a division of the Diocese of Northampton. The allocation of priests prior to that date are pro rata to the actual proportions afterwards.
[4] The Diocese of Hallam was formed in 1980 by a division of the Diocese of Leeds and Nottingham. The allocation of priests prior to that date are pro rata to the actual proportions afterwards.
[5] The Diocese of Wrexham was formed in 1987 by a division of the Diocese of Minevia. The allocation of priests prior to that date are pro rata to the actual proportions afterwards.
[6] There are no figures for 1971 and 1972 as the *Catholic Directory for England and Wales* was not published in these years.

	Membership	Churches	Priests
TABLE 8.11.1 Total Orthodox Churches			
1900	–	–	–
1910	–	–	–
1920	–	–	–
1930	10,000	9	7
1940	20,000	21	13
1950	80,650	33	26
1960	107,240	92	77
1970	159,170	124	108
1980	171,735	154	135
1990	184,745	207	156
2000	207,930	256	197
1991	186,444	208	158
1992	188,525	212	158
1993	190,767	215	159
1994	192,996	221	163
1995	195,895	234	174
1996	198,487	238	184
1997	199,733	243	190
1998	202,236	248	192[12]

	Membership	Churches	Priests[3]
TABLE 8.11.2 Patriarchate of Antioch: Vicariate of Western Europe[2]			
1900	–	–	–
1910	–	–	–
1920	–	–	–
1930	–	–	–
1940	–	–	–
1950	–	–	–
1960	–	–	–
1970	–	–	–
1980	240	0	0
1990	200	5[1]	2[1]
2000[9]	500	16	14
1991	200	6[1]	3[1]
1992	200	7[1]	4[1]
1993	200	8[1]	5[1]
1994	200	9[1]	6[1]
1995	200	10	7
1996[1]	300	10	10
1997[1]	300	11	11
1998[1]	500	14	13

	Membership[10]	Churches	Priests[3]
TABLE 8.11.3 Patriarchate of Bulgaria: Diocese of Western Europe			
1900	–	–	–
1910	–	–	–
1920	–	–	–
1930	–	–	–
1940	–	–	–
1950	–	–	–
1960[1]	10	1	0
1970	30[1]	1	0
1980	30	1	0
1990	30	1	1
2000	82[4]	1	1
1991	50	1	1
1992	50	1	1
1993	65	1	1
1994	70	1	1
1995	80[4]	1	1
1996[1]	80	1	1
1997[1]	80	1	1
1998[1]	80	1	1

	Membership	Churches	Priests[3]
TABLE 8.11.4 Byelorussian Autocephalous Orthodox[7]			
1900	–	–	–
1910	–	–	–
1920	–	–	–
1930	–	–	–
1940	–	–	–
1950[1]	150	2	1
1960[1]	350	5	1
1970[1]	550	7	2
1980	450	7	2
1990	260	4	2
2000[1]	160	3	2
1991	260	3[1]	2
1992	255	3	2
1993[1]	254	3	2
1994	252[1]	4	2
1995[1]	250	4	2
1996[1]	220	4	2
1997[1]	200	4	2
1998[1]	180	3	2

	Membership[6]	Churches	Priests[3]
TABLE 8.11.5 Patriarchate of Constantinople Greek Orthodox[5]			
1900	–	–	–
1910	–		
1920	–		
1930	10,000	9[1]	7[1]
1940	20,000	21[1]	13[1]
1950	80,000	29[1]	22[1]
1960	100,000	40[1]	34[1]
1970	150,000[1]	53	48[9]
1980	160,000	61	57[9]
1990	170,000[9]	90	68[9]
2000[9]	190,000	103	82
1991[1]	173,000	91	70[1]
1992	174,000[9]	92	71[1]
1993	176,000[9]	92	72[1]
1994	178,000[9]	93	73[1]
1995	180,000[9]	93	73[1]
1996[1]	182,000	96	76
1997[1]	183,000	99	79
1998[1]	185,000	102	80[11]

	Membership	Churches	Priests[3]
TABLE 8.11.6 Patriarchate of Constantinople: Ukranian Diocese in Great Britain[8]			
1900	–	–	–
1910	–	–	–
1920	–	–	–
1930	–	–	–
1940	–	–	–
1950[1]	500	2	3
1960[1]	600	2	3
1970[1]	800	3	4
1980[1]	1,000	4	5
1990[1]	1,500	6	7
2000[1]	2,000	9	10
1991[1]	1,550	6	7
1992[1]	1,600	7	8
1993[1]	1,700	7	8
1994[9]	1,750	8	9
1995[9]	1,800	8	9
1996[1]	1,850	9	10
1997[1]	1,900	9	10
1998[1]	2,000	9	10

[1] Estimate
[2] Made up of the Antiochian Arab Orthodox Church and the British Orthodox Deanery
[3] All male
[4] Patriarchate's own estimate
[5] The full title is "The Œcumenical Patriarchate of Constantinople, Archdiocese of Thyateira and Great Britain". It is a jurisdiction composed 99% of Greek and Cypriot members in the British Isles. It began in 1922, membership taken as approximately two-thirds community
[6] Figures proportional to number of churches
[7] Began 1948
[8] Formerly listed as Byelorussian Orthodox
[9] Revised figures
[10] Active membership taken as one-tenth of community
[11] 1999 Figure is 81 priests
[12] The 1999 total for all priests in UK Patriarchates is 167. The others are from those not in communion with the Orthodox Church

	Membership	Churches	Priests[4]
TABLE 8.12.1 Patriarchate of Constantinople Latvian Orthodox Church			
1960[1]	200	1	1
1970	200	1	1
1980	200[3]	1	1
1990	200[1]	1	1[1]
2000[1]	200	1	1
1991	200[1]	1	1[1]
1992	200[1]	1	1[1]
1993	200[1]	1	1[1]
1994	200[1]	1	1[1]
1995	200[3]	1	1[1]
1996[1]	200	1	1
1997[1]	200	1	1
1998[1]	200	1	1

	Membership	Churches	Priests[4]
TABLE 8.12.2 Polish Orthodox Church[11]			
1960[1]	800	1	1
1970[1]	700	1	1
1980	500	1	1
1990[1]	400	1	1
2000	–	–	–
1991	–	–	–
1992	–	–	–
1993	–	–	–
1994	–	–	–
1995	–	–	–
1996	–	–	–
1997	–	–	–
1998	–	–	–

	Membership[10]	Churches	Priests[4]
TABLE 8.12.3 Patriarchate of Romania			
1960[1]	15	1	1
1970	20	1[1]	1[1]
1980	20	1	1
1990	35	1	1
2000[3]	68	2	1
1991	40[1]	1	1
1992	50	1	1
1993	53	1	1
1994	56	1	1
1995	60	2	2
1996[1]	62	2	2
1997[1]	64	2	2
1998[1]	66	2	1

	Membership	Churches	Priests[4]
TABLE 8.12.4 Patriarchate of Moscow[12] Russian Orthodox			
1960[1]	400	6	10
1970[1]	800	11	17
1980	1,500	20	17
1990	2,200[1]	24	18
2000[1]	2,620	30	15
1991[1]	2,220	25	18
1992[1]	2,240	25	18
1993[1]	2,260	26	18
1994[1]	2,280	27	18
1995	2,300[1]	28	19
1996[1]	2,350	28	18
1997[1]	2,400	28	17
1998	2,500	29	15

	Membership	Churches	Priests[4]
TABLE 8.12.5 Russian Orthodox Church Outside Russia[5]			
1960[1]	1,500	6	4
1970	2,000	8	4
1980	1,300	8	5
1990	1,000	6	4[3]
2000[3]	1,000	7	8
1991	1,000[1]	6[1]	4
1992	1,000	7	3
1993	1,000[1]	6	2
1994	1,000[1]	5	2
1995	1,000[1]	5	4
1996	950	5	6
1997	900	5	7
1998[13]	900	5	8

	Membership[7]	Churches	Priests[4]
TABLE 8.12.6 Patriarchate of Serbia[6]			
1960[1]	500	5	3
1970	1,000	10	6
1980	2,000	15	8
1990	3,000	25[8]	9
2000[1]	3,760	20[3]	9[3]
1991[1]	3,000	24	9
1992[1]	3,000	23	9
1993	3,100	23	9
1994	3,200[1]	22[3]	9[3]
1995	3,300	22[3]	9[3]
1996[1]	3,400	21	9
1997[1]	3,500	21	9
1998	3,600	20	9

	Membership[7]	Churches	Priests[4]
TABLE 8.12.7 Ukranian Autocephalous Patriarchate[14]			
1960[1]	900	10	6
1970[1]	1,000	12	8
1980	1,100	13[1]	9
1990	1,250	15	10
2000[1]	1,600	21	10
1991[1]	1,250	15	10
1992	1,250	16	9
1993[1]	1,250	18	9
1994	1,250[1]	20	10
1995	1,500[1]	20	9
1996[1]	1,500	20	9
1997[1]	1,550	20	9
1998[1]	1,550	20	10

	Membership	Churches	Priests[4]
TABLE 8.12.8 Ukranian Orthodox Church Kiev Patriarchate in Great Britain and Ireland[2,14]			
1960	–	–	–
1970	–		
1980	–		
1990	–		
2000[1]	100[3]	7	3
1991	–	–	–
1992	–	–	–
1993	–	–	–
1994	–	–	–
1995	205	7	3
1996[1]	200	7	3
1997[1]	150	7	3
1998[1]	100	7	3

	Membership	Churches	Priests[4]
TABLE 8.12.9 Armenian Church (Monophysite)[9]			
1960[1]	450	3	5
1970[1]	450	3	5
1980	450	3	5
1990	1,000	3	4
2000[1]	1,500	3	3
1991[1]	1,000	3	4
1992	1,000	3	4
1993[1]	1,000	3	4
1994[1]	1,000	3	4
1995	1,200	3	3
1996[1]	1,300	3	3
1997[1]	1,350	3	3
1998[1]	1,400	3	3

[1] Estimate
[2] Began 1995
[3] Revised figures
[4] All male
[5] Diocese of Berlin and Great Britain
[6] Diocese of Western Europe
[7] Active members taken as 25% of the community
[8] Meeting in six churches
[9] Formerly known as Oriental Orthodox
[10] Active members taken as 10% of the community
[11] Merged with the Greek Orthodox Patriarchate in 1991
[12] Diocese of Sourozh
[13] 1999 figures are 1,000, 7 and 8 respectively
[14] Not in communion with any Orthodox Church

TABLE 8.13.1 — Coptic Church[8] (Monophysite)

	Membership	Churches	Priests[7]
1960[1]	1,500	7	2
1970	1,500	7[1]	2[1]
1980	1,500	7	2
1990	1,500	6	2
2000[1]	1,500	6	3
1991[1]	1,500	6	2
1992[1]	1,500	6	2
1993[1]	1,500	6	2
1994[1]	1,500[1]	6[1]	3
1995	1,500[1]	6	3
1996[1]	1,500	6	3
1997[1]	1,500	6	3
1998[1]	1,500	6	3

TABLE 8.13.2 — Eritrean[3] Church[5] (Monophysite)

	Membership	Churches	Priests[7]
1960	–	–	–
1970	–	–	–
1980	–	–	–
1990	–	–	–
2000[1]	200	1	1
1991	–	–	–
1992	–	–	–
1993	–	–	–
1994	–	–	–
1995	–	–	–
1996	200	1	1
1997[1]	200	1	1
1998[1]	200	1	1

TABLE 8.13.3 — Ethiopian Church[9] (Monophysite)

	Membership	Churches	Priests[7]
1960	–	–	–
1970	–	–	–
1980	400	2	2
1990	600	5	5
2000[1]	700	6	6
1991[1]	600	5	5
1992[1]	600	5	5
1993[1]	600	5	5
1994[1]	600	5	5
1995	600[1]	5	5
1996[1]	600	5	5
1997[1]	650	6	6
1998[1]	650	6	6

TABLE 8.13.4 — Indian (Syrian) Church[10] (Monophysite)

	Membership	Churches	Priests[7]
1960	–	–	–
1970	–	–	–
1980	100[1]	1	2[1]
1990	400	4	3
2000[16]	500	4	3
1991[1]	400	4	3
1992[1]	400	4	3
1993[1]	400	4	3
1994[1]	450	4	3[1]
1995	500[1]	4	3
1996[1]	500	4	3
1997[1]	500	4	3
1998[1]	500	4	3

TABLE 8.13.5 — Assyrian Church of the East[4] (Nestorian)

	Membership[6]	Churches	Priests[7]
1960	–	–	–
1970	–	–	–
1980	800	1	6
1990[1]	1,000	1	3[1]
2000[1]	1,100	1	2
1991[1]	1,000	1	3
1992[1]	1,000	1	2
1993[1]	1,000	1	2
1994	1,000[1]	1[1]	1
1995	1,000	1	2
1996[1]	1,000	1	2
1997[1]	1,000	1	2
1998[1]	1,000	1	2

TABLE 8.13.6 — Ancient Othodox[2,11]

	Membership	Meetings[12]	Priests[7]
1960	–	–	–
1970	100[1]	1[1]	0
1980[16]	110	2[1]	1
1990[16]	120	2	1
2000[16]	130	2	1
1991[16]	120	2	1
1992[16]	120	2	1
1993[16]	120	2	1
1994[16]	120	2	1
1995[16]	125	2	1
1996[1]	125	2	1
1997[1]	125	2	1
1998[1]	125	2	1

TABLE 8.13.7 — British Orthodox Church[11,14]

	Membership[13]	Churches	Priests[7]
1960[1]	15	4	6
1970[16]	20	5[1]	8
1980[16]	30	5	10
1990[16]	40	6	13
2000[16]	80	7	13
1991[1]	42	7	13[16]
1992[1]	45	7	13[16]
1993[1]	47	7	13[16]
1994[1]	48	7[16]	13[16]
1995	50	7[16]	13[16]
1996[1]	55	7	13
1997[1]	59	7[1]	13
1998[1]	70	7[1]	13[1]

TABLE 8.13.8 — Celtic Orthodox Church of Brittany[11,15]

	Membership	Churches	Priests[7]
1960	–	–	–
1970	–	–	–
1980	–	–	–
1990	–	–	–
2000[1]	100	5	8
1991	–	–	–
1992	–	–	–
1993	–	–	–
1994	–	–	–
1995	60	4	4
1996[1]	70	4	5
1997[1]	80	4	6
1998[1]	90	4	7

TABLE 8.13.9 — Coptic Orthodox Church of Scotland[3,11]

	Membership[13]	Churches	Priests[7]
1960	–	–	–
1970	–	–	–
1980[3,16]	5	1	0
1990[16]	10	1	1
2000[16]	30	1	1
1991	12[1]	1	1
1992	15[1]	1	1
1993	18[1]	1	1
1994	20[1]	1	1
1995[16]	25	1	1
1996[1]	25	1	1
1997[1]	25	1	1
1998	25	1	1

[1] Estimate
[2] Began 1970
[3] Began 1977
[4] Diocese of Europe; also known as "Nestorian" by outsiders, and "Church of the East" by its own adherents. Began in UK 1977
[5] Began 1996
[6] Taken as one third of the community
[7] All male
[8] Excludes British Orthodox Church and Coptic Orthodox Church of Scotland which is listed separately
[9] Began 1974
[10] Non-Chalcedonian; began 1975
[11] Not in communion with any Orthodox Church
[12] Meeting in church halls, meeting rooms, public halls, private houses etc.
[13] Active membership taken as one-tenth of community
[14] Full title is The Coptic Orthodox Patriarchate (The Apostolic See of St Mark): The British Orthodox Church of the British Isles. Previously known as the Orthodox Church of the British Isles, it was received into canonical union with the Coptic Orthodox Patriarchate of Alexandria, in 1994
[15] Previously part of the Orthodox Church of the British Isles, joined the Celtic Orthodox Church of Brittany in 1995
[16] Revised estimate

TABLE 8.14.1
Total Presbyterian Church

	Membership	Churches	Ministers
1900	1,649,119	5,923	5,632
1910	1,765,904	5,988	5,594
1920	1,815,768	6,117	5,159
1930	1,828,638	5,857	4,956
1940	1.822,320	5,399	4,605
1950	1,796,393	5,090	4,182
1960	1,813,584	4,822	3,761
1970	1,559,137	4,409	2,764
1980	1,437,474	5,920[2]	3,633[2]
1990	1,213,540	5,492	3,122
2000[1]	979,072	5,074	2,641
1991	1,193,626	5,471	3,075
1992	1,171,116	5,454	3,025
1993	1,140,930	5,365	3,079
1994	1,119,333	5,283	3,030
1995	1,088,098	5,284	2,746
1996	1,073,422	5,250	2,696
1997	1,048,488	5,185	2,685
1998	1,030,690	5,152	2,632

TABLE 8.14.2
Associated Presbyterian Churches[3]

	Membership	Churches	Ministers
1900	–	–	–
1910	–	–	–
1920	–	–	–
1930	–	–	–
1940	–	–	–
1950	–	–	–
1960	–	–	–
1970	–	–	–
1980	–	–	–
1990	1,250[1]	33	13
2000[1]	1,200	26	12
1991[1]	1,250	33	13
1992	1,250[1]	32[1]	12
1993[1]	1,250	31	13
1994	1,250	30	15
1995	1,250[4]	30	15
1996[1]	1,240	29	14
1997[1]	1,230	28	13
1998[1]	1,220	27	12

TABLE 8.14.3
Total Church of Scotland[5]

	Membership	Churches	Ministers
1900	662,000	1,828	1,834[1]
1910	714,000	1,643	1,781[1]
1920	739,000	1,704	1,581[1]
1930[6]	1,271,000	2,920	2,889[1]
1940	1,278,000	2,483	2,612[1]
1950	1,271,000	2,340	2,353[1]
1960	1,301,000	2,093	2,094[1]
1970	1,154,211	2,119	1,754
1980	953,933	1,852	1,536
1990	786,787	1,685	1,258
2000[7]	609,450	1,571	1,133
1991	770,217	1,672	1,246[1]
1992	752,719	1,668	1,230[1]
1993	732,963	1,639	1,215
1994	715,571	1,619	1,217
1995	688,552	1,616	1,207
1996	680,082	1,606	1,194
1997	660,954	1,604	1,167
1998[1]	648,930	1,601	1,150[8]

TABLE 8.14.4
Evangelical Presbyterian Church in England and Wales[3]

	Membership	Churches	Ministers
1900	–	–	–
1910	–	–	–
1920	–	–	–
1930	–	–	–
1940	–	–	–
1950	–	–	–
1960	–	–	–
1970	–	–	–
1980	–	–	–
1990	60	3	3
2000[1]	100	6	3
1991[1]	70	3	3
1992[1]	80	4	3
1993[1]	80	4	3
1994[1]	80	4	3
1995	80[9]	4	3
1996	80	4	3
1997	80	5	2
1998	95	5	2

TABLE 8.14.5
Evangelical Presbyterian Church in Ireland[8]

	Membership[10]	Churches	Ministers[11]
1900	–	–	–
1910	–	–	–
1920	–	–	–
1930	200[1]	8	5
1940	200[1]	9	5
1950	300[1]	9	6
1960	350[1]	10	7
1970	396	9	6
1980	432	10	8
1990	430	11	10
2000[7]	580	13	11
1991	430	11	10
1992	428	11[1]	10
1993	438	11[1]	10
1994	476	12[1]	9
1995	500	12	10
1996	512	12	10
1997	525	12	10
1998	532	12	12

TABLE 8.14.6
Percentage Church of Scotland is of total Presbyterian Churches

	Membership	Churches	Ministers
1900	40%	31%	33%
1910	40%	27%	32%
1920	41%	28%	31%
1930	70%	50%	58%
1940	70%	46%	57%
1950	71%	46%	56%
1960	72%	43%	56%
1970	66%	33%	43%
1980	66%	31%	42%
1990	65%	31%	40%
2000[1]	62%	31%	43%

[1] Estimate
[2] This increase is due to the formation of the United Reformed Church in 1972
[3] Began 1989
[4] Based on the 1994 Scottish Church Census
[5] Excluding congregations in England or Ireland but including the Scottish congregations of the United Reformed Church
[6] See Footnote 6 on Page 8.16
[7] Revised estimate
[8] Of whom an estimated 145 are female
[9] 180 in attendance
[10] Excludes adherents
[11] All male

	Membership	Churches	Ministers
TABLE 8.15.1 Free Church of Scotland			
1900	15,740[2]	153[1]	70[1]
1910[1]	30,400	289	130
1920[1]	32,480	290	134
1930[1]	26,620	238	110
1940[1]	22,100	237	95
1950[1]	22,720	237	95
1960[1]	23,050	236	95
1970	22,493	230[1]	95
1980	21,270	224	90
1990	20,000[3]	200	115
2000[4]	15,600	162	92
1991	20,232	195	112
1992[1]	20,000	192	110
1993[1]	19,250	189	107
1994	18,500[3]	182[3]	105
1995[1]	18,400	182	103
1996[1]	17,700	177	100
1997[1]	17,200	173	99
1998[1]	16,700	170	97

	Membership[5]	Churches	Ministers[6]
TABLE 8.15.2 Free Presbyterian Church of Scotland			
1900	6,800	75	11
1910	6,500	72	20
1920	6,200	69	14
1930	6,100	67	23
1940	5,900	65	25
1950	5,800	64	22
1960	5,700	63	28
1970	6,112	68	32
1980	6,280	69	35
1990	4,020[3]	69	22
2000[4]	3,250	64	15
1991[1]	3,900	69	20[1]
1992[1]	3,800	69	19
1993[1]	3,700	69	18
1994	3,650[3]	69	17
1995[1]	3,600	69	16
1996	3,500	70	16
1997	3,450	66	16
1998	3,400	63	17

	Membership	Churches	Ministers[6]
TABLE 8.15.3 Free Presbyterian Church of Ulster[7]			
1900	–	–	–
1910	–	–	–
1920	–	–	–
1930	–	–	–
1940	–	–	–
1950	–	–	–
1960	7,400	27	20
1970	9,400[1]	35[1]	25[1]
1980	9,621[8]	35	35
1990	12,550	60	50
2000[1]	15,520	72	67
1991[1]	12,363	58	50
1992	12,500	58	50
1993	12,700[1]	58	52
1994	13,050	59	54
1995	14,100	66	54
1996[1]	14,200	66	60
1997[1]	14,400	67	61
1998[1]	14,500	67	62

	Membership	Churches	Ministers
TABLE 8.15.4 Non-Subscribing Presbyterian Church of Ireland			
1900	6,798	36	34
1910	7,383	36	30
1920	6,720	35	32
1930	5,718	34	29
1940	5,768	34	20
1950	3,943	34	25
1960	4,594	34	21
1970	5,527	34	17
1980	3,993[8]	34	11
1990	3,815	34	17
2000[1]	3,540[4]	34	13[4]
1991	3,877	34	17
1992	3,933	34	17
1993	3,654	34	15
1994	3,685	34	15
1995	3,640[9]	34	13
1996	3,619	34	13
1997	3,677	34	14
1998	3,650[1]	34	15[10]

	Membership[11]	Churches	Ministers
TABLE 8.15.5 Presbyterian Church in Ireland (Northern Ireland)			
1900	226,986	470[1]	406[1]
1910	226,113	470[1]	404[1]
1920[1]	227,010	470	406
1930[1]	228,683	470	409
1940[1]	230,361	470	412
1950	234,800	470[1]	420[1]
1960	236,456	470[1]	423[1]
1970	232,226	466	415
1980	197,094	461	397
1990	195,576[12]	456	398
2000[1]	193,960	453	360
1991	195,397	456	396
1992	195,228	457	394
1993	195,054	456	400
1994	194,900	456	400
1995	194,718	455	360[13]
1996	194,300	455	360
1997	194,100	455	360
1998	193,990	455	360[14]

	Communicants	Churches	Ministers[15]
TABLE 8.15.6 Presbyterian Church of England[16]			
1900	76,071	326	206
1910	86,828	354	224
1920	83,710	352	222
1930	84,146	353	223
1940	76,815	333	210
1950	69,676	333	210
1960	71,329	318	201
1970[17]	59,473	306[1]	193
1980	–	–	–
1990	–	–	–
2000[1]	–	–	–
1991	–	–	–
1992	–	–	–
1993	–	–	–
1994	–	–	–
1995	–	–	–
1996	–	–	–
1997	–	–	–
1998	–	–	–

[1] Estimate
[2] The continuing body of those not joining the United Free Church of Scotland, estimated as 3.93 (the 1970 proportion) times the number of communicants
[3] Based on the 1994 Scottish Church Census
[4] Revised estimate
[5] Estimated 1900 to 1960 pro rata on average membership per church in 1970 and 1980

[6] All male
[7] Began 1951
[8] 1981 Northern Ireland Census of Population figure
[9] Excluding 552 children
[10] Of whom 1 was female
[11] Active membership taken as 58% of Community figures given in successive Northern Ireland Censuses of Population

[12] Total for all Ireland 276,781 members, 564 churches and 438 ministers
[13] Of whom 13 were female
[14] Of whom 14 were female
[15] Taken as 63% of the number of churches
[16] Became part of the United Reformed Church in 1972
[17] Included in 1972 URC figure

	Membership	Churches	Ministers
TABLE 8.16.1 Presbyterian Church of Wales			
1900	158,000	1,353	1,231
1910	184,000	1,528	1,310
1920	187,000	1,664	1,156
1930	186,000	1,601	1,149[1]
1940	176,000	1,595	1,075
1950	160,000	1,439	913
1960	137,000	1,410	759
1970	108,064	1,300	346
1980	82,653	1,169	220
1990	61,616	1,025	137
2000[1]	41,200	867	100
1991[1]	60,715	1,018	132
1992	59,815	1,012	127
1993	55,690	977	148
1994	54,500[1]	960	135
1995	51,720	939	119
1996	49,356	936	114
1997	47,733	894	116
1998	46,063[1]	880[1]	106

	Membership[2]	Churches	Ministers[5]
TABLE 8.16.2 Reformed Presbyterian Church of Ireland			
1900[1]	3,020	42	28
1910[1]	3,010	42	28
1920[1]	3,020	43	28
1930[1]	3,045	43	28
1940[1]	3,065	43	28
1950[1]	3,125	43	28
1960[1]	3,150	43	28
1970	3,090	43	28
1980	2,800[1]	41	29
1990	2,500	36	32
2000[3]	2,050	33	25
1991	2,500[1]	36	32
1992	2,450[1]	36	30[1]
1993	2,400[1]	36	28[1]
1994	2,350[1]	36	27[1]
1995	2,305	34	25
1996[1]	2,250	34	25
1997[1]	2,200	34	25
1998[1]	2,150	34	25

	Membership[4]	Churches	Ministers[5]
TABLE 8.16.3 Reformed Presbyterian Church of Scotland			
1900[1]	704	10	9
1910[1]	670	9	8
1920[1]	628	8	7
1930[1]	549	7	7
1940[1]	537	7	6
1950[1]	473	6	6
1960[1]	398	5	5
1970	370[5]	5	5
1980	330	5	5
1990	190	5	4
2000[1]	72	4	3
1991[1]	160	5	4
1992	130	5[1]	4[1]
1993	120	5[1]	4[1]
1994	120	5[1]	4[1]
1995	100	4	4
1996[1]	97	4	4
1997[1]	94	4	4
1998	90	4	3

	Membership	Churches	Ministers
TABLE 8.16.4 United Free Church of Scotland[6]			
1900	493,000[7]	1,630	1,803
1910	507,000[7]	1,545	1,659
1920	530,000[7]	1,482	1,579
1930	16,577	116	84
1940	23,574	123	107
1950	24,556	115	104
1960	23,157	113	80
1970	17,248	100	41
1980	11,751	84	39
1990	8,076	75	47
2000[3]	5,300	69	39
1991	7,823	73	45
1992	7,457	73	46
1993	7,094	72	46
1994	6,901	72	44
1995	6,551	71	43[8]
1996	6,294	71	42
1997	5,927	70	42
1998	5,705	70	41

	Membership	Churches	Ministers
TABLE 8.16.5 United Reformed Church[9]			
1900	–	–	–
1910	–	–	–
1920	–	–	–
1930	–	–	–
1940	–	–	–
1950	–	–	–
1960	–	–	–
1970[10]	192,163[1]	2,080	1,314
1980	147,337	1,936	1,228
1990	116,670	1,800	1,016
2000[1]	87,250	1,700	669
1991	114,692	1,808	995
1992	111,326	1,803	973
1993	106,537	1,784	1,020
1994[1]	104,300	1,745	985
1995	102,582	1,768	774[11]
1996	100,192	1,752	741
1997	96,917	1,739	756
1998	93,665	1,730	730

[1] Estimate
[2] Taken as 0.76% (the 1970 percentage) of the Presbyterian community 1900 to 1960
[3] Revised estimate
[4] Membership for 1900 to 1960 has been estimated as 68% (the 1970 percentage) of the communicant figures
[5] All male
[6] The United Presbyterian Church of Scotland merged with the majority of the Free Church of Scotland in 1900 to form the United Free Church of Scotland. The United Free Church of Scotland merged with the Church of Scotland in 1929. Subsequent figures for the United Free Church are for the continuing body
[7] Communicants not members
[8] Of whom 3 were female
[9] The United Reformed Church (URC) in 1972 was a merger of the Presbyterian Church of England and the large majority of the Congregational Church of England and Wales, the figures for the continuing body of which are given in Table 9.6.5. On 26/9/81 the Re-formed Association of Churches of Christ joined the URC. Estimated 1980 figures for the Re-formed Association were 2,317 members, 39 churches and 22 ministers, which are included with the Fellowship of Christ figures in Table 9.8.4. See Footnote 8 on Page 9.8.
[10] 1972 figures
[11] Of whom an estimated 120 were female

TABLE 8.17
Christian and religious membership in thousands in the UK 1900–2000

Year	Anglican	Roman Catholic	Presby-terian	Methodist	Baptist	Others[2]	Total Christian		Other Religions	Total all Religions	
							Number	% Pop[3]		Number	% Pop[3]
1900	3,241	1,912[1]	1,649	849	360	655	**8,664**	33%	164	**8,828**	34%
1905	3,336	1,965[1]	1,739	908	417	726	**9,091**	33%	171	**8,262**	34%
1910	3,480	1,995[1]	1,766	918	412	733	**9,704**	33%	179	**9,883**	34%
1915	3,871	2,064[1]	1,783	900	403	761	**9,782**	32%	183	**9,965**	33%
1920	3,825	2,107[1]	1,816	877	399	779	**9,803**	31%	194	**9,997**	31%
1925	4,120	2,176[1]	1,852	911	404	825	**10,288**	31%	202	**10,490**	31%
1930	4,166	2,190[1]	1,829	918	400	854	**10,357**	29%	209	**10,566**	30%
1935	4,124	2,205[1]	1,840	894	391	838	**10,292**	29%	227	**10,519**	29%
1940	3,911	2,232[1]	1,822	862	376	814	**10,017**	27%	244	**10,261**	28%
1945	3,670	2,247[1]	1,790	815	352	808	**9,682**	26%	258	**9,940**	26%
1950	3,444	2,432[1]	1,796	809	334	799	**9,614**	25%	270	**9,884**	25%
1955	3,397	2,567	1,827	798	320	809	**9,773**	25%	375	**10,148**	26%
1960	3,341	2,845[1]	1,814	789	317	812	**9,918**	24%	421	**10,389**	26%
1965	3,174	2,793[1]	1,791	761	290	839	**9,648**	23%	578	**10,228**	25%
1970	2,987	2,746	1,751	673	272	843	**9,272**	22%	732	**10,004**	24%
1975	2,298	2,525	1,718	602	238	679	**8,060**	19%	885	**8,945**	21%
1980	2,180	2,455	1,437	540	239	678	**7,529**	17%	1,088	**8,617**	19%
1985	1,896	2,281	1,322	497	242	705	**6,943**	15%	1,300	**8,243**	18%
1990	1,728	2,198	1,214	478	230	776	**6,624**	14%	1,527	**8,151**	17%
1995	1,785	1,914	1,088	434	223	841	**6,285**	13%	1,800	**8,085**	17%
2000[1]	1,657	1,722	979	387	209	908	**5,862**	12%	1,962	**7,824**	17%

[1] Estimate
[2] Independent, Congregational, Orthodox, Pentecostal, New and Other Churches. Given in detail in Table 8.18
[3] Adult population, including Northern Ireland population prior to 1921.

Table 8.17 gives the detailed membership for the various main Christian churches in the UK, with the smaller denominations (given in **Table 8.18**) amalgamated together to give the total Christian membership across the 20th Century. It also puts active membership of other religions in for the same period to give the total active religious community over the same time frame, and puts both sets of numbers, given in bold in **Table 8.17**, as percentages of the population.

The *Anglican* figures are the Electoral Roll of the Church of England, with analogous figures for the Episcopal churches in other parts of the UK; these peaked in the late 1920s and 1930s. At its highest point in 1930 12%, or 1 in 8, of the adult population of the UK was on the Electoral Roll of the Church of England or otherwise involved in an Anglican church. These figures are estimated to be declining less fast in the 1990s than in the 1980s.

The *Roman Catholic* figures represent mass attendance which reached a high in the UK in the 1960s and early 1970s, but has been declining since then, more rapidly in the 1990s than in the 1980s. At the highest point in 1960 7% of the adult population in this country, 1 in 14, was attending mass in a Catholic church.

The *Presbyterian* figures largely represent the fortunes of the Church of Scotland which were high in the late 1920s and 1930s, at the same time as the Anglican churches, partly because of the amalgamation of the Church of Scotland with the United Free Church of Scotland in 1929. At their high point in 1925 membership of a Presbyterian church was 6% of the entire adult population in the UK, equivalent to well over half the population (about 57%) in Scotland.

The *Methodist* figures represent the total figures for the different Methodist streams which had their highest point immediately before the first World War in 1910 and subsequently in 1930. In 1910 3% of the adult population of the UK was a member of a Methodist church, 1 person in every 32.

The *Baptist* membership peaked just prior to that of the Methodists in 1905 and was equivalent then of 1½% of the population belonging to a Baptist church, 1 person in every 65.

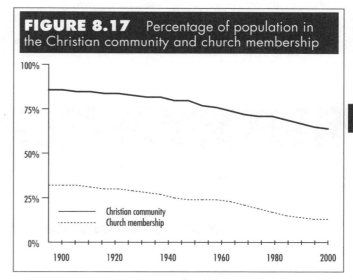

FIGURE 8.17 Percentage of population in the Christian community and church membership

The fortunes of the *smaller denominations* peaked in 1930 and in 1965 and then began to fall until the rise of the Orthodox, Pentecostal and New Churches which impacted the church scene in the UK in the 1980s and saw especially rapid increases in the 1990s. The detail of the smaller denominations is given in **Table 8.18**.

The growth of *other religions* has taken place steadily across the century but has seen particularly great increases towards the latter part of this century. It took 60 years before there were half a million active members of other religions in the UK, but only a further 20 years to get the next half a million, and then a further 10 years to get the next half a million, a rate of growth which has continued in the 1990s.

Figure 8.17 repeats the graph of the Christian community given in **Figure 2.7** and adds underneath it the percentage of the population who are church members. It can be readily seen that the two lines go in tandem. The gap between them is in fact one of the largest gaps for any country across the world, suggesting that we have proportionally more nominal Christians in the UK than almost any other country.

For a similar analysis of church *community* see Page 2.4.

TABLE 8.18.1
Other churches membership in thousands in the UK 1900–2000

Year	Christian Brethren	Congrega-tional	Other Indepen-dent	Orthodox	Salvation Army	Pente-costal	Religious Society of Friends	New Churches[2]	All other denomin-ations	Total Number
1900	79	439	15	0	85	0	18	0	19	**655**
1905	84	499	17	0	89	0	20	0	17	**726**
1910	87	497	18	0	93	0	21	0	17	**733**
1915	91	498	18	0	115	1	20	0	18	**761**
1920	95	495	19	0	131	1	20	0	18	**779**
1925	99	500	22	0	156	12	20	0	16	**825**
1930	102	492	25	10	170	18	20	0	17	**854**
1935	105	477	26	15	150	27	20	0	18	**838**
1940	107	457	27	20	127	36	21	0	19	**814**
1945	106	428	29	51	114	36	22	0	22	**808**
1950	105	392	32	81	106	37	22	0	24	**799**
1955	103	379	34	94	105	45	22	0	27	**809**
1960	101	358	35	107	104	53	22	0	32	**812**
1965	96	334	38	133	100	68	22	0	48	**839**
1970	91	293	39	159	87	86	22	0	66	**843**
1975	91	120[1]	39	170	82	94	20	5	58	**679**
1980	90	108	39	172	72	118	19	10	50	**678**
1985	89	97	44	176	65	129	19	35	51	**705**
1990	88	90	45	185	60	154	19	77	62	**776**
1995	82	75	46	196	57	198	18	104	65	**841**
2000	81	65	49	208	52	233	17	137	66	**908**

[1] This decline is partly due to a change of definition. In 1972 the United Reformed Church (URC) began which included many of the Congregational Churches. The URC is included in Table 8.17 under Presbyterian; this figure is for the continuing Congregational Churches.
[2] Also known as House Churches

FIGURE 8.18
UK Membership of various denominations 1900 and 2000

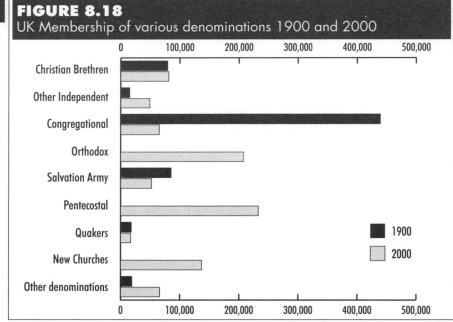

TABLE 8.18.2
Number of Denominations[1] listed in the *UK Christian Handbook* and *Religious Trends*

1977	97
1987	140
1992	208
1994	222
1996	243
1998	247

[1] A denomination is taken as "a Christian organisation uniting a number of local congregations" (John Adair *The Becoming Church*, SPCK, 1997)

FREE CHURCH STATISTICS

Contents

See Notes and Definitions on Page 0.6

9

Source:
Individual denominations and previous editions UK Christian Handbook

	Membership	Churches	Ministers
TABLE 9.2.1 Total			
1900	359,855	4,424	2,910
1910	412,165	5,048	3,195
1920	398,811	4,990	3,118
1930	400,005	5,107	3,102
1940	376,347	5,104	3,069
1950	334,476	5,045	2,872
1960	317,301	4,882	3,005
1970	292,976	3,588	2,459
1980	238,805	3,317	2,414
1990	230,377	3,438	2,615
2000	209,234	3,430	2,774
1991	231,386	3,412	2,755
1992	228,502	3,406	2,814
1993	227,878	3,437	2,883
1994	225,227	3,430	2,866
1995	223,151	3,446	2,860
1996	220,980	3,438	2,817
1997	216,920	3,430	2,815
1998	213,612	3,418	2,777

	Membership	Churches[9]	Ministers[9]
TABLE 9.2.2 Baptist Union of Wales			
1900	106,566	880[1]	255[1]
1910	128,038	1,050[1]	305[1]
1920	125,068	1,040[1]	300[1]
1930	125,704	1,040[1]	302[1]
1940	115,833	995[1]	288[1]
1950	105,922	950[1]	275[1]
1960	93,114	820[1]	238[1]
1970	72,097	692[1]	222[1]
1980	37,770	638	209
1990	26,763	560	117
2000[12]	18,940	501	101
1991[1]	26,146	553	119
1992	25,384	544	121
1993	25,204	549	124
1994	24,178	537	118
1995	23,450	535	118
1996	22,695	524	111
1997	21,224	519	116
1998	20,507	511	102[6]

	Membership	Churches	Ministers
TABLE 9.2.3 Baptist Union of Scotland			
1900	16,899	166	146
1910	20,997	207	181
1920	21,783	214	188
1930	22,841	224	197
1940	23,024	226	198
1950	19,704	194	170
1960	20,067	197	172
1970	16,074	167[1]	146
1980	15,153	159	140
1990	16,212	166	137
2000[12]	14,550	170	104
1991	16,177	166	162
1992	15,287	169	163
1993	15,230	169	169
1994	15,178	170	168
1995	15,781	172	139
1996	15,634	172	133
1997	15,279	172	134
1998	15,050	171	119

	Membership[5]	Membership[5]	Churches	Ministers
TABLE 9.2.4 Baptist Union of Great Britain[2,3]				
1900	239,114	210,300	2,710	1,963
1910	266,224	234,200	3,047	2,098
1920	254,908	224,200	3,019	2,046
1930	253,614	223,100	3,122	2,017
1940	239,241	210,400	3,203	2,026[11]
1950	207,101	182,200	3,277	1,907
1960	198,597	174,700	3,215	2,049
1970	196,301	173,350	2,085	1,555
1980	170,338	153,976	1,872	1,386
1990	159,945	149,262	2,000	1,585
2000[12]	140,050	133,700	1,985	1,692
1991	160,143	150,591	1,972	1,688
1992	158,207	148,911	1,967	1,736
1993	156,939	148,131	1,987	1,779
1994	154,916	146,240	1,988	1,760
1995	152,603	144,159	1,991	1,764
1996	150,289	142,371	1,990	1,728
1997	147,089	139,650	1,982	1,714[4]
1998[1]	144,000	137,000	1,974	1,700

	Membership[7]	Membership[7]	Churches	Ministers
TABLE 9.2.5 Baptist Union of Ireland				
1900	2,696	2,530	31	26
1910	2,935	2,750	33	28
1920	2,785	2,620	32	27
1930	3,649	3,420	41	34
1940	3,743	3,510	42	36
1950	4,476	4,210	51	43
1960	5,582	5,240	63	54
1970	7,186	6,730	81	61
1980	8,060	7,545[8]	88	81
1990	8,500	7,956	101	98
2000[12]	8,300	7,770	113	106
1991	8,563	8,015	102[1]	97[1]
1992	8,602	8,052	103	95
1993	8,695	8,039	103	98
1994	8,770	7,952	104	100
1995	8,445	7,905	109	102[10]
1996[1]	8,430	7,890	109	102
1997[1]	8,410	7,875	109	102
1998[1]	8,400	7,860	109	102

[1] Estimate
[2] Excluding churches which belong to the Baptist Union of Wales or the Baptist Union of Scotland
[3] The Baptist Union of Great Britain and Ireland became the Baptist Union of Great Britain on 26th April 1988
[4] Of whom 120 were female
[5] Churches in Wales may be members of either the Baptist Union of Wales (BUW) or the Baptist Union of Great Britain (BUGB) or both. If they are members of both their membership figures will be double-counted. An estimate of the membership of the churches only belonging to the BUGB is given in the *second* membership column, and it is this column which is used for the overall totals. Prior to 1990 these different figures are not readily available. A detailed church by church count made on the 1975 figures showed that 14.5% of the BUGB churches were also in membership with BUW. Similar figures for 1980, given in the table, showed 16,362 in joint membership (9.6%). Figures for earlier years have been reduced based on the average of these two percentages
[6] Of whom 2 were female
[7] The Baptist Union of Ireland includes the whole of Ireland, and the first membership column gives the total membership for the Union. The *second* membership column estimates the proportion in Northern Ireland which is used for the overall totals. In 1995 the figure was known exactly, but earlier years are estimated, mostly pro rata
[8] Taken as 46% of the community figure given in the Northern Ireland Census in 1981
[9] Pro-rata to membership 1900 to 1960
[10] Of whom 5 were female
[11] Estimated; in 1938 there were 2,008 and in 1939 2,035
[12] Revised figure

	Membership[7]	Churches[8]	Ministers[8]
TABLE 9.3.1 Strict and Particular Baptists[10]			
1900	22,500	600	490
1910	25,000	670	550
1920	24,000	645	525
1930	23,800	640	520
1940	22,500	600	490
1950	19,500	520	430
1960	18,700	500	410
1970[1]	16,300	438	357
1975	13,300[1]	424	410
1990	–	–	–
2000	–	–	–
1991	–	–	–
1992	–	–	–
1993	–	–	–
1994	–	–	–
1995	–	–	–
1996	–	–	–
1997	–	–	–
1998	–	–	–

	Membership[2]	Churches	Ministers[4]
TABLE 9.3.2 Gospel Standard Strict Baptist			
1900	–	–	–
1910	–	–	–
1920	–	–	–
1930	–	–	–
1940	–	–	–
1950	–	–	–
1960	–	–	–
1970	–	–	–
1980	5,600	148	77
1990	6,500	156	45
2000[1]	6,000	140[9]	50
1991[1]	6,400	152	45
1992	6,300[1]	148[1]	45
1993[1]	6,300	144	47
1994	6,300	140	40
1995	6,000	140	50
1996[1]	6,000	140	50
1997[1]	6,000	140	50
1998[1]	6,000	140	50

	Membership[2]	Churches	Ministers[4]
TABLE 9.3.3 Grace Baptist Assembly			
1900	–	–	–
1910	–	–	–
1920	–	–	–
1930	–	–	–
1940	–	–	–
1950	–	–	–
1960	–	–	–
1970	–	–	–
1980	8,800	257	364
1990	10,000[1]	260	416[1]
2000[1]	10,875	270	447[9]
1991[1]	10,000	265	421
1992[1]	10,000	266	427
1993[1]	10,000	267	432
1994	10,000[1]	267	439
1995	10,270	267[3]	440
1996[1]	10,400	267	440
1997[1]	10,500	268	440
1998[1]	10,600	269	440

	Membership	Churches	Ministers[5]
TABLE 9.3.4 Biblical Ministries Worldwide			
1900	–	–	–
1910	–	–	–
1920	–	–	–
1930	–	–	–
1940	–	–	–
1950	–	–	–
1960	–	–	–
1970	–	–	–
1980	35[1]	2	1
1990	63[1]	4	5
2000[1]	99	6	11
1991[1]	67	4	6
1992[1]	70	4	6
1993[1]	74	5	7
1994[1]	79	5	8
1995	86	5	9
1996[1]	90	5	9
1997[1]	92	5	10
1998[1]	95	5	10

	Membership[7]	Churches[8]	Ministers[4,8]
TABLE 9.3.5 Old Baptist Union			
1900	1,060	37	30
1910	1,180	41	33
1920	1,140	40	32
1930	1,140	40	32
1940	1,080	38	31
1950	940	33	27
1960	780	27	22
1970	625	25	18[1]
1980	720	22	20
1990	481	13	9
2000[1]	500[9]	15	8
1991[1]	490	13	9
1992	498	13	8
1993[1]	500	13	9
1994	500[1]	13[1]	10
1995	500	15	9
1996[1]	500	15	9
1997[1]	500	15	9
1998[1]	500	15	9

	Membership[7]	Churches	Ministers
TABLE 9.3.6 Other Baptist Churches[6]			
1900	–	–	–
1910	–	–	–
1920	–	–	–
1930	–	–	–
1940	–	–	–
1950[1]	2,000	20	20
1960[1]	4,700	60	60
1970[1]	7,800	100	100
1980	9,206	131[1]	136
1990	13,140	178	203
2000[1]	16,800	230	255
1991[1]	13,500	185	208
1992[1]	14,000	192	213
1993[1]	14,400	200	218
1994[1]	14,800	206	223
1995[1]	15,000	212	229
1996[1]	15,400	216	235
1997[1]	15,800	220	240
1998[1]	16,000	224	245

[1] Estimate
[2] Figures pro rata to the number of churches
[3] Based on a count from the Grace Baptist Directory
[4] All male
[5] Full-time missionary workers
[6] These figures include non-Baptist Union churches, some of which are or were listed in the Baptist Union of Great Britain Directory
[7] Estimated pro rata to Baptist Union of Great Britain 1900 to 1960
[8] Pro-rata to membership 1900 to 1960
[9] Revised figure
[10] This denomination became two in 1977 – the Gospel Standard Strict Baptist and the Grace Baptist Assemblies. Precise figures for churches and ministers are known for 1975, as given, but other figures have had to be estimated.

TABLE 9.4.1
Other Baptist Union Statistics

	Lay Preachers	Sunday School Scholars	Marriages[4]
1900	5,436	525,136	5,370
1905	5,436	577,936	5,600
1910	5,564	572,686	5,685
1915	5,136	544,919	5,835
1920	5,026	508,759	5,840
1925	5,366	521,219	5,895
1930	5,333	477,929	5,945
1935	5,272	431,592	6,000
1940	5,065	372,174	6,050
1945	4,442[1]	292,567[1]	5,550
1950	4,424	317,688	5,050
1955	4,490	319,701	5,860
1960	4,382	259,742	5,950
1965	4,220	189,683	5,725
1970	4,219	194,126[2]	5,305
1975	2,116	175,700[1]	4,885
1980	1,788	156,372	4,740
1985	1,659	140,400[1]	4,320
1990	1,445	123,590	3,698
1995	1,389	139,342[3]	2,771[5]
2000[1]	1,140	130,800	1,925

TABLE 9.4.2 Baptisms for England and Wales, Isle of Man and Channel Islands 1945–1997

1945	5,566	**1960**	6,729	**1975**	5,066	**1990**	5,544
1946	5,591	**1961**	6,614	**1976**	5,141	**1991**	5,442
1947	6,108	**1962**	7,029	**1977**	5,541	**1992**	5,202
1948	5,968	**1963**	6,694	**1978**	5,655	**1993**	4,828
1949	6,597	**1964**	6,204	**1979**	5,573	**1994**	4,662
1950	6,633	**1965**	5,300	**1980**	6,231	**1995**	3,965
1951	6,980	**1966**	5,307	**1981**	5,748	**1996**	4,029
1952	7,103	**1967**	5,533	**1982**	6,407	**1997**	4,062
1953	6,946	**1968**	5,937	**1983**	6,424		
1954	7,089	**1969**	5,214	**1984**	8,340		
1955	9,130	**1970**	4,450	**1985**	7,940		
1956	8,827	**1971**	4,767	**1986**	7,386		
1957	7,101	**1972**	5,056	**1987**	6,076		
1958	6,469	**1973**	5,263	**1988**	5,726		
1959	6,254	**1974**	5,161	**1989**	6,124		

Source: Revd Darrell Jackson, Mission Adviser, Baptist Union of Great Britain, Didcot

Footnotes for Table 9.4.1

[1] Estimate
[2] From 1970 these numbers are the number of children in Baptist Union churches and not the number of Sunday School Scholars *per se*. In 1970 the number of the latter were 190,315.

[3] 138,826 in 1996 and 135,701 in 1997
[4] All Baptist marriages, estimated from Government figures for various years 1919–1996
[5] 2,564 in 1996

FIGURE 9.4
Baptisms in Baptist Churches in England and Wales 1945 to 1997

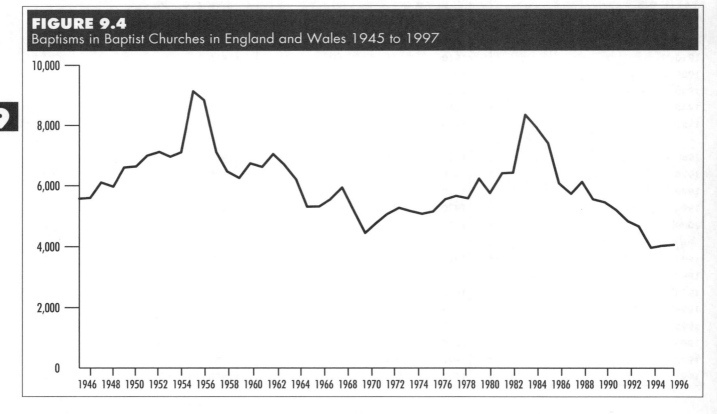

The two peaks in this graph coincide with the two major visits Billy Graham has made to this country – at Haringey in 1954/55 and for Mission Britain 1984/85.

TABLE 9.5.1
Total Brethren Assemblies

	Membership	Churches	Full-time workers
1900	78,900	1,826	0
1910	86,700	1,950	0
1920	94,500	2,065	0
1930	102,300	2,409	0
1940	106,700	2,392	15
1950	104,500	2,337	50
1960	100,595	2,404	94
1970	90,910	2,408	163
1980	90,200	2,229	180
1990	88,230	2,187	223
2000	80,941	1,970	290
1991	87,271	2,139	228
1992	85,945	2,108	239
1993	84,669	2,082	249
1994	83,343	2,050	260
1995	81,926	2,021	270
1996	81,697	2,011	273
1997	81,478	2,002	277
1998	81,357	1,992	277

TABLE 9.5.2
Christian Brethren

	Membership	Churches	Full-time workers
1900	44,000	1,236[1]	0[1]
1910	51,000	1,340[1]	0[1]
1920	58,000	1,440[1]	0[1]
1930	65,000	1,739[1]	0[1]
1940	69,000	1,727[1]	15[1]
1950	67,000	1,677[1]	50[1]
1960	68,000	1,736[1]	80[1]
1970[1]	71,000	1,750	130
1980	72,450	1,610[4]	130[1]
1990	69,165	1,551[4]	165[1]
2000[1]	61,225	1,340	228
1991[1]	68,000	1,510	170
1992	66,750	1,480[1]	180[1]
1993[1]	65,500	1,455	190
1994[1]	64,200	1,425	200
1995	62,865[5]	1,397[5]	210
1996[1]	62,500	1,385	213
1997[1]	62,200	1,374	216
1998[1]	61,900	1,363	220

TABLE 9.5.3
Church of God Brethren

	Membership	Churches	Full-time workers
1960[1]	3,000	112	0
1970[1]	2,875	104	5
1980[1]	2,725	95	10
1990[1]	2,575	86	16
2000[1]	2,425	76	20
1991[1]	2,560	85	16
1992[1]	2,545	84	17
1993[1]	2,530	83	17
1994[1]	2,515	82	18
1995	2,500	80	18
1996[1]	2,485	80	18
1997[1]	2,470	79	19
1998[1]	2,455	78	19

TABLE 9.5.4
Kelly Brethren

	Membership	Churches	Full-time workers[8]
1960[1]	95	4	–
1970[1]	85	4	–
1980[1]	75	4	–
1990[1]	65	4	–
2000[1]	55	4	–
1991[1]	64	4	–
1992[1]	63	4	–
1993[1]	62	4	–
1994[1]	61	4	–
1995	60	4	–
1996[1]	59	4	–
1997[1]	58	4	–
1998[1]	57	4	–

TABLE 9.5.5
Plymouth Brethren No. 4

	Membership[9]	Churches	Full-time workers[6]
1900[1]	30,000	400	0
1910[1]	30,000	400	0
1920[1]	30,000	400	0
1930[1]	30,000	400	0
1940[1]	30,000	400	0
1950[1]	30,000	400	0
1960[1]	25,000	400	10
1970[1]	12,500	400	20
1980	10,500	370	30[1]
1990[1]	12,018	400	30
2000[1]	12,900	420	30
1991[1]	12,250	400	30
1992[1]	12,200	400	30
1993[1]	12,200	400	30
1994[1]	12,200	400	30
1995[1]	12,144	405	30
1996[1]	12,300	408	30
1997[1]	12,400	412	30
1998[1]	12,600	415	30

TABLE 9.5.6
Recruited Brethren[10]

	Membership	Churches	Ministers
1900	4,900	190	0
1910	5,700	210	0
1920	6,500	225	0
1930	7,300	270	0
1940	7,700	265	0
1950	7,500	260	0
1960[1]	4,000	125	4
1970[1]	4,000	125	8
1980[1]	4,000	125	10
1990	4,000	115	12[1]
2000[1]	4,000	107	12
1991[1]	4,000	115	12
1992[1]	4,000	115	12
1993[1]	4,000	115	12
1994[1]	4,000	115	12
1995	4,000	115	12[9]
1996[1]	4,000	111	12
1997[1]	4,000	110	12
1998[1]	4,000	109	12

TABLE 9.5.7
Tunbridge Wells Brethren

	Membership	Churches	Full-time workers
1960[1]	500	27	–
1970[1]	450	25	–
1980[1]	450	25	–
1990	407	25	–
2000[1]	336	23	–
1991[1]	397	25	–
1992[1]	387	25	–
1993[1]	377	25	–
1994[1]	367	24	–
1995	357	23	–
1996[1]	353	23	–
1997[1]	350	23	–
1998	345	23	–

[1] Estimate
[2] *Religious Trends* No 1 1998/1999 gave historical information about the various branches of the Brethren which has not changed. It is not therefore repeated in this volume. Please instead refer to No 1/Page 9.4 , Footnote 6 for the Church of God Brethren, Footnotes 7 and 8 for the Plymouth Brethren No 4, Footnotes 10 and 12 for the Reunited Brethren, Footnote 14 for the Tunbridge Wells Brethren and Footnote 15 for the Kelly Brethren
[3] Of whom an estimated 7% would be female, a proportion estimated by Dr Harold Rowdon
[4] Based on a count in the *Assembly Address Book*, Christian Year Publications (1980 and 1990), and increased by 10% as an estimate for those not listed
[5] Based on estimates by Dr Harold Rowdon on an assumed average congregation size of 45
[6] All male
[7] Of whom 1 was female
[8] No full-time workers are appointed
[9] Figures for 1900 to 1960 very roughly estimated by Dr Neil Summerton
[10] Estimating early numbers for the various Brethren groups with any accuracy is virtually impossible, so the figures shown in this Table combine estimates for the years 1900 to 1950 for the Church of God, Kelly and Tunbridge Wells Brethren

9

TABLE 9.6.1 — Total Congregational Churches

	Membership	Churches	Ministers
1900	439,018	4,903	3,115
1910	496,705	4,939	3,135
1920	494,868	4.751	3,036
1930	492,234	4,700	2,887
1940	456,619	4,643	2,805
1950	391,898	4,305	2,617
1960	358,160	4,121	2,400
1970	292,836	4,132	2,297
1980	107,779	1,275	473
1990	89,785	1,169	371
2000	65,290	1,124	338
1991	84,857	1,165	365
1992	81,580	1,149	365
1993	76,880	1,126	355
1994	76,627	1,143	365
1995	75,240	1,138	329
1996	72,431	1,134	332
1997	69,494	1,132	334
1998	69,236	1,131	336

TABLE 9.6.2 — Congregational Union of England and Wales: England[2]

	Membership	Churches[4]	Ministers
1900	257,435	3,515[1]	2,386[1]
1910	287,952	3,529[1]	2,396[1]
1920	290,203[1]	3,401[1]	2,319[1]
1930	286,716	3,363[1]	2,197[1]
1940	256,804[1]	3,314[1]	2,128[1]
1950	209,590	3,074[1]	1,994
1960	193,341	2,941	1,829[1]
1970	151,212	2,853[1]	1,684[1]
1980	–	–	–
1990	–	–	–
2000	–	–	–
1991	–	–	–
1992	–	–	–
1993	–	–	–
1994	–	–	–
1995	–	–	–
1996	–	–	–
1997	–	–	–
1998	–	–	–

TABLE 9.6.3 — Congregational Union of England and Wales: Wales[2]

	Membership	Churches[4]	Ministers
1900	21,248	226[1]	85[1]
1910	22,693	228[1]	85[1]
1920	24,717[1]	219[1]	87[1]
1930	26,781	219[1]	85[1]
1940	23,556	213[1]	82[1]
1950	20,078	197[1]	73[1]
1960	21,242	189	70[1]
1970	16,590	179	65[1]
1980	–	–	–
1990	–	–	–
2000	–	–	–
1991	–	–	–
1992	–	–	–
1993	–	–	–
1994	–	–	–
1995	–	–	–
1996	–	–	–
1997	–	–	–
1998	–	–	–

TABLE 9.6.4 — Union of Welsh Independents[2]

	Membership	Churches[4]	Ministers
1900	126,265	977[1]	495[1]
1910	146,000[1]	994[1]	498[1]
1920	139,000	946[1]	475[1]
1930	136,000	931[1]	452[1]
1940	133,000	929[1]	444[1]
1950	124,000	862[1]	410[1]
1960	106,000	825[1]	392[1]
1970	88,932	761	362
1980	67,501	718	200
1990	53,027	632	131
2000[9]	35,440	576	118
1991	50,612	630	126
1992	49,850	615	130
1993	48,450	610	121
1994	46,924	605	118
1995	45,885[12]	600[8,12]	121
1996	42,757	594	121
1997	39,874	590	121
1998	39,561	587	121[11]

TABLE 9.6.5 — Congregational Federation[2]

	Membership	Churches	Ministers
1900	–	–	–
1910	–	–	–
1920	–	–	–
1930	–	–	–
1940	–	–	–
1950	–	–	–
1960	–	–	–
1970	7,968[1]	196	57
1980	10,139	293	97
1990	9,275	286	68
2000[9]	12,000	325	80
1991[1]	9,275	285	67
1992	9,278	284	65
1993	9,284	284	67
1994[6]	11,923	313	90
1995	11,922	316	69[8]
1996[1]	11,935	318	71
1997[1]	11,950	320	73
1998[1]	11,970	322	75

Footnotes for Pages 9.6 and 9.7

[1] Estimate
[2] The Congregational Union of England and Wales and the Presbyterian Church of England merged in 1972 to form the United Reformed Church. Table 9.6.2 gives the membership of the churches in England, Table 9.6.3 gives the English speaking members of the churches in Wales, and Table 9.6.4 gives the Welsh speaking members who formed the Union of Welsh Independents (UWI) in 1927. The UWI did not join the 1972 merger. After the merger the Congregational Federation became the continuing body for those not joining the union, although some churches joined the Evangelical Fellowship of Congregational Churches which began in 1967
[3] 1972 figure, not included in the total
[4] Figures relate to the year after that shown
[5] Formed in 1994; previously the Congregational Union of Scotland
[6] Between 1993 and 1994 25 congregations left the Scottish Congregational Church and were accepted into membership of the Congregational Federation in October 1994
[7] Of whom 1 was female
[8] Of whom 12 were female
[9] Revised figure
[10] All male
[11] Of whom 5 were female
[12] Official membership stood at 42,442 based on 555 churches who are in full membership, but a further 45 churches are in associate membership
[13] 36% of the community figure of 8,265 in the 1981 N Ireland Census
[14] 36% of the community figure of 8,176 in the 1991 N Ireland Census
[15] Estimated at 98% of total for all Ireland
[16] Membership for 1900 to 1940 pro rata on 1950 to Congregational Union of England and Wales: England

	Membership	Churches	Ministers[10]
TABLE 9.7.1 Evangelical Fellowship of Congregational Churches[2]			
1900	–	–	–
1910	–	–	–
1920	–	–	–
1930	–	–	–
1940	–	–	–
1950	–	–	–
1960	–	–	–
1972[3]	5,500	105[1]	42[1]
1980	6,176	141	69
1990	6,200	132	65
2000[9]	5,500[9]	134	70
1991[1]	6,200	134	70
1992	6,200	133	73
1993	6,100	134	73[1]
1994	6,100	135	73[1]
1995	5,900	134	70
1996[1]	5,800	134	70
1997[1]	5,700	134	70
1998[1]	5,600	134	70

	Membership	Churches	Ministers
TABLE 9.7.2 Scottish Congregational Church[5]			
1900	30,170	158[1]	120[1]
1910	35,660	159[1]	125[1]
1920	36,498	156[1]	123[1]
1930	38,337	158[1]	123[1]
1940	39,309	159[1]	123[1]
1950	35,030	147[1]	114[1]
1960	34,537	141[1]	104[1]
1970	25,284	119	105
1980	20,988	99	86
1990	18,340	94	81
2000[1]	9,550	63	40
1991	15,850[1]	92	75
1992	13,362	91	70
1993	10,166	72	62
1994	8,810[6]	64	53
1995	8,673	62	39[7]
1996	9,089	62[1]	40[1]
1997[1]	9,130	62	40
1998[1]	9,275	62	40

	Membership[16]	Churches	Ministers[10]
TABLE 9.7.3 Congregational Union of Ireland			
1900	3,900	27[1]	29[1]
1910	4,400	29[1]	31[1]
1920	4,500	29[1]	32[1]
1930	4,400	29[1]	30[1]
1940	3,950	28[1]	28[1]
1950	3,200	25	26
1960[1]	3,040	25	25
1970	2,850[15]	24	24
1980	2,975[13]	24	21
1990	2,943[14]	25	26
2000[9]	2,800	26	30
1991	2,920[9]	24	27
1992	2,890[1]	26	27
1993	2,880[1]	26	32
1994	2,870[1]	26	31[1]
1995[1]	2,860	26	30
1996[1]	2,850	26	30
1997[1]	2,840	26	30
1998[1]	2,830	26	30

For Footnotes see Page 9.6

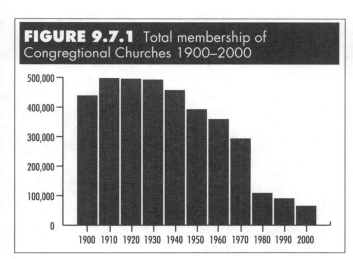

FIGURE 9.7.1 Total membership of Congregational Churches 1900–2000

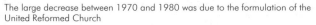

The large decrease between 1970 and 1980 was due to the formulation of the United Reformed Church

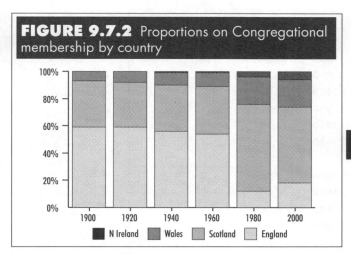

FIGURE 9.7.2 Proportions on Congregational membership by country

Legend: ■ N Ireland ▨ Wales ▥ Scotland ▢ England

9

TABLE 9.8.1
Total All Independent Churches[12]

	Membership	Churches	Ministers
1900	532,797	7,015	3,249
1910	601,507	7,231	3,290
1920	608,829	7,184	3,196
1930	619,660	7,588	3,127
1940	590,547	7,568	3,113
1950	528,079	7,287	3,046
1960	493,506	7,181	2,987
1970	422,544	7,280	3,044
1980	236,706	4,294	1,274
1990	222,918	4,101	1,242
2000	195,498	3,889	1,274
1991	217,237	4,051	1,239
1992	212,991	4,005	1,252
1993	207,286	3,955	1,251
1994	206,053	3,940	1,275
1995	203,594	3,907	1,251
1996	200,872	3,905	1,230
1997	198,462	3,906	1,239
1998	198,974	3,904	1,254

TABLE 9.8.2
Fellowship of Independent Evangelical Churches (FIEC)[3]

	Membership[2]	Churches	Ministers[4]
1900	–	–	–
1910	–	–	–
1920	–	–	–
1930	5,400	102	78
1940	6,000	114	83
1950	11,950	226	175
1960	13,950	264	215
1970	20,760	393	296
1980	21,923	443	323
1990	30,000[5]	423	347
2000[5]	33,200	472	334
1991[1]	30,100[5]	424	348
1992	30,250[5]	425	350
1993	30,500[5]	425	350[1]
1994	30,750[5]	426	355[1]
1995	31,000[5]	430	350
1996	31,279	443	319
1997	32,056	454	324
1998	32,762	464	334

TABLE 9.8.3
Union of Evangelical Churches (UEC)[7]

	Membership[6]	Churches	Ministers[4]
1960[1]	2,500	28	60
1970	2,000	27	57
1980	1,500	26	41
1990	554	20	32[1]
2000[5]	800	20	30
1991	544	20	30
1992	544	20	28
1993	551	20	27
1994	520	20	28
1995	675	20	29
1996[1]	700	20	30
1997[1]	700	20	30
1998[1]	750	20	30

TABLE 9.8.5
Non-Instrumental Churches of Christ[8,10]

	Membership	Churches	Ministers[4]
1900	–	–	–
1910	40	1	0
1920[1]	50	1	0
1930[1]	630	12	2
1940[1]	280	34	8
1950[1]	4,920	134	54
1960[1]	3,900	101	44
1970[1]	2,800	85	40
1980	2,510	84[1]	40[1]
1990	2,470	85	52
2000[5]	2,225	74	40
1991[1]	2,450	84	50
1992[1]	2,425	82	49
1993[1]	2,400	82	47
1994[1]	2,375	80	46
1995	2,350[11]	79	45
1996[1]	2,325	78	44
1997[1]	2,300	77	43
1998	2,275	76	42

TABLE 9.8.4
Fellowship of Churches of Christ[8]

	Membership	Churches[9]	Ministers[9]
1900	12,379	236	84
1910	15,562	291	105
1920	17,011	317	110
1930	16,596	315	110
1940	14,948	285	100
1950	9,811	185	50
1960	7,921	152	42
1970	5,248	100	29
1980	3,229	71	40
1990	1,204	39	20
2000[1]	1,267	35	22
1991	1,243	39	22
1992	1,236	38	20
1993	1,202	38	22
1994	1,153	37	19
1995	1,168	35	22
1996	1,164	35	22
1997	1,061	35	20
1998	1,142	34	22

Footnotes

[1] Estimate
[2] Figures proportioned to number of churches
[3] Began 1922
[4] All male
[5] Revised figure
[6] Attendance is about 25% higher than membership
[7] Founded 1956; previously the Peculiar People or Plumstead Peculiars in 1838, a faith healing evangelical community largely in Kent and Essex
[8] The first Conference (later Association) of the Churches of Christ was held in the UK in 1842; they were formed in 1827 in the United States as the Disciples of Christ. A separate American Association of Churches of Christ working in the UK merged with the UK Association of the Churches of Christ in the 1920s; the figures for the UK Association for membership, churches and ministers have been increased by 5% for 1900 to 1920 to take these into account.
This merger helped to cause others to leave, some of whom came loosely to be called the Non-Instrumental Churches of Christ (Table 9.8.5), called because they use no instruments for worship. They began to leave in the 1920s, and especially after the end of the Second World War. One church, now called Above Bar Church, Southampton, left in 1922 but did not join the Non-Instrumentals; its figures are included within Table 9.8.4.
In 1979 the Association split into two groups: the Fellowship of Churches of Christ and the Re-formed Association of the Churches of Christ which had 2,899 members, 52 churches and 16 ministers in 1975, and 2,317, 39 and 22 respectively in 1980. The Re-formed Association joined the United Reformed Church on 26th September 1981, and are included since then with the URC in Table 8.16.5.
At the time of the merger 8 congregations of the old Association joined neither group: 2 joined the Non-Instrumental Churches of Christ and are included in Table 9.8.5, 2 became independent and are included in Table 9.9.9, 1 became Baptist and is assumed included in Table 9.3.6, 1 became Pentecostal and is assumed included in Table 9.15.7, and 2 closed down. 2 other Churches of Christ are assumed incorporated with the Fellowship figures since 1960, membership 100 with 2 ministers.
The London Church of Christ, detailed in Table 10.3.4, is not part of the Fellowship of Churches of Christ.
Information on the early years for the Churches of Christ compiled with the kind help of Rev Dr Martin Robinson, and his father, Alan.
[9] Figures 1900 to 1960 proportioned to number of members
[10] Includes groups called "Two by Two", "Cooneyites" and "People of the Way"
[11] The 1995 *Christian Worker Directory* gives membership information for 57 of the 75 congregation listed, totalling 1,719 people. This estimate is based on that figure
[12] Total for ALL Independent Churches that is, the total of Tables 9.5.1, and 9.6.1, 9.8.2–5 and 9.9.1–9. A figure of 5,000 members, 100 churches and 100 ministers is added to the total for 1940 and 1950, and half these numbers for 1900 to 1930 for churches given on Page 9.9 as a round estimate for those in existence between 1900 and 1950 for which no detailed figures are available

	Membership	Churches	Ministers[2]
TABLE 9.9.1 Christian and Missionary Alliance[3]			
1960	–	–	–
1970	–	–	–
1980	35	2	1
1990	130	5	4
2000[11]	300	7	13
1991	127	6	5
1992	215	6	5
1993	279	6	6
1994	320	6	6
1995[1]	280	7	10
1996	232[14]	7	13
1997	250[14]	7	13
1998[1]	270	7	13

	Membership	Churches	Priests
TABLE 9.9.2 Catholic Apostolic Church[4]			
1960[1]	70	3	0
1970[1]	60	3	0
1980[1]	40	3	0
1990[1]	25	3	0
2000[1]	10	3	0
1991[1]	25	3	0
1992[1]	20	3	0
1993[1]	20	3	0
1994[1]	15	3	0
1995[1]	15	3	0
1996[1]	14	3	0
1997[1]	13	3	0
1998[1]	12	3	0

	Membership	Churches	Ministers
TABLE 9.9.3 Hutterian Brethren			
1960[1]	350	1	5
1970[1]	350	1	5
1980[1]	350	1	5
1990[1]	350	1	5
2000[1]	350	1	5
1991[1]	350	1	5
1992[1]	350	1	5
1993[1]	350	1	5
1994[1]	350	1	5
1995[1]	350	1	5
1996[1]	350	1	5
1997[1]	350	1	5
1998[1]	350	1	5

	Membership	Churches	Priests[2]
TABLE 9.9.4 Independent Old Catholic Orthodox Church[5]			
1960[1]	60	3	3
1970[1]	60	3	3
1980[1]	60	3	3
1990[1]	20	1	1
2000[1]	–	–	–
1991	20	1	1
1992	20	1	1
1993	10	1	1
1994	10	1	0
1995	–	–	–
1996	–	–	–
1997	–	–	–
1998	–	–	–

	Membership	Churches[6]	Ministers[2]
TABLE 9.9.5 London City Mission			
1960[1]	1,500	34	34
1970[1]	1,500	34	34
1980[1]	1,500	34	31
1990[1]	1,400	31	31
2000[1]	1,200	27	27
1991[1]	1,350	30	30
1992[1]	1,350	30	30
1993[1]	1,300	29	29
1994[1]	1,300	29	29
1995[1]	1,250	28	28
1996[1]	1,230	28	28
1997[1]	1,220	28	28
1998[1]	1,210	28	27

	Membership	Churches	Lay Preachers[2]
TABLE 9.9.6 New Apostolic Church (UK)[7]			
1960[1]	500	10	20
1970	1,000	20[1]	40
1980	1,400[1]	34	53
1990	1,950	37[1]	56
2000[11]	2,200	35	57
1991[1]	1,975	37	56
1992[1]	2,000	36	56
1993[1]	2,000	36	56
1994[1]	2,040	36	57
1995	2,040	35	57
1996[1]	2,080	35	57
1997[1]	2,100	35	57
1998[1]	2,150	35	57

	Membership	Churches	Ministers
TABLE 9.9.7 The Reformed Liberal Catholic Church (Old Catholic)[8]			
1960	–	–	–
1970	–	–	–
1980	–	–	–
1990	–	–	–
2000	65	5	6
1991	–	–	–
1992	–	–	–
1993	–	–	–
1994	–	–	–
1995	–	–	–
1996	–	–	–
1997	–	–	–
1998	–	–	–

	Membership	Churches	Ministers
TABLE 9.9.8 Universal Fellowship of Metropolitan Community Churches[9]			
1960	–	–	–
1970[10]	20	1	0
1980	80	4	1
1990	200	8	12
2000[1]	500	14	18
1991[1]	275	9	13
1992	356	11[12]	15
1993[1]	375	11	15
1994[1]	400	12	15
1995[1]	400	12	15
1996[1]	420	12	16
1997[1]	440	13	16
1998[1]	460	13	17

	Membership	Churches	Ministers
TABLE 9.9.9 Other Independent Churches[13]			
1960	4,000	60	70
1970	5,000	73	80
1980	6,100	85	83
1990	6,600	92	88
2000	7,150	102	94
1991	6,650	93	89
1992	6,700	94	89
1993	6,750	95	89
1994	6,850	96	90
1995	6,900	97	91
1996	6,950	98	91
1997	7,000	99	92
1998	7,000	100	93

[1] Estimate
[2] All male
[3] Began in UK in 1973
[4] Started in Albury and London in 1832
[5] Closed 1994
[6] These are preaching centres, whose attenders are encouraged to attend worship another local churches. There is no formal membership
[7] Began 1948; more information is given in Footnote 5 Page 9.7 of

Religious Trends No 1, 1998/1999
[8] This church started 23rd May 1999 and has broken all ties with the Liberal Catholic Church. It affirms "Christ as Lord and Saviour in His death and resurrection in accordance with spiritual truth."
[9] Part of the European and North Sea (E&NS) District, one of 13 global Districts. The E&NS covers Scandinavia, Germany and the UK; in 1992 there were 11 churches in the UK and 9 elsewhere in this District
[10] 1972 figures

[11] Revised figure
[12] One in Bath, Birmingham, Bournemouth, Brighton, Bristol, Exeter, Glasgow, London (3 churches) and Manchester
[13] All estimated
[14] Sunday morning attendance in 1996 was 288 adults plus 151 children, of which 120 and 70 respectively were Chinese. In 1997 the figures were, respectively, 303 adults, 155 children, 118 and 83 Chinese

	Membership	Churches	Ministers
TABLE 9.10.1 Total Methodist Church[9]			
1900	849,446	7,404	3,952
1910	917,897	7,772	4,270
1920	877,106	8,121	4,057
1930	917,661	8,507	4,243
1940	862,358	8,891	4,005
1950	809,119	9,249	3,750
1960	788,562	9,613	3,646
1970	673,256	9,950	3,090
1980	539,804	8,517	2,430
1990	477,540	7,625	2,467
2001[1]	386,590	6,746	2,408
1991	469,326	7,543	2,461
1992	460,849	7,439	2,461
1993	453,213	7,352	2,475
1994	444,396	7,259	2,465
1995	434,410	7,156	2,441
1996	424,531	7,086	2,437
1997	414,394	6,998	2,428
1998	405,039	6,918	2,411

	Membership	Churches	Ministers[10]
TABLE 9.10.2 Methodist Church in Great Britain			
1900	770,406	6,681[1]	3,320[1]
1910	841,294	7,067[1]	3,625[1]
1920	801,721	7,453[1]	3,450[1]
1930	841,462	7,839[1]	3,625[1]
1940	792,192	8,225[1]	3,410[1]
1950	744,321	8,611[1]	3,210[1]
1960	728,589	8,997[1]	3,140[1]
1970	617,018	9,383	2,690[1]
1980	487,972	7,990	2,102
1990	424,540	7,129	2,167
2000[11]	335,000	6,280	2,137
1991	416,131	7,052	2,157
1992	408,107	6,950	2,159
1993	399,322	6,864	2,181
1994	389,818	6,772	2,175
1995	380,269[3]	6,678	2,162
1996	371,430	6,613	2,158
1997	362,584	6,528	2,154
1998	353,332	6,452	2,138[4]

	Membership	Churches	Ministers
TABLE 9.10.3 Methodist Church in Ireland[8]			
1900	63,573	381	206
1910	59,868	357	202
1920	59,458	327	196
1930	58,886	333	191
1940	54,760	333	181
1950	50,634	310	181
1960	46,507	299	177
1970	44,853	264	147
1980	42,303	242	126
1990	45,150	234	124
2000[1]	45,400	229	116
1991	45,471	233	129
1992	45,146	234	129
1993	46,372	234	123
1994	47,487	234	120
1995	47,360	234	120
1996	46,554	233	122
1997	45,423	232	118
1998	45,426	229	118[5]

	Membership	Churches	Ministers[6]
TABLE 9.10.4 Wesleyan Reform Union			
1900	6,864	188	23[1]
1910	7,859	197	24[1]
1920	7,229	191	24[1]
1930	7,866	187	23[1]
1940	6,915	182	23[1]
1950	5,970	177	22[1]
1960	5,649	166	21[1]
1970	4,681	153	19
1980	3,785	143	26
1990	2,996	131	22
2000[1]	2,075	112	19
1991[1]	2,900	127	21
1992	2,804	123	21
1993[1]	2,720	123	20
1994	2,628	122	19
1995	2,523	118	21
1996	2,401	116[1]	21[1]
1997	2,326	114[1]	21[1]
1998	2,279	113	21

	Membership	Churches	Ministers[6]
TABLE 9.10.5 Free Methodist Church[2]			
1900	–	–	–
1910	–	–	–
1920	–	–	–
1930	–	–	–
1940	–	–	–
1950	–	–	–
1960[1]	100	2	1
1970	237	5	4
1980	656	14	15
1990	1,007	20	19
2000[1]	1,115	23	24
1991	1,042[1]	21[1]	20[1]
1992	1,076	23	20
1993	1,057	22	19
1994	1,057	22	21
1995	980	20	22
1996	979	20	20[1]
1997	948	20	20[1]
1998	927	20	20[1]

	Membership	Churches	Ministers
TABLE 9.10.6 Independent Methodist Churches			
1900	8,303	148	397
1910	8,576	145	413
1920	8,398	144	381
1930	9,147	142	398
1940	8,191	145	385
1950	7,894	145	331
1960	7,517	145	302
1970	6,167	139	224
1980	4,788	122	155
1990	3,547	105	129
2000[1]	2,700	96	106
1991	3,482[1]	104[1]	128[1]
1992	3,416	103	126
1993	3,442	103	126
1994	3,106	103	124
1995	2,978	100	110[7]
1996	2,867	98	110
1997	2,813	98	109
1998	2,775	98	108

[1] Estimate
[2] Began 1960
[3] The community roll was 1,239,476
[4] Of whom, 399 were female
[5] Of whom, 10 were female

[6] All male
[7] Of whom 29 were female
[8] Figures updated since previous edition
[9] These totals include 300 members, 6 churches and 6 ministers throughout as an estimate of

Methodist churches not given on this page
[10] Numbers 1900 to 1960 pro rata to membership
[11] Revised figure

TABLE 9.11.1
Nineteenth century membership of what is now the Methodist Church of Great Britain

1820	208,412
1830	302,048
1840	451,333
1850	518,156
1860	525,332
1870	602,727
1880	653,403
1890	726,106

Footnotes for Table 9.11.2

[1] Estimate
[2] Of whom 10,385 were active; there were 13,126 in 1992 in total, with 10,414 active
[3] Figures for 1900 to 1930 include a 10.5% increase on the total number in the Wesleyan Methodist Church and the Primitive Methodist Church as an estimate for the United Methodist Church (UMC) (which all combined in 1932) as the UMC and its forebears did not publish this information.
[4] Total of the figures for the WMC, PMC and the UMC and its forebears for 1900 to 1930.
[5] All Methodist marriages, estimated from Government figures for various years 1919–1996. The number of Methodist marriages in Scotland will be very small as the Methodist Church in Scotland has less than 5,000 members. Northern Ireland estimated from figures for 1937 to 1997.
[6] After 1991 series became "Children and Young People at Worship".

TABLE 9.11.2 Other Methodist Statistics

	Local Preachers[3]	Sunday School Scholars[4] & % of children under 15		Infant baptisms & % of live births		Marriages[5] England & Wales	Northern Ireland
1900	40,253	1,753,511	14.7%	Not available		17,140	257
1905	39,315	1,801,093	14.7%	Not available		17,250	278
1910	39,594	1,760,653	14.0%	Not available		17,360	300
1915	38,639	1,655,510	13.7%	Not available		17,470	320
1920	36,301	1,538,426	13.0%	Not available		17,581	340
1925	35,688	1,501,018	13.3%	Not available		17,690	362
1930	35,129	1,356,624	12.8%	Not available		17,800	383
1935	34,412	1,187,056	11.1%	Not available		17,915	404
1940	31,307	929,942	8.7%	Not available		18,025	425
1945	28,144	717,021	6.7%	Not available		17,350	446
1950	25,159	799,873	7.4%	Not available		16,715	467
1955	23,605	769,733	6.8%	Not available		16,860	488
1960	22,304	587,276	5.0%	Not available		17,000	509
1965	20,991	482,420	3.9%	47,866	5.6%	17,070	530
1970	18,782	287,330[1]	2.1%	39,405	5.3%	17,085	551
1975	16,350[1]	227,960[1]	1.8%	29,681	5.2%	17,100	511
1980	14,852	175,794	1.5%	29,511	4.8%	17,110	442
1985	12,212[1]	136,240[1]	1.3%	30,636	4.9%	17,130	441
1990	12,965[2]	96,980[1]	0.9%	29,356	4.4%	16,867	380
1995	12,611	74,172[6]	0.7%	23,426	3.8%	12,846	286
2000[1]	10,800	51,870	0.4%	21,380	3.4%	9,340	215

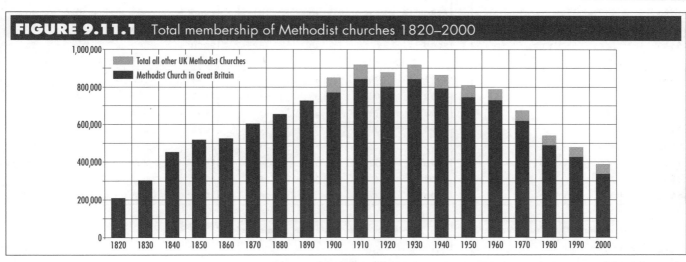

FIGURE 9.11.1 Total membership of Methodist churches 1820–2000

Legend:
- Total all other UK Methodist Churches
- Methodist Church in Great Britain

9

TABLE 9.11.3
Average attendance on Sunday

1980	451,329
1990	412,008
1991	398,157
1992	385,238
1993	372,510
1994	358,849
1995	347,795
1996	338,286
1997	322,770
1998	311,397

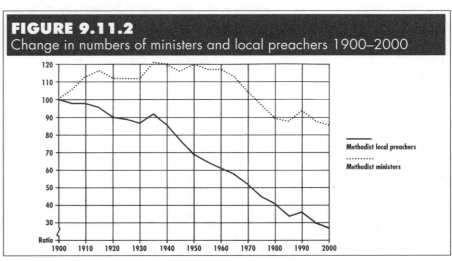

FIGURE 9.11.2
Change in numbers of ministers and local preachers 1900–2000

Legend:
—— Methodist local preachers
······ Methodist ministers

	Membership	Churches	Ministers
TABLE 9.12.1 New Churches[13]			
1960	–	–	–
1970	225	1	20
1980	10,037	205	156
1990	76,485	1,113	1,145
2000[1]	137,225	1,818	1,805
1991	78,950	1,203	1,226
1992	85,468	1,226	1,255
1993	91,763	1,272	1,308
1994	97,859	1,348	1,377
1995	104,101	1,414	1,435
1996	108,594	1,495	1,530
1997	113,730	1,574	1,574
1998	122,887	1,659	1,604

	Membership	Churches	Ministers
TABLE 9.12.2 Association of Vineyard Churches[5]			
1960	–	–	–
1970	–	–	–
1980	–	–	–
1990	2,000	4	2[1]
2000[1]	8,000	65	30
1991	2,500[1]	5	3[1]
1992	3,000[1]	10	6[1]
1993	3,500[1]	12	7[1]
1994	4,000[1]	17	9[1]
1995	4,300	24	11[6]
1996	5,000[1]	32	16[1]
1997	5,500	46	24[1]
1998	6,200	52	26[1]

	Membership	Churches	Ministers
TABLE 9.12.3 Bristol Christian Fellowship			
1960	–	–	–
1970	–	–	–
1980	150	3	2
1990	400	8	5
2000[1]	750	12	5
1991	600	11	5
1992	500	11	4
1993	500	11	4
1994	500	10	4
1995	600	9	3
1996	600	9	5
1997	550	7	4
1998	500	4	4[6]

	Membership	Churches	Ministers
TABLE 9.12.4 Christian Fellowship Church[5]			
1960	–	–	–
1970	–	–	–
1980	–	–	–
1990[1]	700	4	3
2000[1]	2,000	12	9
1991[1]	850	4	3
1992[1]	1,000	5	4
1993[1]	1,200	6	5
1994[1]	1,350	7	5
1995	1,475	8	6
1996[1]	1,600	8	6
1997[1]	1,700	9	7
1998[1]	1,800	10	7

	Membership	Churches	Ministers
TABLE 9.12.5 Cornerstone			
1960	–	–	–
1970	–	–	–
1980[1,4]	1,250	10	10
1990[1]	3,750	30	30
2000[1]	5,000	40	38
1991[1]	3,900	32	30
1992[1]	4,000	33	31
1993[1]	4,200	34	31
1994[1]	4,300	35	32[1]
1995	4,415	36	33[7]
1996[1]	4,525	37	34
1997[1]	4,650	38	35
1998[1]	4,775	38	36

	Membership	Churches	Ministers
TABLE 9.12.6 Covenant Ministries[2,8]			
1960	–	–	–
1970	–	–	–
1980[1]	2,000	20	20
1990[1]	5,000	50	50
2000[1]	2,000	14	14
1991[1]	2,000	15	15
1992[1]	2,200	17	17
1993[1]	2,300	18	18
1994[1]	2,400	19	19
1995	2,500	20	20
1996[9]	2,250	18	18[1]
1997[1]	2,000	15	15
1998[9]	1,780	13	13[1]

	Membership	Churches	Ministers
TABLE 9.12.7 Ground Level			
1960	–	–	–
1970	–	–	–
1980[4]	–	–	–
1990[1]	1,000	25	18
2000[1]	4,500	64	45
1991[1]	1,400	27	21
1992[1]	1,800	29	24
1993[1]	2,200	31	27
1994[1]	2,500	33	30
1995	2,800[9]	35	32[11]
1996[1]	3,100	40	35
1997[1]	3,400	45	38
1998[1]	3,700	50	40

	Membership	Churches	Ministers
TABLE 9.12.8 Ichthus Christian Fellowship[3,12]			
1960	–	–	–
1970	–	–	–
1980	570	10	15[1]
1990	1,701	33	43[1]
2000[1]	2,600	32	35
1991	1,949	33	45[1]
1992	2,217	42	52
1993	2,120	28	39
1994	1,930	29	37
1995	2,200	27	30
1996	1,800	24	30
1997	2,000[9]	25	30
1998	2,300	28[9]	32[10]

Footnotes

[1] Estimate
[2] Began 1977
[3] Began 1975
[4] Began 1982
[5] Founded 1987
[6] Of whom one was female
[7] Of whom 5 were female
[8] Formerly Harvestine; see also Table 9.14.5
[9] Based on *Body Book* 7 numbers increased by 20% for under reporting
[10] Of whom 6 were female
[11] Of whom four were female
[12] Excludes Ichthus linked churches outside the London area
[13] Total includes all churches on pages 9.12, 9.13 and new churches on page 9.14

	Membership	Churches[2]	Ministers[3]
TABLE 9.13.1 Jesus Fellowship Church and Multiply Network			
1960	–	–	–
1970	225	1	20
1980	431	3	47
1990	1,260	11	99
2000[1]	4,500	45	160
1991	1,460	13	108
1992	1,640	16	118
1993	2,020	20	123
1994	2,480	24	128
1995	2,600	26	130
1996	3,160	30	145
1997	3,390	35	146
1998	3,715	38	150[4]

	Membership	Churches	Ministers
TABLE 9.13.2 Kingdom Faith Ministries[5]			
1960	–	–	–
1970	–	–	–
1980	–	–	–
1990	–	–	–
2000[8]	1,000	5	12
1991	–	–	–
1992	500	1	4
1993[1]	550	1	5
1994[1]	650	2	6
1995	750	3	7[6]
1996[1]	800	3	7
1997[1]	850	4	9
1998	900[7]	5[7]	11

	Membership	Churches	Ministers[10]
TABLE 9.13.3 Kings Church[9]			
1960	–	–	–
1970	–	–	–
1980	460	8	9
1990[1]	1,750	15	20
2000[1]	700	6	12
1991[1]	500	5	10
1992[1]	540	5	10
1993[1]	560	5	10
1994[1]	580	5	10
1995	600	5	10
1996[1]	620	5	10
1997[1]	640	5	11
1998[1]	660	6	11

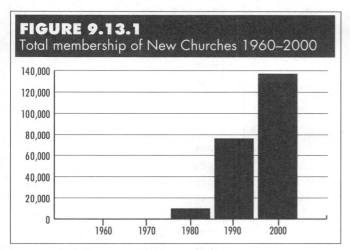

FIGURE 9.13.1
Total membership of New Churches 1960–2000

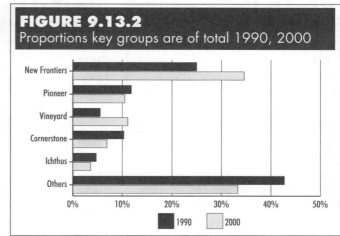

FIGURE 9.13.2
Proportions key groups are of total 1990, 2000

New Frontiers / Pioneer / Vineyard / Cornerstone / Ichthus / Others
0% 10% 20% 30% 40% 50%
■ 1990 □ 2000

	Membership	Churches	Ministers
TABLE 9.13.4 Lifeline Community Churches[11]			
1960	–	–	–
1970	–	–	–
1980	–	–	–
1990	500[1]	4	8[1]
2000[1]	500	4	8
1991[1]	500	4	8
1992[1]	250	2	4
1993[1]	250	2	4
1994[1]	275	2	4
1995	298	2	4
1996[1]	320	2	4
1997[1]	400	3	5
1998[1]	420	3	6

	Membership	Churches	Ministers
TABLE 9.13.5 New Frontiers International[12]			
1960	–	–	–
1970	–	–	–
1980	176	1	3
1990[1]	9,000	60	150
2000[1]	25,000	170	383
1991[1]	11,000	72	175
1992[1]	13,000	84	200
1993[1]	15,000	96	225
1994[1]	17,000	108	250
1995[1]	19,000	120	275
1996	20,000	135	306
1997	21,000[1]	140	300[1]
1998	23,250[1]	157	280

	Membership	Churches	Ministers
TABLE 9.13.6 Pioneer[13]			
1960	–	–	–
1970	–	–	–
1980	–	–	–
1990[1]	4,300	45	85
2000[8]	9,600	88	170
1991[1]	4,600	48	90
1992[1]	4,900	51	95
1993[1]	5,200	54	100
1994[1]	5,500	57	108
1995	5,816	59	114[14]
1996[7]	6,000	70	135[1]
1997[1]	6,500	74	143[1]
1998[7]	7,400	79	153[1]

[1] Estimate
[2] Church households
[3] Nearly all part-time
[4] Of whom 2 were female
[5] Began 1992

[6] Of whom 1 was female
[7] Based on *Body Book* 7th edition, Pioneer, 1998, with some numbers increased by 20% for under reporting
[8] Revised figure(s)
[9] Formerly Antioch Ministries

[10] All male
[11] Began 1981 as Community Resources
[12] Began 1980
[13] Began 1982
[14] Of whom 30 were female

TABLE 9.14.1 — Plumbline Ministries[2]

	Membership	Churches	Ministers
1960	–	–	–
1970	–	–	–
1980	–	–	–
1990	124	4	4
2000[3]	875	15	22
1991	150	4	6
1992	225	4	9
1993	250	5	11
1994	277	7	14
1995	440	7	14[4]
1996	527	8	15
1997[1]	620	10	17
1998	712	13	19

TABLE 9.14.2 — Proclaimers International

	Membership	Churches	Ministers
1960	–	–	–
1970	–	–	–
1980	–	–	–
1990	–	–	–
2000[1]	350	1	4
1991	–	–	–
1992	–	–	–
1993[5]	50	1	1
1994[1]	150	1	2
1995	240	1	3[6]
1996[1]	260	1	3
1997[1]	280	1	3
1998[1]	300	1	3

TABLE 9.14.3 — Rainbow Churches[7]

	Membership	Churches	Ministers
1960	–	–	–
1970	–	–	–
1980	–	–	–
1990	–	–	–
2000[1]	250	5	10
1991	391	4	8
1992	396	3	8
1993	413	4	8
1994	367	6	8
1995	317	5	11[9]
1996	132[8]	4	8
1997[1]	150	4	8
1998[1]	175	4	8

TABLE 9.14.4 — Salt and Light Ministries[12]

	Membership	Churches	Ministers
1960	–	–	–
1970	–	–	–
1980	–	–	–
1990	5,000	20[3]	28[3]
2000[3]	6,600	40	48
1991[1]	5,150	22	28
1992[1]	5,300	23	29
1993[1]	5,450	24	30
1994[1]	5,600	26	31
1995[3]	5,750	27	32
1996	5,900[11]	28	33
1997[1]	6,100	33	39
1998	6,300[11]	38	45

TABLE 9.14.5 — Abundant Life Ministries[18]

	Membership	Churches	Ministers
1960	–	–	–
1970	–	–	–
1980	–	–	–
1990	–	–	–
2000	3,000	5	9
1991	–	–	–
1992	–	–	–
1993	–	–	–
1994	–	–	–
1995	–	–	–
1996	–	–	–
1997	–	–	–
1998	2,000	4	7[19]

TABLE 9.14.6 — Other Non-Denominatinal Churches[13]

	Membership	Churches	Ministers
1960	–	–	–
1970	–	–	–
1980	5,000	150	50
1990	40,000	800	600
2000	60,000	1,200	800
1991	42,000	840	620
1992	44,000	880	640
1993	46,000	920	660
1994	48,000	960	680
1995	50,000	1,000	700
1996	52,000	1,040	720
1997	54,000	1,080	740
1998	56,000	1,120	760

TABLE 9.14.7 — Church of God of Prophecy[16]

	Membership	Churches	Ministers
1960[1]	800	10	25
1970	2,074	23	77
1980	5,290	95	341
1990	5,027	91	483
2000[1]	4,700	84	688
1991[1]	4,937	90	500
1992[1]	4,936	88	525
1993[1]	4,937	87	550
1994[1]	4,939	86	575
1995	4,785	85[14]	600
1996[1]	4,770	85	615
1997[1]	4,755	85	630
1998[1]	4,740	85	650

TABLE 9.14.8 — New Testament Church of God[16]

	Membership	Churches	Ministers
1960[1]	1,840	19	50
1970	3,423	39	108
1980	6,369	86	190
1990	6,632	100	237
2000[6]	8,000	106	275
1991	6,750[6]	103[1]	225
1992	6,870[6]	105	214
1993[1]	7,006[6]	106	220
1994[1]	7,100[6]	107	225
1995	7,220	110	230
1996	7,328	110	247
1997	7,554	106	250
1998	7,728	103	263[15]

TABLE 9.14.9 — Other Pentecostal Churches[17]

	Membership	Churches	Ministers
1960	–	–	–
1970	1,000	32	22
1980	2,300	58	40
1990	3,895	87	60
2000	5,505	118	82
1991	4,050	90	62
1992	4,200	93	64
1993	4,350	96	66
1994	4,500	99	68
1995	4,660	102	70
1996	4,830	105	72
1997	5,000	108	75
1998	5,170	111	77

[1] Estimate
[2] Began 1986
[3] Revised figure(s)
[4] Of whom 4 were female
[5] Began 1993
[6] Of whom 1 was female
[7] Began 1991
[8] Membership fell in 1996 due to the loss of 1 congregation
[9] Of whom 5 were female
[10] All male
[11] Based on *Body Book* 7th edition, Pioneer, 1998, with some numbers increased by 20% for under reporting
[12] Began 1985
[13] All estimated
[14] In 39 buildings
[15] Of whom 26 were female
[16] Began 1953
[17] All estimated, but see footnotes to Table 9.12.7 in *Religious Trends* No 1 1998/99 for evidence of where substantive numbers exist. Includes Peniel Pentecostal Church, Brentwood, started 1976; in 1997 had 1 church with 9 ministers and 600 members. Also includes the Apostolic Faith Church, Bournemouth, out of which came the United Apostolic Faith Church, which is listed.
[18] Established 1997; previously part of the Covenant Ministries Network
[19] Of whom 2 are female

	Membership	Churches	Ministers
TABLE 9.15.1 Total All Pentecostal Churches[16]			
1900	–	–	–
1910	50	2	1
1920	1,100	26	16
1930	18,040	402	321
1940	36,050	782	632
1950	37,050	809	652
1960	52,905	1,092	960
1970	86,090	1,357	1,362
1980	117,582	1,808	2,279
1990	153,962	2,178	3,279
2000	233,234	2,649	4,322
1991	158,005	2,210	3,425
1992	165,910	2,252	3,513
1993	177,499	2,292	3,593
1994	179,854	2,334	3,707
1995	197,602	2,429	3,897
1996	207,491	2,463	3,997
1997	212,929	2,481	4,038
1998	221,520	2,529	4,138

	Membership	Churches[4]	Ministers[5,9]
TABLE 9.15.2 Apostolic Church[2]			
1900	–	–	–
1910[1]	50	2	1
1920[1]	300	11	3
1930[1]	2,040	78	21
1940[1]	4,050	155	42
1950[1]	4,050	155	42
1960[1]	5,050	193	53
1970	5,149	197	54
1980	4,904	176	58
1990	6,100	145	81
2000[1]	4,380[6]	92	72
1991[1]	5,850	145	83
1992	5,600[1]	145	85
1993	5,388	138	80
1994	5,463	135	77
1995	5,385	114	76
1996[1]	5,200	110	75
1997[1]	5,000	105	74
1998[1]	4,700	110	73

	Membership	Churches	Ministers
TABLE 9.15.3 Assemblies of God[7]			
1900	–	–	–
1910	–	–	–
1920	–	–	–
1930	10,000[1]	218	210[1]
1940	17,000[1]	357	350[1]
1950	20,000[1]	420	410[1]
1960	26,000[1]	516	502[1]
1970	28,000[1]	532	518
1980	35,000	571	662
1990	48,000[8]	605[10]	695
2000[1]	61,150	664	836
1991	48,584	608	780
1992	49,381	607	790[1]
1993	54,114	614	800[1]
1994	55,000[1]	630	810[1]
1995	54,655	646	818[14]
1996	56,000[1]	658	835
1997	57,500[1]	651	821
1998	58,500	656	842[11]

	Membership	Churches	Ministers
TABLE 9.15.4 Elim Pentecostal Church[12]			
1900	–	–	–
1910	–	–	–
1920	800[1]	15	13[1]
1930	6,000[1]	106	90[1]
1940	15,000[1]	270	240[1]
1950	13,000[1]	234	200[1]
1960	16,400	294	250[1]
1970	30,000[1]	297	250[6]
1980	30,750[1]	354	310
1990	36,100[6]	437	483
2000[1]	80,000	700	688
1991	36,795	444	481
1992	42,125	461	495
1993	47,618	500	483
1994	46,763	513	494
1995	62,650	577	600
1996	68,750	585	615
1997	70,000	595	622
1998	75,000	620	631[13]

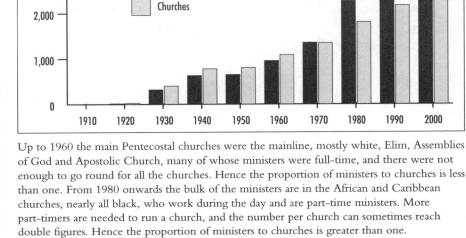

FIGURE 9.15
Total Pentecostal ministers and churches 1910–2000

Up to 1960 the main Pentecostal churches were the mainline, mostly white, Elim, Assemblies of God and Apostolic Church, many of whose ministers were full-time, and there were not enough to go round for all the churches. Hence the proportion of ministers to churches is less than one. From 1980 onwards the bulk of the ministers are in the African and Caribbean churches, nearly all black, who work during the day and are part-time ministers. More part-timers are needed to run a church, and the number per church can sometimes reach double figures. Hence the proportion of ministers to churches is greater than one.

[1] Estimate
[2] Began 1904
[3] See also Tables 9.14.6, 7, 8 and 9.21.4 and 5
[4] Numbers estimated on general trend of those in Tables 9.15.3 and 4
[5] Figures 1910 to 1960 pro rata on number of ministers
[6] Revised figure(s)

[7] Began in 1924 with 74 churches
[8] English Church Census 1989 data suggests that Sunday attendance could be 40% higher than membership
[9] All male
[10] In the 1980s 132 new churches were started but others closed or left to become independent or New Churches
[11] Of whom 23 were female

[12] Began 1915
[13] Of whom 31 were female
[14] Of whom 13 were female
[15] Of whom 22 were female
[16] This Table totals the figures in Tables 9.14.6, 7, 8; Tables 9.15.2, 3, 4; Table 9.16.1; Tables 9.21.4, 5 and Table 9.22.1

TABLE 9.16.1 — Total African and Caribbean Churches

	Membership	Churches	Ministers[7]
1960	1,445	36	46
1970	12,804	177	243
1980	25,639	348	523
1990	35,902	520	971
2000[1]	48,581	589	1,231
1991	36,905	525	1,007
1992	37,814	534	1,035
1993	38,683	529	1,072
1994	39,956	531	1,109
1995	41,497	552	1,133
1996	43,055	558	1,150
1997	44,525	566	1,164
1998	46,127	575	1,182

TABLE 9.16.2 — Aladura International Church[3]

	Membership	Churches	Ministers
1960	–	–	–
1970	100	1	1
1980	300	1	3
1990	500	3	7[2]
2000[1]	–	–	–
1991[1]	400	3	6
1992[1]	300	3	5
1993[1]	200	2	2
1994	–	–	–
1995	–	–	–
1996	–	–	–
1997	–	–	–
1998	–	–	–

TABLE 9.16.3 — All Saints Pentecostal Assembly

	Membership	Churches	Ministers
1960	–	–	–
1970	–	–	–
1980[1]	30	1	1
1990	20	1	4
2000[1]	15	1	5
1991[1]	20	1	4
1992[1]	20	1	4
1993[1]	20	1	4
1994[1]	20	1	4
1995	20	1	4[1]
1996[1]	20	1	4
1997[1]	20	1	4
1998[1]	20	1	4

TABLE 9.16.4 — Apostolic Faith Church

	Membership	Churches	Ministers
1960[1]	50	1	1
1970[1]	60	1	1
1980	70	1	1
1990	180	1	5
2000[1]	330	4	7
1991[1]	200	1	1
1992[1]	220	2	2
1993[1]	230	2	3
1994[1]	240	2	4
1995	250	3	5[4]
1996	300	4[1]	5[1]
1997[1]	310	4	5[1]
1998[1]	320	4	5[1]

TABLE 9.16.5 — Beneficial Veracious Christ Church[5]

	Membership	Churches	Ministers
1960	–	–	–
1970	–	–	–
1980	–	–	–
1990	100	1	1
2000[1]	1,100[8]	7	8
1991[1]	300	2	4
1992[1]	500	3	7
1993[1]	700	4	6
1994	972	5	6[1]
1995	980	6	6
1996[1]	990	6	6
1997[1]	1,000	6	6
1998[1]	1,025	6	6

TABLE 9.16.6 — Beulah United Church of God

	Membership	Churches	Ministers
1960	–	–	–
1970	–	–	–
1980[1]	100	2	2
1990	100[1]	2	2
2000[1]	100	2	2
1991[1]	100	2	2
1992[1]	100	2	2
1993[1]	100	2	2
1994[1]	100	2	2
1995[1]	100	2	2
1996[1]	100	2	2
1997[1]	100	2	2
1998[1]	100	2	2

TABLE 9.16.7 — Born Again Christ Healing Church

	Membership	Churches	Ministers
1960	–	–	–
1970	20	1	4
1980[1]	40	1	4
1990	60	1	4[2]
2000[1]	80	1	4
1991[1]	65	1	4
1992	65	1	4
1993[1]	68	1	4
1994	70[1]	1[1]	4[1]
1995[1]	70	1	4
1996[1]	70	1	4
1997[1]	75	1	4
1998[1]	75	1	4

TABLE 9.16.8 — Chalvey Community Church

	Membership	Churches	Ministers
1960	–	–	–
1970	–	–	–
1980	10[1]	1	0
1990	25	1	0
2000[1]	45	1	0
1991[1]	28	1	0
1992	30	1	0
1993[1]	32	1	0
1994	35[1]	1	0
1995[1]	35[1]	1	0
1996[1]	38	1	0
1997[1]	40	1	0
1998[1]	42	1	0

TABLE 9.16.9 — Cherubim and Seraphim Church Council[9]

	Membership	Churches	Ministers
1960	–	–	–
1970	400	1	1
1980	750[1]	3	2
1990[1]	1,300	9	6
2000[1]	2,200	18	13
1991[1]	1,400	10	7
1992[1]	1,500	11	8
1993[1]	1,550	12	9
1994[1]	1,800	13	10
1995	1,900	15	11[6]
1996[1]	1,950	16	11
1997[1]	2,000	17	12
1998[1]	2,100	18	12

[1] Estimate
[2] Of whom two were female
[3] Began 1970, but believed closed in 1994
[4] Of whom 3 were female
[5] Began 1988
[6] Of whom 4 were female
[7] In 1990 74% of ministers were part time
[8] Revised estimate
[9] Began 1965

	Membership	Churches	Ministers
TABLE 9.17.1 Christ Apostolic Church Mount Bethel[2]			
1960	–	–	–
1970	–	–	–
1980	100[1]	1	2[1]
1990	300	1	9
2000[1]	600	7	18
1991[1]	350	1	11
1992	400	1	13
1993[1]	425	2	13
1994	450	4	13
1995	500	7	14[4]
1996[1]	525	7	15
1997[1]	550	7	16
1998[1]	575	7	17

	Membership	Churches	Ministers
TABLE 9.17.2 Christ the King Pentecostal Church[5]			
1960	–	–	–
1970	–	–	–
1980	–	–	–
1990	100[1]	1	2
2000[1]	200	1	2
1991[1]	110	1	2
1992[1]	120	1	2
1993[1]	130	1	2
1994[1]	140	1	2
1995[1]	150	1	2
1996[1]	160	1	2
1997[1]	170	1	2
1998[1]	180	1	2

	Membership	Churches	Ministers
TABLE 9.17.3 Christian Care Ministries[6]			
1960	–	–	–
1970	–	–	–
1980	–	–	–
1990	75	1	2
2000[1]	75	1	2
1991[1]	75	1	2
1992[1]	75	1	2
1993[1]	75	1	2
1994[1]	75	1	2
1995[1]	75	1	2
1996[1]	75	1	2
1997[1]	75	1	2
1998[1]	75	1	2

	Membership	Churches	Ministers
TABLE 9.17.4 The Christ Family[7]			
1960	–	–	–
1970	–	–	–
1980	–	–	–
1990	75	1	0
2000[1]	147	5	1
1991[1]	75	1	0
1992[1]	75	1	0
1993[1]	75	1	0
1994[1]	75	1	0
1995	105	3	0
1996[1]	110	3	0
1997[1]	115	3	0
1998[1]	120	4	0

	Membership	Churches	Ministers
TABLE 9.17.5 Church of God Assembly			
1960	–	–	–
1970	–	–	–
1980	40	1	4[1]
1990	150	7	18
2000[1]	250	10	32
1991[1]	160	7	19
1992[1]	170	7	20
1993[1]	185	7	22
1994[1]	200	7	24
1995[1]	200	7	25
1996[1]	210	7	26
1997[1]	220	8	27
1998[1]	230	9	29

	Membership	Churches	Ministers
TABLE 9.17.6 Church of God Ground of Truth			
1960	–	–	–
1970	–	–	–
1980[1]	100	2	8
1990	60	2	5
2000[1]	40	2	4
1991[1]	65	2	5
1992[1]	70	2	5
1993[1]	75	2	5
1994[1]	80	2	5
1995[1]	60	2	5
1996[1]	55	2	5
1997[1]	50	2	5
1998[1]	45	2	5

	Membership	Churches	Ministers
TABLE 9.17.7 Church of God Reformation Movement			
1960[1]	100	2	2
1970[1]	150	3	3
1980[1]	200	3	3
1990	300	5	6
2000[1]	250	6	7
1991[1]	280	5	5
1992[1]	260	5	4
1993[1]	240	5	4
1994[1]	220	5	5[1]
1995	200	5	5
1996[1]	210	5	5
1997[1]	220	5	5
1998[1]	230	5	6

	Membership	Churches	Ministers
TABLE 9.17.8 Deeper Christian Life Ministry[3]			
1960	–	–	–
1970	–	–	–
1980[1]	200	5	3
1990	400[1]	9[1]	5
2000[1]	600	13	7
1991[1]	420	9	5
1992[1]	440	10	5
1993[1]	460	10	6
1994[1]	480	11	6[8]
1995	500	11	7
1996[1]	520	11	7
1997[1]	540	12	7
1998[1]	560	12	7

	Membership	Churches	Ministers
TABLE 9.17.9 Deeper Life Bible Church[3]			
1960	–	–	–
1970	–	–	–
1980	–	–	–
1990	20	1	1
2000[1]	60	1	1
1991[1]	25	1	1
1992	30	1	1
1993	35	1	1
1994	40	1	1
1995	40	1	1[1]
1996[1]	40	1	1
1997[1]	45	1	1
1998[1]	50	1	1

[1] Estimate
[2] Began 1974
[3] Began 1985
[4] Of whom 7 were female
[5] Began 1984
[6] Began 1989
[7] Began 1988
[8] Of whom two were female

TABLE 9.18.1
Forest Gate Brethren in Christ[8]

	Membership	Churches	Ministers
1960	–	–	–
1970	–	–	–
1980	20[1]	1	1
1990	60	2	2
2000[1]	60	1	1
1991[1]	60	2	2
1992	60	2	2
1993[1]	50	1	1
1994	40	1	1
1995	40	1	1[1]
1996[1]	45	1	1
1997[1]	50	1	1
1998[1]	55	1	1

FIGURE 9.18
Growth in African and Caribbean ministers and Churches 1960–2000

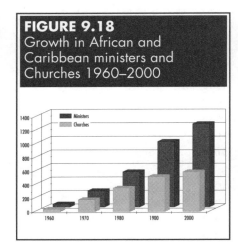

TABLE 9.18.2
Full Gospel Revival Centre

	Membership	Churches	Ministers
1960	–	–	–
1970	–	–	–
1980[1]	50	1	3
1990	120	1[1]	3[1]
2000[1]	200	1	3
1991[1]	130	1	3
1992[1]	140	1	3
1993[1]	150	1	3
1994[1]	160	1	3
1995[1]	170	1	3
1996[1]	175	1	3
1997[1]	180	1	3
1998[1]	190	1	1

TABLE 9.18.3   The Gospel Faith
Mission International[6]

	Membership	Churches	Ministers
1960	–	–	–
1970	–	–	–
1980	–	–	–
1990	180	2	7
2000[1]	400	3	4
1991[1]	190	2	8
1992[1]	200	2	10
1993[1]	230	2	7
1994[1]	260	2	4
1995	289	2	3
1996[1]	310	2	3
1997[1]	330	2	3
1998[1]	350	3	4

TABLE 9.18.4
Gospel Tabernacle Assembly[2]

	Membership	Churches	Ministers
1960[1]	40	1	1
1970[1]	100	2	2
1980[1]	150	2	4[1]
1990	120	3	4
2000[1]	75	3	4
1991[1]	110	3	4
1992[1]	100	3	4
1993[1]	95	3	4
1994[1]	90	3	4[1]
1995[1]	90	3	4
1996[1]	85	3	4
1997[1]	80	3	4
1998[1]	80	3	4

TABLE 9.18.5
Healing Church of God in Christ[7]

	Membership	Churches	Ministers
1960	–	–	–
1970[1]	50	1	2
1980[1]	120	2	3
1990	80	2	3
2000[1]	50	2	3
1991[1]	75	2	3
1992[1]	75	2	3
1993[1]	75	2	3
1994[1]	70	2	3
1995[1]	70	2	3
1996[1]	65	2	3
1997[1]	60	2	3
1998[1]	60	2	3

TABLE 9.18.6
Jesus Vine Church[3, 10]

	Membership	Churches	Ministers
1960	–	–	–
1970	–	–	–
1980	–	–	–
1990	54	1	3
2000[1]	500	2	3
1991[1]	75	1	3
1992	95	1	3
1993[1]	200	1	3
1994	350	1	2
1995[1]	350	1	2
1996[1]	400	1	2
1997[1]	400	1	2
1998[1]	400	1	2

TABLE 9.18.7
The Latter – Rain Outpouring Revival[4]

	Membership	Churches	Ministers
1960	–	–	–
1970[1]	25	1	1
1980[1]	40	2	2
1990	170[1]	6[1]	8
2000[1]	320	10	11
1991[1]	180	6	8
1992[1]	200	6	8
1993[1]	220	6	8
1994	240[1]	6[1]	8
1995	250[1]	8[1]	8[9]
1996[1]	260	8	9
1997[1]	280	9	9
1998[1]	290	9	10

TABLE 9.18.8
Leghorn Baptist Church of God

	Membership	Churches	Ministers
1960	–	–	–
1970[1]	40	1	5
1980	80[1]	1	10[1]
1990	61	1	10
2000[1]	51	1	10
1991[1]	70	1	10
1992	60	1	10
1993[1]	60	1	10
1994[1]	60	1	10
1995	60	1	10
1996[1]	55	1	10
1997[1]	55	1	10
1998[1]	55	1	10

[1] Estimate
[2] Began 1960
[3] Began 1988
[4] Began 1964
[5] Began 1958
[6] Began 1984
[7] Began 1963
[8] Formerly called Kensal Rise Fellowship Brethren in Christ
[9] Of whom 4 were female
[10] Formerly called House of Prayer International Church

	Membership	Churches	Ministers
TABLE 9.19.1 London's Happy Church[7]			
1960	–	–	–
1970	–	–	–
1980	–	–	–
1990	120	1	2
2000[1]	120	1	2
1991[1]	120	1	2
1992[1]	120	1	2
1993[1]	120	1	2
1994[1]	120	1	2
1995[1]	120	1	2
1996[1]	120	1	2
1997[1]	120	1	2
1998[1]	120	1	2

	Membership	Churches	Ministers
TABLE 9.19.2 Miracle Church of God in Christ[2]			
1960[2]	40[1]	1[1]	1
1970	84	2[1]	2
1980	200	3[1]	3
1990	210	3	3
2000[1]	185	5	7
1991	245	3	4
1992	192	3	5
1993	194	3	5
1994	190	4	5
1995	201	5	7
1996	198	5	7
1997	211	5	7
1998	200	5	7

	Membership	Churches	Ministers
TABLE 9.19.3 Mustard Seed Church[5]			
1960	–	–	–
1970	–	–	–
1980	–	–	–
1990	60	1	1
2000[1]	140	1	1
1991[1]	70	1	1
1992	80	1	1
1993[1]	95	1	1
1994[1]	100	1	1
1995[1]	100	1	1
1996[1]	110	1	1
1997[1]	120	1	1
1998[1]	130	1	1

	Membership	Churches	Ministers
TABLE 9.19.4 New Covenant Church[3]			
1960	–	–	–
1970	–	–	–
1980	–	–	–
1990	300	4	4
2000[1]	1,500	18[10]	30
1991[1]	450	7	8
1992	600	11	11
1993[1]	800	11	12
1994	1,000	10	13
1995	1,120	17	8[8]
1996[1]	1,200	17	10
1997[1]	1,300	17	15
1998[1]	1,400	17	20

	Membership	Churches	Ministers
TABLE 9.19.5 New Testament Assembly (Pentecostal)[4]			
1960	–	–	–
1970[1]	1,000	6	10
1980	2,500	12	25
1990	3,500	18	42
2000[1]	4,400	21	54
1991[1]	3,500	19	43
1992[1]	3,500	20	45
1993[1]	3,500	20	45
1994[1]	3,500	20	45
1995	3,900	18	45
1996[1]	4,000	18	47
1997[1]	4,100	19	49
1998[1]	4,200	20	50

	Membership	Churches	Ministers
TABLE 9.19.6 Pentecostal Assembly of Mount Calvary			
1960	–	–	–
1970	–	–	–
1980[1]	80	4	5
1990	60	4	5
2000[1]	50	4	5
1991[1]	60	4	5
1992[1]	60	4	5
1993[1]	60	4	5
1994[1]	60	4	5
1995[1]	60	4	5
1996[1]	60	4	5
1997[1]	55	4	5
1998[1]	55	4	5

	Membership	Churches	Ministers
TABLE 9.19.7 Pentecostal GospelChurch[3]			
1960	–	–	–
1970	–	–	–
1980	–	–	–
1990	100	1	1
2000[1]	500	2	3
1991[1]	150	1	1
1992	200	1	2
1993[1]	250	1	3
1994[1]	300	1	3
1995	300	1	2
1996[1]	350	1	2
1997[1]	400	1	2
1998[1]	450	2	3

	Membership	Churches	Ministers
TABLE 9.19.8 Pentecostal Revival Church of Christ[6]			
1960	–	–	–
1970	–	–	–
1980	50	1	2
1990	200	1	6
2000[1]	320	1	8
1991[1]	225	1	6
1992	250	1	6
1993[1]	250	1	6
1994	250	1	6
1995[1]	250	1	6[9]
1996[1]	270	1	6
1997[1]	280	1	6
1998[1]	300	1	6

	Membership	Churches	Ministers
TABLE 9.19.9 The People's Christian Fellowship			
1960[1]	15	1	1
1970[1]	20	1	1
1980[1]	30	1	1
1990	50	1	1
2000[1]	150	2	2
1991[1]	53	1	1
1992	57	1	1
1993[1]	58	1	1
1994	60	1	1
1995	52	1	1
1996	65	1	2
1997	90	1	2
1998	100	1	2

[1] Estimate
[2] Began 1960
[3] Began 1986
[4] Began 1961
[5] Began 1987
[6] Began 1973
[7] Began 1988
[8] Of whom 1 was female
[9] Of whom 2 were female
[10] Revised figure

	Membership	Churches	Ministers
TABLE 9.20.1 Ransom Church of God Universal Fellowship[4]			
1960	–	–	–
1970[1]	30	1	3
1980[1]	55	1	6
1990	100	2	12
2000[1]	125	1	6
1991[1]	110	2	12
1992	120	2[1]	12
1993[1]	125	2	12
1994	130	2[1]	12
1995	100	1	3
1996[1]	110	1	4
1997[1]	115	1	4
1998[1]	120	1	5

	Membership	Churches	Ministers[10]
TABLE 9.20.2 Redemption Church of God[5]			
1960	–	–	–
1970[1]	40	1	2
1980[1]	50	1	3
1990	40	1	4
2000[1]	35	1	3
1991[1]	38	1	4
1992[1]	35	1	4
1993[1]	35	1	3
1994	35	1	3
1995	40	1	3
1996[1]	37	1	3
1997[1]	35	1	3
1998[1]	35	1	3

	Membership	Churches	Ministers
TABLE 9.20.3 Redemption Ministries, London[9]			
1960	–	–	–
1970	–	–	–
1980	–	–	–
1990	175	1	2
2000[1]	175	1	2
1991[1]	175	1	2
1992[1]	175	1	2
1993[1]	175	1	2
1994[1]	175	1	2
1995[1]	175	1	2
1996[1]	175	1	2
1997[1]	175	1	2
1998[1]	175	1	2

	Membership	Churches	Ministers
TABLE 9.20.4 Shiloh Pentecostal Church[6]			
1960	–	–	–
1970[1]	100	1	1
1980[1]	130	1	1
1990[1]	160	1	2
2000[1]	260	1	2
1991[1]	170	1	2
1992[1]	180	1	2
1993[1]	190	1	2
1994	200	1	2
1995	210	1	2
1996[1]	220	1	2
1997[1]	230	1	2
1998[1]	240	1	2

	Membership	Churches	Ministers
TABLE 9.20.5 Triumphant Church of God in Christ[7]			
1960	–	–	–
1970[1]	15	1	2
1980[1]	30	2	4
1990	50	2	4
2000[1]	70	2	4
1991[1]	55	2	4
1992[1]	60	2	4
1993[1]	65	2	4
1994[1]	70	2	4
1995[1]	60	2	4
1996[1]	62	2	4
1997[1]	64	2	4
1998[1]	65	2	4

	Membership	Churches	Ministers
TABLE 9.20.6 True Vine Church[3]			
1960	–	–	–
1970	–	–	–
1980	–	–	–
1990	80	1	3
2000[1]	80	1	3
1991[1]	80	1	3
1992[1]	80	1	3
1993[1]	80	1	3
1994[1]	80	1	3
1995[1]	80	1	3
1996[1]	80	1	3
1997[1]	80	1	3
1998[1]	80	1	3

	Membership	Churches	Ministers
TABLE 9.20.7 Universal Prayer Group Ministries[2]			
1960	–	–	–
1970[1]	40	1	1
1980	75	1	1
1990	300	1	5
2000[1]	1,000	3	15
1991[1]	350	1	6
1992[1]	400	1	7
1993[1]	450	1	8
1994[1]	500	1	9
1995	500	3	9
1996[1]	600	3	10
1997[1]	700	3	11
1998[1]	800	3	12

	Membership	Churches	Ministers
TABLE 9.20.8 Victory Pentecostal Church of God in Christ[8]			
1960	–	–	–
1970[1]	30	1	1
1980	50[1]	1	1[1]
1990	30	1	2
2000[1]	28	1	2[11]
1991[1]	30	1	2
1992[1]	30	1	2
1993[1]	30	1	2
1994[1]	30	1	2
1995	30	1	2
1996[1]	30	1	2
1997[1]	30	1	2
1998[1]	30	1	2

	Membership	Churches	Ministers
TABLE 9.20.9 Vision International Ministries[3]			
1960	–	–	–
1970	–	–	–
1980	–	–	–
1990	50	1	1
2000[1]	500	5	3
1991[1]	100	1	1
1992[1]	150	1	1
1993[1]	200	1	1
1994[1]	250	1	1
1995	300	1	1
1996	400	2	2[1]
1997[1]	425	3	2
1998	450[1]	4	3

[1] Estimate
[2] Began 1962
[3] Began 1989
[4] Began 1965
[5] Began 1961
[6] Began in UK 1968
[7] Began in UK 1965
[8] Began 1962
[9] Began 1987
[10] All male
[11] Revised figure

	Membership	Churches	Ministers
TABLE 9.21.1 Victory Church International			
1960	–	–	–
1970[1]	–	–	–
1980[1]	–	–	–
1990	200	2	5[1]
2000[1]	200	2	5
1991[1]	200	2	5
1992[1]	200	2	5
1993[1]	200	2	5
1994[1]	200	2	5
1995[1]	200	2	5
1996[1]	200	2	5
1997[1]	200	2	5
1998[1]	200	2	5

	Membership	Churches	Ministers[10]
TABLE 9.21.2 World Missions Outreach[2]			
1960	–	–	–
1970	–	–	–
1980	–	–	–
1990	55	1	3
2000	–	–	–
1991[1]	60	1	3
1992[1]	70	1	3
1993[1]	30	1	3
1994	–	–	–
1995	–	–	–
1996	–	–	–
1997	–	–	–
1998	–	–	–

	Membership	Churches	Ministers
TABLE 9.21.3 Other African and Caribbean Churches[3]			
1960	1,200	30	40
1970	10,500	150	200
1980	20,080[4]	289[4]	414
1990	24,865	390	741
2000	30,195[4]	386	876
1991	25,044	389	758
1992	25,223	388	775
1993	25,587	386	808
1994	25,950	385	840
1995	26,675	385	872
1996	27,420	386	873
1997	28,190	386	873
1998	29,000	386	875

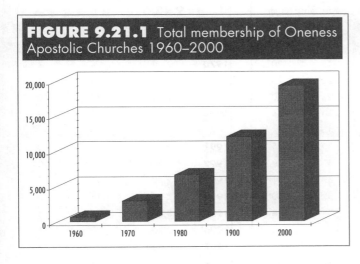

FIGURE 9.21.1 Total membership of Oneness Apostolic Churches 1960–2000

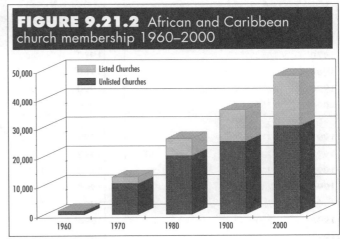

FIGURE 9.21.2 African and Caribbean church membership 1960–2000

- Listed Churches
- Unlisted Churches

[1] Estimate
[2] Began 1987 and closed in 1994
[3] All estimated
[4] Revised estimate
[5] Began 1983; linked to Hampstead Bible College

	Membership	Churches	Ministers
TABLE 9.21.4 Foursquare Gospel Church of Great Britain			
1960	–	–	–
1970	–	–	–
1980	–	–	–
1990	587	17	9
2000[1]	800	27	37
1991[1]	657	17	10
1992	727	18	10
1993	409	14	15
1994	489	15	22
1995	520	18	25
1996[1]	580	20	28
1997[1]	640	22	31
1998[1]	700	24	33

	Membership	Churches	Ministers
TABLE 9.21.5 United Apostlic Faith Church[3]			
1960	750	10	15
1970	750	10	15
1980	750	10	15
1990	750	10	15
2000	750	10	15
1991	750	10	15
1992	750	10	15
1993	750	10	15
1994	750	10	15
1995	750	10	15
1996	750	10	15
1997	750	10	15
1998	750	10	15

9

TABLE 9.22.1 — Total Onenes Apostolic Churches[5]

	Membership	Churches	Ministers
1960	620	14	18
1970	2,890	55	75
1980	6,580	110	140
1990	11,969	166	245
2000[1]	19,368	259	398
1991	12,727	178	262
1992	13,507	191	280
1993	14,250	198	292
1994	14,894	208	312
1995	15,480	215	330
1996	16,228	222	344
1997	17,205	233	356
1998	18,105	245	372

TABLE 9.22.2 — Assembly of the First Born[2]

	Membership	Churches	Ministers
1960	100	1	2
1970[1]	600	6	8
1980[1]	1,300	12	15
1990	2,000	18	25
2000[1]	2,700	21	35
1991[1]	2,200	20	27
1992[1]	2,300	20	28
1993[1]	2,320	20	29
1994	2,350[1]	21	30[1]
1995	2,350[1]	21	30[1]
1996[1]	2,400	21	31
1997[1]	2,450	21	32
1998[1]	2,500	21	33

TABLE 9.22.3 — Bethany Fellowship of Great Britain

	Membership	Churches	Ministers
1960	–	–	–
1970[1]	500	1	1
1980[1]	1,000	2	2
1990	2,000[1]	4[1]	5
2000[1]	2,500	5	9
1991[1]	2,000	4	6
1992[1]	2,000	4	7
1993[1]	2,000	4	7
1994[1]	2,000	4	7
1995	2,000[1]	4[1]	7
1996[1]	2,100	4	7
1997[1]	2,200	4	7
1998[1]	2,300	4	8

TABLE 9.22.4 — Bible Truth Church of God

	Membership	Churches	Ministers
1960	–	–	–
1970[1]	50	2	5
1980[1]	190	6	10
1990	200	7	18
2000[1]	255	9	26
1991[1]	210	7	19
1992	220	7[1]	20[1]
1993[1]	230	7	21
1994[1]	240	7	22
1995[1]	250	8	22
1996[1]	250	8	23
1997[1]	250	8	24
1998[1]	250	8	25

TABLE 9.22.5 — Bibleway Church of Our Lord Jesus Christ[3]

	Membership	Churches	Ministers
1960[1]	100	3	4
1970[1]	400	15	20
1980[1]	600	20	25
1990	1,004	28	40
2000[1]	1,950	38	66
1991[1]	1,050	30	45
1992	1,100[1]	33	49
1993	1,300[1]	32	51[9]
1994	1,500	32	50[9]
1995	1,500	34	58[9]
1996	1,750	35	60
1997[1]	1,800	36	61
1998[1]	1,850	37	63

TABLE 9.22.6 — Christ Apostolic Church Great Britain[4]

	Membership	Churches	Ministers
1960	–	–	–
1970	–	–	–
1980[1]	500	2	2
1990	2,100	11	10
2000[1]	3,800	23	19
1991[1]	2,300	12	10
1992	2,500[1]	14	10
1993[1]	2,700	15	10
1994	2,900[1]	17[1]	10
1995	3,000[1]	18[1]	15
1996	3,200	19	16
1997[1]	3,400	20	17
1998[1]	3,500	21	18

TABLE 9.22.7 — Church of God in Christ Congregational Independent

	Membership	Churches	Ministers
1960	–	–	–
1970	10	1	1
1980	35[1]	4[1]	5
1990	106	6	7
2000[1]	155	8	9
1991[1]	115	5	6
1992	125	7	8
1993[1]	120	7	8
1994	116	7	8
1995	120	7	8[10]
1996[1]	130	7	8
1997[1]	135	7	8
1998[1]	140	7	8

TABLE 9.22.8 — Church of God in Christ United[3]

	Membership	Churches	Ministers
1960[1]	150	3	3
1970[1]	250	5	5
1980	310	7[1]	7[1]
1990	272	7	7
2000[1]	220	9	9
1991[1]	265	7	7
1992	260	7[1]	7
1993	250	9	9
1994	250	9	9
1995	240	9	9[11]
1996[1]	235	9	9
1997[1]	230	9	9
1998[1]	225	9	9

TABLE 9.22.9 — Church of Jesus Christ Apostolic Faith[6]

	Membership	Churches	Ministers
1960[1]	20	1	1
1970[1]	20	1	1
1980	20[1]	1	1
1990	20	1	1
2000[1]	20	1	1
1991[1]	20	1	1
1992[1]	20	1	1
1993[1]	20	1	1
1994[1]	20	1	1
1995	20[1]	1	1[1]
1996[1]	20	1	1
1997[1]	20	1	1
1998[1]	20	1	1

[1] Estimate
[2] Began 1960
[3] Began 1958
[4] Began 1979
[5] Total of churches listed on pages 9.22, 9.23 and 9.24.1–4
[6] Began 1960, UK
[7] All part-time
[8] All male
[9] 38 were part-time
[10] Of whom 3 were female

TABLE 9.23.1 — Eagles Nest Community[6,8]

	Membership	Churches	Ministers
1960	–	–	–
1970	–	–	–
1980	–	–	–
1990	150	1	2
2000[1]	500	5	7
1991[1]	200	2	3
1992	300	3	5
1993[1]	325	3	5
1994[1]	350	4	6
1995	350[1]	4	6[1]
1996[1]	400	4	6
1997[1]	425	4	6
1998[1]	450	4	7

TABLE 9.23.2 — Elijah Tabernacle[2]

	Membership	Churches	Ministers
1960	–	–	–
1970	–	–	–
1980	–	–	–
1990	30	1	2
2000[1]	40	2	3
1991	21	1	3
1992	22	1	3
1993	25	1	3
1994	28	1	3
1995	40	1	3[9]
1996	28	1	2
1997[1]	30	1	2
1998[1]	30	2	2

TABLE 9.23.3 — First United Church of Jesus Christ

	Membership[10]	Churches	Ministers
1960[1]	150	5	7
1970[1]	500	15	20
1980[1]	950	30	40
1990	1,055	45[1]	60[1]
2000[1]	1,250	63	80
1991[1]	1,100	48	63
1992[1]	1,200	50	66
1993[1]	1,200	52	68
1994[1]	1,200	55	70
1995	1,200	55	70
1996[1]	1,210	56	72
1997[1]	1,220	58	74
1998[1]	1,230	60	76

TABLE 9.23.4 — Hackney Pentecostal Apostolic Church[4]

	Membership	Churches	Ministers
1960	–	–	–
1970[1]	10	1	1
1980[1]	30	1	3
1990	100	1[1]	7
2000[1]	235	1	12[11]
1991[1]	125	1	8
1992[1]	150	1	10
1993[1]	175	1	10
1994[1]	200	1	10
1995[1]	200	1	10
1996[1]	210	1	10
1997[1]	215	1	10
1998[1]	220	1	11

TABLE 9.23.5 — The Immaculate Conception Spiritual Baptist Church[12]

	Membership	Churches	Ministers
1960	–	–	–
1970	–	–	–
1980	–	–	–
1990	70	1	3
2000[1]	400	1	7
1991	120	1	4
1992	200	1	4
1993	210	1	4
1994	250	1	5[13]
1995	250	1	5
1996[1]	280	1	6
1997[1]	300	1	6
1998[1]	320	1	6

TABLE 9.23.6 — Mount Zion Holiness Assembly[7]

	Membership	Churches	Ministers[11]
1960	–	–	–
1970	–	–	–
1980[1]	20	1	1
1990	12	1	1
2000[1]	8	1	1
1991[1]	11	1	1
1992[1]	10	1	1
1993[1]	10	1	1
1994[1]	10	1	1
1995[1]	10	1	1
1996[1]	10	1	1
1997[1]	10	1	1
1998[1]	10	1	1

TABLE 9.23.7 — Mount Zion Pentecostal Apostolic Church[5]

	Membership	Churches	Ministers
1960	–	–	–
1970[1]	100	1	3
1980	250	1[1]	5[1]
1990	250	1	17
2000[15]	1,000	12	20
1991[1]	300	1	17
1992	320[15]	1	17[1]
1993[1]	350	1	17
1994[1]	200	1[1]	17
1995[1]	200	1	15
1996[1]	300	2	16
1997[1]	600	6	17
1998[1]	900	10	18

TABLE 9.23.8 — Shiloh United Church of Christ Apostolic World Wide[3,14]

	Membership	Churches	Ministers
1960	–	–	–
1970[1]	200	5	7
1980[1]	550	12	10
1990[1]	400	8	10
2000[1]	225	4	10
1991[1]	375	8	10
1992[1]	350	7	10
1993[1]	325	7	10
1994[1]	300	6	10
1995[1]	300	6	10
1996[1]	275	6	10
1997[1]	250	6	10
1998[1]	250	6	10

TABLE 9.23.9 — United Church of God

	Membership	Churches	Ministers[11]
1960	–	–	–
1970	–	–	–
1980[1]	25	1	1
1990	120	1	1
2000[1]	230	1	2
1991[1]	135	1	1
1992[1]	150	1	1
1993[1]	165	1	1
1994[1]	180	1	1
1995[1]	180	1	1
1996[1]	190	1	1
1997[1]	200	1	1
1998[1]	210	1	1

[1] Estimate
[2] Began 1985
[3] Began 1968, UK
[4] Began 1970
[5] Began in UK 1965
[6] Began 1983
[7] Began 1978, UK
[8] Formerly called Deliverance
Ministries International
[9] All female
[10] Active membership taken as 10% of the community
[11] All part-time
[12] Formerly called Apostle of Melchizedek Spiritual Baptist Church
[13] Of whom 3 were female
[14] Including Shiloh Church of Christ
[15] Revised figure

	Membership	Churches	Ministers
TABLE 9.24.1 United Pentecostal Church of Great Britain and Ireland[2]			
1960[1]	100	1	1
1970[1]	250	2	3
1980[1]	700	7	10
1990	1,980	22	26
2000[1]	3,600	46	68
1991[1]	2,080	25	28
1992	2,180	29	30
1993	2,424	32	34
1994	2,700[1]	36	49
1995	2,900[1]	38	54
1996[1]	3,000	40	57
1997[1]	3,200	42	60
1998[1]	3,400	44	63

	Membership	Churches	Ministers
TABLE 9.24.2 Universal Church of the Kingdom of God[3]			
1960	–	–	–
1970	–	–	–
1980	–	–	–
1990	–	–	–
2000[1]	100	5	10
1991	–	–	–
1992	–	–	–
1993	–	–	–
1994	–	–	–
1995[1]	20	1	2
1996[1]	40	1	4
1997[1]	60	2	6
1998[1]	80[1]	3	8[1]

	Membership	Churches	Ministers
TABLE 9.24.3 Universal Pentecostal Church			
1960	–	–	–
1970	–	–	–
1980[1]	100	3	3
1990	100[1]	3	3[1]
2000[1]	100	3	3
1991[1]	100	3	3
1992[1]	100	3	3
1993[1]	100	3	3
1994[1]	100	3	3
1995[1]	100	3	3
1996[1]	100	3	3
1997[1]	100	3	3
1998[1]	100	3	3

	Membership	Churches	Ministers
TABLE 9.24.4 Well of Living Water Ministries[4]			
1960	–	–	–
1970	–	–	–
1980	–	–	–
1990	–	–	–
2000[1]	80	1	1
1991	–	–	–
1992	–	–	–
1993	–	–	–
1994	–	–	–
1995	–	–	–
1996[1]	50	1	1
1997[1]	60	1	1
1998[1]	70	1	1

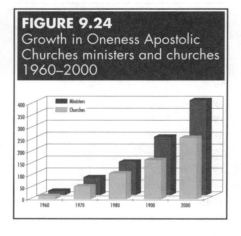

FIGURE 9.24
Growth in Oneness Apostolic Churches ministers and churches 1960–2000

[1] Estimate
[2] Began 1958
[3] Began 1977 by Emmanuel Macedo in Brazil, and in UK 1995; linked to the Rainbow Theatre
[4] Began 1996

TABLE 9.25.1
Total Central Denominations[10]

	Membership	Churches	Ministers
1900	115,569	1,843	3,256
1910	125,948	1,888	2,699
1920	162,815	1,795	3,399
1930	200,574	2,299	3,724
1940	158,297	2,247	3,599
1950	138,901	2,243	2,996
1960	140,106	2,243	2,389
1970	125,582	1,744	1,870
1980	111.841	1,715	1,601
1990	103,491	1,890	2,029
2000	93,970	1,774	1,749
1991	102,599	1,862	2,023
1992	102,359	1,822	1,993
1993	101,551	1,841	1,996
1994	100,538	1,841	1,987
1995	99,941	1,848	1,915
1996	98,912	1,855	1,885
1997	96,821	1,835	1,848
1998	95,102	1,761	1,812

TABLE 9.25.2
British Conference of Mennonites

	Membership	Churches	Ministers[2]
1900	–	–	–
1910	–	–	–
1920	–	–	–
1930	–	–	–
1940	–	–	–
1950	–	–	–
1960	–	–	–
1970	–	–	–
1980	12	1	1
1990	30	1	0
2000[1]	30	1	1
1991[1]	30	1	0
1992	30	1	0
1993	30[1]	1[1]	0[1]
1994	30[1]	1[1]	0[1]
1995	30	1	1
1996[1]	30[1]	1[1]	1[1]
1997[1]	30[1]	1[1]	1[1]
1998[1]	30	1	1

TABLE 9.25.3
Countess of Huntingdon's Connection

	Membership	Churches	Ministers[2]
1900[1]	5,000	70	55
1910[1]	4,000	63	51
1920[1]	3,000	55	44
1930[1]	2,000	45	36
1940[1]	1,000	33	27
1950[1]	1,000	33	24
1960[1]	1,000	33	20
1970	1,100	35	16
1980	860	29	22
1990	853	24	14
2000[6]	700	23	20
1991	875[1]	24	14
1992	900	24	15[1]
1993	925[1]	24	16
1994	950[1]	24	19
1995	970[1]	24[1]	19[1]
1996	1,000	24	20
1997	880	24	19
1998	800	23	19

TABLE 9.25.4
Moravian Church in Great Britain and Ireland

	Membership	Communicants	Churches	Ministers
1900	6,023[1]	3.342[1]	60[1]	43[1]
1910	6,487	3,803	62[1]	44[1]
1920	5,279	3,484	56[1]	40[1]
1930	3,801	3,365	47[1]	33[1]
1940	3,555	3,206	45[1]	32[1]
1950	3,440	3,015	44[1]	31[1]
1960	3,107	2,843	42[1]	30[1]
1970	2,564	4,643[9]	38	27
1980	2,651	4,600	41	32
1990	2,579	4,000[1]	40	27
2000[1]	1,800[6]	3,800	36	23
1991	2,565[1]	4,035[1]	40	28[1]
1992	2,551	4,060[1]	40	29
1993	2,518	4,100	39	29
1994	2,418	4,013	39	26
1995	2,326	4,000[1]	36	25
1996	2,121	3,960[1]	36	24
1997	2,071[1]	3,902[1]	36	24
1998	1,996[1]	3,880[1]	36	24[5]

TABLE 9.25.5
Religious Society of Friends (Quakers)

	Membership[3,6]	Great Britain	N Ireland	Churches[7]	Ministers[4]
1900	18,346	17,346	1,000[1]	403[1]	–
1910	20,522	19,522	1,000[1]	425[1]	–
1920	20,049	19,049	1,000[1]	424[1]	–
1930	20,117	19,117	1,000[1]	431[1]	–
1940	20,827	19,827	1,000[1]	443[1]	–
1950	21,795	20,795	1,000[1]	453[1]	–
1960	22,222	21,222	1,000[1]	457[1]	–
1970	21,572	20,572	1,000[1]	450	–
1980	19,313	18,549	764[8]	474	–
1990	19,008	18,084	924[8]	487	–
2000[6]	17,130	16,180	950[1]	489	–
1991	18,994	18,072	922	486	–
1992	18,992	18,072	920	487	–
1993	18,726	17,802	924	505	–
1994	18,503	17,579	924	506	–
1995	18,221	17,296	925[1]	513	–
1996	18,649	17,719	930[1]	519[1]	–
1997	17,934	16,999	935[1]	509[1]	–
1998[1]	17,246	16,306	940[1]	494[1]	–

9

[1] Estimate
[2] All male
[3] Includes children
[4] There are no ministers
[5] Of whom 6 were female

[6] Revised figure(s)
[7] 15 churches have been added each year 1900 to 1970 to include estimates for Northern Ireland; numbers as given in the 1995/6 *Irish Christian Handbook* Table 13c have been used for later years

[8] Taken from N Ireland Census
[9] Figures from 1970 include adherents and children. The previous series gave 2,740 communicants in 1970
[10] This Table gives the total of Tables 9.25.2–5 and 9.26.1–3

TABLE 9.26.1
Salvation Army

	Soldiers[2]	Corps[3]	Officers
1900	85,000	1,297	3,149[1]
1910	93,000	1,316	2,590[1]
1920	131,000	1,221	3,290
1930	170,000	1,724[1]	3,621[1]
1940	127,000	1,660	3,497[1]
1950	106,000	1,638	2,893[1]
1960	104,000	1,597	2,267[1]
1970	86,701	1,065	1,724
1980	72,277	966	1,451
1990	60,285	1,032	1,793[4]
2000[6]	52,320	940	1,560
1991	59,268	1,026	1,802
1992	58,698	985	1,807
1993	58,068	990	1,776
1994	57,191	988	1,770[1]
1995	57,124	973	1,703[5]
1996	56,188	992	1,680[1]
1997	54,719	982	1,650[1]
1998	53,470	923	1,620[1]

TABLE 9.26.2
Seventh-Day Adventist

	Membership	Churches	Ministers
1900	1,200[1]	13	9
1910	1,939	22	14
1920	3,487	39	25
1930	4,656	52	34
1940	5,915	66	43
1950	6,666	75	48
1960	9,277	104	67
1970	12,145	136	88
1980	14,569[7]	164	79
1990	17,739	232	144
2000[6]	19,690	240	131
1991	17,864	241	153
1992	18,200	241	118
1993	18,297	239	153
1994	18,565	241	152
1995	18,734	256	150
1996	18,845	238	146
1997	19,066	238	140
1998	19,390	239	134[1]

TABLE 9.26.3
Worldwide Church of God[8]

	Membership	Churches	Ministers
1900	–	–	–
1910	–	–	–
1920	–	–	–
1930	–	–	–
1940	–	–	–
1950	–	–	–
1960[1]	500	10	5
1970	1,500[1]	20	15[1]
1980	2,159	40	16
1990	2,997	44	28
2000[6]	2,300	45	14
1991	3,003	44	26[1]
1992	2,988	44	24[1]
1993	2,987	43	22[1]
1994	2,881	42	20[1]
1995	2,536	45	17
1996	2,079	45[1]	14[1]
1997	2,121	45[1]	14[1]
1998	2,200	45[1]	14[1]

TABLE 9.26.4
Emmanuel Holiness Church[9]

	Membership	Churches	Ministers
1900	–	–	–
1910	–	–	–
1920[1]	20	1	1
1930[1]	40	1	1
1940[1]	70	2	2
1950[1]	75	2	2
1960[1]	150	6	9
1970[1]	200	10	15
1980	370	8	10
1990	439	7	2
2000[1]	430	5	2
1991[1]	437	7	2
1992	435	7	2
1993[1]	431	7	2
1994[1]	430	7	2
1995	430	5	2[1]
1996[1]	430	5	2
1997[1]	430	5	2
1998[1]	430	5	2

TABLE 9.26.5
Swedish Lutheran

	Paying households[10]	Churches	Ministers
1900	1,000[1]	5	5
1910	1,500[1]	6	6
1920	2,000[1]	7	7
1930	2,000[1]	7	7
1940	2,500[1]	8	8
1950	3,500[1]	8	8
1960	2,800[1]	6	6
1970	2,300[1]	4	4
1980	2,300	4	5
1990	2,300	4	5
2000[1]	1,900	4	4
1991[1]	2,100	4	5
1992	1,900[1]	4	5[1]
1993	1,497[1]	4	5[1]
1994	1,451	4	4
1995	1,630[1]	4	4
1996	1,808	4	4
1997	1,623	4	4
1998	1,889	4	4

TABLE 9.26.6
Other Lutheran Churches[11]

	Membership	Churches	Ministers
1900[1]	1,500	4	1
1910[1]	1,500	4	1
1920[1]	2,000	5	1
1930[1]	2,000	5	1
1940[1]	2,000	5	1
1950[14]	4,000	7	1
1960[1]	4,800	12	1
1970[1]	5,650[12]	17	1
1980	4,630	17	1
1990	4,206[12]	13	1
2000[6]	5,775	14	3
1991[1]	4,630	13	1
1992	5,050[12]	13	2
1993[1]	5,130	13	2[6]
1994[13]	5,200	14[6]	3[6]
1995[6]	5,300	14	3
1996[1]	5,400	14	3
1997[1]	5,500	14	3
1998[1]	5,600	14	3

[1] Estimate
[2] Includes adherents
[3] Church buildings 1900 to 1960. In 1970 there were 1,326 church buildings
[4] Increase due to inclusion of officers in other forms of ministry not previously included
[5] Of whom 1,188, or 70%, were female
[6] Revised figure(s)
[7] Figures up to 1970 are for Great Britain only; figures for 1980 and beyond include the Republic of Ireland with about 80 members, 4 churches and 3 ministers, and Northern Ireland with about 200 members, 7 churches and 4 ministers. Churches and ministers 1900 to 1960 are pro rata to membership in 1970
[8] Began 1957. See Footnote 11 on Page 29 of *Religious Trends* No 1 1998/99 for a description of its current theological position
[9] Began 1916
[10] In 1985 the Swedish community in the UK was 18,999 people; it was an estimated 15,000 in 1995. The 1993 community comprised 6,179 households, of which 1,497 paid towards the Swedish Lutheran churches. In 1994, the numbers were respectively 6,200 and 1,451, and in 1995 6,514 and an estimated 1,630. The "membership" column consists of actual or estimated numbers of paying households, roughly pro rata to the number of churches, rather than a membership based on the fluctuating numbers of visitors, seamen, etc.
[11] In the 1851 Census which included church attendance, there were 6 Lutheran churches with a total attendance of 1,416. Extrapolated to 1900 pro rata to the general population this gives a total of 2,600 attenders, which reduces to 1,500 shown after subtracting 1900 figures in Tables 9.24.3, 4 and 6
[12] An exact figure of 5,435 Other Lutherans was obtained for 1975 by subtracting constituent churches from the Lutheran Council of Great Britain figures, and for 1990 and 1992
[13] Includes the London Chinese Lutheran Church which began 1994 with 50 members, 1 church and 1 minister
[14] The Lutheran Council of Great Britain began in 1948

	Membership	Churches	Ministers
TABLE 9.27.1			
Total Holiness Churches[2]			
1900	–	–	–
1910	330	8	6
1920	790	21	16
1930	860	22	16
1940	1,071	28	22
1950	1,216	31	23
1960	2,346	62	55
1970	4,470	121	108
1980	5,247	132	137
1990	6,948	153	192
2000	7,815	157	198
1991	7,022	152	190
1992	7,095	152	187
1993	7,321	152	192
1994	7,440	154	198
1995	7,110	149	179
1996	7,360	150	184
1997	7,470	152	187
1998	7,590	153	191

	Membership	Churches	Ministers
TABLE 9.27.2			
African Methodist Episcopal Church			
1960	–	–	–
1970[1]	100	4	6
1980	200[1]	6	8[1]
1990	300	8	10[1]
2000[1]	350	9	11
1991[1]	300	8	10
1992[1]	300	8	10
1993[1]	300	8	10
1994[1]	300	8	10
1995[1]	300	8	10
1996[1]	310	8	10
1997[1]	320	8	10
1998[1]	330	8	10

	Membership	Churches	Ministers
TABLE 9.27.3 African Methodist			
Episcopal Zion Church			
1960	–	–	–
1970	150[1]	5	7[1]
1980	280[1]	8	10[1]
1990	450[1]	12	15[1]
2000[1]	530	14	18
1991[1]	450	12	15
1992[1]	450	12	15
1993[1]	450	12	15
1994[1]	450	12	15
1995[1]	450	12	15
1996[1]	470	12	16
1997[1]	480	12	17
1998[1]	500	13	17

	Membership	Churches	Ministers
TABLE 9.27.4			
Church of the Nazarene[5]			
1900	–	–	–
1910[1]	330	8	6[1]
1920[1]	770	20	15[1]
1930[1]	820	21	15
1940	1,001	26[1]	20[1]
1950	1,141	29[1]	21[1]
1960	2,096	54[1]	41[1]
1970[1]	3,550	91	68
1980	3,792	93	87
1990	4,736	96	118
2000[1]	5,425[6]	96	116
1991[1]	4,790	96	115
1992	4,847	96	111
1993[1]	5,050	96	115
1994[1]	5,150	97	120
1995	4,950	95	111[3]
1996[1]	5,150	95	113
1997[1]	5,220	95	113
1998[1]	5,290	95	115

	Membership	Churches	Ministers
TABLE 9.27.5			
Holiness Churches of God[4]			
1960	–	–	–
1970	–	–	–
1980	–	–	–
1990	150	4	5
2000[1]	150	4	5
1991[1]	150	4	5
1992[1]	150	4	5
1993[1]	150	4	5
1994[1]	150	4	5
1995[1]	150	4	5
1996[1]	150	4	5
1997[1]	150	4	5
1998[1]	150	4	5

	Membership	Churches	Ministers
TABLE 9.27.6			
Pentecostal Holiness Church[9]			
1960	–	–	–
1970[1]	20	1	2
1980	50[1]	3	5[1]
1990	220	6	16[10]
2000[1]	330	8	25
1991[1]	235	6	18
1992	250[1]	6	20[1]
1993[1]	260	7	20
1994[1]	270	7	20
1995[1]	280	7	20
1996[1]	290	7	21
1997[1]	300	8	22
1998[1]	310	8	23

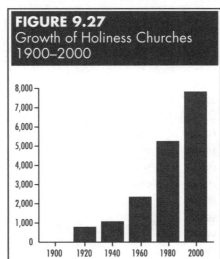

FIGURE 9.27
Growth of Holiness Churches
1900–2000

	Membership	Churches	Ministers
TABLE 9.27.7			
Wesleyan Holiness Church[7]			
1960[1]	100	2	5
1970[1]	450	10	10
1980[1]	555	14	17
1990	653[8]	20	26
2000[1]	600	21	21
1991[1]	660	19	25
1992	663	18	24
1993[1]	680	18	25
1994[1]	680	19	26
1995	550	18	16
1996[1]	560	19	17
1997[1]	570	20	18
1998[1]	580	20	19

[1] Estimate
[2] This Table is the total of Tables 9.27.2–7 and 9.26.4
[3] Of whom 6 are female
[4] Began 1988
[5] Began in 1908 as Pentecostal Church of Scotland, changed its name in 1915, united with International Holiness Mission in 1952 and Calvary Holiness Church in 1955
[6] Revised figure(s)
[7] Began 1958
[8] 2000 in attendance
[9] Full title is "Fellowship of Pentecostal Holiness Churches of Great Britain"
[10] 8 were part-time

	Membership	Churches	Ministers
TABLE 9.28.1 Total Lutheran Churches[6]			
1900	3,600	28	20
1910	4,500	34	25
1920	5,700	40	26
1930	5,880	41	26
1940	6,450	42	28
1950	11,280	68	34
1960	13,350	81	34
1970	15,810	100	38
1980	16,967	116	48
1990	15,470	103	48
2000	16,315	101	48
1991	15,645	103	46
1992	15,800	103	48
1993	15,442	103	48
1994	15,416	104	48
1995	15,650	101	49
1996	15,908	101	49
1997	15,803	101	49
1998	16,149	101	49

	Membership	Churches	Ministers
TABLE 9.28.2 Estonian Evangelical Lutheran Synod[2]			
1900	–	–	–
1910	–	–	–
1920	–	–	–
1930	–	–	–
1940	–	–	–
1950[1]	100	1	1
1960[1]	500	3	1
1970[1]	800	5	2
1980	1,200	7	2
1990	710	5	3
2000[1]	550[8]	5	3
1991[1]	700	5	3
1992	680	5	3
1993[1]	665	5	3
1994[1]	665	5	3
1995[1]	640	5	3
1996[1]	620	5	3
1997[1]	600	5	3
1998[1]	580	5	3

	Membership[5]	Churches[5]	Ministers
TABLE 9.28.3 Evangelical Lutheran Church of England[4]			
1900[1]	800	13	12
1910[1]	1,000	16	15
1920[1]	1,000	16	14
1930[1]	1,080	17	16
1940[1]	1,000	16	15
1950[1]	880	14	13
1960[1]	850	12	12
1970[8]	960	15	12
1980	1,077	17	16
1990	854	16	16
2000[1]	890	15	16
1991[1]	840	16	14
1992	820[1]	16	15
1993[1]	780	16	15
1994[1]	880	16	15
1995	880	15	16
1996[1]	880	15	16
1997[1]	880	15	16
1998[1]	880	15	16

	Membership	Churches[6]	Ministers
TABLE 9.28.4 German Evangelical Lutheran Synod[3]			
1900[1]	50	1	1
1910[1]	100	2	2
1920[1]	100	2	2
1930[1]	100	2	2
1940[1]	50	1	1
1950[3]	200	3	3
1960	500	8	3
1970	1,000	15	5
1980[8]	2,000	25	8
1990	2550[1]	31	11
2000[1]	2,500[8]	30	11
1991[1]	2,500	31[1]	11[1]
1992	2,500[1]	31	11
1993[1]	2,500	31[1]	11[1]
1994[1]	2,500	31[1]	11[1]
1995	2,500	30	11[7]
1996[1]	2,500	30	11
1997[1]	2,500	30	11
1998[1]	2,500	30	11

	Membership	Churches	Ministers
TABLE 9.28.5 Latvian Evangelical Lutheran Synod[2]			
1900	–	–	–
1910	–	–	–
1920	–	–	–
1930	–	–	–
1940	–	–	–
1950[1]	100	1	1
1960[1]	1,000	3	3
1970[8]	1,000	5	5
1980	2,680	7	7
1990	2,150	7	7
2000[8]	2,000	7	7
1991	2,125[1]	7	7
1992	2,100	7	7
1993	2,100	7	7
1994	2,070	7	7
1995	2,000	7	7
1996	2,000	7	7
1997[1]	2,000	7	7
1998[1]	2,000	7	7

	Membership	Churches	Ministers
TABLE 9.28.6 Polish Evangelical Church of the Augsburg Confessions Abroad			
1900[1]	250	5	1
1910[1]	400	6	1
1920[1]	600	10	2
1930[1]	700	10	2
1940[1]	900	12	3
1950[1]	2,700	35	8
1960[1]	2,900	37	8
1970[1]	3,100[8]	39	9
1980	3,080	39	9
1990	2,750	27	5
2000[1]	2,700	26	4
1991	2,750	27[1]	5[1]
1992[1]	2,750	27	5
1993[1]	2,750	27	5
1994[1]	2,750	27	5
1995[1]	2,700	26	5
1996[1]	2,700	26	5
1997[1]	2,700	26	5
1998[1]	2,700	26	5

[1] Estimate
[2] Began 1947 in UK
[3] Began 1955 as a Synod; prior to that just German Christ Church
[4] Began 1896
[5] Figures proportional to number of churches, 1980 onwards. Prior to 1980 to Church of England, but halved
[6] This Table is a total of Tables 9.28.2–6, and 9.26.5 and 6
[7] Of whom 2 were female
[8] Revised figure(s)

	Membership	Churches	Ministers
TABLE 9.29.1 American Church in London[2]			
1960[1]	150	1	1
1970	160[1]	1	1[1]
1980	200[1]	1	2[1]
1990	591	1	3
2000[1]	420[8]	1	2
1991	617	1	3
1992	612	1	3
1993	515	1	3
1994	532	1	3
1995	487	1	2
1996	480	1	1
1997	486	1	1
1998	450	1	2

	Membership	Churches	Ministers
TABLE 9.29.2 Chinese Churches			
1960[1]	250	4	2
1970[1]	500	15	8
1980	3,020	40	10
1990	4,500	45	20
2000[8]	5,800	78	40
1991[1]	4,500	48[8]	22[8]
1992	4,500	53[8]	24[8]
1993[1]	4,700	57[8]	26[8]
1994[1]	5,000	63[8]	28[8]
1995[1]	5,100	68	30
1996[1]	5,200	70	32
1997[1]	5,300	72	34
1998[1]	5,500	75	36

	Membership	Churches	Ministers
TABLE 9.29.3 Danish Churches			
1960[1]	180	2	2
1970[1]	200	2	2
1980	180	2	2
1990	80	2	2
2000[1]	100	1	2
1991[1]	85	2	2
1992	88	2	2
1993	94	1	2
1994	96	1	2
1995	100[1]	1	2
1996[1]	100	1	2
1997[1]	100	1	2
1998[1]	100	1	2

	Membership	Churches	Ministers
TABLE 9.29.4 Dutch Churches			
1960[1]	350	1	1
1970	400	1	1
1980	400	1	1
1990	270	1	1
2000[1]	300[3]	1	1
1991	270	1	1
1992	270	1	1
1993	270	1	1
1994	270	1	1
1995	260	1	1
1996	270	1	1
1997	270	1	1
1998	260	1	1

	Membership[6]	Churches	Ministers
TABLE 9.29.5 Finnish Church and Seaman's Mission[4]			
1960[1]	50	1	2
1970[1]	50	1	2
1980	50	1	2
1990	50	1	2
2000[1]	50	1	2
1991[1]	55	1	2
1992	60[1]	1	2
1993[1]	60	1	2
1994[1]	60	1	2
1995	50[1]	1	2[1]
1996[1]	50	1	2
1997[1]	50	1	2
1998[1]	50	1	2

	Membership[9]	Churches	Ministers
TABLE 9.29.6 French Protestant Church in UK[5]			
1960[1]	50	1	1
1970	60	1	1
1980	80	1	1
1990	200	3	3
2000[1]	300[8]	3	3
1991[1]	225	3	3
1992	250[1]	3	3
1993	250	3	3
1994	250	3	3
1995	250[1]	3	3
1996	260[1]	3	3
1997	270[1]	3	3
1998	280[1]	3	3

	Membership	Churches	Ministers
TABLE 9.29.7 Greek Christian Fellowship			
1960	–	–	–
1970	–	–	–
1980	–	–	–
1990	12	1	0
2000[1]	18	1	0
1991	14[1]	1	0
1992	15	1	0
1993	15[1]	1[1]	0
1994	15[1]	1[1]	0
1995[1]	15	1	0
1996[1]	16	1	0
1997[1]	16	1	0
1998[1]	17	1	0

	Membership[7]	Churches	Ministers
TABLE 9.29.8 Hungarian Reformed Church in the UK			
1960[1]	50	1	2
1970[1]	70	1	2
1980	100	1	2
1990	100	1	1
2000[1]	70	1	1
1991	110	1	1
1992	100	1	1
1993	100	1	1
1994	90	1	1
1995	90	1	1
1996	90	1	1
1997	85	1	1
1998	80	1	1

	Membership	Churches	Ministers
TABLE 9.29.9 International Presbyterian Church			
1960	–	–	–
1970	–	–	–
1980	200[1]	3	2[1]
1990	500[1]	6	4[1]
2000[1]	800	8	6
1991[1]	530	6	4
1992	560[1]	6	4
1993[1]	590	6	4
1994	620[1]	7	5
1995	680	7[10]	5
1996[1]	700	7	5
1997[1]	725	8	6
1998[1]	750	8	6

[1] Estimate
[2] In membership with the United Reformed Church; numbers are excluded from the total, except for 1960 and 1970
[3] Addresses in Greater London

[4] Membership figures are particularly subject to wide fluctuation due tor random incidence of seamen, visitors etc.
[5] Includes churches in Brighton, Canterbury & London.
[6] Active membership taken as 1% of community

[7] Active members taken as one-tenth of community
[8] Revised figure(s)
[9] Numbers are double attendance
[10] 5 Korean and 2 English congregations

TABLE 9.30.1 Iranian Christian Fellowship[3]

	Membership	Churches	Ministers
1960	–	–	–
1970	–	–	–
1980	–	–	–
1990	50	1	2
2000[1]	90	1	3
1991	55	1	2
1992	60	1	3
1993	70	1	3
1994	80	1	3
1995	90	1	3
1996[1]	90	1	3
1997[1]	90	1	3
1998[1]	90	1	3

TABLE 9.30.2 Italian Pentecostal

	Membership	Churches	Ministers
1960	–	–	–
1970	10[1]	0	1[1]
1980	20	0	2
1990	75	4	4
2000[1]	120	7	5
1991	80[1]	4	3
1992	85[1]	4	3
1993	90	5	4
1994	90	5	4
1995	95[1]	5	4
1996[1]	100	6	4
1997[1]	105	6	4
1998[1]	110	7	5

TABLE 9.30.3 Japanese Christian[4]

	Membership	Churches	Ministers
1960	–	–	–
1970[1]	90	2	1
1980	60	2	2
1990	–	–	–
2000[1]	40	1	0
1991	–	–	–
1992	–	–	–
1993[1]	10	1	0
1994[1]	10	1	0
1995	20	1	0
1996[1]	25	1	0
1997[1]	30	1	0
1998[1]	35	1	0

TABLE 9.30.4 Korean Churches[5]

	Membership[6]	Churches	Ministers
1960[1]	70	1	2
1970[1]	200	3	5
1980[1]	600	10	20
1990	1,100[1]	16	30[1]
2000[1]	1,520	21	39
1991[1]	1,300	17	32
1992	1,300	17	35
1993[1]	1,300	17	35
1994[1]	1,300	17	35
1995[1]	1,300	17	35
1996[1]	1,350	18	36
1997[1]	1,400	19	37
1998[1]	1,450	20	38

TABLE 9.30.5 London Messianic Congregation[11]

	Membership	Churches	Ministers
1960	–	–	–
1970	–	–	–
1980	50[1]	1[1]	0
1990	100[1]	2	2
2000[1]	200[1]	4	4
1991[1]	125	2	2
1992	150	3	3
1993[1]	150	3	3
1994[1]	150	3	3
1995[1]	150	3	3
1996[1]	160	3	3
1997[1]	170	3	3
1998[1]	180	4	4

TABLE 9.30.6 Norweigan Church and Seaman's Mission: St Olav's Church[7]

	Membership	Churches	Ministers
1960[1]	150	4	3
1970[1]	200	4	3
1980	300	5	3
1990	440	6	3
2000[1]	540	7[12]	4[12]
1991[1]	445	6	3
1992	450	6	3
1993[1]	460	6	3
1994[1]	470	6	3
1995	500[1]	7	4
1996	520	7	4
1997	530	7	4
1998[1]	540	7	4

TABLE 9.30.7 Bread of Life Ministries (Portugese)[8,9]

	Membership	Churches	Ministers
1960	–	–	–
1970	–	–	–
1980	–	–	–
1990	6	0	1
2000[1]	400	7	5
1991	40	0	1
1992	60	0	1
1993	80	1	3
1994	120	5	4
1995	350	6	4
1996	380	7	7
1997	420	10	10
1998	480	10	12

TABLE 9.30.8 Scottish Asian Christian Fellowship[2]

	Membership	Churches	Ministers
1960	–	–	–
1970	–	–	–
1980	–	–	–
1990	–	–	–
2000[1]	40	1	1
1991	–	–	–
1992	–	–	–
1993	–	–	–
1994	–	–	–
1995	–	–	–
1996	–	–	–
1997	–	–	–
1998	23	1	0

TABLE 9.30.9 Spanish Evangelical[10]

	Membership	Churches	Ministers
1960	10	1	1
1970[1]	10	1	2
1980	30	2	4
1990	60	1	3
2000[1]	135	2	3
1991[1]	79	1	3
1992	80	1	3
1993	80[1]	1[1]	3
1994	85[1]	1[1]	3
1995	120	2	3
1996[1]	125	2	3
1997[1]	130	2	3
1998[1]	130	2	3

[1] Estimate
[2] Began 1998
[3] Began 1985
[4] Closed 1986; another church opened in 1993
[5] Excludes two Korean congregations in the International Presbyterian Church but includes the World Mission Korean Church in Surrey (50 members 1995)
[6] Figures proportional to number of churches
[7] Membership figures are particularly subject to wide fluctuations due to random incidence of visitors, seamen etc.
[8] Began officially 1993
[9] In membership with Elim Pentecostal Church
[10] Began 1960
[11] Began 1980
[12] Revised figure

	Membership	Churches	Ministers
TABLE 9.31.1 Swahili Church			
1960[1]	40	1	1
1970[1]	50	1	2
1980	70	1	2
1990	90	1	1
2000[1]	105	1	1
1991[1]	90	1	1
1992	90	1	1
1993[1]	90	1	1
1994[1]	95	1	1
1995[1]	95	1	1
1996[1]	95	1	1
1997[1]	100	1	1
1998[1]	100	1	1

	Membership	Churches	Ministers
TABLE 9.31.2 Swiss Churches[2]			
1960[1]	1,200	3	3
1970[1]	1,400[3]	3	3
1980	1,016	3	2
1990	1,600	3	3
2000[1]	1,730	3	3
1991[1]	1,550	3	3
1992	1,500[1]	3	3[1]
1993[1]	1,550	3	3
1994[1]	1,575	3	3
1995[1]	1,600	3	3
1996[1]	1,625	3	3
1997[1]	1,650	3	3
1998[1]	1,680	3	3

	Membership	Churches	Ministers
TABLE 9.31.3 Syrian Church, Mar Thoma			
1960[1]	150	1	1
1970[1]	250	1	2
1980	300	1	2
1990	400	1	1
2000[1]	480	1	2
1991[1]	400	1	1
1992	400	1	1
1993[1]	410	1	1
1994	420[1]	1[1]	2
1995[1]	430	1	2
1996[1]	440	1	2
1997[1]	450	1	2
1998[1]	460	1	2

	Membership	Churches	Ministers
TABLE 9.31.4 Tamil Language Congregations[4]			
1960	–	–	–
1970	–	–	–
1980	–	–	–
1990	220	3	4
2000[1]	1,100	14	17
1991[1]	330	5	5
1992[1]	450	7	6
1993[1]	570	9	6
1994[1]	680	11	7
1995	880[1]	12[5]	15
1996[1]	920	12	15
1997[1]	960	12	16
1998[1]	1,000	13	16

	Membership	Churches	Ministers
TABLE 9.31.5 Urdu and Punjabi			
1960[1]	25	1	1
1970[1]	50	1	1
1980	50[1]	1	1
1990	50[1]	1	1
2000[1]	50	1	1
1991[1]	50	1	1
1992	50[1]	1	1
1993[1]	50	1	1
1994[1]	50	1	1
1995[1]	50	1	1
1996[1]	50	1	1
1997[1]	50	1	1
1998[1]	50	1	1

	Membership	Churches	Ministers
TABLE 9.31.6 Other Language Groups[6]			
1960	300	6	3
1970	400	8	4
1980	400	8	4
1990	600	12	6
2000	850	17	9
1991	650	13	7
1992	650	13	7
1993	700	14	7
1994	700	14	7
1995	750	15	8
1996	750	15	8
1997	800	16	8
1998	800	16	8

[1] Estimate
[2] Includes the Swiss Church in London, the Swiss Reformed Church and the Swiss Evangelical Brotherhood Church
[3] Revised figure
[4] First congregation began 1983
[5] Of which 8 belong to established denominations
[6] All estimated

9

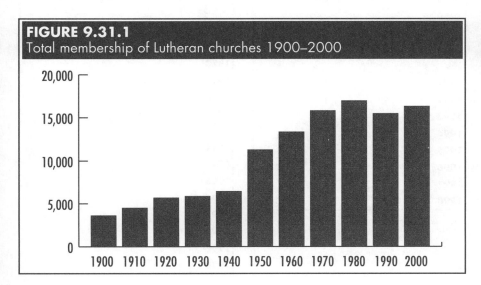

FIGURE 9.31.1
Total membership of Lutheran churches 1900–2000

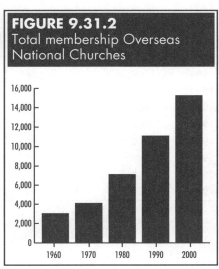

FIGURE 9.31.2
Total membership Overseas National Churches

	Membership	Churches	Ministers
TABLE 9.32.1 Total All Other Denominations[10]			
1900	119,169	1,871	3,276
1910	130,778	1,930	2,730
1920	169,305	1,856	3,441
1930	207,314	2,362	3,766
1940	166,018	2,318	3,650
1950	152,547	2,352	3,062
1960	159,427	2,429	2,536
1970	150,762	2,031	2,097
1980	142,241	2,068	1,897
1990	138,153	2,284	2,416
2000	134,363	2,250	2,194
1991	137,909	2,262	2,411
1992	138,039	2,228	2,385
1993	137,523	2,255	2,398
1994	137,127	2,270	2,400
1995	137,123	2,279	2,319
1996	136,901	2,294	2,300
1997	135,276	2,286	2,277
1998	134,438	2,227	2,251

	Membership	Churches	Ministers
TABLE 9.32.2 Total All Overseas Nationals[2]			
1900	–	–	–
1910	–	–	–
1920	–	–	–
1930	–	–	–
1940[1]	200	1	1
1950[1]	1,100	9	8
1960	3,025	29	26
1970	4,100	46	41
1980	7,126	84	64
1990	11,094	112	97
2000	15,258	183	154
1991	11,591	119	102
1992	11,780	127	110
1993	12,204	136	115
1994	12,758	149	121
1995	13,462	159	132
1996	13,796	164	137
1997	14,257	172	147
1998	14,592	179	153

	Membership	Churches	Ministers
TABLE 9.32.3 Liberal Catholic Church (Grail Community)[3]			
1960	–	–	–
1970	–	–	–
1980	–	–	–
1990	150[1]	3	6[1]
2000[1]	150	3	6
1991[1]	150	3	6
1992[1]	150	3	6
1993[1]	150	3	6
1994[1]	150	3	6
1995[1]	150	3	6
1996[1]	150	3	6
1997[1]	150	3	6
1998	150	3	6

	Membership	Churches	Ministers
TABLE 9.32.4 Liberal Catholic Church (Theosophia Synod)[3,4]			
1960	–	–	–
1970	–	–	–
1980	–	–	–
1990	100[1]	2	14
2000[1]	100	2	14
1991[1]	100	2	14
1992[1]	100	2	14
1993[1]	100	2	14
1994[1]	100	2	14
1995[1]	100	2	14
1996[1]	100	2	14
1997[1]	100	2	14
1998[1]	100	2	14

	Membership	Churches	Ministers
TABLE 9.32.5 The Christian Community[9]			
1900	–	–	–
1910	–	–	–
1920	–	–	–
1930	–	–	–
1940	–	–	–
1950[1]	50	1	1
1960[1]	300	6	7
1970[1]	800	12	15
1980	1,060	13	22
1990	800[1]	18	25
2000[1]	470	16	17
1991[1]	760	17	24
1992[1]	720	15	22
1993[1]	680	14	21
1994[1]	640	13	20
1995	600	12	18[8]
1996[1]	550	13	18
1997[1]	500	14	18
1998[1]	500	15	18

	Membership	Churches	Ministers
TABLE 9.32.6 Life-Changing Ministries[5]			
1900	–	–	–
1910	–	–	–
1920	–	–	–
1930	–	–	–
1940	–	–	–
1950	–	–	–
1960	–	–	–
1970	–	–	–
1980	–	–	–
1990	–	–	–
2000[6]	250	11	3
1991	7	1	0
1992	25	1	0
1993	40	1	1
1994	50	1	1
1995	75	2	1
1996	90	3	2
1997	140	4	3
1998	220	7	3

	Membership	Churches	Ministers
TABLE 9.32.7 Gnostic Church of Sophia[7]			
1960	–	–	–
1970	–	–	–
1980	–	–	–
1990	–	–	–
2000[1]	35	3	5
1991	35	3	5
1992[1]	35	3	5
1993[1]	35	3	5
1994[1]	35	3	5
1995[1]	35	3	5
1996[1]	35	3	5
1997[1]	35	3	5
1998[1]	35	3	5

[1] Estimate
[2] Total of Tables 9.29.1–9, 9.30.1–9 and 9.31.1–6 and then extrapolated backwards for earlier years
[3] A breakaway group from the Liberal Catholic Church, with different theology
[4] Began 1990 in the UK
[5] Began 1991, an independent Pentecostal church
[6] Church's own estimates
[7] An independent church in the Catholic tradition which says it is Trinitarian, began 1991
[8] Of whom 6 were female
[9] Previously in the Non-Trinitarian Section
[10] Total of Tables 9.25.1, 9.27.1, 9.28.1 and 9.32.2

OTHER RELIGIOUS AND NON-TRINITARIAN STATISTICS

Contents

10

Sources:
Individual churches and religions, previous editions of the *UK Christian Handbook* and *Churches and Churchgoers* by Robert Currie et al, OUP, 1974

	Membership	Churches	Ministers
TABLE 10.2.1 Total Non-Trinitarian Churches			
1900	70,982	871	512
1910	110,805	1,174	756
1920	172,080	1,694	1,052
1930	175,533	1,888	1,675
1940	172,499	1,953	2,596
1950	177,942	2,121	3,641
1960	212,159	2,440	6,189
1970	276,120	2,673	8,083
1980	348,756	3,090	10,431
1990	454,557	3,297	15,347
2000	548,433	3,492	11,127
1991	464,403	3,311	15,294
1992	466,339	3,283	15,818
1993	479,453	3,320	18,359
1994	493,883	3,338	16,397
1995	507,936	3,369	15,420
1996	524,595	3,385	14,569
1997	531,990	3,416	13,724
1998	537,311	3,442	12,739

	Membership	Ecclesias	Ministers[3]
TABLE 10.2.2 Christadelphians			
1900[1]	6,000	110	–
1910[1]	9,000	160	–
1920[1]	12,000	220	–
1930[1]	15,000	270	–
1940[1]	18,000	325	–
1950[1]	18,000	325	–
1960[1]	20,000	360	–
1970[1]	21,000	379	–
1980[1]	22,000[1]	360	–
1990[1]	20,000	320	–
2000[1]	18,465	278	–
1991[1]	20,000	320	–
1992[1]	19,500	318	–
1993[1]	19,400[11]	310	–
1994[1]	19,300[11]	300	–
1995[1]	19,200[11]	297	–
1996[1]	19,000	292	–
1997[1]	18,900	287	–
1998[1]	18,700	282	–

	Membership	Churches	Practitioners[15]
TABLE 10.2.3 Church of Christian Scientist			
1900	500[1]	5	12
1910	7,700[1]	65	193[1]
1920	12,800[1]	113	320[1]
1930	30,400[1]	206	761[1]
1940	44,200[1]	313	1,104
1950	36,400[1]	341	909[1]
1960	27,000[1]	336	680[12]
1970	22,000[1]	311	540[11]
1980	15,000[1]	261	420[11]
1990	11,000	225[1]	350[11]
2000[1]	7,500	183	278[11]
1991[1]	10,750	218	340[11]
1992[1]	10,500	210	330[11]
1993[1]	10,500	205	320[11]
1994[1]	9,750	200	310[11]
1995[1]	9,500	200	305[11]
1996[1]	9,000	195	300[11]
1997[1]	8,500	190	290[11]
1998[1]	8,000	185	280[11]

	Membership	Churches	Ministers
TABLE 10.2.4 Jehovah's Witnesses			
1900	–	–	–
1910	–	–	–
1920[13]	550[1]	11[1]	60[1]
1930[1]	2,740	46[1]	300[1]
1940	8,823	108[1]	900[1]
1950	20,936	260[1]	2,200[1]
1960	43,650	536[1]	4,500[1]
1970	59,705	733[1]	6,200[1]
1980	85,321	1,163	8,109
1990	116,612	1,318	12,733
2000[11]	134,000	1,485	8,500
1991	125,836	1,332	12,692
1992	126,173	1,362	13,275[5]
1993	127,395	1,371	15,796
1994	129,852	1,388	13,831
1995[1]	129,400	1,403	12,860
1996[1]	130,600	1,420	12,000
1997[1]	131,800	1,437	11,140
1998[1]	131,981	1,452	10,138

	Membership	Churches	Ministers
TABLE 10.2.5 Liberal Catholic Church[1]			
1900	–	–	–
1910	–	–	–
1920[2]	750	10	20
1930	1,200	25	30
1940	800	22	25
1950	1,000	22	28
1960	1,000	22	28
1970	650	22	35
1980	650	20	38
1990	550	17	36
2000[16]	150	5	15
1991[1]	525	15	35
1992[1]	500	13	32
1993[1]	475	11	30
1994[1]	450	11	28
1995[1]	425	11	25
1996[1]	400	11	23
1997[1]	375	11	22
1998[1]	350[18]	11	21

	Membership	Churches	Ministers
TABLE 10.2.6 Church of Jesus Christ of Latter Day Saints (Mormons)			
1900	5,683[14]	8[1]	8[1]
1910	8,364[14]	12[1]	12[1]
1920	8,297[14]	12[1]	12[1]
1930	7,991[14]	11[1]	11[1]
1940	7,864[14]	11[1]	11[1]
1950	7,857[14]	11[1]	11[1]
1960	21,332	28[1]	28[1]
1970	85,217	110[1]	110[1]
1980	114,458	197	197
1990	159,789	329	329
2000[1]	185,000[8]	480	480
1991	160,068	331	331
1992	162,560	313[9]	313
1993	165,025	362	362
1994	168,302	382	382
1995[1]	174,000[11]	400[11]	400[11]
1996[1]	177,000	410	410
1997[1]	180,000	430	430
1998[1]	182,000	450	450

[1] Estimate
[2] Began 1916 as the old Catholic Church being named the Liberal Catholic Church (old Catholic)
[3] No full time ministers
[4] The Christian Science Catholic has a byelaw which forbids publication of membership numbers; these are all estimated
[5] Of which 2,200 were female
[6] The Liberal Catholic Church is Trinitarian but included here because 'The man Jesus', the second person of the Trinity, is seen as being overshadowed by a greater being 'The Christ (one) essential divinity within a man', a position distinct from Jesus Christ as the only Son of God in the traditional creeds
[7] Attendance is slightly higher than membership. For instance in 1987 there were 166,000 attenders to 142,310 members
[8] Churches own estimate
[9] In 239 religious meeting houses
[10] All 'worthy' males from the age of 12 are ordained as 'ministers'. There are no paid clergy, but each congregation is headed by a Bishop
[11] Revised figure
[12] 567 in 1967, 581 in 1969
[13] First members were made in Britain in 1914
[14] Actual figures for Great Britain plus 1,500 for N. Ireland
[15] Members and Churches pro rata to practitioners 1900–1960
[16] Reduced because of the formation of the Reformed Liberal Catholic
[17] All Bishops are also members of the Theosophical Society
[18] 41% are members of the Theosophical Society

	Membership	Churches	Ministers
TABLE 10.3.1 Church of God International			
1960	–	–	–
1970	–	–	–
1980	5	1	1
1990	35[1]	2	1
2000[1]	120	15	2
1991[1]	44	4	1
1992	52	6	1
1993[1]	60	7	1
1994[1]	68	8	1
1995[1]	75	9	1
1996[1]	80	10	1
1997[1]	90	11	1
1998[1]	100	12	2

	Membership	Churches	Ministers
TABLE 10.3.2 The Family[8]			
1960[1]	1,000	20	40
1970[1]	1,000	20	40
1980[1]	200	5	10
1990[1]	200	5	10
2000[1]	200	5	10
1991[1]	200	5	10
1992[1]	200	5	10
1993[1]	200	5	10
1994[1]	200	5	10
1995[1]	200	5	10
1996[1]	200	5	10
1997[1]	200	5	10
1998[1]	200	5	10

	Membership	Churches	Ministers
TABLE 10.3.3 Global Church of God[2]			
1960	–	–	–
1970	–	–	–
1980	–	–	–
1990	–	–	–
2000[1]	50	5	2
1991	–	–	–
1992	–	–	–
1993	–	–	–
1994	–	–	–
1995[1]	50	5	2
1996[1]	50	5	2
1997[1]	50	5	2
1998[1]	50	5	2

	Membership	Churches	Ministers
TABLE 10.3.4 London Church of Christ[3,9]			
1960	–	–	–
1970	–	–	–
1980	–	–	–
1990	1,000	8[10]	4[1]
2000[1]	2,000	15	7
1991[1]	1,000	9	4
1992[1]	1,200	10	4
1993[1]	1,300	10	5
1994[1]	1,400	11	5
1995[1]	1,500	12	6
1996[1]	1,600	12	6
1997[1]	1,700	13	6
1998[1]	1,800	14	7

	Membership	Churches	Ministers
TABLE 10.3.5 Philadelphia Church of God[4]			
1960	–	–	–
1970	–	–	–
1980	–	–	–
1990	50[1]	3	3
2000	30	3	3
1991[1]	50	3	3
1992[1]	50	3	3
1993[1]	50	3	3
1994[1]	50	3	3
1995[1]	50	3	3
1996[1]	50	3	3
1997[1]	50	3	3
1998[1]	40	3	3

	Membership	Churches	Ministers
TABLE 10.3.6 Reorganized Church of Jesus Christ of Latter Day Saints[11]			
1960[1]	2,700	21	145
1970	2,400	20	140[1]
1980[1]	2,100	20	140
1990	1,824[12]	21	143
2000[1]	1,303	21	157
1991	1,795[1]	21	144
1992	1,765	22	146
1993	1,758	22	148
1994	1,753	21	150
1995	1,446	21	155[1,13]
1996[1]	1,420	21	155
1997[1]	1,400	21	156
1998[1]	1,370	21	156

	Membership	Churches	Ministers
TABLE 10.3.7 Scientology, Church of[15]			
1960[1]	5,000	4	100
1970[1]	10,000	8	200
1980	30,000	16	450
1990	75,000	13	700
2000[1]	144,400	17	760
1991	78,000[1]	13	725[1]
1992	80,000[1]	13	730[6]
1993	90,000[1]	13	735[6]
1994	100,000	13	737[6]
1995	121,800	17	739[14]
1996[1]	125,000	17	745
1997[1]	130,000	17	750
1998[1]	135,000	17	755

	Membership	Churches	Ministers
TABLE 10.3.8 United Church of God[5]			
1960	–	–	–
1970	–	–	–
1980	–	–	–
1990	–	–	–
2000[1]	200	10	8
1991	–	–	–
1992	–	–	–
1993	–	–	–
1994	–	–	–
1995	–	–	–
1996[1]	50	2	2
1997[1]	100	5	4
1998[1]	150	7	6

[1] Estimate
[2] Began 1995 as a breakaway group from the Worldwide Church of God
[3] Began 1982
[4] Began 1994 as a breakaway group of the Worldwide Church of God
[5] Began 1995 as a breakaway group of the Worldwide Church of God with 150 members
[6] Revised estimate
[7] An offshoot of the Worldwide Church of God; they believe the Holy spirit is divine but not part of the Godhead
[8] Previously called The Children of god which officially disbanded in February 1978. The remnant were then called the Family of Love, but have since abbreviated their name. They have been active in over 100 countries, and are currently particularly strong in Australia. The family is Trinitarian but is included here because of its close association with the writings of its founder Father David, and previous controversial outreach methods such as 'Flirty Fishing'
[9] The London Church of Christ is Trinitarian but included here because whilst it emphasises salvation is through Jesus Christ. It also teaches that salvation is only through their church
[10] Including one in Edinburgh, others in Birmingham, Leeds, Liverpool, London, Manchester, Newcastle and Oxford
[11] Whilst the Church 'firmly holds to a trinity of God, Christ and the Holy Spirit' it is included here because the Book of Mormon is also regarded as containing inspired writings which provide an added testimony of the divinity of Jesus Christ
[12] Worldwide membership in 1991 was 245,413
[13] Of whom an estimated 35 were female
[14] Of whom 250 were female
[15] Since 10 December 1996 Scientology has been officially recognised as a religion by the Home Office replacing its previous status as a cult
[16] Revised estimate

10

	Community	Churches	Ministers
TABLE 10.4.1 Total Spiritualists[6]			
1900[1]	25,000	250	83
1910[1]	50,000	400	133
1920[1]	100,000	760	253
1930[1]	84,000	715	238
1940[1]	61,600	638	213
1950[1]	64,000	650	217
1960[1]	61,300	636	212
1970[1]	44,934	600	207
1980	52,404	578	290
1990	45,000[7]	550	310
2000[1]	35,000	520	260
1991[1]	43,000	548	295
1992[1]	41,000	545[8]	280
1993[1]	40,500	540	275
1994[1]	40,000	535	270
1995[1]	40,000	535	270
1996[1]	39,000	532	268
1997[1]	38,000	530	266
1998[1]	37,000	527	264

	Membership	Churches	Ministers
TABLE 10.4.2 Swedenborgian New Church[10]			
1900	6,335	100[1]	43[1]
1910	6,684	100[1]	45[1]
1920	6,486	94[1]	44[1]
1930	6,096	86[1]	41[1]
1940	5,461	76[1]	37[1]
1950	4,852	66[1]	33[1]
1960	4,081	56[1]	28[1]
1970	3,104	49	21
1980	2,161	42	21
1990	1,712	36	16
2000[1]	1,240	30	13
1991	1,665	36	15
1992	1,639	36	15
1993	1,580	35	14
1994	1,528	36	15
1995	1,450	34	15
1996[1]	1,400	33	15
1997[1]	1,350	32	14
1998[1]	1,300	32	14

	Membership	Churches	Ministers
TABLE 10.4.3 Unification Church (Moonies)			
1960	–	–	–
1970[1]	50	2	5
1980	597	29	35[1]
1990	385[2]	31[1]	53[1]
2000[1]	400	31	57
1991[1]	350	30	53
1992[1]	360	30	53
1993[1]	370	30	54
1994[1]	380	30	54
1995[1]	390	31	55
1996[1]	395	31	55
1997[1]	395	31	56
1998[1]	395	31	56

	Membership	Churches	Ministers
TABLE 10.4.4 The Way			
1960	–	–	–
1970[1]	100	2	1
1980	300	25	5
1990	600[1]	45	6
2000[1]	875	58	8
1991[1]	600	45	6
1992	600[1]	45	6[1]
1993	640	46	6
1994[1]	680	47	6
1995[1]	725	48	7
1996[1]	750	50	7
1997[1]	800	52	7
1998[1]	825	54	8

	Membership	Lodges	Ministers[11]
TABLE 10.4.5 Theosophists[13,14]			
1900[1]	1,464	30	–
1910	2,057	63[1]	–
1920	6,197	113[1]	–
1930	5,106	187	–
1940	3,751	120[1]	–
1950	3,897	112[1]	–
1960	3,096	68[1]	–
1970	2,960	65	–
1980	2,560[9]	60[1]	–
1990	2,300[9,12]	58[9]	–
2000[1]	2,000	51	–
1991[1]	2,270	56	–
1992[1]	2,240	55	–
1993[1]	2,200	55	–
1994[1]	2,170	55	–
1995[1]	2,140	54	–
1996[1]	2,100	53	–
1997[1]	2,080	53	–
1998[1]	2,050	52	–

	Membership	Churches	Ministers
TABLE 10.4.6 Unitarian and Free Christian Churches			
1900	26,000[1]	368	366
1910	27,000[1]	374	373
1920	25,000[1]	361	343
1930	23,000[1]	348	294
1940	22,000[1]	340	306
1950	21,000[1]	334	243
1960	18,000[1]	313	228
1970	15,000[1]	272	184[9]
1980	11,000	213	155
1990	8,500	216	153
2000[4]	5,500	180	67
1991[1]	8,250	225	140[9]
1992[1]	8,000[1]	197	120[9]
1993[1]	8,000	195	100[9]
1994[1]	8,000	193	80[9]
1995[1]	6,700	184	67[3]
1996[1]	6,500	183	67
1997[1]	6,500	181	70
1998[1]	6,000	181	67

	Membership	Churches	Ministers
TABLE 10.4.7 Other Non-Trinitarian[5]			
1960	4,000	40	200
1970	8,000	80	400
1980	10,000	100	500
1990	10,000	100	500
2000	10,000	100	500
1991	10,000	100	500
1992	10,000	100	500
1993	10,000	100	500
1994	10,000	100	500
1995	10,000	100	500
1996	10,000	100	500
1997	10,000	100	500
1998	10,000	100	500

[1] Estimate
[2] 1985 & 1990 figures exclude an estimated 8,000 associate members, and 100 'practising' members. Membership numbers from New Religious Movements, Dr Eileen Barker, HMSO 1989
[3] Of whom 14 were female
[4] Churches own estimate
[5] All estimated, but includes Local Church Movement and the True Jesus Church
[6] A summation of figures of the Greater World Christian Spiritual Associations (GWESA), the Spiritual Association of Great Britain and others (SAGB)
[7] Including 2,440 members of SAGB and 670 members of GWCSA
[8] Including 125 affiliated to GWCSA
[9] Revised estimate

Continued on Page 10.5

FIGURE 10.5.1
Distribution of Mormons 1967

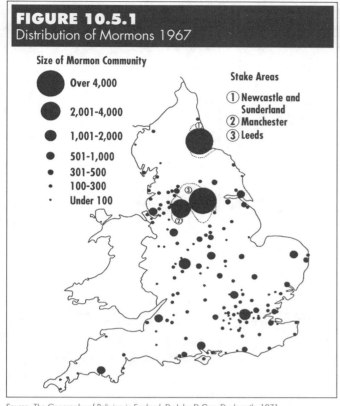

Size of Mormon Community

- Over 4,000
- 2,001–4,000
- 1,001–2,000
- 501–1,000
- 301–500
- 100–300
- Under 100

Stake Areas
1. Newcastle and Sunderland
2. Manchester
3. Leeds

Source: The Geography of Religion in England, Dr John D Gay, Duckworth, 1971

FIGURE 10.5.2
Number of Mormon churches by county 1994

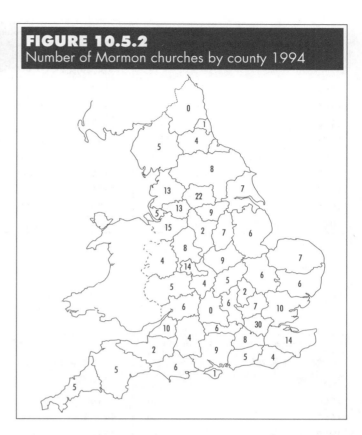

FIGURE 10.5.3
Membership of largest churches, 2000

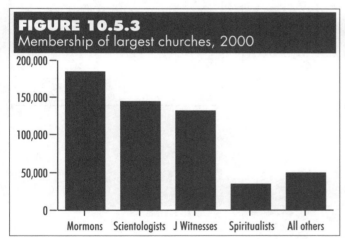

FIGURE 10.5.4
Growth of Non-Trinitarian church membership, 1900–2000

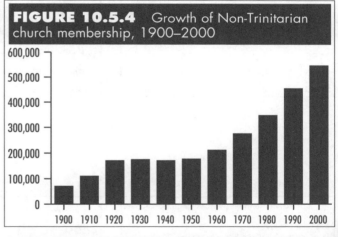

FIGURE 10.5.5
Christian Science Practitioners worldwide 1903–1998

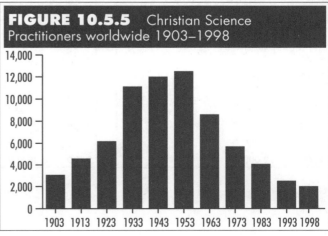

Source: 'The Rise and Fall of Christian Science' by Richard Singelenberg in Journal of Contemporary Religion, Volume 14, Number 1, 1999, Page 131.

Footnotes from Page 10.4 continued

[10] Not to be confused with the New (House) Churches. The New Church is Trinitarian but is included with the Non-Trinitarian Churches because it worships the Lord Jesus Christ as One God in whom is a Trinity of essentials of Father, Son and Holy Spirit, rather than the One God in Three Persons of the traditional creeds
[11] No full-time ministers
[12] Including 1,500 members of the Theosophical Society in England, and 35 of the United Lodge of Theosophists
[13] Figures for the Theosophical Society in England augmented by 21.4% to include Scottish, Welsh members and of the United Lodge to 1970
[14] The first English Lodge of the Theosophical Society was founded in 1878. A separate Theological Society in Scotland was chartered in 1910 and in Wales in 1922

	Active Members	Groups	Leaders
TABLE 10.6.1 Total Other Religions			
1960	258,870	548	814
1965	335,680	663	1,122
1970	456,042	855	1,795
1975	572,742	1,091	2,213
1980	739,560	1,233	3,188
1985	898,854	1,563	4,024
1990	1,072,844	1,858	4,786
1995	1,292,039	2,347	5,560
2000	1,460,430	2,650	6,385

	Active Members	Groups	Imams[2]
TABLE 10.6.2 Ahmadiyya Movement			
1960[1]	6,000	20	5
1965[1]	6,500	25	8
1970[1]	7,000	30	10
1975[1]	7,000	32	10
1980[1]	7,250	35	15
1985[1]	7,500	37	17
1990[1]	7,700	38	18
1995[1]	7,900	40	18
2000[1]	8,125	42	20

	Community	Groups[6]	Leaders[2]
TABLE 10.6.3 Bahái's			
1960[1]	250	20	1
1965[1]	500	50	2
1970[1]	1,000	100	3
1975[1]	2,000	150	5
1980[1]	3,000	200	7[5]
1985[1]	4,000	250	10[5]
1990	5,000[3]	320	12[5]
1995[3]	6,000	380	14
2000[1]	7,000	440	17[5]

	Active Members	Groups	Priests[2]
TABLE 10.6.4 Buddhists[7]			
1960[1]	1,000	3	10
1965[1]	4,000	14	60
1970[1]	8,000	22	110
1975	13,000	36	150
1980	17,000	50	210
1985	23,000	92	290
1990	31,500[8]	155[10]	350[1]
1995	45,000[9]	180[11]	400[1]
2000[1]	52,400	234	470

	Active Members	Temples	Priests[2]
TABLE 10.6.5 Hindus[12]			
1960[1]	40,000	50	40
1965[1]	60,000	70	60
1970[1]	80,000	90	80
1975[1]	100,000	110	105
1980[1]	120,000	125	120
1985[1]	130,000	130	140
1990	140,000[13]	140	150
1995	155,000[4]	161[4]	150[1]
2000[1]	165,000	169	165

	Active Members	Groups	Full-time Leaders
TABLE 10.6.6 IskCon, International Society for Krishna Consciousness[14]			
1960[1]	–	–	–
1965[1]	–	–	–
1970[1]	50	1	30
1975[1]	80	2	60
1980[1]	300	5	250
1985[1]	350	3	300
1990[1]	425	3	400
1995[1]	600	13	500[15]
2000[1]	670	18	575

	Active Members	Groups/Temples	Leaders
TABLE 10.6.7 Jains			
1960[1]	100	0	–
1965[1]	500	1	–
1970[1]	2,000	4	–
1975[1]	4,000	6	–
1980[1]	6,000	8	–
1985[1]	8,000	10	–
1990	10,000[3]	12[1]	–
1995	10,000[4]	15[4]	–
2000[1]	12,000	17	–

	Heads of Households	Congregations[20]	Full-time Leaders[2]
TABLE 10.6.8 Jews			
1960[1]	130,000	380	400
1965[1]	125,000	378	400
1970	119,642[17]	375	390[1]
1975	114,500[18]	339[18]	400[1]
1980	110,915	321	416
1985	105,455	337[1]	432[1]
1990	101,229	356	440
1995	93,684[19]	365	440[1]
2000[1]	88,800	383	440

[1] Estimate
[2] All male
[3] Based on *Religion: Aspects in Britain.* HMSO 1992
[4] Based on *Religions in the UK: A Multi-Faith Directory,* 1997
[5] Revised figure
[6] Including 41 Dharma Centres in 1995
[7] Figures up to 1990 based on surveys of all Buddhist groups in 1975, 1980 and 1985
[8] Including approximately 5,000 Soka Gakkai (Nichiren Shoshu) members, 5,000 lay and 300 ordained members of Friends of the Western Buddhist Order and 15,000 practitioners of Tibetan Buddhism (so the Office of Tibet) given in *Religion Today,* Volume 8, Number 2, Spring 1993. The total is approximately one-sixth of the total European and Asian community in the UK
[9] Taken as approximately one-third of the estimated community figure of 130,000 given in *Religions in the UK: A Multi-Faith Directory,* 1997
[10] M Baumann in *Journal of Contemporary Religion,* Volume 10, Number 1, 1995, states there were 213 Buddhist groups and centres in Great Britain in 1991
[11] Chris Forster in *Planting for a Harvest* (Challenge 2000, 1996) gives a total of 509 groups of 'Buddhist-type religions' in 1994, but the *Religions in the UK: A Multi-Faith Directory,* 1997, lists only 117
[12] Active members taken as one-third of the community
[13] Including perhaps 10,000 Satya Sai Baba followers, from *The Spirit of Hinduism,* Dr David Burnett, Monarch, 1992
[14] The 'Hare Krishna' Movement, which began 1969
[15] Of which 145 were female
[16] Male and female, affiliated to synagogues. These figures are about one-third of the community
[17] Based on the assumption that a quarter are female. In 1970 there were 88,434 male-headed households and 78,899 in 1983
[18] In 1977 there were 111, 459 active members and 324 congregations
[19] Based on a community figure of 300,000; in 1996 the number is 93,447
[20] These congregations use slightly fewer synagogues; for example in 1983 there were 328 congregations but 290 synagogues

FIGURE 10.7.1
Distribution of Jewish Population 1967

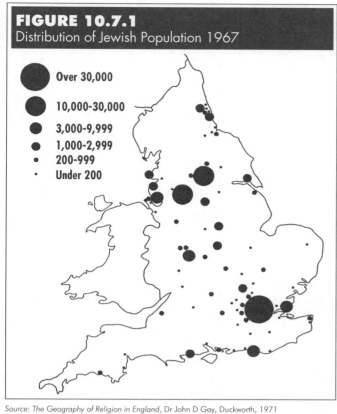

Source: *The Geography of Religion in England*, Dr John D Gay, Duckworth, 1971

FIGURE 10.7.2
Number of Jewish Synagogues by county 1994

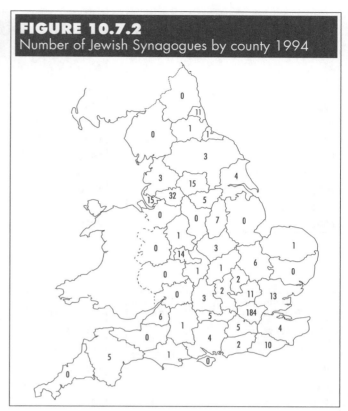

Source: *Planting for a Harvest*, Chris Forster, Challenge 2000

FIGURE 10.7.3 Largest non-Christian religious active membership, 2000

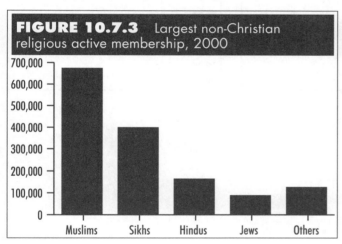

FIGURE 10.7.4
Growth of other religions, 1960–2000

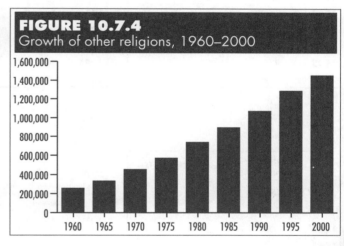

FIGURE 10.7.5 Percentage increase in other religions from 1960 to 2000

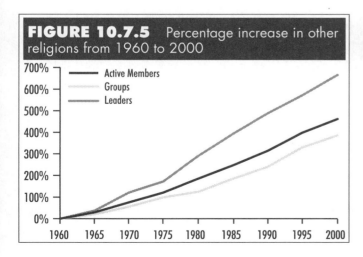

FIGURE 10.7.6 Active members of other religions as percentage of UK population 1960–2000

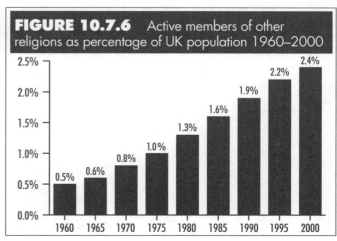

10

TABLE 10.8.1 — Muslims[2]

	Active Members[3,7]	Registered Mosques[6]	Full-time Leaders
1960[1]	30,000	40	300
1965[1]	60,000	65	450
1970[1]	130,000	130	900
1975	204,000	150	1,000
1980[1]	306,000	193	1,540
1985	434,979	314	2,077
1990	495,000[4]	350[7]	2,500[8]
1995[1]	580,000[5]	587	2,900
2000[1]	675,000	660	3,377

TABLE 10.8.2 — New Religious Movements Total[9]

	Active Members	Groups	Leaders
1960[1]	0	0	0
1965[1]	250	10	25
1970[1]	750	25	70
1975[1]	2,250	87	190
1980	3,825	152	250
1985	5,530	204	300
1990	7,285	267	386
1995	8,785	336	429
2000	10,150	392	488

TABLE 10.8.3 — Satanists[10]

	Active Members[11]	Groups	Leaders
1960[1]	20	1	1
1965[1]	30	3	1
1970[1]	50	5	2
1975[1]	50	8	3
1980	100	16	5
1985[1]	200	33	8
1990[1]	280	35	10
1995[1]	330	38	19[12]
2000[1]	420	41	16

TABLE 10.8.4 — School of Meditation

	Continuing Practitioners[13]	Buildings	Full-time Leaders[14]
1960[1]	200	1	7
1965[1]	1,400	1	25
1970[1]	2,750	2	40
1975	3,862	2	50
1980	4,820[1]	2	75[1]
1985[1]	6,000	2	100
1990	7,000[1]	2[1]	100
1995	9,000	2[1]	120
2000[1]	11,000	3	130

TABLE 10.8.5 — Sikhs[15]

	Active Members	Temples	Priests[14]
1960[1]	50,000	30	35
1965[1]	75,000	40	50
1970	100,000	60	80
1975	115,000	75	120
1980	150,000	105	140
1985	160,000	125	150
1990	250,000	149	180
1995	350,000[16]	202[17]	200
2000[1]	400,000	225	220

TABLE 10.8.6 — Zoroastrians

	Active Members[18]	Firehouses	Priests
1960[1]	300	1	0
1965[1]	500	1	0
1970[1]	800	1	0
1975	1,000[19]	1	0
1980[1]	1,350	1	0
1985[1]	1,670	1	0
1990	2,000[20]	1	0
1995	2,250[21,22]	1	0
2000[1]	2,500[21]	1	0

TABLE 10.8.7 — Other Religions

	Active Members	Groups	Leaders
1960[1]	1,000	2	15
1965[1]	2,000	5	40
1970[1]	4,000	10	80
1975[1]	6,000	15	120
1980[1]	9,000	20	160
1985[1]	12,000	25	200
1990[1]	15,000	30	240
1995[1]	20,000	35	280
2000[1]	23,000	40	320

[1] Estimate
[2] Including non-South Asians
[3] Taken as 50% of the estimated Muslim community as being the attendance at one of the main Muslim festivals in Great Britain, from *Mosque Attendance*, a survey by Dr Jim Holway, reported in the 1987/88 Edition of *UK Christian Handbook*
[4] Community taken as 990,000
[5] Community taken as 1.16 million. This figure is disputed and estimates range from 1,070,000 (Prof Ceri Peach, 1995), and 1.5 million (Muhammed Anwar, *Muslims in Britain*, 1991)
[6] These are registered mosques but many other buildings are used for worship. For example in 1985 612 buildings were used for 926 groups. In 1995 there were about 800 buildings in use, 200 of which were houses
[7] 1,020 groups meeting
[8] Of whom 100 were female
[9] This Table repeats Table 10.9.1 for 1980 to 2000; the figures for 1960 to 1975 are estimates based on the total figures 1980 to 2000
[10] Including members of the Temple of Set, Northern Order of the Prince, Society of the Dark Lily and Order of the Nine Angels
[11] Active members taken as one per cent of community
[12] Of whom 7 were female
[13] Estimates of continuing practioners, not number enrolling (10,000 per month in October 1972)
[14] All male
[15] All figures based on the Sikh Cultural Society's own estimates
[16] Includes 10,000 Namdhari Sikhs (*Religions in the UK: A Multi-Faith Directory* 1997). The Sikh Cultural Society estimated the Community to be 500,000
[17] Based on *Religions in the UK: A Multi-Faith Directory*, 1997
[18] Active members taken as about one-third of the community
[19] Community given as 3,000 in 1976 in *Zoroastrians*, Mary Boyce, Routledge & Kegan Paul, 1979, Page 226
[20] From tribute to rock musician Freddie Mercury in the *Independent* of 27 Nov 1991. An article by Harriot Crout-Tree in *Inter-faith Network* on 17 Feb 1992 put the community as 5,000 rather than 6,000
[21] Revised estimate
[22] *Religions in the UK: A Multi-faith Directory*, 1997, gives a community figure of 5–10,000

TABLE 10.9.1 Total	Active Members	Groups	Leaders
1980	3,825	152	250
1985	5,700	204	300
1990	7,710	267	386
1995	12,275	328	519
2000	14,515	377	635

TABLE 10.9.2 The Aetherius Society[2]	Active Members	Groups	Leaders
1980	100[1]	5	5
1985	300[1]	6	6
1990	500	7	8
1995	600[1]	8	9
2000[1]	700	14	5

TABLE 10.9.3 Brahma Kumaris[3]	Active Members	Groups	Leaders
1980[1]	700	28	40
1985[1]	800	35	50
1990[1]	900	38	60
1995[1]	1,000	45	45
2000[1]	1,500	50	30

TABLE 10.9.4 Chrisemma[4]	Active Members	Groups	Leaders
1980	–	–	–
1985	–	–	–
1990	5[1]	1	2
1995[1]	20	1	3
2000[1]	50	1	4

TABLE 10.9.5 Creme[5]	Active Members	Groups	Leaders
1980[1]	250	10	10
1985[1]	300	15	15
1990[1]	375	25	18
1995	450[1]	35[1]	25
2000[1]	510	43	30

TABLE 10.9.6 Da Free John[6]	Active Members	Groups	Leaders
1980[1]	35	1	8
1985[1]	40	1	10
1990[1]	50	2	14
1995[1]	55	2	25
2000[1]	70	5	50

TABLE 10.9.7 Eckankar[7]	Active Members	Groups	Leaders
1980[1]	250	24	100
1985[1]	300	25	102
1990[1]	350	26	105
1995[1]	400	27	110
2000[1]	450	28	113

TABLE 10.9.8 Elan Vital[8]	Active Members	Groups	Leaders
1980[1]	1,200	–	1
1985[1]	1,500	–	1
1990[1]	1,800	–	1
1995[1]	2,100	–	1
2000[1]	2,400	–	1

TABLE 10.9.9 Fellowship of Isis[9]	Active Members	Groups	Leaders[11]
1980[1]	150	25	25
1985[1]	200	30	30
1990[1]	250	35	35
1995[1]	300	30	35
2000[1]	400	20	35

10

[1] Estimate
[2] The Aetherius Society have had contact with perhaps 900 people in the UK, between 50 and 80 people attended their Sunday service, frequently including newcomers. Branches are located in Bristol, Derby, Hull, London, Manchester, Merseyside and Sheffield, with 12 further unofficial locations with representatives
[3] Brahma Kumaris have been holding meditation courses in the UK since 1972. 2,500 attended for the first time in 1992, with a total of about 30,000 who have attended since 1972. The number of actual members is about 10 times the numbers given,which are of regular attenders. One-fifth of these are in London, as are a third of their full-time workers
[4] Full name is 'The Chrisemma Foundation', founded by Chris Orchard and Emma Lea in November 1990. About 60 people have tried their teachings, and many of these were Sannyasins, or members of Rajneesh. Figures given are for the committed, who all live near Totnes, Devon
[5] Benjamin Creme. There is no organisation as such; meetings began in the Friends' Meeting House, London in 1974. Its sphere of influence could be 10,000 people. All workers are voluntary
[6] Teach a combination of Tibetan Buddhism, Hinduism, and elements of Zen, est and Rajneesh. About 1,000 people have come to their weekly introductory talks started in 1984, but their mailing list numbers only 110, including 60 friends. Of the 52 regular attenders, 40 are practitioners and 12 novices. Sixteen members live in the Ashram in Norwich, of whom 8 are priests doing pujas every day, and the others work voluntarily. Also called Adi Dam.
[7] Eckankar has had contact with 50,000 people worldwide and 700 in the UK. There are no full-time workers, but each of the 27 local directors has three helpers. Each major centre has a building, including Birmingham, London and Nottingham
[8] The old Divine Light Mission is no longer operational. The previous instructors have left, except for Maharaji. The group is no longer considered a religion and has renounced its Hindu connections, but is included here for usefulness. Presentations take place to give Knowledge. In 1992 between 7,000 and 10,000 practiced the Knowledge, with 150 currently receiving it, and 700 aspirants waiting
[9] The Fellowship of Isis was founded in 1976 in Huntingdon Castle by Rev. Durdin Robertson with his wife and sister. They have a following of 11,500 worldwide in 70 countries, being especially strong in West Africa. Their UK mailing list numbers 5,000
[10] Barry Long, a 'Master of the West', began teaching in the UK in 1982. They hold two 'Residential' events each year for 300–500 people at the Olympia Conference Centre, London. Has now moved to Holland.
[11] Taken as one-tenth of the total priests and priestesses.

TABLE 10.9.10 The Barry Long Foundation[10]	Active Members	Groups	Leaders
1980	–	–	–
1985	400[1]	0	1
1990	400[1]	0	1
1995	400[1]	0	1
2000[1]	0	0	0

	Active Members	Groups	Leaders
TABLE 10.10.1 Life Training[2]			
1980	–	–	–
1985[1]	200	1	2
1990[1]	250	1	3
1995	300[1]	1	4[1]
2000[1]	350	2	5

	Active Members	Groups	Leaders
TABLE 10.10.2 Mahikari[3]			
1980	–	–	–
1985	–	–	–
1990[1]	220	1	5
1995[1]	250	1	5
2000[1]	280	1	5

	Active Members	Groups	Leaders
TABLE 10.10.3 Outlook Seminar Training[4]			
1980	–	–	–
1985[1]	60	0	2
1990[1]	100	0	2
1995[1]	200	2	3
2000[1]	250	2	3

	Active Members	Groups	Leaders
TABLE 10.10.4 Pagan Federation[5]			
1980[1]	500	30	25
1985[1]	700	50	30
1990[1]	900	80	35
1995[1]	3,000	110	150
2000[1]	5,000	132	220

	Active Members	Groups	Leaders
TABLE 10.10.5 The Raelin Movement[6]			
1980[1]	100	0	0
1985[1]	100	0	0
1990[1]	100	0	0
1995[1]	100	0	0
2000[1]	100	0	0

	Active Members	Groups	Leaders
TABLE 10.10.6 Sahaja Yoga[7]			
1980[1]	220	18	10
1985[1]	250	20	10
1990[1]	280	22	10
1995	330[8]	25[1]	10[1]
2000[1]	365	27	10

	Active Members	Groups	Leaders
TABLE 10.10.7 Shinnyeon UK[9]			
1980[1]	10	1	1
1985[1]	20	1	1
1990[1]	30	1	2
1995	50	1[1]	3[1]
2000[1]	60	1	4

	Active Members	Groups	Leaders
TABLE 10.10.8 Solara[10]			
1980	–	–	–
1985	–	–	–
1990[1]	140	0	0
1995[1]	160	0	0
2000[1]	180	0	0

	Active Members	Groups	Leaders
TABLE 10.10.9 3HO[11]			
1980[1]	60	0	15
1985[1]	60	0	15
1990[1]	60	0	15
1995[1]	60	0	15
2000[1]	60	0	15

	Active Members	Groups	Leaders
TABLE 10.10.10 Others[12]			
1980[1]	250	10	10
1985[1]	500	20	25
1990[1]	1,000	30	50
1995[1]	1,500	40	75
2000[1]	1,900	50	100

[1] Estimate
[2] Life Training began in 1981 by Dr K Bradford Brown, with W Roy Whitten. It is especially strong in the South African townships. 2,500 in the UK have undertaken one course. Of the active members, 100 teach. One of the leaders is part-time
[3] Mahikari is especially strong in Martinique and Guadeloupe, where they have over 10,000 followers. Mahikari was founded in Japan in 1959 by Sukui Nushi Soma, and whilst they came to Britain in 1983 they only began their talks in 1989. About 1,300 have attended, with half this number coming in 1989
[4] Previously called 'I am Grove' after its founder Pat Grove, with Tony Weisman. Seven courses are held every year with an average of 23 people at each. There are 2,000 graduates; 65 have done all three courses. I am Associates began in 1984; the Seminars in London in 1988
[5] The actual membership is about 2,000, with half this number being 'committed'. Their 40 leaders work voluntarily and part-time in 19 regions with 100 informal meeting places. It was founded in 1971
[6] There are 25,000 Roelians in 67 countries and are especially strong in Belgium, Canada [Quebec], France, Italy, Japan and Switzerland. It was begun by racing driver Mr Claude Rael in December 1973, after encountering an alien who appointed him as prophet to the world
[7] Founded early 1970s
[8] Regular attenders about 200; community 1,000
[9] Shinnyeon is one of Japan's largest new religions and has been active in the UK since 1979. The Journal of Contemporary Religion Vol 10 No 2 1995 estimates the number of active members in 1995 in the UK to be about 50, although Shinnyeon UK claims 100 followers
[10] Solara is also called Star-Borne Unlimited, with a membership of about 800. They started in 1986
[11] 3HO stands for 'Healthy, Happy, Holy', and is made up of teachers and followers of Kundalini Yoga as taught by Yogi Bhajan. They came to the UK in the early 1970s, and have two annual events. Six of their Kundalini teachers are in London, three in the Midlands, and one in Scotland
[12] Including 40 members, 2 groups, 3 leaders in 1980, 30, 2 and 3 in 1990, and 25, 2 and 3 in 1995 for the British Mazdaznan Association, members taken as a tenth of the community

ECCLESIASTICAL BOUNDARIES

Contents

For the boundaries of other denominations, see Religious Trends No 1 Section 11

Sources:
Individual denominations and John Whitehorn © John Whitehorn/Graham Turner 1997, 1999

FIGURE 11.2 COUNTY AND UNITARY AUTHORITY MAP OF THE UNITED KINGDOM

A
City of Edinburgh
City of Glasgow
East Dunbartonshire
East Renfrewshire
Falkirk
Inverclyde
North Lanarkshire
Renfrewshire
West Dunbartonshire
West Lothian

B
Gateshead
Newcastle upon Tyne
North Tyneside
South Tyneside
Sunderland

C
Darlington

D
Hartlepool
Middlesborough
Redcar and Cleveland
Stockton on Tees

E
Bolton
Bury
Knowsley
Liverpool
Manchester
Oldham
Rochdale
Salford
St Helens
Sefton
Stockport
Tameside
Trafford
Wigan
Wirral

F
Barnsley
Bradford
Calderdale
Doncaster
Kirklees
Leeds
Rotherham
Sheffield
Wakefield

G
Birmingham
Coventry
Dudley
Sandwell
Solihull
Walsall
Wolverhampton

H
Blaeau Gwent
Bridgend
Cardiff
Caerphilly
Merthyr Tydfil
Monmouthshire
Neath Port Talbot
Newport
Rhondda Cynon Taff
Swansea
The Vale of Glamorgan
Torfaen

I
Bath and NE Somerset
City of Bristol
NW Somerset
South Gloucestershire

J Leicester

K Milton Keynes

L Luton

M Stoke

N Derby

O Thamesdown

P
Barking and Dagenham
Barnet
Bexley
Brent
Bromley
Camden
City of London
Croydon
Ealing
Enfield
Greenwich
Hackney
Hammersmith and Fulham
Harrow
Haringey
Havering
Hillingdon
Hounslow
Islington
Kensington and Chelsea
Kingston upon Thames
Lambeth
Lewisham
Merton
Newham
Redbridge
Richmond upon Thames
Southwark
Sutton
Tower Hamlets
Waltham Forest
Wandsworth
Wesminster, City of

RELIGIOUS SOCIETY OF FRIENDS
Boundaries England, Wales, Scotland and Ireland

Britain Yearly Meeting:
General Meetings
1 Bedfordshire
2 Berks and Oxon
3 Bristol and Somerset
4 Cumberland
5 Derbyshire, Lincolnshire and Nottinghamshire
6 Devon and Cornwall
7 Durham
8 Essex and Suffolk
9 Hampshire, Isle of Wight and Channel Islands
10 Kent
11 Lancashire and Cheshire
12 London and Middlesex
13 Norfolk, Cambridge and Huntingdon
14 Sussex and Surrey
15 Warwick, Leicester and Stafford
16 Western
17 Westmorland
18 Yorkshire

(Boundaries between General Meetings are not recognised by the London Yearly Meeting but are included for comparisons with other denominations.)

Ireland Yearly Meeting:
Quarterly Meetings
1 Ulster
2 Leinster (and Connaught)
3 Munster

Scotland General Meeting:
Monthly Meetings
A North of Scotland
B East of Scotland
C South East Scotland
D West Scotland

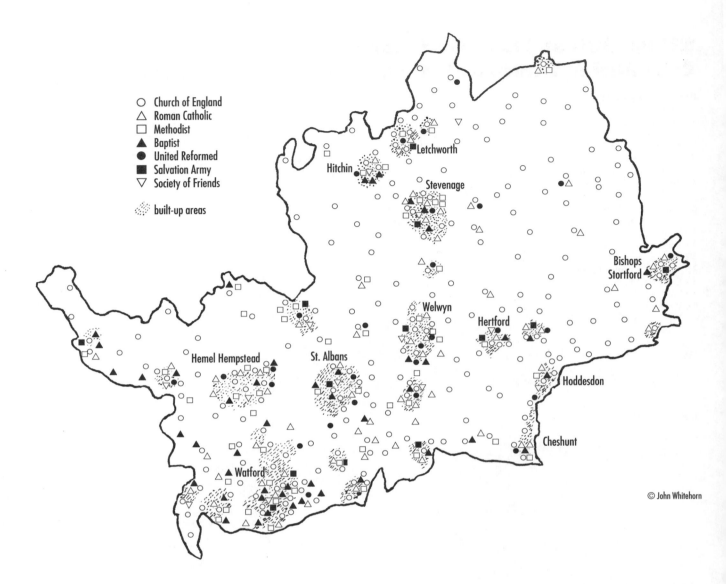

Legend:
○ Church of England
△ Roman Catholic
□ Methodist
▲ Baptist
● United Reformed
■ Salvation Army
▽ Society of Friends

░ built-up areas

© John Whitehorn

This map of Hertfordshire shows the location of 460 churches from 7 of the denominations which publish lists identifying where their congregations worship. This is 77%, over three-quarters, of the total of 599 churches in the county in 1998. It excludes the Independent, New, Orthodox and Pentecostal churches, Baptist churches outside the Baptist Union, and some of the churches in smaller denominations, though includes those of the Society of Friends and Salvation Army.

Of these 460, 234 are Church of England, 69 Roman Catholic, 54 Methodist, 48 Baptist Union, 28 United Reformed, 14 Society of Friends and 13 Salvation Army.

As would be expected the map naturally shows that there are more churches in built-up areas. There are however considerable numbers of churches in the rural parts of Hertfordshire. In the 1989 English Church Census, 39% of the then 624 churches were in (self-designated) rural areas, 22% in towns, 26% in suburban areas, 9% in Council Estates, and 4% elsewhere, such as city centres.

The map shows that it is the Church of England which is predominantly in the rural areas, but there are quite a few Catholic and Methodist in these areas too. The map highlights the close proximity of some churches of the same denomination in some places, such as the two Catholic churches in Cheshunt, or the three Baptist churches in the south of Hitchin, with none in nearby Letchworth, doubtless all with good historical reasons.

Hertfordshire, part of the Southeast (North) Region described in detail on **Page 12.15**, had 967,000 attending church on Sunday in 1989, a figure which dropped 13% to 843,000 by 1998. There was also a net drop of 25 congregations in that period. A third of those attending church were Anglican in 1989, but this had dropped to a quarter in 1998. The reverse happened to Catholic attendance: over a quarter attended Catholic churches in 1989, but this had increased to a third by 1998.

In 1989, 9.8% of the population of Hertfordshire attended church on Sunday. By 1998 this had dropped to 8.2%, both figures higher than for the Southeast (North) Area as a whole. The average congregation was 150 in 1989, but this had dropped to 140 nine years later.

The age of those attending church is however very similar to those in the general area. Hertfordshire has a slightly smaller percentage of children, and just a few more of those in their twenties, but the differences are not significant and within the margins of measurement error. Hertfordshire is therefore a fairly average county within the Southeast Area, and it is the differences of the entire Area which will make it different rather than any special characteristics of itself.

ENGLISH CHURCH ATTENDANCE SURVEY 1998

Contents

Survey sponsored by:

The Centre for Black & White Christian Partnership
Campaigners
Christian Aid
Christian Book Club
Christian Healing Mission
Covenanters
Church Pastoral Aid Society
Ecclesiastical Insurance Group
English Heritage
Moorlands Bible College
Operations Mobilisation
Premier Radio
Scripture Union
Youth for Christ

12

Source:
12,446 Individual churches of all denominations across England

Abbreviations

★   Less than 50 attenders/members
†   Too few churches to justify giving any percentages
12   Figures in *italics* are percentages
12   Upright figures are actual numbers
⇒   Percentages sum to 100% horizontally
⇓   Percentages sum to 100% vertically
–   There are none in the category
n/a No information is available

Introduction

In September 1998, the English Church Attendance Survey (ECAS) was undertaken under the auspices of Christian Research, sponsored by the 14 organisations listed on the previous page. The full report of this study is published separately under the title *The Tide is Running Out*, providing a commentary on the results as well as highlighting the key results. It contains a description of the reasons for the study, how it was prepared, the pilot study and a copy of the questionnaire used.

Page 12.3 gives a summary of selected features from this survey. This data was broken down into the 10 English Economic Regions, with the South Eastern Region broken into three areas: South East (North), South East (Greater London) and South East (South), the North and South parts being respectively the counties in the Region north and south of the River Thames. The data on **page 12.3** is broken down for each Region or Area in the subsequent pages, one page per region.

The figures given for comparison for 1979 and 1989 come from the English Church Censuses conducted in those years, full details of which were published in 1991 in two volumes, *'Christian' England* (the commentary) and *Prospects for the Nineties* (regional and county tables).

The response

There were an estimated 37,717 churches at the time of the Survey, and usable replies were received from 12,446, a third, 33.0%.

It is now known that not every church was in fact included. This is largely due to the difficulty of locating new independent churches. The number omitted is estimated at about 200 churches, with a probably additional church attendance in the New Church sector of 10,000 adults. The Tables here exclude these.

Who was included?

The Survey was intended to cover all Christian denominations, including all Free, Protestant, Anglican, Catholic and Orthodox churches, that is, all those accepting the Trinitarian formula of belief in God the Father, God the Son, and God the Holy Spirit in one Essence. This excluded Jehovah's Witnesses, Mormons, Christian Scientists, Christadelphians, Jews, Muslims, Hindus and other non-Trinitarian or non-Christian groups.

We separately identified and counted churches with two or more places of worship in distinct communities, such as linked Church of England parishes where the parish churches were still in use. In team ministries each congregation counted as a unit, unless they all met unitedly together when they were treated as one congregation.

The basic unit

The basic unit of the Survey was a *congregation*, which was defined as a "body of people meeting on a Sunday in the same premises primarily for public worship at regular intervals". The key elements of this definition are:

"*a body of people*", that is, a congregation is the basic unit rather than a church. This means that where a church building is used by more than one group, each separate group counted as a unit. Where a church had united into one congregation, it was counted as such.

"*on a Sunday*" meant that those groups only meeting for prayer and/or Bible Study mid-week, and services at crematoria, were excluded. But a modification from Sunday to Saturday was allowed for the Seventh-Day Adventists and Saturday evening Catholic services. Whilst this means that the survey concentrated on numbers attending on Sundays, questions were also asked about mid-week activities and services. Details of these are not on the pages included here, but are given in the commentary.

"*primarily for public worship*". Public worship was taken to mean where ordinary members of the public could attend. Thus religious communities holding services not open to the public, prisons, hospitals and services in old folks' homes were excluded. Schools, colleges, university chaplaincies, military bases, religious orders and others that advertise service times were taken to be open to the public, and therefore included.

"*at regular intervals*" allowed for the situation, common in rural areas, where services are not held every week. If a service was held at least monthly numbers were included; those held less regularly were not. This eliminated special events such as Christian holiday gatherings, conferences, conventions and private chapels used for occasional services.

"*in the same premises*". This identified a congregation specifically by its geographical location. Where a group of people have been known to rotate around people's houses Sunday by Sunday they have generally not been included.

The above definition meant that a few worshippers were excluded from the Survey count. The numbers we do have however relate to public worshippers coming to church or chapel in the normally understood sense of what it means to "go to church".

Details collected

Average Sunday Church attendance was collected for September 1998, broken down by adults and children (under 15). A subsequent question asked for the frequency with which the adults in the congregation attended. In the Tables in this volume, this information is summarised into three groups:

- "52+" gives the total percentage of those attending either once a week or more than once a week

- "13-26" gives the total percentage of those attending either monthly or fortnightly

- "2-4" gives the total percentage of those attending either twice a year or quarterly

Age and sex of attenders. These were generally estimated by the person completing the questionnaire.

Each congregation was given a **denomination code**. The different denominations were grouped into ten categories for ease of analysis. Which denominations were included in which group are given in the detailed Tables in Sections 8 and 9 of this volume. The number attending church on Sunday in each of these 10 denominational groups is given in **Table 2** on each page in Section 12. The proportion of attenders that each denomination is of the total is also given for 1979, 1989 and 1998 in each **Table 2**, and the frequency with which these attenders actually attend on a Sunday. The number of churches by denomination in 1989 and 1998 is also given.

The population per church, across all denominations, is given for 1979, 1989 and 1998 in **Table 1** on each page. Estimates based on the civil population in the relevant county were made.

Continued on Page 12.21

FIGURE 12.3.1

FIGURE 12.3.2

TABLE 12.3.1 Overall figures

	1979	1989	1998
Total population	46,396,100	47,735,300	49,658,300
Usual Sunday church attendance	5,441,000	4,742,800	3,714,700
% attending on Sunday	11.7%	9.9%	7.5%
Number of churches	39,064	38,607	37,717
Population per church	1,190	1,240	1,320

TABLE 12.3.2 Sunday attendance by denomination

	Anglican	Baptist	Catholic	Independent	Methodist	New	Orthodox	Pentecostal	URC	Others	TOTAL
1979	1,671,000	290,000	1,991,000	235,000	621,000	64,000	10,000	228,000	190,000	141,000	5,441,000
% ↓	−24	−7	−14	+27	−18	+161	+23	+4	−21	−19	−13
1989	1,266,300	270,900	1,715,900	298,500	512,300	167,000	12,300	236,700	149,300	113,600	4,742,800
% ↓	−23	+2	−22	−46	−26	+38	+105	−9	−18	−18	−22
1998	**980,600**	**277,600**	**1,230,100**	**161,600**	**379,700**	**230,500**	**25,200**	**214,600**	**121,700**	**93,100**	**3,714,700**
1979 →	31	5	37	4	11	1	0	4	4	3	100%
1989 →	27	6	36	6	11	4	0	5	3	2	100%
1998 →	**26**	**8**	**33**	**4**	**10**	**6**	**1**	**6**	**3**	**2**	**100%**
Number of churches											
1989	16,373	2,339	3,824	3,097	6,740	1,026	114	1,951	1,681	1,462	38,607
% ↓	−1	+3	−1	−28	−7	+63	+126	+8	−7	−20	−2
1998	**16,281**	**2,413**	**3,771**	**2,243**	**6,240**	**1,673**	**258**	**2,105**	**1,564**	**1,169**	**37,717**
Frequency of attendance in weeks per year, 1998											
↓ % 52 +	46	73	64	74	61	79	15	72	59	66	58
↓ % 13–26	26	17	11	15	23	15	20	17	25	19	20
↓ % 2–4	28	10	25	11	16	6	65	11	16	15	22

TABLE 12.3.3 Sunday attendance by churchmanship

	Anglo-Catholic	Broad	Catholic	Evangelical Broad	Evangelical Mainstream	Evangelical Charismatic	Evangelical Total	Liberal	Low Church	Others	TOTAL
1989	178,300	434,000	1,867,500	414,600	384,600	631,200	1,430,400	479,900	280,500	72,200	4,742,800
% ↓	0	−19	−48	−47	+68	−16	−3	−11	−2	+56	−22
1998	**177,600**	**352,400**	**980,000**	**217,900**	**645,500**	**527,900**	**1,391,300**	**425,500**	**275,400**	**112,500**	**3,714,700**
1989 →	4	9	39	9	8	13	30	10	6	2	100%
1998 →	**5**	**9**	**27**	**6**	**17**	**14**	**37**	**12**	**7**	**3**	**100%**
Number of churches											
1989	2,050	6,056	6,205	4,190	4,344	5,107	13,641	5,258	4,441	956	38,607
% ↓	−2	−18	−6	−16	+41	−6	+6	−12	+1	+42	−2
1998	**2,012**	**4,996**	**5,824**	**3,505**	**6,105**	**4,790**	**14,400**	**4,622**	**4,501**	**1,362**	**37,717**
Frequency of attendance in weeks per year, 1998											
↓ % 52 +	50	50	63	55	71	72	69	49	54	59	58
↓ % 13–26	25	23	12	23	16	17	17	25	24	16	20
↓ % 2–4	25	27	25	22	13	11	14	26	22	25	22

TABLE 12.3.4 Sunday attendance by ethnic groups, 1998

	White	BCA	CKJ	IPB	OA	ONW	Total (=100%)
% →	88.1	7.2	1.5	1.5	1.0	0.1	3,714,700

BCA = Black Caribbean/African/Other Black   CKJ = Chinese/Korean/Japanese   IPB = Indian/Pakistani/Bangladeshi
OA = Other Asian   ONW = Other Non-white

TABLE 12.3.5 Percentage in each age-group

	Churchgoers 1979 %	Churchgoers 1989 %	Churchgoers 1998 %	Population 1979 %	Population 1989 %	Population 1998 %
Under 15	26	25	19	21	19	19
15 to 19	9	7	6	8	8	6
20 to 29	11	10	9	14	16	13
30 to 44	16	17	17	19	20	23
45 to 64	20	22	24	23	22	23
65 or over	18	19	25	15	15	16

[1] Including 312 residential schools/colleges

FIGURE 12.3.3
Percentage of population in church by age-group, 1979, 1989 and 1998

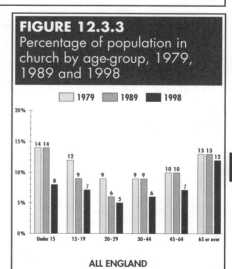

ALL ENGLAND

12

FIGURE 12.4.1

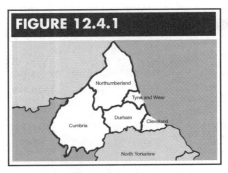

FIGURE 12.4.2

TABLE 12.4.1 Overall figures

	1979	1989	1998
Total population	3,087,400	3,071,000	3,085,800
Usual Sunday church attendance	365,300	312,500	225,100
% attending on Sunday	11.8%	10.2%	7.3%
Number of churches	2,638	2,550	2,443
Population per church	1,170	1,200	1,260

TABLE 12.4.2 Sunday attendance by denomination

	Anglican	Baptist	Catholic	Independent	Methodist	New	Orthodox	Pentecostal	URC	Others	TOTAL
1979	98,700	5,700	165,200	7,700	55,000	2,100	300	7,300	12,200	11,100	365,300
% ↓	−23	+18	−15	+52	−20	+195	–	+16	−20	−20	−14
1989	76,100	6,700	140,500	11,700	43,800	6,200	300	8,500	9,800	8,900	312,500
% ↓	−27	−18	−37	−32	−4	+3	−33	−32	−14	−47	−28
1998	**55,200**	**5,500**	**88,800**	**7,900**	**41,900**	**6,700**	**200**	**5,800**	**8,400**	**4,700**	**225,100**
1979 →	27	2	45	2	15	1	0	2	3	3	100%
1989 →	24	2	45	4	14	2	0	3	3	3	100%
1998 →	**25**	**2**	**40**	**3**	**19**	**3**	**0**	**2**	**4**	**2**	**100%**
Number of churches											
1989	990	72	320	203[1]	592	45	1	71	130	126	2,550
% ↓	−2	−7	−1	−23	−4	+56	+300	+13	−5	−30	−4
1998	**973**	**67**	**316**	**156**[1]	**566**	**70**	**4**	**80**	**123**	**88**	**2,443**
Frequency of attendance in weeks per year, 1998											
↓ % 52 +	57	80	74	87	67	89	5	60	56	61	68
↓ % 13–26	21	15	8	12	20	6	90	18	25	21	15
↓ % 2–4	22	5	18	1	13	5	5	22	19	18	17

TABLE 12.4.3 Sunday attendance by churchmanship

	Anglo-Catholic	Broad	Catholic	Evangelical Broad	Evangelical Mainstream	Evangelical Charismatic	Evangelical Total	Liberal	Low Church	Others	TOTAL
1989	9,400	28,800	147,900	24,500	22,600	26,800	73,900	28,500	18,600	5,400	312,500
% ↓	+15	−26	−45	−70	+58	−38	−19	−9	−8	+48	−28
1998	**11,000**	**21,300**	**81,900**	**7,400**	**35,700**	**16,700**	**59,800**	**26,000**	**17,100**	**8,000**	**225,100**
1989 →	3	9	47	8	7	9	24	9	6	2	100%
1998 →	**5**	**9**	**36**	**3**	**16**	**8**	**27**	**12**	**7**	**4**	**100%**
Number of churches											
1989	122	403	573	210	297	234	741	279	351	81	2,550
% ↓	−5	−38	+5	−20	+25	−31	−6	−3	+12	+43	−4
1998	**116**	**250**	**599**	**167**	**370**	**161**	**698**	**271**	**393**	**116**	**2,443**
Frequency of attendance in weeks per year, 1998											
↓ % 52 +	71	56	74	63	75	69	72	52	63	59	68
↓ % 13–26	15	23	8	24	18	16	18	21	21	25	15
↓ % 2–4	14	21	18	13	7	15	10	27	16	16	17

TABLE 12.4.4 Sunday attendance by ethnic groups, 1998

	White	BCA	CKJ	IPB	OA	ONW	Total (=100%)
% →	95.6	1.4	0.9	1.1	1.9	0.1	225,100

BCA = Black Caribbean/African/Other Black   CKJ = Chinese/Korean/Japanese   IPB = Indian/Pakistani/Bangladeshi
OA = Other Asian   ONW = Other Non-white

TABLE 12.4.5 Overall figures

	Churchgoers 1979 %	Churchgoers 1989 %	Churchgoers 1998 %	Population 1979 %	Population 1989 %	Population 1998 %
Under 15	25	23	16	22	19	19
15 to 19	9	7	5	8	8	6
20 to 29	9	10	8	14	16	13
30 to 44	17	15	16	18	20	22
45 to 64	23	24	26	24	22	24
65 or over	17	21	29	14	15	16

[1] Including 13 residential schools/colleges

FIGURE 12.4.3
Percentage of population in church by age-group, 1979, 1989 and 1998

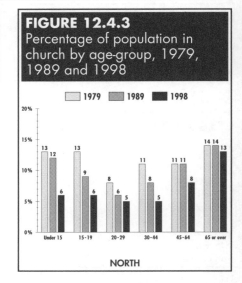

NORTH

FIGURE 12.5.1

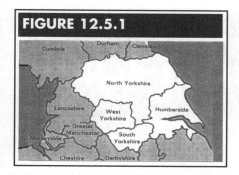

FIGURE 12.5.2

TABLE 12.5.1 Overall figures

	1979	1989	1998
Total population	4,878,200	4,912,800	5,052,200
Total Sunday church attendance	512,200	429,600	296,400
% attending on Sunday	10.5%	8.7%	5.7%
Number of churches	3,896	3,827	3,606
Population per church	1,250	1,280	1,400

TABLE 12.5.2 Sunday attendance by denomination

	Anglican	Baptist	Catholic	Independent	Methodist	New	Orthodox	Pentecostal	URC	Others	TOTAL
1979	145,200	13,100	179,300	11,000	98,000	3,000	500	30,300	18,000	13,800	512,200
% ↓	−26	−6	−17	−7	−14	+353	+40	−21	−24	−5	−16
1989	107,900	12,300	149,600	10,200	84,700	13,600	700	23,900	13,600	13,100	429,600
% ↓	−20	+19	−42	+26	−47	+25	+100	−49	−36	−34	−33
1998	**84,700**	**14,600**	**86,400**	**7,500**	**45,300**	**17,000**	**1,400**	**12,200**	**8,700**	**8,600**	**286,400**
1979 →	28	3	35	2	19	1	0	6	3	3	100%
1989 →	25	3	35	2	20	3	0	6	3	3	100%
1998 →	**30**	**5**	**30**	**3**	**16**	**6**	**0**	**4**	**3**	**3**	**100%**
Number of churches											
1989	1,555	129	388	140[1]	1,082	58	8	166	148	153	3,827
% ↓	0	−3	−1	−23	−14	+91	+188	−31	−10	−20	−6
1998	**1,559**	**125**	**385**	**108[1]**	**926**	**111**	**23**	**114**	**133**	**122**	**3,606**
Frequency of attendance in weeks per year, 1998											
↓ % 52 +	51	74	75	64	58	90	31	74	62	57	64
↓ % 13–26	27	16	8	12	26	8	17	15	24	28	18
↓ % 2–4	22	10	17	24	16	2	52	11	14	15	18

TABLE 12.5.3 Sunday attendance by churchmanship

	Anglo-Catholic	Broad	Catholic	Evangelical Broad	Evangelical Mainstream	Evangelical Charismatic	Evangelical Total	Liberal	Low Church	Others	TOTAL
1989	17,300	50,000	151,700	34,600	30,600	55,700	120,900	49,100	32,200	8,400	429,600
% ↓	−16	−23	−58	−53	+31	−46	−29	−12	−11	+50	−33
1998	**14,500**	**38,300**	**63,100**	**16,200**	**40,100**	**29,900**	**86,200**	**43,200**	**28,500**	**12,600**	**286,400**
1989 →	4	12	35	8	7	13	28	11	8	2	100%
1998 →	**5**	**13**	**22**	**5**	**14**	**11**	**30**	**15**	**10**	**5**	**100%**
Number of churches											
1989	185	684	599	363	374	427	1,164	521	568	119	3,827
% ↓	+2	−12	−16	-6	+26	−20	−1	−13	−1	+22	-6
1998	**188**	**601**	**503**	**342**	**471**	**340**	**1,153**	**451**	**565**	**145**	**3,606**
Frequency of attendance in weeks per year, 1998											
↓ % 52 +	60	56	73	49	71	72	67	55	57	52	64
↓ % 13–26	23	18	8	26	19	18	20	28	24	12	18
↓ % 2–4	17	26	19	25	10	10	13	17	19	36	18

TABLE 12.5.4 Sunday attendance by ethnic groups, 1998

	White	BCA	CKJ	IPB	OA	ONW	Total (=100%)
% →	93.0	4.2	1.2	0.7	0.7	0.2	286,400

BCA = Black Caribbean/African/Other Black   CKJ = Chinese/Korean/Japanese   IPB = Indian/Pakistani/Bangladeshi
OA = Other Asian   ONW = Other Non-white

TABLE 12.5.5 Overall figures

	Churchgoers 1979 %	Churchgoers 1989 %	Churchgoers 1998 %	Population 1979 %	Population 1989 %	Population 1998 %
Under 15	24	25	19	22	19	19
15 to 19	9	7	5	8	8	7
20 to 29	10	9	8	14	16	13
30 to 44	16	16	17	18	20	22
45 to 64	21	22	25	23	22	23
65 or over	20	21	26	15	15	16

FIGURE 12.5.3
Percentage of population in church by age-group, 1979, 1989 and 1998

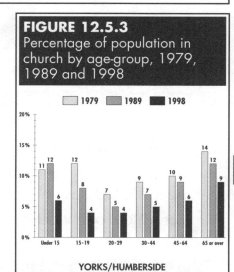

YORKS/HUMBERSIDE

12

[1] Including 15 residential schools/colleges

What do you use SALT for?

Sumo wrestlers throw it over their shoulder before a fight

Drivers use it in winter to melt snow

Cooks use it to flavour food

At **Scripture Union** we use **SALT** to teach about the Bible.

In fact we've been doing it for more than 50 years and now over 85,000 busy children's leaders use it every week.

For a **FREE** one week sample of **SALT** ring **01908 856182**

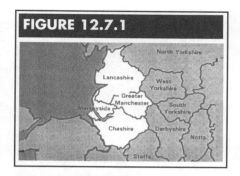

FIGURE 12.7.1

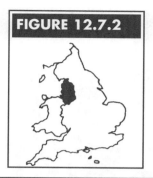

FIGURE 12.7.2

TABLE 12.7.1 Overall figures

	1979	1989	1998
Total population	6,476,100	6,427,800	**6,461,000**
Usual Sunday church attendance	960,500	793,100	**556,800**
% attending on Sunday	14.8%	12.3%	**8.6%**
Number of churches	4,206	4,039	**4,044**
Population per church	1,540	1,590	**1,600**

TABLE 12.7.2 Sunday attendance by denomination

	Anglican	Baptist	Catholic	Independent	Methodist	New	Orthodox	Pentecostal	URC	Others	TOTAL
1979	219,900	19,600	526,100	24,900	97,600	6,800	300	23,800	29,200	12,300	960,500
% ↓	−26	−5	−18	+33	−16	+57	−67	−9	−21	−21	−17
1989	162,800	18,600	430,900	33,100	82,300	10,700	100	21,700	23,200	9,700	793,100
% ↓	−36	+1	−32	−54	−25	+10	+300	+3	−9	−18	−30
1998	**104,800**	**18,800**	**292,800**	**15,200**	**61,500**	**11,800**	**400**	**22,300**	**21,200**	**8,000**	**556,800**
1979 →	23	2	55	3	10	1	0	2	3	1	100%
1989 →	21	2	54	4	11	1	0	3	3	1	100%
1998 →	**19**	**3**	**53**	**3**	**11**	**2**	**0**	**4**	**4**	**1**	**100%**
Number of churches											
1989	1,369	186	706	306[1]	846	54	5	158	269	140	4,039
% →	0	−1	−1	−2	−6	+94	+400	+32	−4	−25	0
1998	**1,366**	**184**	**696**	**300**[1]	**795**	**105**	**25**	**209**	**259**	**105**	**4,044**
Frequency of attendance in weeks per year, 1998											
↓ % 52 +	55	77	65	68	61	75	39	85	61	64	64
↓ % 13–26	26	16	8	18	23	15	35	11	23	21	15
↓ % 2–4	19	7	27	14	16	10	26	4	16	15	21

TABLE 12.7.3 Sunday attendance by churchmanship

	Anglo-Catholic	Broad	Catholic	Evangelical Broad	Evangelical Mainstream	Evangelical Charismatic	Evangelical Total	Liberal	Low Church	Others	TOTAL
1989	13,300	56,300	439,200	62,400	44,400	62,500	169,300	58,200	52,500	4,300	793,100
% ↓	+33	−9	−49	−44	+87	−32	−5	−9	−23	+126	−30
1998	**17,700**	**51,000**	**224,700**	**35,200**	**83,200**	**42,200**	**160,600**	**52,700**	**40,400**	**9,700**	**556,800**
1989 →	2	7	55	8	5	8	21	7	7	1	100%
1998 →	**3**	**9**	**40**	**6**	**15**	**7**	**29**	**10**	**7**	**2**	**100%**
Number of churches											
1989	156	601	855	465	476	411	1,352	512	519	44	4,039
% ↓	0	−24	−5	−7	+47	+2	+15	−9	0	+102	0
1998	**156**	**458**	**809**	**433**	**698**	**418**	**1,549**	**465**	**518**	**89**	**4,044**
Frequency of attendance in weeks per year, 1998											
↓ % 52 +	60	58	64	62	70	74	69	56	55	71	64
↓ % 13–26	24	20	8	21	17	19	18	27	24	10	15
↓ % 2–4	16	22	28	17	13	7	13	17	21	19	21

TABLE 12.7.4 Sunday attendance by ethnic groups, 1998

	White	BCA	CKJ	IPB	OA	ONW	Total (=100%)
% →	93.8	3.0	1.6	0.8	0.4	0.4	556,800

BCA = Black Caribbean/African/Other Black   CKJ = Chinese/Korean/Japanese   IPB = Indian/Pakistani/Bangladeshi
OA = Other Asian   ONW = Other Non-white

TABLE 12.7.5 Overall figures

	Churchgoers 1979 %	Churchgoers 1989 %	Churchgoers 1998 %	Population 1979 %	Population 1989 %	Population 1998 %
Under 15	27	26	18	23	19	20
15 to 19	9	7	6	8	8	6
20 to 29	11	9	8	14	16	13
30 to 44	16	16	16	18	21	22
45 to 64	19	23	25	23	21	23
65 or over	18	19	27	14	15	16

[1] Including 11 residential schools/colleges

FIGURE 12.7.3
Percentage of population in church by age-group, 1979, 1989 and 1998

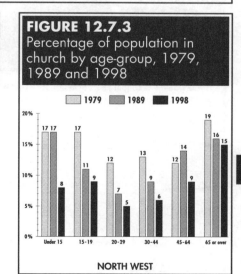

NORTH WEST

12

When you think of a **famine**, what springs to mind? A hot, arid country far away, droughts, no water or food? Mass starvation?

What if we said there was a famine on your **doorstep**? In your own **church**?

This country is facing a famine like its never seen before. **A youth famine**. Statistics show that we are losing young people from our churches at an alarming rate. In 1991 we discovered that 300 young people left the church each week. Today that number is higher and the age is younger.

The Church is being **starved of young people** and Youth For Christ is committed to fighting this famine. That s why we work closely with the Church. That s why we send out hundreds of young people each year to reach their peers with the gospel.

We need you to help us in this fight. We re looking for fired up young people to join our teams. We also need churches to partner with us so that we can serve you and strengthen you. Together we must stem the flow before it s too late.

Youth For Christ... Fighting the famine. Fanning the flames of revival. Serving the Church.

If you would like to join YFC s fight against **Youth Famine**, please fill in this coupon and **send it back to us** at the address on the left.

RT 99

Name _____

Address _____

_____ **Postcode** _____

Telephone _____ **Email** _____

Church _____

☐ **Yes.** I would like more information on Youth Famine
☐ **Yes.** I would like a Youth Famine Resource Pack
Please tick box

Youth for Christ, PO Box 5254
Halesowen, West Midlands B63 3DG
Tel: 0121 550 8055
Email: YFC@compuserve.com

Registered Charity 263446

12

FIGURE 12.9.1

FIGURE 12.9.2

TABLE 12.9.1 Overall figures

	1979	1989	1998
Total population	3,765,800	3,970,200	4,181,400
Usual Sunday church attendance	384,200	328,600	260,800
% attending on Sunday	10.2%	8.3%	6.2%
Number of churches	4,072	3,911	3,856
Population per church	920	1,020	1,080

TABLE 12.9.2 Sunday attendance by denomination

	Anglican	Baptist	Catholic	Independent	Methodist	New	Orthodox	Pentecostal	URC	Others	TOTAL
1979	141,000	23,800	97,800	9,700	59,700	2,600	500	19,700	14,600	14,800	384,200
% ↓	−23	−4	−13	+25	−15	+281	+40	−13	−23	−29	−14
1989	108,400	22,900	84,700	12,100	51,000	9,900	700	17,200	11,200	10,500	328,600
% ↓	−22	−12	−31	+13	−20	+62	+29	−12	−29	−33	−21
1998	**84,700**	**20,200**	**58,600**	**13,700**	**40,600**	**16,000**	**900**	**15,200**	**7,900**	**7,000**	**260,800**
1979 →	37	6	25	3	15	1	0	5	4	4	100%
1989 →	33	7	26	4	16	3	0	5	3	3	100%
1998 →	**32**	**8**	**22**	**5**	**16**	**6**	**0**	**6**	**3**	**3**	**100%**
Number of churches											
1989	1,913	235	251	169[1]	877	89	7	134	122	114	3,911
% ↓	−1	+5	−1	−32	−5	+70	+186	+8	+2	−25	−1
1998	**1,900**	**246**	**248**	**104[1]**	**832**	**151**	**20**	**145**	**124**	**86**	**3,856**
Frequency of attendance in weeks per year, 1998											
↓ % 52 +	39	69	54	67	52	82	2	76	64	68	54
↓ % 13–26	32	17	11	18	25	15	87	19	26	14	22
↓ % 2–4	29	14	35	15	23	3	11	5	10	18	24

TABLE 12.9.3 Sunday attendance by churchmanship

	Anglo-Catholic	Broad	Catholic	Evangelical Broad	Evangelical Mainstream	Evangelical Charismatic	Evangelical Total	Liberal	Low Church	Others	TOTAL
1989	13,700	36,100	102,500	36,800	20,800	48,400	106,000	38,600	26,000	5,700	328,600
% ↓	+2	−15	−43	−47	+97	−14	−4	−30	−22	+49	−21
1998	**14,000**	**30,700**	**58,000**	**19,500**	**41,000**	**41,600**	**102,100**	**27,200**	**20,300**	**8,500**	**260,800**
1989 →	4	11	31	11	6	15	32	12	8	2	100%
1998 →	**5**	**12**	**22**	**7**	**16**	**16**	**39**	**11**	**8**	**3**	**100%**
Number of churches											
1989	229	738	557	449	265	437	1,151	534	581	121	3,911
% ↓	−6	−7	−9	−6	+76	−3	+14	−17	−3	+4	−1
1998	**215**	**688**	**508**	**421**	**467**	**425**	**1,313**	**442**	**564**	**126**	**3,856**
Frequency of attendance in weeks per year, 1998											
↓ % 52 +	30	41	53	52	72	69	67	44	42	41	54
↓ % 13–26	50	30	12	26	13	20	14	27	28	35	22
↓ % 2–4	20	29	35	22	15	11	19	29	30	24	24

TABLE 12.9.4 Sunday attendance by ethnic groups, 1998

	White	BCA	CKJ	IPB	OA	ONW	Total (=100%)
% →	90.5	6.3	1.1	1.1	0.3	0.7	260,800

BCA = Black Caribbean/African/Other Black   CKJ = Chinese/Korean/Japanese   IPB = Indian/Pakistani/Bangladeshi
OA = Other Asian   ONW = Other Non-white

TABLE 12.9.5 Overall figures

	Churchgoers 1979 %	Churchgoers 1989 %	Churchgoers 1998 %	Population 1979 %	Population 1989 %	Population 1998 %
Under 15	27	26	20	22	18	19
15 to 19	7	7	5	8	8	6
20 to 29	9	8	8	14	16	13
30 to 44	16	16	17	19	21	22
45 to 64	21	22	23	23	22	24
65 or over	20	21	27	14	15	16

FIGURE 12.9.3
Percentage of population in church by age-group, 1979, 1989 and 1998

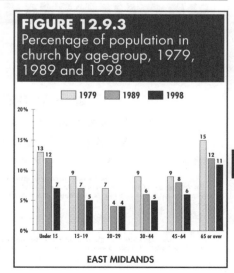

EAST MIDLANDS

12

[1] Including 14 residential schools/colleges

12

FIGURE 12.11.1

FIGURE 12.11.2

TABLE 12.11.1   Overall figures

	1979	1989	1998
Total population	5,152,200	5,206,600	**5,329,500**
Usual Sunday church attendance	574,800	516,700	**363,000**
% attending on Sunday	11.2%	9.9%	**6.8%**
Number of churches	4,054	3,868	**3,790**
Population per church	1,270	1,350	**1,410**

TABLE 12.11.2   Sunday attendance by denomination

	Anglican	Baptist	Catholic	Independent	Methodist	New	Orthodox	Pentecostal	URC	Others	TOTAL
1979	169,900	22,600	218,400	23,200	67,200	6,300	400	41,000	14,900	10,900	574,800
% ↓	−23	+11	−6	+23	−13	+103	+150	−14	−26	−36	−10
1989	131,300	25,000	206,100	28,600	58,400	12,800	1,000	35,400	11,100	7,000	516,700
% ↓	−31	−5	−37	−37	−33	+16	+20	−18	−9	−7	−30
1998	**91,100**	**23,700**	**129,600**	**17,900**	**39,100**	**14,900**	**1,200**	**28,900**	**10,100**	**6,500**	**363,000**
1979 →	29	4	38	4	12	1	0	7	3	2	100%
1989 →	25	5	40	6	11	3	0	7	2	1	100%
1998 →	**25**	**6**	**36**	**5**	**11**	**4**	**0**	**8**	**3**	**2**	**100%**
Number of churches											
1989	1,782	195	344	282[1]	665	88	4	250	132	126	3,868
% ↓	−1	+7	−1	−29	−7	+59	+625	+4	−8	−13	−2
1998	**1,760**	**209**	**342**	**200**[1]	**618**	**140**	**29**	**261**	**121**	**110**	**3,790**
Frequency of attendance in weeks per year, 1998											
↓ % 52 +	47	72	68	74	60	76	0	72	57	69	63
↓ % 13–26	25	19	8	14	23	19	100	10	26	18	16
↓ % 2–4	28	9	24	12	17	5	0	18	17	13	21

TABLE 12.11.3   Sunday attendance by churchmanship

	Anglo-Catholic	Broad	Catholic	Evangelical Broad	Evangelical Mainstream	Evangelical Charismatic	Evangelical Total	Liberal	Low Church	Others	TOTAL
1989	29,600	49,700	214,000	39,300	30,900	63,900	134,100	57,300	25,300	6,700	516,700
% ↓	−26	−27	−65	−19	+113	−28	+7	−12	+7	+40	−30
1998	**22,000**	**36,300**	**74,100**	**31,700**	**65,800**	**45,900**	**143,400**	**50,700**	**27,100**	**9,400**	**363,000**
1989 →	6	10	41	8	6	12	26	11	5	1	100%
1998 →	**6**	**10**	**21**	**8**	**18**	**13**	**39**	**14**	**7**	**3**	**100%**
Number of churches											
1989	187	420	591	328	494	781	1,603	721	265	81	3,868
% ↓	−5	−19	−17	0	+52	−9	+12	−13	−7	+47	−2
1998	**177**	**340**	**493**	**327**	**749**	**714**	**1,790**	**624**	**247**	**119**	**3,790**
Frequency of attendance in weeks per year, 1998											
↓ % 52 +	56	49	69	59	74	72	70	49	54	67	63
↓ % 13–26	21	23	8	17	10	16	13	25	23	12	16
↓ % 2–4	23	28	23	24	16	12	17	26	23	21	21

TABLE 12.11.4   Sunday attendance by ethnic groups, 1998

	White	BCA	CKJ	IPB	OA	ONW	Total (=100%)
% →	88.6	8.8	0.6	0.9	0.4	0.7	363,000

BCA = Black Caribbean/African/Other Black   CKJ = Chinese/Korean/Japanese   IPB = Indian/Pakistani/Bangladeshi
OA = Other Asian   ONW = Other Non-white

TABLE 12.11.5   Overall figures

	Churchgoers 1979 %	Churchgoers 1989 %	Churchgoers 1998 %	Population 1979 %	Population 1989 %	Population 1998 %
Under 15	26	24	20	22	19	20
15 to 19	9	7	6	8	8	6
20 to 29	11	9	8	14	16	13
30 to 44	18	16	17	19	20	22
45 to 64	21	23	25	23	22	23
65 or over	15	21	24	14	15	16

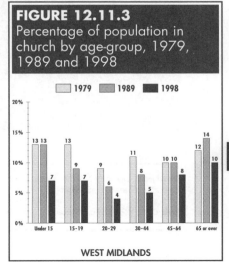

FIGURE 12.11.3
Percentage of population in church by age-group, 1979, 1989 and 1998

WEST MIDLANDS

12

[1] Including 25 residential schools/colleges

bible • community • worship

"Covies aims to serve the local church as it establishes children and young people in the Christian Faith."

We help churches right across the denominations become more effective in their Ministry. as we move into the millennium.

"Whether you are going all out or on the verge of going under, Covies can offer all the local support, ideas and encouragement YOU need. Let Covies share over 70 years of experience in children's and youth work with YOU."

Paul Wilcox, National Director

■ Support
Expert advice, information and encouragement from experienced staff both nationally and regionally.

■ Training
All types from national residential to regional, area, and local church training.

■ Structure
Help with every age group from birth to 25.

■ Materials
Knowledge of and access to all areas of past, present and new cutting edge materials for working with children and young people.

■ Events
Including holidays, competitions, fun days, sports, worship and celebrations, aiming to supplement your local programme.

Your partners in reaching children and young people

Contact: Dorothy Mason, Operations Manager, Mill House, Mill Lane, Cheadle, Cheshire, SK8 2NT

Tel: 0161-428 5566 **Email:** covies@dial.pipex.com   Registered Charity: 282122

Talk to us!
0161 428 5566

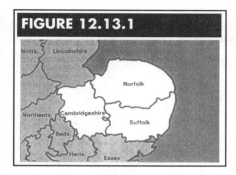

FIGURE 12.13.1

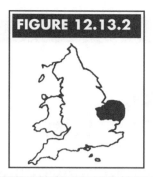

FIGURE 12.13.2

TABLE 12.13.1 Overall figures

	1979	1989	1998
Total population	1,863,200	2,033,700	2,174,400
Usual Sunday church attendance	250,700	224,400	162,400
% attending on Sunday	13.5%	11.0%	7.5%
Number of churches	2,887	2,769	2,662
Population per church	650	730	760

TABLE 12.13.2 Sunday attendance by denomination

	Anglican	Baptist	Catholic	Independent	Methodist	New	Orthodox	Pentecostal	URC	Others	TOTAL
1979	97,000	19,000	67,000	15,600	23,000	4,300	400	3,200	11,100	10,100	250,700
% ↓	−21	−1	−16	+34	−15	+95	+25	+28	−19	+3	−10
1989	76,300	18,900	56,300	20,900	19,600	8,400	500	4,100	9,000	10,400	224,400
% ↓	−17	−6	−41	−61	−32	+42	+20	−37	−40	−44	−28
1998	**63,600**	**17,800**	**33,200**	**8,200**	**13,300**	**11,900**	**600**	**2,600**	**5,400**	**5,800**	**162,400**
1979 →	39	8	27	6	9	2	0	1	4	4	100%
1989 →	34	9	25	9	9	4	0	1	4	5	100%
1998 →	**39**	**11**	**21**	**5**	**8**	**7**	**0**	**2**	**3**	**4**	**100%**
Number of churches											
1989	1,507	210	161	158[1]	419	77	6	39	93	99	2,769
% ↓	−1	−3	−1	−39	−9	+47	+133	+8	−3	−26	−4
1998	**1,488**	**204**	**160**	**97[1]**	**381**	**113**	**14**	**42**	**90**	**73**	**2,662**
Frequency of attendance in weeks per year, 1998											
↓ % 52 +	40	77	65	71	78	85	53	64	74	71	60
↓ % 13–26	23	15	17	14	13	11	29	21	18	19	18
↓ % 2–4	37	8	18	15	9	4	18	15	8	10	22

TABLE 12.13.3 Sunday attendance by churchmanship

	Anglo-Catholic	Broad	Catholic	Evangelical Broad	Evangelical Mainstream	Evangelical Charismatic	Evangelical Total	Liberal	Low Church	Others	TOTAL
1989	8,800	27,600	62,700	27,100	26,400	26,500	80,000	24,600	17,600	3,100	224,400
% ↓	−15	−21	−72	−48	+31	−18	−12	−13	+14	+26	−28
1998	**7,500**	**21,700**	**17,600**	**14,100**	**34,600**	**21,600**	**70,300**	**21,300**	**20,100**	**3,900**	**162,400**
1989 →	4	12	28	12	12	12	36	11	8	1	100%
1998 →	**5**	**13**	**11**	**9**	**21**	**13**	**43**	**13**	**12**	**3**	**100%**
Number of churches											
1989	132	549	420	312	296	229	837	335	409	87	2,769
% ↓	−5	−23	−11	−20	+47	−2	+8	−21	+9	+43	−4
1998	**125**	**421**	**374**	**250**	**434**	**224**	**908**	**263**	**447**	**124**	**2,662**
Frequency of attendance in weeks per year, 1998											
↓ % 52 +	47	50	57	57	71	77	70	51	50	73	60
↓ % 13–26	22	23	20	21	16	12	16	18	21	15	18
↓ % 2–4	31	27	23	22	13	11	14	31	29	12	22

TABLE 12.13.4 Sunday attendance by ethnic groups, 1998

	White	BCA	CKJ	IPB	OA	ONW	Total (=100%)
% →	94.8	2.8	0.8	0.8	0.5	0.3	162,400

BCA = Black Caribbean/African/Other Black   CKJ = Chinese/Korean/Japanese   IPB = Indian/Pakistani/Bangladeshi
OA = Other Asian   ONW = Other Non-white

TABLE 12.13.5 Overall figures

	Churchgoers 1979 %	Churchgoers 1989 %	Churchgoers 1998 %	Population 1979 %	Population 1989 %	Population 1998 %
Under 15	25	25	20	22	20	19
15 to 19	7	7	5	8	7	6
20 to 29	12	8	8	15	16	13
30 to 44	16	16	16	19	20	21
45 to 64	21	22	23	22	20	24
65 or over	19	22	28	14	17	17

[1] Including 31 residential schools/colleges

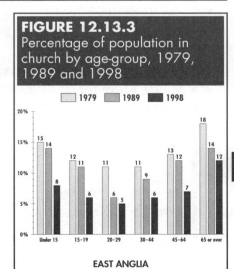

FIGURE 12.13.3
Percentage of population in church by age-group, 1979, 1989 and 1998

☐ 1979 ▨ 1989 ■ 1998

EAST ANGLIA

12

The Centre for Black and White Christian Partnership

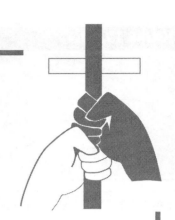

Promoting Better Relations
Between Different Christian Traditions In Britain

We seek to build bridges between African, Asian, Caribbean and European cultural expressions of Christianity. We work with all Christian denominations in furthering the cause of Mission in our nation and world. We offer our services in the following ways:

COURSES
- Theology at Certificate, Diploma and Degree levels
- Counselling at Certificate and Diploma levels
- Teaching Preparation at Certificate level
- Race Awareness Training non-accredited

PUBLICATIONS
- Black Christians: Black Church Traditions in Britain £10.00
- Preaching With Power: Sermons by Black Preachers £9.99
- Black Theology in Britain: A Journal of Contextual Praxis £12.50 PA (Twice Yearly)
- Directory of Black-majority Churches (UK)
- Partnership News, three times a year newsletter

RESOURCES
A specialist intercultural library of books, periodicals, theses and archival materials
- Ten Tips for Partnership leaflet
- Database of Black-led and Black-majority churches
- Database of Racial Justice organisations
- Intercultural Christian Consultancy

NETWORKING
Workshops, Forums, Seminars, Visits

For further information contact us at:
The Centre for Black and White Christian Partnership
Selly Oak Colleges
Bristol Road
Birmingham
B29 6LQ
Tel: 0121 472 7952
Fax: 0121 415 2400
E-mail: cbwcp@sellyoak.ac.uk

Registered Charity Number 328998

12

FIGURE 12.15.1

FIGURE 12.15.2

TABLE 12.15.1 Overall figures

	1979	1989	**1998**
Total population	4,657,400	4,999,600	**5,289,100**
Usual Sunday church attendance	520,400	445,300	**386,900**
% attending on Sunday	11.2%	8.9%	**7.3%**
Number of churches	3,790	3,943	**3,800**
Population per church	1,230	1,270	**1,390**

TABLE 12.15.2 Sunday attendance by denomination

	Anglican	Baptist	Catholic	Independent	Methodist	New	Orthodox	Pentecostal	URC	Others	TOTAL
1979	174,800	46,900	157,400	28,000	45,800	7,600	1,100	18,800	20,400	19,600	520,400
% ↓	−22	−4	−20	+29	−22	+166	+9	−14	−18	−35	−14
1989	135,500	45,200	125,800	36,200	35,600	20,200	1,200	16,100	16,800	12,700	445,300
% ↓	−24	+15	−9	−39	−11	+19	+50	−17	−21	−16	−13
1998	**103,600**	**51,900**	**114,500**	**22,100**	**31,600**	**24,000**	**1,800**	**13,400**	**13,300**	**10,700**	**386,900**
1979 →	34	9	30	5	9	1	0	4	4	4	100%
1989 →	30	10	28	8	8	5	0	4	4	3	100%
1998 →	**27**	**14**	**30**	**6**	**8**	**6**	**0**	**3**	**3**	**3**	**100%**
Number of churches											
1989	1,676	352	392	413[1]	460	120	10	156	197	167	3,943
% ↓	0	−3	0	−29	−2	+55	+160	−8	−14	−23	−4
1998	**1,674**	**340**	**391**	**293[1]**	**449**	**186**	**26**	**144**	**169**	**128**	**3,800**
Frequency of attendance in weeks per year, 1998											
↓ % 52 +	41	73	59	72	60	83	20	74	61	65	59
↓ % 13–26	26	16	15	17	27	13	16	19	26	15	19
↓ % 2–4	33	11	26	11	13	4	64	7	13	20	22

TABLE 12.15.3 Sunday attendance by churchmanship

	Anglo-Catholic	Broad	Catholic	Evangelical Broad	Evangelical Mainstream	Evangelical Charismatic	Evangelical Total	Liberal	Low Church	Others	TOTAL
1989	14,600	39,700	141,000	39,400	44,400	77,300	161,100	59,100	26,000	3,800	445,300
% ↓	+41	−7	−38	−45	+61	−23	−5	−18	+19	+153	−13
1998	**20,400**	**36,900**	**88,000**	**21,500**	**71,400**	**59,700**	**152,600**	**48,400**	**31,000**	**9,600**	**386,900**
1989 →	3	9	32	9	10	17	36	13	6	1	100%
1998 →	**5**	**9**	**23**	**6**	**19**	**15**	**40**	**13**	**8**	**2**	**100%**
Number of churches											
1989	191	586	561	453	425	559	1,437	657	428	83	3,943
% ↓	−6	−4	−5	−21	+37	−19	−3	−19	+6	+82	−4
1998	**179**	**564**	**531**	**358**	**582**	**454**	**1,394**	**529**	**452**	**151**	**3,800**
Frequency of attendance in weeks per year, 1998											
↓ % 52 +	42	48	59	48	69	72	67	49	50	63	59
↓ % 13–26	28	25	15	23	18	18	19	26	28	17	19
↓ % 2–4	30	27	26	29	13	10	14	25	22	20	22

TABLE 12.15.4 Sunday attendance by ethnic groups, 1998

	White	BCA	CKJ	IPB	OA	ONW	Total (=100%)
% →	91.3	4.4	1.6	1.4	0.8	0.5	386,900

BCA = Black Caribbean/African/Other Black   CKJ = Chinese/Korean/Japanese   IPB = Indian/Pakistani/Bangladeshi
OA = Other Asian   ONW = Other Non-white

TABLE 12.15.5 Overall figures

	Churchgoers			Population		
↓	1979 %	1989 %	1998 %	1979 %	1989 %	1998 %
Under 15	28	27	19	24	19	20
15 to 19	9	8	6	8	8	6
20 to 29	11	10	9	14	16	14
30 to 44	17	18	19	20	22	23
45 to 64	20	20	24	22	21	23
65 or over	15	17	23	12	14	14

FIGURE 12.15.3
Percentage of population in church by age-group, 1979, 1989 and 1998

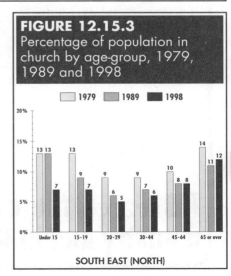

SOUTH EAST (NORTH)

[1] Including 74 residential schools/colleges

GET A JOB/ADVERTISE A JOB IN THE ONE-STOP JOB SHOP

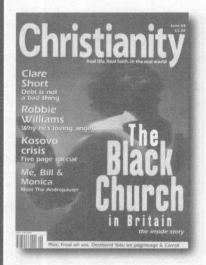

Published every month in both *Christianity* and *Youthwork* magazines, **JOB**search is THE place to find a job, or place a job advert, for posts in all forms of Christian ministry/work. In the past 12 months over 500 vacancies appeared in **JOB**search.

If you're looking for a job, OR looking to appoint someone at a Christian company, church, mission agency, charity or organisation – look no further!

The most frequently advertised posts in **JOB**search include:

- Youth Worker/Youth Pastor
- Community Worker
- Chaplain
- Executive Director
- Minister/Pastor
- Children's Worker
- Project Manager
- Field Officer
- Financial Controller
- Schools Worker
- Chief Executive

JOBsearch appears every month in both *Christianity* and *Youthwork* magazines, which have a joint readership of over 20,000. These magazines are available from all good Christian bookstores, church agents and by subscription.

- To subscribe to *Christianity* or *Youthwork* call during office hours on 01903 602100.

- To advertise in **JOB**search phone Pamela Chaston an 0207 316 1456.

*'We received several applications directly from **JOB**search and would certainly use it again to advertise staff posts.'*
Highfield Church, Southampton

*'We were very pleased with the number and calibre of the candidates that responded to our advert in **JOB**search.'*
Norwich Youth For Christ

JOBsearch the one-stop shop for jobs in Christian ministry and in Christian companies/organisations.

FIGURE 12.17.1

FIGURE 12.17.2

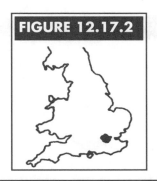

TABLE 12.17.1 Overall figures

	1979	1989	1998
Total population	6,877,100	6,735,000	7,145,900
Usual Sunday church attendance	696,000	649,600	617,900
% attending on Sunday	10.1%	9.6%	8.6%
Number of churches	3,350	3,549	3,743
Population per church	2,050	1,900	1,910

TABLE 12.17.2 Sunday attendance by denomination

	Anglican	Baptist	Catholic	Independent	Methodist	New	Orthodox	Pentecostal	URC	Others	TOTAL
1979	140,500	46,600	333,700	29,800	35,000	8,100	5,300	57,500	19,600	19,900	696,000
% ↓	−30	−12	−12	+37	−26	+227	+21	+44	−16	−9	−7
1989	98,500	41,100	293,000	40,900	25,900	26,500	6,400	82,700	16,400	18,200	649,600
% ↓	+3	+11	−19	−52	−8	+51	+145	+13	+1	+32	−5
1998	**101,100**	**45,800**	**237,200**	**19,700**	**23,700**	**39,600**	**16,400**	**93,700**	**16,600**	**24,100**	**617,900**
1979 →	20	7	48	4	5	1	1	8	3	3	100%
1989 →	15	6	45	6	4	4	1	13	3	3	100%
1998 →	**16**	**8**	**38**	**3**	**4**	**6**	**3**	**15**	**3**	**4**	**100%**
Number of churches											
1989	987	287	422	342[1]	252	132	53	709	174	191	3,549
% ↓	0	+20	−1	−26	−4	+79	+25	+21	−13	−3	+5
1998	**989**	**345**	**417**	**254**[1]	**243**	**236**	**66**	**856**	**152**	**185**	**3,743**
Frequency of attendance in weeks per year, 1998											
↓ % 52 +	51	68	65	73	59	75	13	67	46	69	62
↓ % 13–26	28	20	13	17	25	15	10	21	30	19	18
↓ % 2–4	21	12	22	10	16	10	77	12	24	12	20

TABLE 12.17.3 Sunday attendance by churchmanship

	Anglo-Catholic	Broad	Catholic	Evangelical Broad	Evangelical Mainstream	Evangelical Charismatic	Evangelical Total	Liberal	Low Church	Others	TOTAL
1989	16,400	24,900	301,500	37,100	67,300	112,400	216,800	46,300	19,600	24,100	649,600
% ↓	+22	−9	−29	−52	+73	+8	+18	+10	+56	+58	−5
1998	**20,000**	**22,700**	**199,700**	**17,900**	**116,700**	**121,200**	**255,800**	**51,000**	**30,600**	**38,100**	**617,900**
1989 →	3	4	46	6	10	17	33	7	3	4	100%
1998 →	**3**	**4**	**32**	**3**	**19**	**20**	**42**	**8**	**5**	**6**	**100%**
Number of churches											
1989	208	243	582	299	634	785	1,718	442	243	113	3,549
% ↓	+2	−20	+9	−33	+28	+4	+6	−5	+10	+63	+5
1998	**213**	**195**	**633**	**201**	**810**	**817**	**1,828**	**422**	**268**	**184**	**3,743**
Frequency of attendance in weeks per year, 1998											
↓ % 52 +	50	49	65	49	67	71	68	46	62	61	62
↓ % 13–26	23	28	14	31	19	18	19	28	25	11	18
↓ % 2–4	27	23	21	20	14	11	13	26	13	28	20

TABLE 12.17.4 Sunday attendance by ethnic groups, 1998

London	White	BCA	CKJ	IPB	OA	ONW	Total (=100%)
Inner	48.8	37.4	2.8	3.6	4.1	3.3	239,700
Outer	73.2	15.2	3.3	5.0	2.2	1.1	378,200

BCA = Black Caribbean/African/Other Black   CKJ = Chinese/Korean/Japanese   IPB = Indian/Pakistani/Bangladeshi
OA = Other Asian   ONW = Other Non-white

TABLE 12.17.5 Overall figures

	Churchgoers 1979 %	Churchgoers 1989 %	Churchgoers 1998 %	Population 1979 %	Population 1989 %	Population 1998 %
Under 15	33	24	21	19	18	19
15 to 19	8	7	6	8	7	6
20 to 29	11	12	12	14	18	16
30 to 44	14	20	20	19	22	26
45 to 64	18	21	22	24	20	20
65 or over	16	16	19	16	15	13

[1] Including 19 residential schools/colleges

FIGURE 12.17.3
Percentage of population in church by age-group, 1979, 1989 and 1998

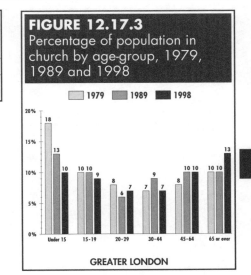

GREATER LONDON

12

FIGURE 12.18.1

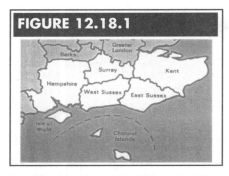

FIGURE 12.18.2

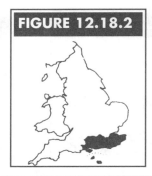

TABLE 12.18.1 Overall figures

	1979	1989	1998
Total population	5,323,000	5,744,800	6,040,300
Usual Sunday church attendance	615,900	544,100	479,000
% attending on Sunday	11.6%	9.5%	7.9%
Number of churches	4,305	4,297	4,212
Population per church	1,240	1,340	1,430

TABLE 12.18.2 Sunday attendance by denomination

	Anglican	Baptist	Catholic	Independent	Methodist	New	Orthodox	Pentecostal	URC	Others	TOTAL
1979	252,800	52,700	150,200	45,600	49,700	12,400	500	13,200	24,500	14,300	615,900
% ↓	−24	−17	−8	+15	−28	+212	−20	−13	−17	−22	−12
1989	192,200	43,900	137,600	52,300	36,000	38,700	400	11,500	20,400	11,100	544,100
% ↓	−20	+2	−9	−49	−16	+53	+150	+3	−9	−21	−12
1998	**152,800**	**44,900**	**125,000**	**26,700**	**30,300**	**59,100**	**1,000**	**11,900**	**18,500**	**8,800**	**479,000**
1979 →	41	9	24	8	8	2	0	2	4	2	100%
1989 →	35	8	25	10	7	7	0	2	4	2	100%
1998 →	**32**	**9**	**26**	**6**	**6**	**12**	**0**	**3**	**4**	**2**	**100%**
Number of churches											
1989	1,869	334	474	501[1]	396	225	9	117	203	169	4,297
% ↓	0	+6	−4	−39	−1	+56	+111	+12	−5	−21	−2
1998	**1,875**	**353**	**457**	**307[1]**	**392**	**352**	**19**	**131**	**192**	**134**	**4,212**
Frequency of attendance in weeks per year, 1998											
↓ % 52 +	47	76	56	78	59	75	32	80	60	69	60
↓ % 13–26	24	15	16	13	29	16	15	12	28	20	19
↓ % 2–4	29	9	28	9	12	9	53	8	12	11	21

TABLE 12.18.3 Sunday attendance by churchmanship

	Anglo-Catholic	Broad	Catholic	Evangelical Broad	Evangelical Mainstream	Evangelical Charismatic	Evangelical Total	Liberal	Low Church	Others	TOTAL
1989	29,300	59,100	174,900	50,000	49,900	90,300	190,200	60,200	28,400	2,000	544,100
% ↓	−3	−29	−27	−43	+72	+5	+10	−13	+8	+50	−9
1998	**28,500**	**41,700**	**113,200**	**28,400**	**86,000**	**95,100**	**209,500**	**52,500**	**30,600**	**3,000**	**494,000**
1989 →	6	11	32	9	9	17	35	11	5	0	100%
1998 →	**6**	**8**	**24**	**6**	**17**	**19**	**42**	**11**	**6**	**1**	**100%**
Number of churches											
1989	295	725	690	453	507	650	1,610	549	381	47	4,297
% ↓	0	−30	−6	−28	+51	+4	+10	−9	+1	+132	−2
1998	**296**	**506**	**649**	**326**	**765**	**675**	**1,766**	**50**	**386**	**109**	**4,212**
Frequency of attendance in weeks per year, 1998											
↓ % 52 +	40	51	57	54	71	73	70	47	53	58	60
↓ % 13–26	23	25	16	25	17	16	18	27	22	25	19
↓ % 2–4	37	24	27	21	12	11	12	26	25	17	21

TABLE 12.18.4 Sunday attendance by ethnic groups, 1998

	White	BCA	CKJ	IPB	OA	ONW	Total (=100%)
% →	94.1	2.7	1.0	0.7	0.9	0.6	479,000

BCA = Black Caribbean/African/Other Black   CKJ = Chinese/Korean/Japanese   IPB = Indian/Pakistani/Bangladeshi
OA = Other Asian   ONW = Other Non-white

TABLE 12.18.5 Overall figures

	Churchgoers 1979 %	Churchgoers 1989 %	Churchgoers 1998 %	Population 1979 %	Population 1989 %	Population 1998 %
Under 15	23	25	20	21	18	18
15 to 19	10	8	6	8	8	6
20 to 29	11	8	9	14	16	13
30 to 44	17	18	17	18	20	22
45 to 64	20	21	24	23	21	24
65 or over	19	20	24	16	17	17

FIGURE 12.18.3
Percentage of population in church by age-group, 1979, 1989 and 1998

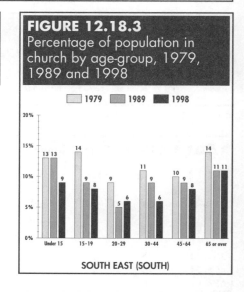

SOUTH EAST (SOUTH)

[1] Including 72 residential schools/colleges

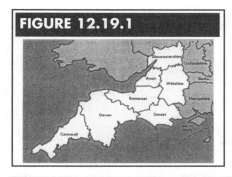

FIGURE 12.19.1

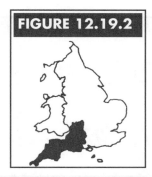

FIGURE 12.19.2

TABLE 12.19.1 Overall figures

	1979	1989	**1998**
Total population	4,315,700	4,633,800	**4,898,700**
Usual Sunday church attendance	561,000	498,900	**381,400**
% attending on Sunday	13.0%	10.8%	**7.7%**
Number of churches	5,866	5,854	**5,561**
Population per church	740	790	**880**

TABLE 12.19.2 Sunday attendance by denomination

	Anglican	Baptist	Catholic	Independent	Methodist	New	Orthodox	Pentecostal	URC	Others	TOTAL
1979	231,200	40,000	95,900	39,500	90,000	10,800	700	13,200	25,500	14,200	561,000
% ↓	−23	−9	−5	+33	−17	+85	+43	+18	−30	−15	−11
1989	177,300	36,300	91,400	52,500	75,000	20,000	1,000	15,600	17,800	12,000	498,900
% ↓	−22	−5	−30	−49	−30	+48	+30	−45	−35	−26	−25
1998	**139,000**	**34,400**	**64,000**	**26,700**	**52,400**	**29,500**	**1,300**	**8,600**	**11,600**	**8,900**	**376,400**
1979 →	41	7	17	7	16	2	0	2	5	3	100%
1989 →	36	7	18	11	15	4	0	3	4	2	100%
1998 →	**37**	**9**	**17**	**7**	**14**	**8**	**0**	**2**	**3**	**3**	**100%**
Number of churches											
1989	2,725	339	366	583[1]	1,151	138	11	151	213	177	5,854
% ↓	−1	0	−2	−27	−10	+51	+191	−19	−6	−22	−5
1998	**2,697**	**340**	**359**	**424[1]**	**1,038**	**209**	**32**	**123**	**201**	**138**	**5,561**
Frequency of attendance in weeks per year, 1998											
% 52 +	40	73	52	79	62	78	9	84	58	63	56
% 13–26	23	16	12	12	19	19	19	8	23	19	18
% 2–4	37	11	36	9	19	3	72	8	19	18	26

TABLE 12.19.3 Sunday attendance by churchmanship

	Anglo-Catholic	Broad	Catholic	Evangelical Broad	Evangelical Mainstream	Evangelical Charismatic	Evangelical Total	Liberal	Low Church	Others	TOTAL
1989	25,900	61,800	132,100	63,400	47,300	67,400	178,100	58,000	34,300	8,700	498,900
% ↓	−15	−16	−55	−59	+50	−20	−15	−9	−13	+11	−24
1998	**22,000**	**51,800**	**59,700**	**26,000**	**71,000**	**54,000**	**151,000**	**52,500**	**29,700**	**9,700**	**381,400**
1989 →	5	12	26	13	9	14	36	12	7	2	100%
1998 →	**6**	**14**	**16**	**7**	**19**	**14**	**40**	**14**	**8**	**2**	**100%**
Number of churches											
1989	345	1,107	790	858	576	594	2,028	708	696	180	5,854
% ↓	+1	−12	−8	−21	+32	−5	−1	−7	−5	+11	−5
1998	**347**	**973**	**725**	**680**	**759**	**562**	**2,001**	**655**	**661**	**199**	**5,561**
Frequency of attendance in weeks per year, 1998											
↓ % 52 +	53	41	53	54	73	72	69	40	50	45	56
↓ % 13–26	23	21	14	24	15	18	18	16	24	27	18
↓ % 2–4	24	38	33	22	12	10	13	44	26	28	26

TABLE 12.19.4 Sunday attendance by ethnic groups, 1998

	White	BCA	CKJ	IPB	OA	ONW	Total (=100%)
% →	96.0	1.8	0.9	0.5	0.4	0.4	376,400

BCA = Black Caribbean/African/Other Black   CKJ = Chinese/Korean/Japanese   IPB = Indian/Pakistani/Bangladeshi
OA = Other Asian   ONW = Other Non-white

TABLE 12.19.5 Overall figures

	Churchgoers 1979 %	Churchgoers 1989 %	Churchgoers 1998 %	Population 1979 %	Population 1989 %	Population 1998 %
Under 15	24	24	19	21	18	18
15 to 19	8	8	5	8	8	6
20 to 29	9	8	7	14	15	12
30 to 44	16	15	16	18	20	21
45 to 64	21	22	23	23	21	24
65 or over	22	23	30	16	18	19

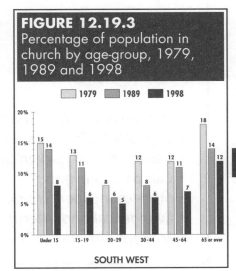

FIGURE 12.19.3
Percentage of population in church by age-group, 1979, 1989 and 1998

◻ 1979 ◼ 1989 ◼ 1998

SOUTH WEST

12

[1] Including 38 residential schools/colleges

Campaigners has the Answer!

A Church integrated Youth Organisation that works!

Campaigners -

Young People discovering LIFE

A proven heritage-and a modern relevance!
- *Boys AND Girls from 6 to late teens*
- *Varied, action packed programme;*
- *Camps and events;*
- *Modern inexpensive designer uniform;*
- *Evangelical and Interdenominational;*
- *Modern alternative peer led teenage programme*

Rush me details about the Youth Work Programme that will work for my Church

Name _____
Address _____
_____
Phone _____
Campaigners, Campaigner House, St. Mark's Close, Colney Heath, St Albans, Herts AL4 0NQ.
Tel: 01727 824065 Fax: 01727 825049
www.charitynet.org/~Campaigners

12

Continued from Page 12.2

A comparison of the percentage both of the general population and those attending church on Sunday in each of the six age-groups used are given in **Table 5** on each page of Section 12. This comparison is given for 1979, 1989 and 1998. **Figure 3** on each page takes these percentages and expresses the churchgoing numbers as a proportion of the population in that age-group for each of these three years. The overall proportion attending church on Sunday for these three years is given in **Table 1**.

Churchmanship. Respondents were invited to tick up to three boxes in a list of nine categories, and were able to use an "other, please specify" category as well. The nine categories used were the same as in the 1989 English Church Census to allow comparisons. The information was completed by the minister, or leader, to describe his/her congregation not their own personal position.

A few churches gave more than three ticks. These were reduced to the main three classifications using the same rules as were adopted for the 1989 English Church Census, as described in *Prospects for the Nineties*. The actual combinations of codes were the same as used in 1989. Three combinations not found in 1989 were coded as follows: ABCDEI (BDE), BCDEHI (BEH) and CDEFG (CDF).

Details of the numbers by each churchmanship are given in **Table 3** on each page in Section 12, with a comparison for 1998 both in attendance terms and in the number of churches.

Answers to the following questions are given only in the commentary:

- **Age of church/congregation.** The date the congregation started to meet rather than the age of the building per se, the difference being especially important for those who have taken over redundant churches, or who hire school halls, etc to meet in.

- **Listed building and facilities.** If the church was a listed building, the grade of listing was also requested, if known. Whether the church, not hall, had a publicly available toilet, and/or wheelchair access, was also requested.

- **Midweek and other services.** If the church had a regular mid-week worship service, and/or a regular Youth worship service was requested, and if so, the approximate number of attenders. The number of adults and children who might also attend mid-week church-run activities but who do not regularly attend worship services was also requested.

- **Healing ministry and the future.** If the church had one of four types of healing services or ministries, they were asked to indicate. Likewise an estimate was requested as to whether the church might have grown, remained static, declined or closed by 2010.

Ethnic mix. The average number of adults in the congregation by six ethnic groups was asked. The groups used were the same as used in the 1991 Population Census, which allows therefore a comparison of the answers. In the Tables in this volume, the breakdown of the adult congregation is given in percentage terms in **Table 4** on each page in Section 12.

Arrows

To help the reader more easily understand the numbers in the following pages arrows have been used to indicate the direction in which the percentages have been taken.

Thus a horizontal arrow (→) indicates that the percentages sum to 100% horizontally; the number on which the percentages are based is given in the final column. A vertical arrow (↓) indicates that the percentages sum to 100% vertically, although the number on which these percentages are based is not usually given since they can be easily derived from the horizontal percentage figures.

Rates of change have been calculated over the ten or nine year periods 1979 to 1989 and 1985 to 1998 to give an historical perspective whenever possible.

Greater London. In the 1979 Census, Inner London was taken as the boundary of the then Inner London Education Authority. For consistency in analysis the same boundaries have been used for both the 1989 Census and the 1998 English Church Attendance Survey. The actual boroughs included within each grouping are listed below:

Inner London: Camden, City of London, City of Westminster, Greenwich, Hackney, Hammersmith and Fulham, Islington, Kensington and Chelsea, Lambeth, Lewisham, Southwark, Tower Hamlets, Wandsworth (13 in total). Inner London as officially defined includes Haringey and Newham but excludes Greenwich.

Outer London: Barking and Dagenham, Barnet, Bexley, Brent, Bromley, Croydon, Ealing, Enfield, Haringey, Harrow, Havering, Hillingdon, Hounslow, Kingston-upon-Thames, Merton, Newham, Redbridge, Richmond-upon-Thames, Sutton, Waltham Forest (20 in total).

For more details contact Dr Peter Brierley, at the address on Page 0.2

Investments.
Insurances.
Mortgages.
Pensions.
Principles.

Principles?

Isn't it refreshing to discover a company that's not only progressive and successful but also shares your Christian ideals?

Discover Ecclesiastical and, whether you're in need of a competitive insurance quotation, or a chat with one of our locally based financial consultants, you'll find it's an enriching experience.

For an appointment with your local Ecclesiastical Financial Consultant call (01452) 33 49 78.

For household or motor insurance quotations call 0800 33 66 22.

ECCLESIASTICAL
INSURANCE YOU CAN BELIEVE IN

Head Office: Beaufort House,
Brunswick Road, Gloucester GL1 1JZ.
email:gbeigmkg@ibmmail.com   www.eigonline.co.uk

YOUR HOME IS AT RISK IF YOU DO NOT KEEP UP REPAYMENTS ON A MORTGAGE OR ANY OTHER LOAN SECURED ON IT. Any advice you may receive on financial services products will only relate to the products offered by Ecclesiastical Group, members of which are regulated by the Personal Investment Authority and IMRO. A representative of the company may call to discuss your requirements, without obligation. Financial advice offered by Ecclesiastical is open to residents of the UK only. The value of investments may fall as well as rise. Calls may be monitored or recorded.

ALPHABETICAL INDEX

See also Subject Index on Page 7.14
The "2/" in front of an entry refers to *Religious Trends* Number 2, and the "1/" to *Religious Trends* Number 1, thus forming a cumulative index

13

13

13

13